CYPRUS 1974

CONFLICT IN THE MEDITERRANEAN:
NO CONTROL, NO CONSPIRACY

ANDREW SOUTHAM

FRONTLINE
BOOKS

CYPRUS 1974
Conflict in the Mediterranean: No Control, No Conspiracy

First published in Great Britain in 2025 by
Frontline Books
An imprint of Pen & Sword Books Ltd
Yorkshire – Philadelphia

ISBN 9781036124182

Typeset by Lapiz Digital
Printed and bound in the UK by CPI Group (UK) Ltd, Croydon, CR0 4YY.

MIX
Paper | Supporting
responsible forestry
FSC® C013604

The Publisher's authorised representative in the EU for product safety is Authorised Rep Compliance Ltd., Ground Floor, 71 Lower Baggot Street, Dublin D02 P593, Ireland.
www.arccompliance.com

For a complete list of Pen & Sword titles please contact

PEN & SWORD BOOKS LIMITED
47 Church Street, Barnsley, South Yorkshire, S70 2AS, England
E-mail: enquiries@pen-and-sword.co.uk
Website: www.pen-and-sword.co.uk
or
PEN AND SWORD BOOKS
1950 Lawrence Road, Havertown, PA 19083, USA
E-mail: uspen-and-sword@casematepublishers.com
Website: www.penandswordbooks.com

For my mother and stepfather.

'The police eventually found the person who had put the bomb in the car; it was a paediatrician who had gone to Harvard Medical School. In true, from my biased point of view, Greek fashion, to protest, he didn't pick on the Greeks allied to the colonels, he picked on the Americans.'

Charles Stuart Kennedy,
United States Consul General,
Athens, 1970–1974[1]

'We were blamed for the junta, we were blamed for the Cyprus situation and we were blamed for not stopping it…'

Colonel Frank Athanason,
United States Military Attaché,
Athens, 1974[2]

CONTENTS

Introduction vii

Chapter 1   An Intractable Problem 1
Chapter 2   British Exposure 21
Chapter 3   Turkish Independence 29
Chapter 4   American Distraction 36
Chapter 5   Greek Misjudgement 49
Chapter 6   An Incomplete Picture: January to June 1974 55
Chapter 7   An Unexpected Coup: Monday, 15 July 1974 78
Chapter 8   Turkey Goes Through the Motions: Tuesday,
                16 July 1974 88
Chapter 9   Tones of Difference Emerge: Wednesday,
                17 July 1974 95
Chapter 10 Don't Legitimise Makarios: Thursday, 18 July 1974 105
Chapter 11 The Sisco Mission: Friday, 19 July 1974 113
Chapter 12 The First Assault: Saturday, 20 July 1974 122
Chapter 13 Turkish Prevarication: Sunday, 21 July 1974 142
Chapter 14 Relief: Monday, 22 July 1974 156
Chapter 15 Greek Fall: Tuesday, 23 July 1974 166
Chapter 16 Karamanlis Returns: Wednesday, 24 July 1974 177
Chapter 17 The First Conference 182
Chapter 18 Fall of a President 192
Chapter 19 Second Assault 198
Chapter 20 Recrimination, Reappraisals and Assassination 215

Chapter 21 Creation of a Villain. 222

Chapter 22 The Battle for Aid Begins 236

Chapter 23 Return of the King. 245

Chapter 24 Out of Time. 253

Chapter 25 A Long Shadow 262

Acknowledgments 271

Bibliography 272

Notes 277

Index 297

INTRODUCTION

Early morning on Monday, 15 July 1974 an apprehensive Greek-Cypriot bodyguard appeared through French doors on the lower-ground floor of the Presidential Palace in Nicosia, Cyprus. He walked over to the elected president of Cyprus, Archbishop Makarios III, who was sitting at the desk of his official residence preparing to greet Greek orthodox school children visiting from Cairo in Egypt later that day, told him tanks were approaching and asked if they should leave.

Makarios removed his black archbishop's tunic and hastened through a secret passage to the back of the palace, where he crossed the lawn, flagged down a car with his three aides and sped off as four tanks arrived to cut off the exit.

This Cypriot president, a man of immaculate charm, sophistication and a consummate political manipulator avoided another assassination attempt by minutes as tanks pounded the palace.

Coup plotters, thinking they had him, announced his death at midday and installed a new leader, a thug called Nikos Sampson, known as a killer of Turks and British soldiers. This proved a red flag for the Turkish government, which, having to protect Turkish Cypriots and resolve long-held defence concerns that Greece might one day take over the island, consequently occupied a third of the island in July and August 1974.

Here unfolded the first example in Europe since the Second World War (1939–1945) of an intractable ethnic conflict risking war between fellow North Atlantic Treaty Organization (NATO) countries Greece and Turkey, for which, in summer 1974, neither the United States (US) nor western European nations were prepared. They were instead consumed by Cold War (1947–1991) politics pitching the West against the communism of the Soviet Union and China in the east; and although the 1970s saw de-escalating tension through the *détente* process, allowing for nuclear weapon reduction talks, both sides continued outwitting each other in different theatres across the world from South America to the Mediterranean.

Western economies also reeled from a fourfold increase in oil prices introduced by Arab countries following the Arab-Israeli War (1973), over which American Secretary of State Dr Henry Kissinger expended enormous energy to broker a lasting peace. The Vietnam War (1955–1975), at the time the United States' longest war and one without victory, still cast a shadow with American combat troops only having left in March 1973; and, in fact, the war did not end until 1975. And the world was engrossed by the unravelling of American President Richard M. Nixon over the Watergate political scandal.

These preoccupations and the realities of influence meant that the United States and Britain struggled to manage affairs when Cyprus fell apart in 1974. This island conflict saw 3,000 people die, overturned the Greek military dictatorship, threatened British service personnel and their dependents, had Cypriot refugees flee to British bases for safety, and forced the transfer of vast numbers of Cypriots: the Greek community to the south and the Turkish community to the north. One American ambassador was recalled, another was assassinated in his own embassy and a year later the Central Intelligence Agency (CIA) station chief in Athens, Greece was murdered. The long-term consequence was a divided island, which still remains at the time of writing.

Fifty years of initiatives have not resolved that lasting division, which I saw as a young cadet in the Royal Air Force (RAF) Air Training Corps staying at the British sovereign base in Akrotiri on the island for two weeks during a hot Easter in 1981. My abiding memory of Cyprus is the buffer zone known as the 'Green Line', patrolled by the United Nations (UN), separating the Greek and Turkish communities in the heart of the capital Nicosia, and also my first experience of armed men.

An RAF squadron leader, incapable of smiling and somewhat miserable at being charged with our safety in those two exciting weeks, briefed us about avoiding 'the line'. His message was reinforced by the airmen and soldiers that we integrated with at meal times, who proffered stories of occasional trigger-happy shooting by Turkish guards and various other incidents.

Such memories stayed with me as I researched a doctoral thesis on the Mediterranean, which never quite came to conclusion, and have ever since remained frustrated by the absence of an accurate narrative history explaining what happened for the general reader. The absence of this work has allowed misleading theories that accuse the United States and sometimes Britain of manufacturing the terrible events of 1974 to flourish without proper challenge.

These conspiracy fabulations take various forms, alleging that the United States supported the Greek coup against Makarios to remove a troublesome president, or cooperated with Turkey to divide the island, or other themes, all of which do not stand in the face of evidence. Such allegations have been convincingly countered by serious historical works, but there is still no widely available narrative for the general reader showing what happened and why.

My book tries to meet that need, describing in simple terms the story for those unfamiliar with the background and events. It seeks to reveal the scale of complexity, competing demands, confusion and moral dilemmas faced by Henry Kissinger in Washington DC and British Foreign Secretary Leonard James 'Jim' Callaghan in London, tackling a problem with limited power and incomplete information.

I have tried to do this without overwhelming the reader with details of every single telephone call, meeting and piece of paper, but by setting out the thrust of events in two parts. The first five chapters describe the background of the main affected countries: Cyprus, Greece, Turkey, Britain and the United States. The following twenty chapters narrate the principal events as they happened starting in January 1974. In some cases, there is a deliberate repetition of events and people as I lock together the background with the narrative so you can easily follow what is going on.

Errors may well have crept in when trying to distil a huge body of information into a mid-sized book, though I am confident that the general thrust of events is accurate. And as this book is written for the 'person in the street' and not experts in their field, I have used an entertaining and informative style. All my sources are, however, set out in the Bibliography and I have credited the sources of any quotations in the end notes.

My intention in writing this work is not to blame, but to understand and explain decisions in a readable manner, showing how neither the United States nor Britain had control of the terrible situation in Cyprus throughout the summer of 1974.

Chapter 1

AN INTRACTABLE PROBLEM

Archbishop Makarios III was the last of the twentieth-century priest-politicians who held an incomparable commanding presence over Cypriot political, religious and social life, yet stoked ethnic division with Turkish Cypriots and created complications for the West when making Cyprus a neutral country during the Cold War.

Born in 1926 in Paphos, Cyprus and christened Michael Christodoulou Mouskos to a goat herdsman and a mother who died when he was but 9 years old, Makarios immersed himself in 2,000-year-old Greek orthodox monasticism and Greek culture. After local schooling in Nicosia, he entered the Cypriot Orthodox Church at 13, and then studied theology at the University of Athens during the Second World War, before being ordained in 1946. He went on to study theology and sociology at the University of Massachusetts in Boston in the United States with aspirations of becoming a theology professor before returning to Cyprus in 1948 as the Bishop of Kition, assuming the name Makarios.

Here was a man possessing gifts destined for a public stage with his tall frame and handsome looks completed by a musical voice and mesmerising eyes. This role came when, aged 37, he was elected Archbishop of Cyprus on 18 September 1950 to an office independent of the Greek Orthodox Church, a privilege highlighted by the right to sign documents in distinctive purple ink and to bear an imperial sceptre rather than carry a normal hooked staff. Makarios simultaneously became an *ethnarch* – a political and spiritual leadership position – guarding the traditions and identity of Greek culture on the island, and an informal form of ethnic leadership for Greek Cypriots.

His archbishopric was an ancient office, which like Cyprus itself had outlived invading foreign empires and ruling dynasties. Cyprus, as with much of the Greek-speaking world, was at first subsumed into the Roman Empire until this immense classical civilisation divided in the fourth century AD with the eastern half becoming an independent state run by its own emperor. When the western empire eventually fell to invading Germanic tribes, the eastern world slowly evolved into the Christian Byzantium Empire ruled from Constantinople (now modern-day Turkey). It was as part of this new empire that Cyprus established its independent Greek orthodox archbishopric in AD 431.

A Christian Cyprus remained under Byzantine rule for 800 years apart from a 300-year intermission when Arab leaders from the powerful Umayyad Caliphate – the vast Islamic empire that incorporated Iberia and Sicily – shared ownership with Constantinople emperors. A revitalised Byzantium regained full control in the tenth century AD.

Medieval European rulers then intervened. In 1191, King Richard I of England (Richard the Lionheart) seized control of Cyprus during his crusading quest to the Holy Land. Within a year, he sold the island to the Knights Templar who equally swiftly sold it to the Franks, the House of Lusignan. This minor and haphazard dynasty stayed for 300 years establishing the first kings of Cyprus, with the last one, James II, marrying the daughter of a Venetian merchant, allowing the Republic of Venice to assume control in 1489. All the while raiders and Arab kingdoms, including the Sultan of Egypt, continued to pillage the island. Yet amid all these developments, the independent Greek archbishopric survived despite suppression by the Roman Latin Church when Venice took control.

Ottoman Muslim Turks, who captured Constantinople in 1453 and nearly overcame Europe to establish another of the world's great empires, took the island in 1571 when Sultan Mehmed II (Mehmed the Conqueror) defeated Venetian forces after a year-long siege of Famagusta, a city famous for its deep harbour. William Shakespeare used these events thirty years later as the setting for *Othello*, portraying a Moorish general serving Venetian masters sent to protect the 'warlike island'[3] of Cyprus from the Turks.

These new masters ruled for three centuries, but notably never built a significant fortress to defend the island. They did, however, introduce over time around 40,000 Muslim strangers – mostly Turkish soldiers who settled on the island in return for land grants – into a predominantly Christian Greek orthodox culture creating a new mix of peoples, who generally rubbed together well for over 450 years, but with elements capable of violence at certain points.

Ottoman rulers also let the orthodox archbishopric continue ruling its Greek flock under a practice known as the *millet* system, allowing non-Muslim communities some self-rule. This cemented the role of the now centuries-old Cypriot archbishopric as both a religious office and a Greek community leadership position – the Roman Catholic Church having been evicted when the Venetians left.

Britain became the final empire to take over Cyprus from the waning power of the Ottomans, who had already allowed Greek independence in 1821 and suffered defeat at the hands of an encroaching Russia from 1877 to 1878. The completion of the Suez Canal in Egypt opened a new route for British Imperial interests in the east making Britain anxious about a menacing Russia, a country they had tussled with throughout the nineteenth century in the 'Great Game'. Britain, therefore, forced the sultan to make Cyprus a British protectorate in 1878 in return for protecting other Ottoman lands against Russia. Under the terms of this deal, Cyprus was to be 'occupied and administered'[4] by Britain for as long as desired, though the paper deeds and sovereignty stayed with the Ottomans.

This protectorate, which started a defence and social relationship between Britain and Cyprus – and is still current today, caused diplomats some scratching of heads. For having grabbed the island for political as much as military reasons to defend the Ottomans and win their own share of the spoils if that eastern empire collapsed, they were not entirely sure what to do with their new possession. Eventually, they decided the island should be an eastern version of Gibraltar, a type of impregnable outpost of the British Empire in the Eastern Mediterranean and a defensive chain linking Gibraltar and Malta.

The British occupation of Egypt in the following decade diminished this concept and again left defence planners pondering over the worth of Cyprus. They even offered it back to Greece during the London Peace Conference (1912–1913) in return for building a deep-water base on another Greek island. These considerations continued until Britain placed Cyprus under military occupation in 1914 when Turkey became a First World War (1914–1918) enemy. Britain again offered Cyprus back to Greece in October 1915, providing that Greece joined the war effort and protected Serbia from Bulgarian incursions. Greek King Constantine I rejected the offer fearing that new gains were not worth the risk of losing other territory in battle – a decision also swayed by his marriage to the sister of German Kaiser Wilhelm I.

After the First World War, Britain for a third time considered returning Cyprus to Greece, but decided against it because of the complication of Turkish-Cypriot interests and instead made the island a Commonwealth Crown Colony in 1925, ending the paper sovereignty exercised by the now finished Ottoman Empire. Cyprus proved an important supply base for the Allies during the Second World War, but no one actually fought over Cyprus as they did for the Greek island of Crete.

Against this 1,500-year record, Makarios took up his religious office, which had outlasted the Romans, Byzantines, Crusaders, Arabs and Turks, and was as old as the papacy in Rome. No one could ever fathom how the weight of this past informed Makarios's mentality about becoming the guardian of Greek culture thousands of years old. For here was a man of supreme cunning, large political appetite and undecipherable complexity, who never revealed his feelings. Few forget his piercing eyes and fewer came to understand his real intentions for Cyprus or himself.

He instigated the effort to rid Cyprus of its final foreign power – the British – by helping found *enosis*, a campaign to unite Cyprus with Greece and create the past glories of a large complete Hellenistic region. Crete, which had escaped Ottoman hands in 1898, provided the latest precedent when it became part of Greece in 1913 and one of its sons, Eleftherios Venizelos, became a noted Greek prime minister.

Nineteenth-century Greek Cypriots had believed that Britain's protectorate would be a stepping stone to union with Greece. After all, they thought, Britain had helped Greece achieve independence from the Ottomans seventy years earlier and had also returned the Ionian Islands to Greece in 1864. This aspiration was soon thwarted, causing the rise of an anti-British sentiment, which was particularly strong in the Troodos Mountains at the Kykkos Monastery founded by a Byzantine emperor in the eleventh century. This was also where Makarios began his life as a novice monk. This early push for *enosis* fomented a limited but bloody revolt when Greek Cypriots burnt down Government House in Nicosia in 1931 before reinforcements from neighbouring colonies restored order two months later.

Turkish Cypriots who knew that fellow Turks had been forced to migrate from other islands when uniting with Greece favoured British rule to protect them. Their equivalent variant of union with mainland Turkey, *taksim*, emerged in the 1920s, partly to counter *enosis* but also in response to the revival of Turkish mainland pride when General Mustafa Kemal Atatürk became president of Turkey in 1923 after the fall of the Ottomans and the defeat by the Allies during the First World War. *Taksim* though did not attract the same strength as *enosis* among Cypriot Turks, who tended to regard themselves a notch up from their mainland neighbours.

What Makarios meant by *enosis* is puzzling. Whether he favoured union with the Greek mainland, making him simply another regional bishop among many or used this as means for independence – and what that meant in respect of Greek-Cypriot control over Turkish-Cypriot neighbours – is not clearly understood and may never be. His interest probably lay more in his version of *enosis* or his version of independence – which was possibly the same thing – granting him a national platform. In any event, during the 1950s, he became the figure head and public voice for *enosis*, consistently summoning international support for the cause and knocking on the doors of the UN for sponsorship to join Greece.

He worked uneasily with a fellow founding member, Georgios 'George' Grivas, a small, austere old-school romantic hero to the Greeks and veteran of the Greco-Turkish War (1919–1922) and the Second World War fight against Germany. Grivas, a dyed-in-the-wool warrior who adopted the name of Digenis – a hero of legend from Byzantium, became the military leader of *enosis*. He formed a right-wing guerilla organisation called the Ethniki Organosis Kyprion Agoniston (National Organisation of Cypriot Fighters or abbreviated to EOKA), which began a campaign of assassination against British and Greek-Cypriot soldiers as well as Turkish Cypriots. Britain put a price on his head for this cause, which targeted civilians and led to 660 deaths.

Makarios was uneasy about the guerilla campaign but helped plan and direct some activities. His influence caused the British to expel him into pleasant exile on the Seychelles in 1956. Here, his arrival created a last-minute panic when diplomats realised the potential public relations disaster of placing the archbishop in comfortable surroundings unfortunately named 'La Bastille'. The governor general quickly relinquished his own residence where the exiled archbishop lived in impressive surroundings renamed Makarios House. During his brief stay, Makarios was helped with his English by the wife of a retired Indian Army officer, who possibly became one of the very few people in whom he confided.

Meanwhile, British use of Turkish police officers to restore order in Cyprus caused Grivas to declare open season on Turkish Cypriots, poisoning community relations as never before and causing them to make louder calls for *taksim*. Turkish generals in Ankara, Turkey, helped their Cypriot cousins form the Türk Mukavemet Teşkilatı (Turkish Resistance Organisation or abbreviated to TMT) to counter EOKA and sometimes used similar terrorist tactics.

Britain deployed 17,000 servicemen between 1955 and 1959 to quell EOKA's campaign, which numbered around 1,200 fighters, in a conflict known as the Cyprus Emergency. Some features were captured in the 1964 film thriller, *The High Bright Sun* (1964), starring dashing British film star Dirk Bogarde as a British intelligence officer falling in love with an American student, who happens to live at the house where the fictional leader of the rebellion – supposedly Grivas – is staying. This was no fiction though, for EOKA's hidden assassins killed over 300 British servicemen and injured many more through ambushes of bombs and sniper fire.

After eventually gaining the upper hand, Britain released Makarios and then invited his participation in independence discussions. Whitehall brokered these discussions in both London and Zürich, Switzerland, between Greek Prime Minister Konstantinos G. Karamanlis – a stalwart in politics and later to play a crucial role in 1974, who agreed to give up any idea of *enosis* from the perspective of Athens – and his Turkish counterpart, Prime Minister Ali Adnan Ertekin Menderes, and authorities in Cyprus, including Makarios as well as Dr Fazil Küçük for the Turkish Cypriots. In February 1959, at Lancaster House in London, they agreed an independent republic of Cyprus under a presidential system of a Greek-Cypriot president, a Turkish-Cypriot vice president and a parliament of five-year terms allocating thirty-five seats for the first community and fifteen for the second.

These well-intentioned arrangements, which tried to balance power between Greek Cypriots and Turkish Cypriots, soon broke down increasing tension between both communities.

Makarios, however, benefitted by returning to the island and winning the first presidential election in December 1959. He now exercised power like no other Cypriot before him, securing all 3 Cypriot leaderships positions combining the 1,500-year-old office of archbishop and *ethnarch* with the modern-day role of elected head of state. Fazil Küçük won the election as the unopposed vice president representing the Turkish community. Georgios Grivas was by contrast exiled to Greece – a point Britain insisted on, having twice narrowly missed arresting him – where he enjoyed a hero's welcome, many honours including promotion to general and temporarily settled into Greek politics and gardening.

Makarios formally assumed the presidency in August 1960 becoming the most prominent political figure in the Greek-speaking world giving him a platform to deal with world leaders from Washington to Moscow. He made Cyprus neutral by joining the non-aligned bloc of countries in 1961 and courted third-world countries, all to play off the superpowers in his favour and build alternative sources of strength for a small island at the mercy of larger countries. Before long the Western press portrayed him as the 'Fidel Castro of the Mediterranean'.

His power over Cyprus was not complete, however, for not only were constitutional rights granted to Turkish Cypriots, but an associated Treaty of Guarantee obliged Britain, Greece and Turkey to protect the constitution and the island's independence, territorial integrity and constitution. One notable article allowed them to consult together in the event of any violations and, if collective action by all three was not possible, unilaterally intervene. These clauses not only tied a reluctant Britain to Cypriot domestic affairs but gave Turkey justification to intercede in certain circumstances.

Under these new arrangements, Britain also obtained sovereign land – in other words permanent territory – for military bases in Akrotiri on the south coast of the island and Dhekelia on the east coast. It also leased small pockets of land for scattered facilities, including listening posts, which until 1966 included RAF Nicosia when the airport became passed into civilian hands, but with Britain retaining residual responsibilities.

An accompanying Treaty of Alliance also bound Greece, Cyprus and Turkey to prevent any aggression against the island. Greece and Turkey had the right to station troops – 950 and 650 respectively – supposedly under a tripartite headquarters in Cyprus, which instead of providing comfort to their respective communities proved a thin mask for importing numerous weapons and soldiers quickly exceeding the treaty numbers.

Despite helping to shape these London and Zürich agreements, including a provision to permanently renounce *enosis*, Makarios conveniently denounced them to create the illusion for his supporters that he was forced to sign other people's bits of paper. He especially repudiated the guarantees permitting other countries to interfere with the self-determination of Cyprus and his new authority. He further regretted giving Turkish Cypriots a separate status and veto powers; and spent the next decade undoing their rights. In doing so, he chose division over unity, treating the Turkish Cypriots badly and trying in 1963 to change the constitution to establish majority rule for Greek Cypriots.

Ankara, already angered by Makarios's attempt to remove their 650 troops, dismissed his proposals. Vice President Fazil Küçük said 'no' and Turkey's 180,000 strong Cypriot community, some 18 per cent of the population fast becoming second-class citizens, withdrew from the government and started ruling themselves in enclaves dotted around the island with the largest in the north, pitting communities against each other in conditions making violence highly likely.

This violence came to pass in December 1963 when some Greek-Cypriot police officers roughed up a Turkish family causing two deaths, followed a week or so later by a group of Greek nationalists attacking a Turkish village, killing Turks, including a mainland military officer and his family stationed there. Ankara sent in low-flying jets to buzz the conflict zones in support of their regiment, and irregular forces encircled their Turkish communities for defence. By Christmas, 500 people from both sides had died, a memory seared into Cypriot history as the 'Christmas Massacre'. Britain with agreement from Athens restored order.

Some Turkish Cypriots fled northwards to escape their exposed villages and Greek Cypriots moved south with those from either side caught in the wrong place faring badly. American diplomat Barrington King in Cyprus between 1964 to 1967 saw what happened:

> You couldn't travel between those points if you were a Greek or Turk, you'd be killed, that's all there was to it; but you could, if you were a diplomat, but it was risky business and several times when I was driving in both the Greek and the Turkish parts of the island, you'd be stopped by some 15-year-old kid with an automatic weapon poked in your face. There were violent incidents all the time.[5]

British forces commander Major General Peter Young used a green wax pencil in early 1964 to draw out a protective buffer zone on a map dividing Nicosia, consequently dubbed the 'Green Line'. Britain patrolled this new line to maintain order until handing over responsibility in March that year to a newly formed UN peacekeeping force called United Nations Peacekeeping Force in Cyprus (UNFICYP). At the same time, the UN appointed a mediator, former Finnish prime minister, Sakari Severi Tuomioja, who unfortunately suffered a fatal haemorrhage while in Cyprus.

Further fighting still broke out in summer 1964 with both Greek and Turkish militaries equipping their irregular units, reinforcing the separation between the two communities. A strong public reaction in Turkey again pushed the government in Ankara to intervene and protect displaced Turkish Cypriots. Turkish planes flew in to show their presence threatening to cause war with Greece and throwing NATO into disarray. Makarios quickly put together the Cypriot

National Guard to protect against a possible Turkish intervention, which swelled to an 8,000-strong force from Greek soldiers smuggled in from the mainland.

Newly elected Greek Prime Minister Georgios Papandreou – who thought that *enosis* was the answer – allowed the old war dog Georgios Grivas – who had from afar watched his nationalist vision fall apart – to return in June 1964 to take control of all-Greek military forces in Cyprus. Grivas was sent as much to control Makarios as organise the military for the Greek prime minister and he had a common cause in their hatred of communism, which Makarios seemingly now embodied. Makarios's former collaborator eventually became a deadly political foe widening the fissure in Cypriot political infighting between left- and right-wing political forces, but for the time being they looked in lock step, appearing together at a public rally when thousands turned out to see the return of their legendary Cypriot warrior.

Grivas's return and further violence readied Turkish generals to intervene. Lacking in plans and equipment their make-do preparations soon alerted and startled the Americans who feared the collapse of NATO. American President Lyndon B. Johnson sent Ankara a letter – now regarded as one of the most aggressive messages one NATO ally can send another –threatening to leave Turkey defenceless against the Soviets by withdrawing all military equipment, including nuclear cover. American Undersecretary of State George W. Ball described this as 'producing the diplomatic equivalent of an atomic bomb'.[6] The impact of this bomb went deeper than the United States anticipated for while the threat stopped the Turks from intervening, they never forgot nor forgave this message from a close ally stopping them from defending their citizens.

In June 1964, Johnson commissioned Ball and Dean Acheson, a former American secretary of state, to look for a lasting solution, which they went about in intensive discussions with Ankara and Athens, and with Makarios.

Further fighting broke out in the middle of these discussions in August 1964 causing Turkish and Greek fighter jets to strafe positions in support of their own factions. An aghast Johnson again calmed the situation.

Meanwhile Acheson and Ball developed a plan from their hard bargaining that returned Cyprus to Greece but gave Turkey an 80-square mile sovereign base on the Karpas Peninsula to the north of Cyprus and granted Turkish Cypriots protected status. Turkey looked on the plans favourably, but Papandreou prevaricated, so Acheson modified his plan to recommend giving Turkey a fifty-year lease for a base instead of sovereignty. This was not an American imposed plan, but a genuine effort to find common ground and prevent a future conflict over the island.

Makarios predictably refused, claiming that any formal Turkish presence, even with a lease, diminished Cypriot independence and meant Turkish interference. Papandreou, unable to control Makarios, who was the elected leader of an independent nation and arguably the larger personality in the Greek-speaking world, had no alternative but to reject the plan. American political counsellor Herbert Daniel Brewster in Greece at the time thought the

> Greeks shot the plan down, because Makarios would not accept the solution proposed. The Turks were ready to accept it, but it would have taken negotiation ... Makarios wanted the whole piece of pie. He was doing it just as a way of showing that 'nobody can walk over me.'[7]

Greek rejection infuriated Johnson, who at the height of the negotiations had told Papandreou that no other question had taken up so much of his own personal time and attention. When the Greek ambassador explained to him that no Greek government could accept such a plan, Johnson replied in his notable earthy language, 'F**k your Parliament and your Constitution'.[8]

The United States gave up on the diplomatic initiative but could not divorce itself from a crucial NATO front that might collapse in any Greek-Turkish conflict. Tension and incidents continued for the next three years but not enough to disturb a film of uneasy calm across the island.

Then events in mainland Greece provoked another crisis after a military junta in Athens deposed the democratically elected Greek prime minister, Georgios Papandreou, in April 1967 and pushed the cause of *enosis*. This presented an internal threat to Makarios who began to fear the Greek-led National Guard and the Cypriot police, and opened a stronger rift with Georgios Grivas who, inspired by the junta, overran two Turkish-Cypriot villages in November 1967, killing Turkish Cypriots and renewing serious prospect of a Turkish-Greek war. Turkey, facing large demonstrations demanding support for their neighbours, readied its armed forces to intervene and Greece threatened retaliation.

American political officer Thomas 'Tom' David Boyatt in Nicosia – who played a leading role as an expert on Cyprus seven years later – saw the problems in 1967 for himself:

There were several days during which the crisis got worse, and we were expecting a Turkish invasion at any moment. Meanwhile, there was frenzied diplomatic activity in all the capitals essentially trying to avert a Turkish invasion. Anyway it got bad enough so that we evacuated all the women and children, and non-essentials, and got down to the very core group. At that point, myself and the Turkish language officer, were going back and forth between the lines, and that was very dangerous. You know, as always, there were teenage kids manning guard posts with automatic weapons on both sides, nervous as hell. It was very tricky ...[9]

This time Johnson sent out Cyrus Vance, a former undersecretary of defense, as his envoy to mediate an agreement. Robert V. Keeley, political officer at the American Embassy in Athens, stood ready to brief Vance on his arrival but never had the opportunity:

because as soon as the meeting began, Vance said he didn't want to hear anything about the Cyprus problem; he was not in Athens to solve the Cyprus problem. He said that too many people, better qualified than he, had tried to do that over a period of years and had failed and he would, if he tried it, also fail. He added that he didn't even have time to understand it. He had just one mission from the President [Lyndon Johnson] and that was to prevent war between Greece and Turkey over Cyprus.[10]

And that he did, manoeuvring Greece to reluctantly withdraw thousands of troops who had infiltrated the island though leaving the National Guard untouched and again recalling Grivas to the mainland. These actions provided the conditions to start local negotiations between Greek-Cypriot and Turkish-Cypriot community representatives.

Vance also gave Turkey another sharp warning curtailing its intervention for a second time. Playing this ultimate card against the Turks had consequences. Their simmering resentment of twice missing an opportunity – in 1964 and 1967 – to protect their own people and resolve their long-held security concerns about Greek positions in Cyprus weakened American-Turkish relations and created a determination that the United States must never again stay their hand. Vance presciently noted at the end of his mission that 'The next time the Greeks provoke the Turks over Cyprus there will be no stopping them. They'll invade Cyprus and nothing we or anyone else can do will stop them.'[11]

Makarios then constantly frustrated talks between the Greek-Cypriot and Turkish-Cypriot communities and undermined efforts by Athens and Ankara to reach an agreement on Cyprus over his head. His perpetual disturbance of seeming solutions, his reliance on left-wing factions, his flirting with the Soviets and his leadership of the non-aligned countries reinforced a reputation as the 'Fidel Castro of the Mediterranean'. British servicemen stationed in Cyprus called him 'Red Mac'.

But Makarios's professed left-wing leanings are like the man himself, complex and not completely understood. The archbishop, who wore the robes of ancient Greek nationalism and supported the Greek monarchy, used forces from the left as much as for convenience as for any ideological commitment. He manoeuvred them as tactical counterweight to strong right-wing factions lined up against him, which included fellow Greek orthodox bishops, Grivas's guerilla movement, the Cypriot police and the National Guard, and smaller organisations including a National Front party.

For this reason, he relied heavily on the island's communist party, Ανορθωτικό Κόμμα Εργαζόμενου Λαού (Anorthotikó Kómma Ergazómenou Laoú – Progressive Party of Working People or abbreviated to AKEL), founded in 1926, which boasted the largest communist membership per head of population of any in Western Europe. AKEL had close connections to Moscow, which provided funding and training, and dominated some two thirds of unions in Cyprus – the final third falling under the sway of the church – and saw in Makarios a way to remove Western forces from Cyprus. During the Cyprus Emergency, AKEL formed an uneasy alliance with Grivas to support *enosis* despite his killing many of their comrades a decade earlier in the Greek Civil War (which took place between 1944–1945 and 1946–1949). This peace did not last, and periodic violence broke out between the right and left in yet another fracture of the island's political complexity, many a left-wing family fearing a visit by EOKA's masked men to their villages. Violence between Greek Cypriots was a fact of life.

Even closer to Makarios were forces of the island's socialist party, ΕΔΕΚ Σοσιαλιστικό Κόμμα (United Democratic Centre Union or abbreviated to EDEK), formed by his own doctor, Dr Vassos Lyssarides, who was another EOKA veteran and former member of the communist party. Lyssarides recruited paramilitaries to EDEK, which served as a protection force for the archbishop.

By the 1970s, Makarios's sobriquet as the 'Fidel Castro of the Mediterranean' had waned in the West though not in Greece. From the United States' perspective, the archbishop represented a figure more like Egypt's Gamal Abdel Nasser, an opportunist who had close relations with the Soviets. Britain did not seriously think that Makarios would make Cyprus a communist country.

In fact, while a prominent leader in the non-aligned movement, Makarios cooperated with Britain and the United States in relation to Cold War politics, neither protesting nor making any political statement about the nuclear missiles and intelligence operations at British bases or American involvement. William Rex Crawford Jr, the American deputy chief mission in Nicosia from 1968 to 1972, noticed how Makarios 'quietly cooperated in many respects with the United States, in an anti-Communist sense'.[12] He signed an agreement with the United States in 1968 to continue the operation of listening posts on the island and kept quiet about the supposedly secret U2 flights operating from RAF Akrotiri to aid the Arab-Israeli peace process. And even while relying on AKEL for political support, he manoeuvred events to stop this communist party winning an outright election majority in parliament.

In this way, Makarios governed Cyprus as a hugely popular, almost cult-like figure, among less well-educated Greek Cypriots, a towering political presence on both the island and in Greece, courted in the international limelight, accepted but distrusted by Western powers, detested by the Turks and understood by hardly anyone.

Peter Ramsbottom, the British high commissioner from 1969 to 1972, and later the British ambassador in Washington during the crisis, saw him as the 'last surviving priest-king. He was a dignified, cheerful and confident man. I remember that people used to think that they would get his assent as he was so courteous. Not a bit.'[13] But Sir Derek Malcolm Day, counsellor at the High Commission from 1972, thought him

> the single greatest obstacle to any kind of settlement in the Cyprus problem. I don't think he had the vision or the statesmanship to see that accommodation with the Turkish Cypriots would have preserved the unity and identity of Cyprus ... I think he had a very closed mind.[14]

Tom Boyatt thought he

> was probably the most masterful politician diplomat I've ever seen ... He was just terrific at playing off all sides against each other, and playing off the problem, playing off the problem until something changed which put him in less danger, or brought him closer to his goal.[15]

His island was a land of contrasts. Cyprus did not boast much wealth as an agricultural nation vulnerable to drought with a smattering of light industries and shipping and dependent on spending by British forces. It was plagued by political violence. Yet a world away from the sporadic troubles, the island's endless sun and blue waters attracted young families in a burgeoning tourism scene, especially on northern Cypriot beaches and at Famagusta in the east, which hosted sun seekers and international celebrities, including Richard Burton and Elizabeth Taylor.

These juxtapositions were common across the island. In April 1970, four young talented Swedes few people had yet heard of – ABBA – played their first touring concert in Famagusta for the Swedish contingent of UNFICYP. Elsewhere a twice-daily UN armoured convoy had to escort Greek holiday makers who wanted to sunbathe in Kyrenia, returning them before dark. Celebrities also sought out the archbishop, such as Hollywood actor Telly Savalas born to Greek American parents in New York and famous for his highly popular fictional detective character, the lollipop sucking *Kojak*.

Political antagonism still worsened in the 1970s between Makarios and the ruling junta, known as the regime of the colonels, which was led by soldier Georgios Papadopoulos, the Greek prime minister. Makarios's supposed communist leanings rubbed up against these right-wing military officers and their ambitions for Cyprus making the period between 1967 and 1974 a sinister game of cat and mouse. While intercommunal talks struggled to find a solution on the ground, the junta tried unseating Makarios through politics – and possibly through the gun, although assassination attempts against the archbishop were nothing new. William Crawford, the American deputy chief of mission in Nicosia, faithfully recorded the various intrigues against the archbishop for the United States, with his detective work earning him the Department of State's annual reporting award in 1971.

Perhaps the closest came in 1970 when on the morning of Sunday, 8 March, British High Commissioner Ramsbottom asleep at his official residence awoke suddenly to a crackling of gunshot fire in sleepy Nicosia. These same noises were also heard by the recently arrived First Secretary Richard Oliver Miles (known as Oliver Miles), who turned to his wife and said, 'Did you hear that noise, it sounded to me like machine gun fire?' She replied, 'Don't be silly, you aren't in Aden anymore.'[16]

Across the dusty streets of the capital, 2 miles away, Makarios's two-seater helicopter had begun climbing from the President Palace ferrying him to a monastery when machine gun fire riddled the canopy. Four Greek Cypriots, including two police officers, positioned on the flat roof of a nearby house opened fire at close range in a planned attack called Operation Hermes. Despite being shot twice in the stomach, the skilful Greek air force pilot landed in a street avoiding telegraph wires. Makarios, blessed with nine lives, got out unscathed, flagged down a passing car and returned to his palace. The gunmen escaped but were later caught and prosecuted that year.

Which of the Greek military officers on the island were implicated in this attempt and any connection back to the junta is not clear. A week later, on Friday, 13 March 1970, Cypriot police officers boarded a plane bound for Beirut, Lebanon, removing the former Cypriot interior minister, Polykarpos Giorkatzis, the suspected organiser of the plot. He was not arrested, however, and two days later, on Monday, 16 March 1970, two men, quite possibly co-conspirators, walked up to Giorkatzis sitting in a car on a quiet road between Famagusta and Nicosia for an agreed rendezvous and shot him six times.

Nothing highlighted the complications of riven Greek-Cypriot politics more than the assassination of this former minister, a one-time EOKA fighter and former supporter of Makarios who became a rival. Giorkatzis had forged a relationship with the Greek junta and the Americans in anti-communist activity as head of the Cypriot police, which Makarios knew about and tolerated without intervention. Then, in 1968, he bizarrely helped in some fashion a disaffected student enter Greece, who tried to murder the head of the junta Colonel Georgios Papadopoulos with a car bomb. This isolated him from Athens, leading to his sacking from Makarios's Cabinet and establishing a political party called the United Front.

Giorkatzis hoped to win seats in the forthcoming election setting him up as a rival to Makarios, even though his new party espoused a practical view on *enosis* and was closer to the views of the archbishop than more radical *enosis* colleagues. Why then supposedly use his connections to try and kill Makarios in the chaotic helicopter attack? And his own killers could have come from any number of sources: junta links, various Makarios supporters or even from a small National Front party founded the previous year bent on achieving *enosis*.

A year after this assassination attempt, 70-year-old Georgios Grivas, hankering after his obsessive *enosis* cause, slipped back into Cyprus in August 1971. Four years had passed since he was withdrawn for the second time and now had Makarios, the traitor to union with Greece and a communist threat, in his eye. Makarios understood the meaning of Grivas's return telling American Ambassador Robert 'Bob' McCloskey in 1973 that besides *enosis* Grivas 'wants to kill me'.[17]

Grivas renewed the former EOKA guerilla campaign on a smaller scale, creating an offshoot called EOKA-B, recruiting around 700 fighters, some who worked as police officers or served in the Cypriot National Guard. Their objective was *enosis*, at any cost, bombing police stations, police homes and government buildings, and battling

Makarios's supporters. Grivas also fought for the hearts of Greek Cypriots with funds from Greece that enabled three new newspapers to advocate his cause.

Matters peaked with Greece when early that year Makarios tapped his fellow monks at Kykkos Monastery for $2.5 million to buy weapons, including bazookas from Czechoslovakia, and even hid them in the cellars of monastery. Head of the Greek junta Georgios Papadopoulos demanded he hand them over to the UN, form a government of national unity and let community talks proceed. Makarios refused so the Greek leader planned a coup and even warned the Turkish military using a hotline between the respective armed forces, thinking that now was time to improve Greek-Turkish relations by resolving differences over Cyprus. The United States learnt about the operation – as did Makarios who lobbied the Americans – and forestalled Greek action with a strong warning about the consequences.

Makarios had won yet another sparring round with a principal enemy, though he did hand over some of the arms to the UN. His popularity across the Greek community stayed firm as no one stood against him in the presidential election of February 1973, which was consequently cancelled and he was unanimously declared president for a third five-year term.

Violence continued though. In early April 1973, two cars and a bar in Larnaca used by Grivas's supporters were blown up. Grivas's supporters retaliated by gunning down a known supporter of Makarios and setting fire to a petrol station linked to the victim.

Such tit-for-tat operations continued with both leaders in Cyprus careful to avoid evidence incriminating themselves in a move against the other. Makarios could not arrest Grivas because of the guerilla fighters' support, so formed his own personal bodyguard organisation, the police Tactical Reserve Unit. This was yet another paramilitary force around 500 strong, which he used to purge the Cypriot police of Grivas supporters. Grivas replied by kidnapping the minister of justice from his house in July 1973, who, surprisingly, was released unharmed in August of the same year. This resulted in large public demonstrations denouncing Grivas's criminal acts with mainstream Greek Cypriots now turning against the continued unrest. Even the mainland Greek dictator Georgios Papadopoulos had to distance himself from Grivas, publicly calling on him to stop his campaign, which the independently minded Grivas and his deputies took as a betrayal and, in turn, denounced the junta for abandoning *enosis*.

However, Papadopoulos, although dissuaded by the Americans from taking action two years previously and allowing a calm to settle over relations with the archbishop, did not entirely abandon hopes of removing Makarios by other means. That same year, 1973, three conservative bishops in Cyprus who all supported *enosis* tried defrocking Makarios. They convened a synod in April 1973 proclaiming the archbishop in violation of church law for simultaneously holding religious and political office. The hand of Greece seemed to be somewhere in the background. Makarios still proved their match by appealing to the Holy Synod of the Greek Orthodox Church, which found in his favour and ended up defrocking the three bishops themselves.

Makarios then avoided a second serious assassination attempt, on 7 October 1973, when land mines detonated along the road to Famagusta, only five minutes before his car drove him to Sunday mass at a local village, leaving four craters. The perpetrators were never identified.

While this Greek-Cypriot in-fighting dominated the 1970s, relative stability characterised Greek and Turkish community relations as talks proceeded in fits and starts. Imposing on this story were the leaders of each community, Greek Cypriot Glafcos Ioannou Clerides and his Turkish counterpart, Rauf Raif Denktaş, both well-educated barristers and politicians, with portly stomachs concealed by smart three-piece suits, and both masters in persuasive oratory and shrewd manoeuvring to advance their separate causes.

Born in April 1919, Clerides hailed from a prominent barrister father, Ioannis, who had stood against Makarios in the first presidential election. Clerides earned a mention in despatches in the RAF before being shot down over Hamburg, Germany in 1942 seeing out the Second World War as a prisoner. Afterwards, he turned to law like his father studying at King's College London, passing through Lincoln's Inn (one of the four Inns of Court for barristers), then practicing in London where he met his Indian born wife, Lila Irene, who worked for the BBC.

Like his contemporaries, Clerides immersed himself in the EOKA campaign when returning to Cyprus to practice law, assisting the movement under the alias of Hyperides, particularly by defending those prosecuted for their involvement. He participated in the independence negotiations and won election to the Cypriot Parliament in 1960, where he served as speaker, constitutionally elevating him to the role of acting president when Makarios was unavailable. In 1968, the archbishop made him chief negotiator with the Turkish community, though astutely kept his distance to avoid being tarnished by any concessions given to Turkish Cypriots.

Clerides had a testy relationship with Makarios, who worked to constrain and at times undermine him with both of them being undeclared rivals. He was sometimes associated with political intrigues against the archbishop and had helped form the United Front with the assassinated Giorkatzis though Makarios ruled him out of participation in the helicopter plot. Yet for all his moderation and respect from Britain and the United States, which kept in regular private contact, Clerides could not carry the Greek community towards any lasting solutions in the way that Makarios could if he were minded. And neither the archbishop's supporters including the socialist and communist parties nor the right-wing advocates of *enosis* favoured him.

Unlike Makarios though, Clerides crucially earned the trust of Turkish Cypriots and Turkey, and the respect of his counterpart, Rauf Denktaş. Born in Paphos in January 1924, Denktaş, who also came from a legal family, studied law in London where the two met as fellow barrister students. Clerides, for his part, claimed that Denktaş could not hold his beer and that he often carried him back to his digs after a night on the town. Denktaş served as a wartime teacher and civil servant afterwards becoming a state prosecutor of accused EOKA members, sometimes on the same case defended by Clerides, eventually becoming Queen's Counsel.

Denktaş was similarly involved in the 1960 independence discussions, won an election as a member of parliament, eventually becoming the official negotiator opposite Clerides and subsequently winning the vice presidency in the same election in 1973 that returned Makarios unopposed as president. He also had links to the hardmen of his cause, for, despite his gregariousness, he was tough, stubborn and helped form the Turkish-Cypriot paramilitaries, TMT.

Both clever lawyers opposed each but kept up a trustworthy level of communication while arguing intensely. Denktaş, a Greek speaker, once said that Clerides was the only Greek Cypriot he respected. He was the politically stronger of the two with a personal power among the Turkish Cypriots making him in one sense the equivalent of Makarios. Yet despite this authority, his agile mind could be the more inflexible, wedded to a form of partition under a single Cypriot government.

Left alone these two practical lawyers who understood each other might well have thrashed out a deal. Clerides, however, was ever wary of Makarios, and Denktaş was beholden to the Turkish military in Ankara with whom he had good relations, but where authority lay. Their community talks lasted for six years, breaking down in June 1968 and resuming in 1972 under the initiative of UN Secretary General Dr Kurt Waldheim. Twice they appeared near to compromise, but

Makarios stepped in unwilling to concede too much and vehemently opposed changes creating a federal system or cantons.

In any event, dark developments on the Greek mainland eclipsed the progress of community talks. A new hardman, Brigadier General Dimitrios Ioannidis, head of the Greek military police, Ελληνική Στρατιωτική Αστυνομία (abbreviated to ESA), rarely seen in public and careful to avoid photographs, had deposed the junta leaders including Prime Minister Georgios Papadopoulos on 25 November 1973. He stepped in after the junta violently broke up a November student protest at Athens Polytechnic, with numbers killed in double figures, and reimposed martial law.

Right-wing purist Ioannidis had become alarmed by liberal reforms introduced by Papadopoulos, including plans for parliamentary elections in 1974, which he thought the country was not ready for and which the student uprising had, to his mind, conclusively proved. He, therefore, executed this second Greek coup without bloodshed, installing another general, Phaedon Gizikis, as president and an American educated economist Adamantios Androutsopoulos as prime minister, though exercised real power from the shadows. A rabid anti-communist, Ioannidis despised the left-wing Makarios whom he thought intended to turn the island to the Soviet Union, which he would not allow, so this meant only one thing: removing the archbishop.

Back on Cyprus on 27 January 1974, the born-to-be guerilla fighter Georgios Grivas died of a heart attack in his lair at Limassol. The Greek ambassador, all-Greek-Cypriot National Guard commanders and nearly 100,000 Cypriots attended 3 days of mourning as Grivas's body lay on a bed draped in the Greek flag. Thousands streamed past in this unofficial lying- in- state funeral, boycotted by Makarios and his government, including former EOKA fighters and the newer breed of EOKA-B, some holding banners declaring, 'we shall struggle for union with Greece till death'.[18]

Among the mourners was the notorious figure of Nikos Sampson, a strident lieutenant of EOKA-B and former EOKA fighter with a reputation for killing British soldiers, Turks and fellow Greek Cypriots, and playing no small part for the attribution of one street in Nicosia as 'Murder Mile'. He escaped a death sentence in the 1950s for killing a police sergeant when a complaint about torture led to a commuted sentence of life imprisonment, which was lifted when Cyprus became independent. Sampson then led irregular units in attacks on Turkish communities during the 1963 troubles earning him a reputation as the 'Butcher of Omorphita' to Turkish Cypriots and the 'Tourkfogos' ('Turk eater') to the Turks.

The American deputy chief of mission from 1968 to 1972, William Crawford, saw him as

> just a plain despicable man whose claim to fame in history was that he carried in his newspaper during the period of the fight against the British pictures of a British woman and child blown up or shot in the back, lying bleeding to death on a Nicosia Street. The common story was that it was [Nikos] Sampson who had shot them in the back and then stepped up to photograph them and give it more publicity. This was the view that the Cypriots had of him – cheap, unintelligent, ambitious, a killer, a thug.[19]

Glafcos Clerides had the unfortunate pleasure of once being a neighbour. On one occasion when out gardening in a white shirt Sampson went over to him and said that whenever he saw white shirt, he saw blood and blood spreading. Not all his family had the same disposition, for his wife, Vera (née Fessus), was surprisingly charming.

Sampson became a journalist after independence and founded a right-wing newspaper called *Mahi* (meaning combat), advocating union with Greece. He won election as a member of parliament where he displayed his anti-Turk rhetoric without elegance, for Sampson had no formal education and his Greek was corrected by other parliamentarians. An American political officer, James Alan Williams, met him regularly in his duties. One day, he found Sampson sitting at a huge desk in his office with shelves lined with newspapers, magazines and books, which Williams doubted this politician-journalist had read. Instead, he often found him studying the centrefold of *Playboy* magazine: 'He was totally unembarrassed about it, put it to the side, and then would talk rather freely about how he saw the political development within the Greek-Cypriot community, or within Cyprus'.[20]

Sampson arranged EOKA-B members around the casket at Grivas's funeral while he spoke to the crowds of continuing the fight for *enosis* to rounds of applause. Then he slammed his fist on the coffin and shouted out, 'We will avenge you Digenis!'[21] He even left a copy of his *Mahi* magazine in Grivas's casket.

Chapter 2

BRITISH EXPOSURE

Nikos Sampson's name attracted little attention at the Foreign and Commonwealth Office in London where there was otherwise apprehension that fragile Cypriot community relations might collapse as happened closer to home in Northern Ireland. Indeed, Cyprus was similarly a headache without cure, which Britain because of its strong military presence and role as a guarantor power had, on paper, the heaviest responsibility while realistically lacking the means to make any difference.

The newly appointed British Foreign Secretary Jim Callaghan, who took up post in May 1973 under Labour Prime Minister Harold Wilson, did not have this on top of his in tray. Wilson had unexpectedly beaten Edward Heath's Conservatives in the snap general election of February 1973 but fell some thirty-three seats short of an overall majority to form Britain's first post-Second World War minority government. This exposed position dominated the thinking of senior party figures who had to navigate around parliamentary defeats for the rest of the year and into 1974 while planning for the inevitable next early election.

An experienced politician, a former chancellor of the exchequer and home secretary, Callaghan's skills had some limitation in international diplomacy. Born in 1912 to a background of deprivation and Baptist religion in the naval town of Portsmouth and losing his father when he was aged 9, he worked his way up in Labour Party politics through the Inland Revenue Union, joining the Civil Service aged 16. Then, after wartime service in the Royal Navy, he won election as a member of parliament for Cardiff South in 1945.

Although serving as shadow colonial secretary and shadow foreign secretary in the 1960s, Callaghan's upright moral code and straight-talking union negotiating experience struggled when managing politicians of foreign temperaments and cultures. And he did have a temper. His former assistant private secretary, John Weston, saw him as

> rather like a large grizzly bear, I mean very huggable if he was in the right mood, but if he wasn't you'd better jolly well duck or your head would probably come off your shoulders. He was a very cultured man for someone whose formal education ended at quite an early stage. He had a profound sense of British history and knew quite a lot of British literature.[22]

A prominent consideration for him, as both foreign secretary and a senior Labour politician, in any Greek related matters was the influence of a Greek lobby affecting the party's electoral fortunes. Labour had significant links to a largely London-based Greek and Greek-Cypriot community, concentrated in Camden and championed by Labour's Lena Jeger MP, campaigning for censure of the undemocratic Greek junta. This influence caused Wilson's administration to cancel a visit to Greece by HMS *Tiger* and HMS *Charybdis* in March 1974 infuriating junta leader Dimitrios Ioannidis.

British first secretary in Nicosia from 1970 to 1975, Oliver Miles, realised the strength of this connection:

> I began to see what it meant because you go into a remote mountain village and you go into the square and you sit down next to the old village elder who would be sitting there sipping his brandy and ginger, which was typical in Cyprus, and you would try out your Greek on him and you would find actually he had spent thirty years living in the east end of London. And only came back to Cyprus because his family were there. And this sort of relationship has pervaded everything. My wife was at the LSE [London School of Economics] and she decided early on that it would be fun to start an LSE alumni association and she very quickly had more than half the cabinet in it. President Makarios himself was not at the LSE but most of his ministers were.[23]

Another prevalent feature of 1974 was the mentality of retreat from world affairs in London's foreign policy establishment. Harold Macmillan's 1960s 'winds of change' policy returning colonies to independence continued alongside a financial urgency forcing Britain to dramatically reduce defence spending and surrender international responsibilities. Labour's 1966/1967 defence review, under Prime Minister Harold Wilson's second term in office, had considered but rejected handing over the eastern base, RAF Dhekelia, in Cyprus to Turkey fearing American objections.

A further financial crisis a year later upturning Britain's balance of payments forced Whitehall to reconsider this withdrawal. It was again rejected because the bases provided a staging post to complete the drawdown of forces in the Far East and hosted the mighty Vulcan aircraft with their conventional and nuclear armed weapons for the Central Treaty Organization (CENTO) also known as the Baghdad Pact, which offered support to Iraq, Iran and Pakistan. Civil servants were also mindful of repercussions between Greek and Turkish Cypriots who regarded the bases as a source of protection in times of civil strife.

Wilson's government instead reduced the garrison force in Cyprus and, more dramatically, decided on a national defence policy based only on NATO's theatre of operation in Europe, which curtailed hundreds of years of independent worldwide intervention. This 1966/1967 policy, rarely talked about today, marked the moment Britain decided what role to play in the post-Second World War world. The result meant abandoning bases in the Persian Gulf and cancelling new aircraft orders, including the home designed bomber TSR-2 and naval ships.

Edward Heath who harboured romantic yearnings for British power that he could not afford tried reversing these changes when he was prime minister from 1970 to 1974. But a further balance of payment problems caused even him to start another defence review in 1974, which Harold Wilson's third government inherited.

As Labour took over, yet another financial cloud brought pressures for fresh cuts in 1974 with Treasury mandarins arguing that Britain's NATO only policy did not need a Mediterranean island serving Western rather than national defence interests. RAF Akrotiri's staging role was, they argued, redundant since the Middle East and Far East bases had now been relinquished and the CENTO role had withered – points rebutted by defence officials who protested that the station was needed in case troubled brewed in Hong Kong and to cater for the unknown.

Alongside these defence reductions was the tough process of retreating from worldwide bases without disturbing the Cold War balance of power. In most cases, the British strategy was to pass the buck to the United States, which they especially tried doing over Cyprus once the island became independent. When trouble stirred between the communities in late 1963, British Ambassador David Ormsby-Gore famously told George Ball that the United States must now take the lead. This it did, which led to the ill-fated Dean Acheson mission and American efforts to contain the problems in 1964 and 1967 – and ease the situation in 1970.

Neither Democrat President Lyndon Johnson nor his Republican successor, President Richard Nixon, were happy about British withdrawal across the globe, which they lobbied hard against. Johnson was furious about Wilson's failure to send troops into the Vietnam War, making his famous quip that all he wanted was a platoon of bagpipers for presentation purposes. And by March 1974, Nixon's administration disbelievingly heard rumours of more British defence cuts at the very time when the president was threatening to withdraw troops from western Europe if NATO allies did not share more of the defence burden.

On top of these tensions Callaghan and Wilson had, when re-elected in February 1974, to repair the personal relationship with the White House, which Edward Heath's standoffish approach to the United States had severed. Nixon and his secretary of state, Henry Kissinger, fumed at Heath for ending informal briefings with them just so he could prove his credentials to Germany and France in support of Britain's application to join the European Community. This spat came on top of other disagreements about recognising China, dealings with India over the conflict creating Bangladesh in March 1971 and Heath, mindful of British oil interests, denying the United States use of the bases during the Arab-Israeli War in 1973 in case Arab countries misinterpreted them as British support for Israel. Kissinger in a calculated pique of anger even cut off certain types of British-American intelligence cooperation, the only instance in the post-Second World War world until complaining American agencies had it resumed twenty-four hours later.

Callaghan was more naturally disposed towards the United States and worked for a strong relationship with Washington. His views were slightly sentimental in the fashion of Britain playing classical Greece to the United States' Rome, at times adopting the mannerism of an avuncular uncle with Henry Kissinger, one of the most intellectually formidable and powerful American secretaries of state of modern times. Callaghan also had a lingering hesitancy about Britain ever acting without American cooperation from his own experiences during the Suez Crisis in 1956. He and many in the foreign policy establishment never forgot how their former wartime ally disavowed rash French and British action to seize the Suez Canal from Egyptian President Gamal Abdel Nasser, manoeuvring American warships alongside Egyptian ones to protect them, and refused an essential $1 billion loan unless Prime Minister Anthony Eden agreed an immediate ceasefire. As Britain and France withdrew in national humiliation, the Suez debacle became an enduring symbol of national decline in the United Kingdom (UK). This lesson stayed with him.

In 1974, British sovereign bases in Cyprus formed a vital component in the British-American relationship. While the non-aligned status of Cyprus meant Britain could not, on paper, use the bases for NATO or Western purposes, in reality these facilities were of crucial consideration for the balance of power in the Eastern Mediterranean, known as NATO's Southern Flank, and, as a near open secret, operated as a nuclear weapons location.

Washington regarded them as a Western staging facility and stopping the Warsaw Pact – the military alliance formed in 1955 by the Soviet Union and its eastern European satellite countries to oppose NATO – from moving into Cyprus, which could threaten its own Mediterranean-based Sixth Fleet with aircraft and missiles, was a priority. The bases also helped anchor Turkey to the West by reducing any Soviet political-military intimidation on Ankara whose generals had been at war with the Soviet Union more than any other country. And from the United States' perspective, the bases provided stability in Cypriot affairs and by dint of this in Greek-Turkish affairs in the Southern Flank, the most politically fragile and militarily exposed NATO theatre and the only region that saw an increase in Soviet naval capability, now capable of matching the United States Navy, though not necessarily NATO.

In particular, the bases also bolstered American foreign policy in the Middle East – a vital concern to Henry Kissinger – allowing the United States' UFO shaped stealth bomber, the U2, to monitor the ceasefire lines agreed after the Six-Day War in 1967 between Israel and Arab nations. American pilots wore civilian clothing in a pretence of secrecy, though the distinctive presence of the U2s on the RAF Akrotiri runway was harder to disguise: these spy planes were notoriously unsteady in cross winds causing RAF ground crew to dash out and hold up the tips of the long wings before the plane came to a complete halt on landing. Makarios did not protest about them.

And these bases were a vital intelligence asset, which continues to the time of writing. A listening post at Ayios Nikolaos on RAF land was American but operated by the British 9th Signals Regiment and part of the British-American communications network providing intelligence on Warsaw Pact nuclear missile deployments and tests. British bases also provided cover for the United States' own two intelligence operations on the island close to Nicosia.

From a British defence perspective, the reliable summer heat of Cyprus gave the Ministry of Defence a perfect recruiting tool to attract prospective soldiers and airman with stories of an exotic life abroad. RAF pilots adored the routine of flying from 7.00 am to 1.00 pm, sailing in the afternoon and entertaining in the long hot evenings. Chester Armstrong was a young RAF helicopter pilot flying Whirlwinds of 84 Squadron whose 'B' Flight was stationed at Nicosia International Airport to support UNFICYP. He and his wife married in 1973 shortly before his posting and indulged themselves in this exotic lifestyle:

> visiting beaches, swimming, water skiing, and parties. We bought a brand-new yellow Renault 4, and enjoyed exploring the island from Paphos to Famagusta and swimming from remote beaches like Nisi [Nissi]. We had great fun water skiing from the northern beaches by Kyrenia.[24]

Water skiing was a pull in its right for RAF armourer Michael Anderton. He arrived with his wife, Pauline, and young daughter, Susan, in August 1971 to receive married quarters of a spacious two-bedroom bungalow with garden, garage and front balcony in Limassol, which was so large he had to fill it out with rented furniture. They spent the early days visiting tourist spots before Michael Anderton discovered the base water-skiing club at Limassol Bay, next to RAF Akrotiri and never looked back, eventually becoming an instructor. Life was

> really heaven and apart from work, a permanent holiday during the summer months. Pauline was able to sit on the club patio in the shade socialising with all the other members and having a go at snorkelling in the clear water when she wanted to cool down. Susan made many new friends, with the other children and spent most of the time out on the raft learning to dive and swim expertly.[25]

Pauline Anderton accommodatingly agreed to extend their posting in 1974, when her husband stood a good chance of becoming the overall service water skiing champion. Unfortunately, the coup against Makarios happened a month before the competition.

Service families and unmarried airman and soldiers immersed themselves in the local Greek and Turkish-Cypriot culture, living among the local population in rented houses, bungalows and flats, principally in the two large towns of Famagusta and Limassol, and forming many lifelong friendships. They frequented local shops, cafes, restaurants and hairdressers and especially enjoyed a well-known perk of buying second hands cars bought duty free – Renault 4s were particularly popular, that was until Makarios got wind of an opportunity and imposed a new £100.00 tax on all second-hand car purchases thereafter dubbed 'Black Mac's Tax'.

And from these relationships and local tourism came revenue for the island economy. The spending power of the base and its occupants contributed some £35 million per annum or 10 per cent of Cypriot gross national product. Makarios also squeezed Britain for compensation for the land occupied by the bases. In August 1973, he presented Wilson's government with a £76.6 million bill covering the last eight years as a negotiating tactic to force the resumption of a financial assistance Britain was obliged to pay under the 1960 arrangements, which was suspended after the 1960s ethnic clashes and made dependent on community talks progress. Wilson's government deferred the matter until after his defence review in 1974.

What appeal the island offered as recruiting sergeant and its military benefits had to be weighed against the perennial worry that 10,000 servicemen and their families living off base – together with some 2,000 British expats littered across the island – created a potential hostage to fortune in any ethnic conflict. Anti-British sentiment was minimal by the 1970s, apart from lingering stories of former EOKA fighters and a light suspicion that Britain favoured the Turkish community but nothing prominent. Many Cypriots regarded British bases as source of stability against all out conflict between Greek and Turkish communities.

However, the bitter experience of EOKA's 1950s guerrilla campaign made for long memories in London. Not the least the awful occasion when Highland Light Infantry soldiers relaxing from a game of football near a local village leant over a nearby well to drink the cool water and were blown apart by a bomb hidden in the innocent looking drinking hole.

Even without local turmoil, British diplomats grappled with related problems, including a complex relationship with Middle East countries and perennial worries about oil security. Egypt had spread a story that Britain had secretly used Cyprus to aid Israel in an earlier Arab-Israeli war (the Six-Day War) in 1967, what became known as the 'Great Lie', which resulted in short-lived oil sanctions and the prospect in Arab minds that the same could happen again while the sovereign bases remained. By 1974, a strain of thought in the Foreign and Commonwealth Office favoured withdrawal from Cyprus to heal this sore in British-Arab affairs.

These were the problems related to Cyprus Callaghan and Wilson faced when taking office in March 1974, one of many foreign affairs issues demanding their attention in the Cold War world and dwarfed by electoral considerations and an influential hard left pushing for greater social welfare spending at home amid Britain's faltering economic performance.

Helping the new foreign secretary was British high commissioner in Cyprus, Stephen Olver, who, though long in service as a 56-year-old starting off in the Indian police and political service, only took up post in Nicosia in 1973. Within a year, he would be dictating telegrams while lying down to avoid bullets whizzing past the High Commission building (embassies in Commonwealth countries are called high commissions).

At home, Alan Goodison, as head of the South European Department, provided Callaghan's principal advice over Cyprus in 1974. With religious leanings like Callaghan only this time in Methodism, Goodison was a lay reader who preached during his previous diplomatic postings. He also delighted in colourful ties and trousers in the straightlaced Foreign and Commonwealth Office of the 1970s. During one tense moment in the Cyprus crisis, Callaghan turned to him and ask what the initials 'YSL' stood for on his tie. Instead of explaining the design house, Yves St Laurent, the quick witted Goodison replied, 'Young Socialist League, Secretary of State'.[26]

Chapter 3

TURKISH INDEPENDENCE

Turkey, a middle-income country of 38 million people, 2,500 miles from Britain, faced its own social and political problems with a mix of a strong military ready to intervene in politics, a weak civilian government and a population ready to demand action if their Cypriot neighbours were threatened.

Unlike Greece where the military intervened to restore order, the Turkish military intervened to protect the constitution established by its former commander, Mustafa Kemal Atatürk, who founded modern Turkey in 1923. Atatürk restored Turkish pride after the humiliations of the First World War by defeating Greek incursions into Turkey and replacing the Ottoman Empire with a secular and Western looking tradition of parliamentary democracy and the separation of state and religion. His legacy left the military as the custodian of this rigid constitution ever ready to intercede when trouble appeared.

This it did in 1960 against a background of political and economic turmoil, and the seeming desertion of the secular path, seizing power and hanging Ali Adnan Ertekin Menderes, the very prime minister who signed the Cyprus independence arrangements, for a range of offences before handing back power to an elected government in 1965.

More unrest prevailed in the late 1960s with left-wing student organisations bombing and robbing their way towards political ends, opposed by equally violent right-wing factions, particularly the Grey Wolves, an ultranationalist student organisation. Some university campuses and schools resembled Wild West shoot outs rather than seats of learning. A growing Islamist movement and a striking workforce damaging a weak economy exacerbated this sense of chaos.

Disgruntled army chiefs consequently toppled elected politicians in March 1971 in what was dubbed the 'coup by memorandum', because the government, mindful of Menderes's fate, acquiesced without a shot fired and was replaced by a well-regarded Cabinet of technocrats and intellectuals. The generals lifted martial law in September 1973 allowing for an indecisive general election from which emerged the interesting political leader Bülent Ecevit.

Here was a most unusual man in Turkish politics, by background a poet and journalist born in May 1925 to a professor of forensic medicine and parliamentarian and an artistic mother. After graduating in literature from Turkey's answer to Eton College called Robert College in Istanbul, this small and slight-framed man began his journalism, working first in London as a press attaché at the Turkish Embassy, where he studied Sanskrit and art history at the School of Oriental Studies. He then earned a United States Department of State fellowship working on a local paper in North Carolina, including nine months studying at Harvard University and by a remarkable quirk of fate studying under Henry Kissinger, who taught at the university before entering government.

Ecevit returned home and entered Turkish politics with left-wing leanings though also as a nationalist joining Atatürk's Republican People's Party, a secular socialist party, as its youngest member of parliament in 1957. He headed the party from 1966 but resigned from government rather than support military rule in 1971. During these years, he also established a reputation as a man of letters, writing his own poetry and translating Ezra Pound, Dylan Thomas and T.S. Eliot into Turkish.

A romantic socialism ran through Ecevit's personal life. He and his wife famously never owned any apartment in which they lived, and he notably wore a working man's cap, earning him loyalty on the ground and a nickname as 'Karaoglan', the boy known for his moustache and dark hair as the Turkish Robin Hood. Generally favourable to the West, Ecevit nonetheless bore his party's suspicion of a foreign presence in Turkey, especially of the United States, with relations tarred not only by 1964 and 1967, but a continuing bitter dispute about Turkey's legal production of opium, which ended up on the streets of American inner cities.

He had problems from the outset as prime minister in January 1974. Just as Makarios played a balancing game between the left and the right, Clerides had to watch out for the archbishop and Denktaş was controlled from Ankara, so Ecevit had to look over both shoulders, one for the Turkish generals and the other for right-wing parties trying to oust him. Like Callaghan's Labour Party trying to govern without a parliamentary majority, Ecevit had only won 37 per cent of the vote and depended on the cooperation of the Islamic neo-nationalist National Salvation Party (or abbreviated to NSP) as a coalition partner.

An anxious military closely monitored Ecevit's administration. Unrest prevailed with rising unemployment and growing inflation, exacerbated by unprecedented oil price rises. Student disorder remained and a pan-Islamic movement, anti-Western in nature, continued to peck away at Turkey's secular state. The 'Kurdish question', a push for independence by an ethnically solid people in eastern Turkey, caused further demonstrations.

In respect of Cyprus, Ankara had long worried about the island falling into hostile hands when Turkey was already hemmed in by the Soviet Union to the north and east: the distinctive shape of Cyprus led to an analogy of the island as a pistol pointed at the Anatolian heartland. Any Turkish government had also to respond to a public clamour to protect fellow Turks in Cyprus, who had generally come off worse in the ethnic violence of the 1960s and now ran their own enclaves. Ecevit very much regarded himself as a defender of minorities from protesting about treatment of Black Americans during his stay in Carolina or protecting worker's rights in Turkey and had particular concern for Turkish Cypriots.

These two objectives could only be met from the military point of view by permanent access to a seaport in the north of Cyprus, which the tension of the 1960s had highlighted as crucial in an emergency. Yet Turkey had no appetite to interfere in Cyprus in 1974 without provocation, as military intervention would cause partition of some kind, which simply created a new southern border for Turkey rubbing up against a Greek one giving Athens cause to increase its forces on the island and risked damaging relationships with NATO and the United States. Instead, Turkey's aim was to prevent Cyprus falling under Greek or any other country control, particularly a communist one, which meant forestalling any likelihood of *enosis*.

Years of Makarios stifling the progress of community talks certainly created impatience. Alarm arose in Cyprus when Ecevit's party programme in February 1974 called for a federal solution suggesting a change in Turkish policy from allowing both communities to reach their own solution. Yet Ecevit rowed back on these comments the following month when emphasising the formula of a peaceful community solution. In any event, talk of a federal solution was not new: Denktaş preferred it and any observer of the island's recent history might have concluded that federation or a form of separation between the communities seemed inevitable.

Ecevit was prepared for community talks to continue though not indefinitely but any interference was likely to be political and peaceful rather than military. Besides, the start of 1974 focused Turkish minds on the Aegean Islands where disagreement with Greek leader Dimitrios Ioannidis provoked tensions over oil discovery hopes, the ownership of various islands and fly over rights rather than Cyprus.

What was apparent at the start of 1974 was the weakening levers any country had to influence a Turkey concerned about matters of vital national interest. Britain's relationship was respectful but not close. Turks looked favourably on Britain, partly in memory of General Charles Harington, commander of British forces occupying Constantinople and the southern Dardanelles in 1922, who supported Atatürk's aspirations for modern Turkey. The imposition of martial law in 1971 did not harm a state visit by Queen Elizabeth II that year who was greeted by around 1 million people. Prince Philip of England, born Prince Philip of Greece and Denmark even privately met with former president, İsmet İnönü, Atatürk's chief of staff and leader of the opposition, who had defeated his Greek father at the Battle of İnönü in the Turkish War of Independence fifty years earlier (1919–1923).

But these social links lacked the financial, political and defence clout of the United States, which had since the 1950s provided some $6.7 billion in military and financial aid, or the financial influence of West Germany with 700,000 Turkish guest workers still sending pay packets back home and Bonn's large aid and military support bolstering Turkish Gross National Product (GNP). West Germany, since 1964, was the second principal country financial backer for Turkey, after the United States.

Even with this support, American influence was waning. Relations between both countries had soured over Turkey's opium production, which dwarfed any significance of Cyprus in American domestic politics. Richard Nixon's declared war on drugs addiction with congressmen grandstanding on the subject annoyed Turkey, where legal cultivation of poppies accounted for up to 70 per cent of illicit heroin and morphine distribution in the United States. This drugs trade, shipped over from Marseille, provided the basis for the noted film, *The French Connection* (1971).

European countries were similarly affected. That same year naïve British teenager Timothy Davy was arrested in Turkey on his way back from India on drugs charges when used by his mother as a courier as they entered the country in a caravan. Attracting international media attention, Turkey released him in May 1974 under a general amnesty.

Turkey's military stopped the production in June 1971 under heavy American lobbying in return for $35.7 million of economic compensation. Ecevit, worried by the resulting hardship on farmers who had grown the crop for 2,000 years and was one of few plants easily cultivated in the mountains, removed the ban on 6 July 1974, 9 days before the coup against Makarios, despite considerable American protest including the temporary recall of its ambassador, William 'Bill' Butts Macomber Jr.

Lindsey Grant, a senior diplomat in Nicosia from 1972 to 1974, used this example to warn Greek Cypriots, who forever assumed the United States could control Ankara, about the limitations of American power on Turkey:

> Here's something of tremendous importance to the United States, much more important than Cyprus to America – the drug problem. We couldn't stop the Turks from growing opium, and you should take that as a lesson as to what we could do if the Turks decided to move against you. It had absolutely no effect on them.[27]

This defiance on a matter of crucial American interest underlined a growing spirit of independence in Turkish thinking ever since President Lyndon Johnson's interventions in 1964 and 1967 raised doubts, in Turkish minds, about how their interests were served by a leading ally and by NATO. Nearly every Turkish official who met their American counterpart ranted about the Johnson letter of 1964. The deputy chief of mission in Ankara, James W.S. Spain, observed that when within six weeks of presidents Harry S. Truman and Lyndon Johnson dying apart in 1973, Turks lined the streets outside the American Embassy to sign a dozen books of condolences for Truman but barely twenty Turks other than diplomats signed one for Johnson; the most senior Turkish official to do so was only a protocol officer acting out of courtesy. 'The Turks still hated Lyndon Johnson for his 1964 letter telling them that if they invaded Cyprus and the USSR [Union of Soviet Socialist Republics] struck at them, we would not come to their help.'[28]

A recent thawing of relations between the United States and the Soviet Union under *détente* accentuated Ankara's worries of being cast afloat against future Moscow predation. Turkey also disliked its disproportionate contribution to the Alliance compared to its modest economic performance.

Turkish politicians and civil servants understood the strategic significance their country held for the West in containing the Soviet threat on four borders (Thrace, the Black Sea, eastern Turkey and along the southern border) and providing NATO's largest land army. Turkey hosted American nuclear weapons to attack Soviet reinforcements in the event of a surge through eastern Europe, the United States and NATO surveillance bases in the north and American aircraft giving air cover to the Sixth Fleet. And it crucially controlled the Bosporus Strait through which Soviet ships sailed under the Montreux Convention of 1936 to reach the Mediterranean.

The United States stationed 35,000 service personnel across these facilities. Young airman and sailors from the visiting Sixth Fleet often hit the bars around İzmir, Adana and Istanbul creating the attendant nuisance and reputation. On one occasion American Ambassador Bill Macomber inadvertently entertained a group of Turkish sex workers at the American Embassy when inviting a detachment of marines, asking they each bring a Turkish friend so that half the guests were non-Americans under the Department of State guidance. One of the Marine Corps' sergeants lived at a brothel, where he moonlighted as a bouncer and his girlfriend presided as 'the madam'. Enterprising marines closed the business that evening by escorting all the 'employees' to the function, with some of these 'friends' speaking to the unknowing Macomber, who astoundingly later complimented the marines for one of the better receptions held at the embassy.

A heavy American presence did not counter Turkish worries about the reliability of American and Western commitment to their country when push came to shove. Ecevit's civilian coalition government started a defence policy to replace dependence on American aid with home grown resources (any Greek-Turkish conflict would be fought with American weapons with enough ammunition to last only three weeks). Achieving such ambitions when the Turkish economy was faltering was another matter.

Western governments nonetheless worried about where these trends might lead. Perhaps Turkey might develop an independent foreign policy working with but not as part of NATO, become neutral or, though unlikely, reach some form of accommodation with the Soviet Union. NATO could not afford to lose Turkey. This did not mean Greece was not valued, for Athens provided the West with home porting facilities for the Sixth Fleet in Crete, stationed American aircraft, provided ten divisions for NATO and contributed to the West's naval control of the Mediterranean helping the United States operate in the Middle East. From the United States' perspective, Greece provided facilities whereas Turkey provided geography.

Ecevit's relations with Greece had reached their lowest point for a decade by 1974. This was not over Cyprus but the ownership and militarisation of islands, the boundaries between them across the Mediterranean, oil exploration rights, control over air space, the significant Turkish population in western Thrace in Greece and the Greek population in Istanbul. Many Western analysts feared conflict between Greece and Turkey in that summer over competing claims on the Aegean Islands, especially when Dimitrios Ioannidis declared a 12-mile exclusion zone around some of the Greek islands.

Chapter 4

AMERICAN DISTRACTION

Concerns about a Greek-Turkish conflict over the Aegean Islands were but one of many national and international issues jockeying for intention in Washington, which were all dwarfed by the second most eventful drama in post-Second World War American politics.

Watergate overwhelmed even the most powerful American secretaries of state of all time and grand strategist of international diplomacy, Henry Kissinger. A former Harvard University academic in international relations whose impressionable years were forged in Germany under the Nazis from which his Jewish family fled in 1938, he practiced balance of power theories or realpolitik, a view of the world based on calculations of power, balance and counterbalance. Countries were pieces on a chessboard where every movement affected the others in a theory of linkage. Strategy triumphed at the expense of internal politics and details on the ground, with human rights not at the forefront of Cold War political calculations. When presented with a situation by his diplomats, Kissinger's refrain was always 'what is in the best long-term interests of the United States?'

Richard Nixon appointed him national security adviser in 1969 when together they created a new security structure that ran foreign policy from the White House rather than the Department of State. After Nixon's re-election in 1972, Kissinger became both secretary of state and national security adviser placing him at the apex of foreign and intelligence activity.

Applying their foreign policy theories, Nixon and Kissinger dramatically realigned the world order. Kissinger secretly negotiated with the Chinese to pave the way for Nixon's memorable visit to Beijing in February 1972, stepping off Air Force One with an extended arm to end twenty-five years of that communist country's diplomatic isolation known as the 'opening of China'. Their approach to treat the Soviet

36

Union and China as separate communist powers rather than as a single bloc helped drive a wedge in Sino-Soviet relations. Three months later Nixon achieved his second major breakthrough in Moscow under the policy of *détente*, or easing of tensions, where he signed agreements with the Soviet general secretary, Leonid Brezhnev, limiting the deployment of nuclear weapons – Kissinger having done the preparation.

How Kissinger practiced his theory caused tensions and controversy. A man of superior intelligence who sometimes vainly thought he could win people over with his reasoning, he used idiosyncratic methods, sometimes bypassing conventional Department of State communication and avoiding local American ambassadors – and sometimes keeping his own staff in the dark. Kissinger liked picking up the telephone to foreign leaders and ministers or meeting them spontaneously, all of which happened even if no official was present to record the discussion or the Department of State's recording system was not working.

Kissinger's preferred secretive methods reflected elements of paranoia. This came from a suspicion prevalent across Nixon's administration about John F. Kennedy-leaning liberal civil servants in post, his own complicated relationship with Nixon himself (the president manipulating his security adviser so that he did not become too powerful) and the untrusting atmosphere of the White House, especially following the publication of The Pentagon Papers – detailing the Unites States' involvement in Vietnam – in 1971.

Little happened in areas not in Kissinger's interest and when it did, he preferred to become the expert, at times virtually combining the roles of secretary of state, deputy secretary and assistant secretary on the relevant subject. Even the secretariat and coordination of the Department of State was done from his office, such a system imposing limitations on Kissinger's time when crises hit as happened over Cyprus.

He recruited the most intellectually able staff, favouring professionals above political appointees, making the assistant secretaries around him, the sixth and seventh floor crowds of the Department of State, the toughest and most able of a generation. Hardened by their master, they did not have it easy. Kissinger railed at them if instructions were not followed in full, allowing his accomplished diplomats little room for interpretation, and demanded much from brutal workloads. His national security assistant, Peter W. Rodman, noted,

> [He could be] difficult, he was temperamental and he could let off steam. It was not always pleasant to be there. He did this with his immediate entourage but if you stood your ground you realized that most of the

time it was just steam. He respected people who stood up to him. He was capable of debating with people on his staff who, I think, were the most valuable to him ... He did not respect people who didn't stand their ground.[29]

Kissinger had reason to feel strained as the year turned to 1974. He was still managing the effects of the Paris Peace Accords signed in 1974 with North Vietnam leader Lê Đức Thọ, ending American military involvement in its then longest and domestically most divisive conflict since the Second World War, earning both men the Nobel Peace Prize. He was supervising *détente* while trying to outwit the Soviet Union on the ground from South America to the Middle East in a policy that reached another landmark at the Washington Summit in June 1973, when Leonid Brezhnev became the first Soviet leader to address the American people from their own soil. Despite the summit, Kissinger still gloomily predicted an ever-increasing Soviet threat.

Then came another Israeli-Arab conflict, the Yom Kippur War of October 1973, with global implications dominating his attention. The United States supported Israel, and the Soviet Union the Arab nations, both while maintaining *détente*, but not without Kissinger infuriating Western leaders by unilaterally raising the nuclear threat alert for NATO forces. Arab countries discovered oil as a weapon raising prices fourfold embargoing countries they disliked, which imperilled economies in the developing nations, nearly ruining some European nations and contributed to Britain's 24 per cent inflation rate. Western European nations scurried to prove their neutrality credentials, which inflamed relations with the Americans when, apart from Greece, they denied the United States use of bases in their countries to rearm Israel. Kissinger led the subsequent eight-day peace negotiations in January 1974 between Egypt and Israel and then in May 1974 for the Syrian-Israeli agreement in his notable shuttle diplomacy constantly flying between capital cities to propose new positions.

Against these problems, Cyprus was a second-tier issue though still one to be handled through the prism of the strategic chess board denying communist powers any advantage. However, his successes in Vietnam, China, Russia and the Middle East inflated expectations of what an American secretary of state was capable of achieving.

On top of international pressures, Kissinger was drawn into the unfolding political disturbance shaking American politics to its core. By the start of 1974, a siege mentality dominated Richard Nixon's White House as the Watergate investigation, which arose from the June 1972 burglary of the Democratic Party's national headquarters, focused on the president's personal involvement. Nixon, a remarkably complex and insecure personality at the height of his powers having won re-election, faced his undoing as the truth about his efforts to hide the White House's involvement emerged over seventeen months, each one gripping the public as the hunters moved ever closer to their quarry.

Nixon's former counsel, John Dean, gave evidence under immunity to the United States Senate in June 1973, implicating the president and attracting some of the country's highest television ratings. When another White House assistant revealed details of Nixon's hidden tape-recording system, the investigation became an extended Hollywood film production with the ending all rather obvious. Nixon, a fighter to the last, joined battle with the House of Representatives' Judiciary Committee over the second half of 1973 refusing to hand over the secret tapes. This spectacle gripped the nation and the world as the battle passed into 1974. With Nixon preoccupied, Kissinger and several others shouldered the burden of stopping the administration from crumbling, reducing time for other problems.

In equally bad timing, the Department of State was being reorganised which hampered the section managing the Eastern Mediterranean including Cyprus. The Bureau of Near Eastern Affairs was being slowly transferred to the Bureau of European Affairs (EUR), at the request of Kissinger to stop the need for senior officials from both departments accompany him to NATO conferences.

Senior EUR staff familiar with European culture and high politics had thrust upon them a region of which they had no knowledge and experience and which included two NATO allies pitted against each other through 1,000 years of religious and historical acrimony. The EUR's assistant secretary, Arthur 'Art' Adair Hartman, a quiet and courteous diplomat with a penetrating mind and an expert on the Soviets, was told, 'Oh, by the way, we are reorganizing the bureau and you've got three additional countries. It makes more sense for them to be in Europe.' Two of them were NATO members and Cyprus was there'.[30] Hartman realised he did not know a 'damn thing'[31] about Cyprus. Similarly, his deputy, Wells Stabler, felt uncomfortable about the acquisition and unfamiliar with their newly acquired staff.

Sitting over Hartman and Stabler was the newly appointed undersecretary for political affairs, Joseph 'Joe' John Sisco, whose name is rarely mentioned in history studies, but who is one of those civil servants deserving a book in his own right about foreign affairs. This tough-talking, 6-foot 1-inch, Italian American from Chicago, with a doctorate in soviet affairs who loved cooking Italian dishes for foreign diplomats at home, earned his straight-talking reputation in the toughest negotiations from the Middle East to India and Pakistan. With an energy that attracted the nickname 'Jumping Joe', Sisco was considered one of the cleverest bureaucrats of the day. Kissinger sometimes treated him brusquely but respected him immensely – Sisco, in turn, was not shy in telling his boss where to get off – and persuaded him not to leave the department by promoting him early in 1974 to the highest policy position possible for a career diplomat.

These were all some of main protagonists forming the Department of State staff implementing the policy of their White House masters, which was to bring stability to the fragile Eastern Mediterranean and keep NATO's Southern Flank intact. This meant avoiding direct involvement in the intractable affairs of Cyprus and instead supporting UN managed community talks and stopping the country from becoming an international issue in the Security Council creating opportunities for Soviet meddling.

Crucial to this policy was maintaining good relations with Greece and Turkey irrespective of their types of government. Kissinger was haunted by the prospect of either one becoming a rogue state such as Libya, where Colonel Muammar Gaddafi (Qaddafi) and fellow conspirators seized power from King Idris in 1969, sweeping to power on nationalist sentiment and leaning heavily on Soviet Union support, a concept called 'Qaddafism' in Department of State thinking.

In short, the Nixon-Kissinger balance of power approach preferred anti-communist dictators to left-wing socialists, a policy causing angst in the Department of State for it meant supporting the unpopular Greek junta. President Lyndon Johnson's previous administration had kept its distance and cut off some aid, which Nixon and Kissinger restored while increasing contact with the regime unlike other west European nations.

Nixon's first secretary of state, William Rogers, tried walking this tightrope with coded comments encouraging Greece back to democracy while still supporting the regime. His replacement, Kissinger, brooked no public criticism of Greece, occasionally lecturing his ambassadors from Greece to South America that the Department of State was not a political science college but there to work for American interests: if ambassadors could produce a reliable democratic country all well and good but otherwise the United States should work with what there was, and it was not their role to interfere and change regimes. American Vice President Spiro Agnew (himself Greek American) and Secretary of Defense Melvin Laird as well as senior American military commanders all visited the junta to promote good relations.

The United States Navy prized Greece as a Mediterranean home for its Sixth Fleet in Piraeus. One of the most notable of navy chiefs, Admiral Elmo Zumwalt, whose son died in Vietnam from the very Agent Orange chemical he had ordered to be sprayed over the Mekong Delta, had long argued the critical importance of Greek facilities. Zumwalt convinced himself that Piraeus was ideal to overcome navy recruitment problems, much like Cyprus did for the British armed services. The Greek colonels eventually agreed in September 1972, though many in the United States Department of State and Congress fought against it, and the idea never really worked out for only a few service families decided to stay.

A policy of cooperation with the Greek junta created confusion and incoherence when pursued locally in the American Embassy in Athens. A tension existed, sometimes bitter, between diplomats who thought the junta had rescued Greece from left-wing forces – especially from Andreas Papandreou, the son of the deposed Greek prime minister, Georgios Papandreou, who spouted anti-American rhetoric – and those who thought their job was to nurture Greece back to democracy. Diplomat Barrington King serving there between 1967 and 1972 saw the discussions in which there 'were ups and downs. It depended on what was happening. Something would happen that some people in the [American] Embassy would see as an outrage, and others would, as you said, try to excuse. This happened all the time.'[32]

At the heart of this dilemma, sat one of the most problematic and aloof diplomats of any American posting, Ambassador Henry Joseph Tasca, a 58-year-old, squash playing, career diplomat with an economics doctorate, who earned a reputation for secretiveness and being a loner. Charismatic but difficult, somewhat Machiavellian, many staff fretted working under him, though others found him fair. Part of his power came from Nixon. When, as a former vice president, Richard Nixon spent his years in the political wilderness after losing the Californian gubernatorial election in 1964 many American ambassadors, especially political appointees, spurned him. Henry Tasca as American ambassador to Morocco from 1965 to 1969 did the opposite and welcomed the hard-nosed politician, earning Nixon's favouritism and endorsement to became ambassador to Athens in January 1970 and making him hard to move while Nixon remained president.

Tasca arrived in Athens with one of his sons and an opinionated Italian wife, who gained her own reputation as one of the dragons of the American foreign service. Natalina Tasca, an architect, spent much of her time in Rome, her family apparently holding a monopoly in rubbish collection under Benito Mussolini, a notoriety which some of her staff played with to create unappealing nicknames. Her constant redecoration of the American Embassy and apparent disdain for local staff did not go down well with the Greeks who were not minded to take orders from Italians they had defeated during the Second World War.

The American ambassador in Athens had a rough remit carrying out the new Nixon policy of improving relations with the junta and protecting the Southern Flank, while, before Kissinger became secretary of state, gently encouraging the Greek colonels towards democracy. But he involved himself too closely with regime, almost outlawing any criticism of its actions and suppressing alternative views in the embassy, frustrating officers in the political section. He saw much of the first junta leader Prime Minister Georgios Papadopoulos and his chief lieutenants inviting them to parties or attending dinner parties, while reducing contacts with opposition parties. On one occasion, the entire Greek Cabinet save for the three main colonels came to a Tasca party and watched the overlong western, *How the West Was Won* (1962), all of them falling asleep. Harmon Elwood Kirby, the Department of State's expert on Turkey in the EUR worried, like many of his colleagues, about the quality of the embassy's reporting, 'I think most of us in EUR felt that Ambassador [Henry] Tasca and his [American] Embassy were perhaps more inclined to apologize for the Greek Generals and the Colonels than was warranted'.[33]

Tasca also developed a relationship with Thomas 'Tom' Pappas, a prominent Greek American from Boston, who became an oil magnate owning a refinery in Thessaloniki, Greece, among steel interests and tanker fleets. Pappas not only had strong contacts in the regime but had contributed Greek money to Nixon's re-election fund, some of which became hush money to help pay for the Watergate cover up.

Tasca even stopped the American consul general in Thessaloniki submitting reports directly to Washington and instead had them sent through him to remove any anti-junta sentiment. Walter J. Silva, the Greek desk officer from 1969 to 1973, noted,

[How Tasca] was trying, I think honestly, to play both ends. He was trying to support the colonels in order to keep things on an even keel and at the same time make occasional squeaks of displeasure for the sake of the Congress and those in the Department who didn't feel as he did. It didn't work, of course. He was generally reviled in the Department. Even Joe Sisco thought very little of him. It was too bad. He was the wrong guy for the job, obviously. But being unwilling to really go on record with anybody as believing the colonels to be an evil in themselves and something to be rid of, I think he helped perpetuate the colonels reign longer than it should have lasted.[34]

Worse, Tasca, the United States' formal government representative, refused to deal personally with Dimitrios Ioannidis after this shadowy military police officer effectively became the new head of the junta in November 1973. He did initially try but Ioannidis, who took a strong nationalist line against the United States and was paranoid about being seen to cooperate with Washington in case his numerous enemies within the military moved against him, applied so many conditions of secrecy, especially that no word must reach Congress, that further efforts were ruled out. Tasca, therefore, absented himself from communication with the new leader saying dismissively that he did not deal with cops. Instead, he met only with people he considered part of the legitimate government, such as the president and prime minister, who everyone knew were simply puppets of Ioannidis. If an important message had to be passed to the regime, Tasca used intermediaries, such as the head of the Greek Orthodox Church or a contact through the embassy's defence attaché office.

This bewildering approach caused an absence of official communication with the Greek government when Ioannidis was honing his plans to assassinate Makarios and denuded the embassy's political section of any informed understanding about what was really happening in Athens.

Into this void stepped the local CIA, which remarkably Tasca allowed to become an unofficial conduit to Ioannidis. Richard L. Jackson, deputy consul general at the consul in Thessaloniki, knew about these problems:

> Henry Tasca had, by all indications, abdicated contacts with the military regime and turned them over almost exclusively to the CIA station, many of whom were of Greek origin and close to the colonels. That was resented bitterly by the political officers. It was not a happy place ...[35]

The United States' foremost intelligence agency was tasked at the start of the Cold War under President Harry Truman's 1947 doctrine to contest communism across the globe, wherever and whenever it appeared. And Greece was a country where the CIA most successfully executed this charge in the early stages of opposing the influence of the Soviet Union.

Britain and then the United States helped the Greek government battle communist forces in a bitter civil war, which took place from 1944 to 1945 and continued from 1946 to 1949, accounting for 150,000 deaths leaving lasting social divisions. Over the next twenty-five years, the United States established in Athens one of the largest intelligence centres of any in the Western alliance other than in West Berlin, boasting lasting contacts in Greek society, spending large sums to develop underground movements across the decades and fostering military and intelligence contacts. In the process, the CIA helped Greece build its own foreign intelligence agency, the Greek Intelligence Service (KYP), establishing life-long connections with Greek soldiers working there who later achieved positions of influence in the military and government. Among them were the first head of the junta Georgios Papadopoulos who became the KYP liaison officer with the CIA, and the next junta leader Dimitrios Ioannidis.

American CIA operations became highly influential and unusual in boasting many Greek Americans filling lower-grade appointments in such a large operation, including a headquarters for CIA Middle East operations, that journalists knew the names of many an American spy. These Greek Americans numbered among the sixty odd full-time officers in the embassy with others serving as staffers who floated in and out of operations when needed. They knew many in the junta, having served with them in the Greek Civil War or even against the Germans or both, and shared similar humble backgrounds and not the best education. They were valued because they spoke Greek, a difficult language to learn, and had good contacts.

CIA chiefs prided themselves on their influence in Greece. The United States' first CIA director, Allen Welsh Dulles, had nurtured such close contacts with Queen Frederica, wife to Greek King Paul I, that the two were found intimately together in his own office. People even joked that CIA station chief in the 1960s, John M. Maury Jr, pushed the Greek queen's shopping cart in the American commissary when buying American goods for her. CIA officers also had links to the prominent industrialist, Tom Pappas. and his oil refinery in the north of the country.

A large CIA operation was not the only show in town though. Besides it was the United States Army's own intelligence operation run by the Defense Intelligence Agency (DIA), which similarly knew just about everyone in the Greek military. DIA officers likewise achieved influence, though of limited value in the long term, with the Greek royal family who were restored in 1935 as heads of state but then fled in 1973. An American military sergeant from Hawaii and an expert in martial arts even became a confident of the young Prince Constantine (future King Constantine II) in the 1950s, teaching him self-defence in sessions, which included the future King Carlos of Spain visiting as the crown prince. Competition could break out between the intelligence agencies though many DIA staff, like their CIA colleagues, were similarly conservative minded Greek Americans who all tended to side with the junta, causing tension with local American diplomats.

Political officers at the American Embassy fretted over the loyalties of large numbers of Greek Americans in United States operations. Disquiet was already present in the 1960s under Tasca's predecessor, American Ambassador Walter Phillips Talbot, a not especially strong character nor a career diplomat but a former journalist and academic who let the local CIA operation develop an unusually strong influence in his embassy.

CIA station chief from 1968 to 1972, James M. Potts, exemplified this culture nurturing the closest of contacts with head of the junta Georgios Papadopoulos. Political counsellor Elizabeth 'Ann' Brown attended one of her first social events in Athens at Potts's house where she was surprised to find all three of the 'colonels' present. This went too far even for American Ambassador Henry Tasca who, though he himself had invited junta members to formal engagements and suppressed criticism of them, did not want American intelligence officers privately cavorting with them in case this was taken as official American endorsement. Brown saw how he 'subsequently read the riot act to Potts. He told him that he was not to invite such people.'[36] Members of the junta also attended Potts's farewell party in 1972 again annoying Tasca who this time complained to Washington.

An assignment to defeat communism in all forms developed a darker side when the CIA, proud of their contacts and content with a pro-Western government in place, discouraged negative reporting about the junta. When the consul general, Charles Stuart Kennedy, reported people being beaten up by the junta, the CIA station chief tempered such accounts by saying, 'Well, that's not quite the report we get and we know this didn't happen',[37] and mentioned his sources, which Kennedy realised were the very sources administering the beatings. For Kennedy, the 'CIA station chief was in bed with the guys who were beating up the Greeks, and sometimes Greek Americans. To my mind it was too close a relationship.'[38]

A tug of war developed between the political staff on one side and the CIA and the military on the other. Henry Tasca referred his own staff to the CIA station chief if they reported beatings in the streets or other unacceptable regime activities. By 1974, that chief was Stacy Beakes Hulse Jr, a hockey-playing Harvard University graduate from Boston, who continued the approach of his predecessor without being as effective, for he did not get close to Dimitrios Ioannidis, was hampered by a lack of good Greek and had few other relationships in the junta – and was due to leave his post the following year.

Much of the engagement with the junta was, therefore, left to his deputy, Ron Estes, a former baseball playing rifleman in the United States Marines who had fought in the Korean War (1950–1953) and had initially wanted a career helping young offenders before the CIA tapped him on the shoulder at Virginia Tech college. Estes was an able Greek speaker with good contacts from his first assignment there in 1959 and a subsequent posting in Cyprus. After arriving in the second half of 1973, Estes not only became the principal CIA contact in his few meetings with Ioannidis, but by virtue of Tasca's refusal to deal with the dictator, inadvertently became an unofficial American contact with the brigadier general.

Working for Estes and sometimes accompanying him when meeting with Ioannidis was the colourful Gust Lascaris Avrakotos, a tough, blue-collar Greek American from the steel town of Aliquippa, Pennsylvania, in the United States. Avrakotos, who had a reputation for earthy language even within the CIA, became throughout the 1960s a principal CIA liaison with senior figures in the Greek military, knowing both Papadopoulos and Ioannidis. He understood the tough village mentality of old-fashioned anti-communist army types, spoke their language and drank with them. Much has been written and alleged about Avrakotos but, despite boasting unique contacts and a strong personality, he remained subject to the chain of command reporting into Estes, who together with Hulse acted under the direction of CIA headquarters in Virginia.

The Department of State's experts, who were based on the fourth floor of the main office in Washington and advised their principals on the sixth and seventh floors, were sceptical about the quality of CIA reporting by late 1973. These experts, such as Robert 'Bob' S. Dillon (director), Tom Boyatt (expert on Cyprus), John Day (expert on Greece) and Harmon Elwood Kirby (expert on Turkey) not only applied a healthy level of disdain to CIA information, but they were also equally frustrated by the misreporting of Henry Tasca's embassy staff in Athens.

In contrast, apparent alarmist reporting by American Embassy staff in Nicosia confounded the confusing situation. These accounts throughout 1973 and the early months of 1974 describing the latest explosions and shootings between the forces of Makarios and Georgios Grivas accompanied by consistent dire warnings of an imminent implosion fatigued Washington. A bottomless well of messages asserting that it is about to happen now, but never quite did, started to wear thin. Political officer James Williams in Nicosia commented,

> [I did not know whether they] yelled wolf too much or not. I do know there was some ominous comments. Every time you sent one of these cables in that reported a police station or a mailbox had been blown up you'd have a final paragraph as a comment, this is a typical reporting officer's trick, and there were only so many comments you can make on this type of stuff. After a period of time the reader's eyes begin to glaze over ...[39]

By July 1974, American diplomats in Cyprus suspected a move by Ioannidis against Makarios but, rather like their British colleagues, not until September 1974 when Greece and Turkey rotated their troops on the island, giving Athens a chance to install soldiers ready and willing to take on the mission. Williams realised, 'We were so used to this constant peppering of violence by EOKA-B and so we didn't anticipate something big was coming until it really happened. I don't recall anybody predicting that in a timely way.'[40]

Williams and his colleagues were anyway awaiting the arrival of their new boss, American Ambassador Rodger Paul Davies, a universally liked career diplomat from California who learnt Arabic while an army lieutenant in the wartime Middle East and who had formerly run the department's Bureau of Near Eastern Affairs. Davies, his 20-year-old daughter Dana, 15-year-old son John and cat, Ms T., had moved to Cyprus escaping from their personal tragedy of losing a wife and mother, Sally, a year earlier.

As with Britain, a Greek lobby also influenced thinking in the United States though in this case through politicians in Congress rather in government itself. Greek Americans were, at that time, the second most influential ethnic-based lobby group in the country after the Jewish lobby, though, until Cyprus blew up, focused their political sway on local rather than national matters.

Unlike Italian, Irish and Jewish migrations, which congregated in certain American cities, the strength of some 3 million Greek Americans was dispersed across the United States, across political districts and across small businesses. This gave them influence with a range of congressmen (twelve having Greek-American connections, notably Paul Spyros Sarbanes of Maryland and John Brademas of Indiana) and elected officials from the local sheriff to the mayor, affording them a prominent voice in American politics when needed.

They were conservative in nature and not overly vexed when the junta seized power in 1967, which appeared to augur in a period of political stability, and certainly had little sympathy for the political left led by the intellectual Andreas Papandreou, the son of the former prime minister, Georgios Papandreou. A minority of better educated Greeks in the United States including academics and journalists did protest and formed an interest group in Washington to oppose the colonels known as the Greek Mafia, which encouraged Congress to consider aid cuts. But without mainstream Greek Americans their influence was limited, until summer 1974, which galvanised the entire community as never before. By contrast, Turkish Americans numbering fewer than 1 million had limited clout.

Chapter 5

GREEK MISJUDGEMENT

Greece itself was ruled by the seven-year-old military dictatorship, a product of a society bitterly divided between left and right forces since the Greek Civil War, which had struggled to find political stability. These traits were most starkly revealed when Prime Minister Konstantinos Karamanlis, who signed the Cyprus independence agreements, resigned in 1963 after arguing with King Paul I over a royal visit to England. Some temporary figures became prime minister until Georgios Papandreou and his centre union party won the general election that year sparking another constitutional crisis, when he argued with the new young king, Constantine II, over appointments to the army earning him dismissal by the inexperienced monarch in 1965, leading to another two years of weak caretaker governments.

Elections planned for 1967 worried certain sections in the army who predicted a sweeping victory for Papandreou and his son Andreas, a Harvard University educated economist and lecturer who had become virulently anti-American and supported Makarios and the non-aligned status of Cyprus. Andreas Papandreou and his left-wing supporters were anathema to the Greek military, which had fought communism, an enemy considered worse than the Turks and was not about to see blood and tears spent for nothing.

Many in Greece and Western countries therefore anticipated a coup by senior military ranks but were caught off guard when middle-ranking colonels acted instead. Three of them, Georgios Papadopoulos, Stylianos Pattakos and Nikolaos Makarezos, formed a nucleus seizing power in a bloodless coup of April 1967. They were sworn in by the inexperienced 27-year-old King Constantine II, crowned only three years earlier, sealing his own fate with the Greek public who did not forgive this seeming validation of dictators.

49

A takeover by these upstart middle-ranking officers caused division in the military as they kicked out many of their superior officers, who had themselves been planning action with the young king to stop the elections. Six months later, in December 1967, the king and the generals tried executing their delayed plan, this time against the colonels, a rather foolish exercise for many in the junta had an intelligence background and knew every detail of the attempt. The 'king's coup' as it became known failed on the very day it began. King Constantine II flew to the north of the country to announce he was taking control, a message few Greeks heard as the radio transmission was too weak and then by the end of the day flew out, this time to Rome in exile taking twenty-eight bags of luggage and his obstetrician for his expecting wife – the Greek royal family never to return as heads of state.

Now settled into power, the right-wing and ultra-nationalist junta administered intimidation, arrests and beatings, though it was not the most oppressive regime around proving more inept than ruthless and attracting derision rather than fear from Greeks on the street. Its leading members largely came from rural, old-school and virulent anti-communist backgrounds, few speaking English and not especially well educated. Cosmopolitan Greeks regarded them as bumpkins. Pattakos, in particular, had a penchant for cleanliness: he was noted for having his chauffeur pull over when seeing someone throw a cigarette end on the pavement, get out to pick up the butt and admonish the offender.

Violence and roughing up opponents were still a feature of their rule. A then current joke had President Muhammad Anwar Sadat of Egypt escorting Greek leader Georgios Papadopoulos around a pyramid and explaining that no one had been able to identify the pharaoh buried there. After wandering around for fifteen minutes, Papadopoulos proclaimed that the tomb belonged to Ramses II. 'How do you know?' asked Sadat. Papadopoulos smiled and replied, 'He confessed!' However, most people's lives continued without disturbance and Greece actually enjoyed a stable political period, which after the turmoil of the 1960s was not unwelcome.

Both Nixon's and Kissinger's political theories, which would have preferred a stable pro-Western democracy, settled instead for this seemingly stable dictatorship serving Western interests. NATO similarly tolerated the Greek military regime despite the rancour caused within its ranks, which needed careful management to stop Scandinavian delegates making provocative statements causing them or, in turn, the Greeks to walk out of meetings.

An anti-American undertone emerged among average Greeks who mistakenly suspected Washington of participating in the coup, which it had not. This trend, while sometimes causing protests, mainly took the form of quiet opinions, grumblings and mutterings rather than loud expressions of anger.

Occasional incidents happened. Douglas G. Hartley an Eton-educated American economic officer had arrived at his new Athens posting in 1970 with his eldest daughter ahead of the rest of the family, dogs and cats. One day Hartley drove out of the car park next to the American Embassy to collect his pets arriving from Virginia and on his return was met by confusion. Fifteen minutes after leaving, a Greek-Cypriot terrorist and his Italian female accomplice drove into the car park and tried to plant a bomb under an American-owned car, which blew up in their hands, damaging a side of the embassy and killing them instantly. The force of the blast decapitated one of the bombers. Hartley was unhurt by the bomb; the drama was over before he returned to the embassy.

Greeks generally, however, remained pro-Western as the colonels brought a measure of political stability and, in the early years, economic growth; they had no reason to consider themselves humiliated and no strong cause to look for scapegoats.

What the toppling of democracy did achieve was a raised profile for Makarios, who as archbishop, *ethnarch* and president of an independent Cyprus now became the authentic voice of Hellenism or Greek culture, as mainland bishops had lost credibility when blessing the junta. His perceived left-wing credentials and his exercise of an independent foreign policy making Cyprus neutral also stuck in the throat of these vehement anti-communists junta leaders. Prime Minister Georgios Papadopoulos did not have much of a mission, but he did want better relations with Turkey, Cyprus resolved and to remove any chance of Makarios turning the island over to the Soviets.

Georgios Papadopoulos's regime, therefore, soon began intrigues to unseat the archbishop. The junta's role in the attempted assassination of Makarios supposedly by his former interior minister, Polykarpos Giorkatzis, when taking off in a helicopter in 1970 remains a mystery. In any event, moves against Makarios had first to win over Turkish fears about a Greek push for *enosis*, so Papadopoulos wrote to then Turkish prime minister, İsmail Nihat Erim, who regarded Makarios as a nineteenth-century priest running a chauvinistic state, seeking better relations. Erim, welcoming the gesture, replied that Cyprus must first be settled and Turkish minority rights on the island recognised.

Papadopoulos provided sufficient reassuring noises for both countries' foreign ministers to meet at a NATO conference in Lisbon, Portugal, in July 1971, when they thrashed out a loose arrangement for handling Cyprus disputes without involving other countries or the UN and with Greece again agreeing to abandon *enosis*.

This fortified the determination of Papadopoulos to remove the priest. He wrote to Makarios telling him to respect Turkish rights, implying that he should also follow the foreign policy of the Greek government, which the archbishop inevitably refused saying Greek Cypriots would determine their own future. Greece also allowed Grivas to slip back into the island to create a new guerilla organisation, EOKA-B, to oppose him.

Makarios then gave Papadopoulos cause to move against him openly when importing weapons from Czechoslovakia for left-wing paramilitaries to counter the threat from Grivas. Papadopoulos issued an ultimatum in February 1972 telling Makarios to surrender the weapons and form a national unity government or else; and readied plans for the Cypriot National Guard, staffed by mainland Greek officers, to intervene if Makarios said no. The archbishop outsmarted him by alerting the United States to an expected coup. Washington duly had Ambassador Henry Tasca warn Papadopoulos off this dangerous path causing the junta to back down for the time being – though this did not stop the independently minded Grivas who continued his own campaign.

Continued attacks by Grivas even became too much for the junta, which feared a backlash across the Greek-speaking world and violence no one could control. In August 1973, Papadopoulos publicly asked him to stop and support community talks, which Grivas rejected and now considered Papadopoulos an enemy of *enosis*.

Papadopoulos had also become preoccupied with problems at home. Purist military figures who saw their aspirations for the revolution of 1967 squandered by his self-enrichment plotted against him, while public unrest grew. He had already circumvented one army plot in September 1972 and overcame strikes and demonstrations in spring 1973, as well as an abortive navy coup in May of the same year. A manufactured referendum in July 1973 that abolished the monarchy allowing Papadopoulos ambitiously to declare himself regent besides prime minister exacerbated these divisions.

His plans for liberal reforms, including a limited return to democracy, proved the final straw, splitting the junta and the army alike. His peeling away of restrictions prompted students to stage their notable protests at Athens Polytechnic in November 1973, which his restless government broke up with resulting injuries and deaths. This persuaded radical military figures that Greece was not yet ready for democracy and that Papadopoulos must go.

The head of the secret military police, Dimitrios Ioannidis, had realised this for some time and had been planning a coup for six months when the student demonstrations gave him cause to act. On 25 November 1973, he surrounded Papadopoulos's opulent seaside villa, which was rented from the business tycoon Aristotle Onassis, placed him under house arrest and took control from behind the scenes in another bloodless coup. The coup was itself remarkable for catching Papadopoulos – an intelligence expert who had foiled plots against him – off guard.

Though professing a poor background like many Greek soldiers, Ioannidis was born to middle-class parents in Athens in 1923 but grew up in the mountainous area around Epirus in north-east Greece. He had worked with Papadopoulos when they and fellow-minded officers formed in the 1950s a secret organisation in the army called IDEA (the sacred bond of Greek officers) sworn to protect Greece from the communist threat – Ioannidis having forged his unshakeable anti-communist convictions as an army intelligence officer in the Greek Civil War. He held similar contemptuous views about the Turks: when serving as an intelligence colonel in Cyprus during the violence of 1963/1964, he reportedly suggested to Makarios eliminating the entire Turkish-Cypriot population. Makarios's disregard for the idea ignited Ioannidis's hatred of the archbishop.

Ioannidis, much like Grivas, was an ascetic and idealist, both men foreswearing their lives to promote Hellenism and a greater Greece, but he lacked the charisma of Grivas and was overall a plain and colourless character. He participated in the coup of 1967 while serving as a lieutenant colonel at the Greek military academy and earned control of the Greek military police, ESA, which he made a self-sufficient army unit becoming the witchfinder general of communists, feared by regime opponents and even within the military.

ESA became his power base for nurturing a web of informants, including loyal junior officers recruited for their nationalistic views whom he carefully placed in positions of influence and used to perfect his 1973 coup, with few anticipating his action. He purged Papadopoulos supporters and promoted these idealistic and inexperienced junior officers to executive positions, in some cases promoting them about their own seniors creating another cause of simmering resentment in the military. After his clear out – all the lieutenant generals, 80 per cent of the major generals, the brigadier generals and 80 per cent of the colonels in the Hellenic army (the Greek mainland army) had fewer than six months experience, making it virtually incapable of action and very unreliable.

Those generals and admirals who did stay watched without comment for the moment. The navy chief, Admiral Petros Arapakis, who had graduated from the Naval War College in Rhode Island in the United States, remained neutral at best. Other army generals broadly acquiesced in the changes through a dislike of Papadopoulos, who had come to enjoy the trappings of power too much and spurned fellow coup members. Ioannidis did not make that mistake, staying in the shadows and creating a puppet government of ministers as the official face of Greece, earning himself the title of 'invisible dictator'.

Henry Tasca's embassy in Athens and the local CIA unit were again caught off guard by this second coup in Greece though Tasca dismissed Ioannidis's influence as overstated and gave him a year at best. This assessment was largely correct for Ioannidis's dictatorship proved as equally nationalistic and inept as the previous one, soon facing serious economic problems exacerbated by oil price increases. And the Greek people and soldiers who were at first relieved that a corrupt regime had gone soon realised the replacement was not any better with no solutions for the country's woes. Ioannidis, operating behind his official government, could not offer them any personal brand or message to congregate around other than a Hellenistic nationalistic agenda, which he used to concentrate minds in winter 1974 by heightening conflict with Turkey over the Aegean Islands trying to unite the people and the army behind him.

Oil gave him an opportunity. By unlucky timing this black gold was discovered in March 1974 off the Greek island of Thasos in an un-demarcated area of the Aegean Islands, promoting tension between Greece and Turkey, and inflating Ioannidis's ideas of Greece becoming an energy superpower like Arabia. Turkey, disappointed in its own searches for oil, staked a claim but offered to negotiate, which Ioannidis refused and threatened to expand Greek territorial waters from 6 to 12 miles. Turkey placed the military on alert and under the mask of a naval exercise defiantly arranged its own survey in Greek waters for five days in April 1974 prompting, in turn, a Greek military alert. This friction exacerbated tensions in other areas, including fly over rights and the position of 10,000 Turkish citizens in Thrace. The Department of State's experts feared that oil rights rather than Cyprus might cause a Greek-Turkish conflict in 1974.

But they underestimated Ioannidis's single-minded cause to resolve the Cyprus problem and rid the world of the supposed communist, Makarios. Ioannidis saw no reason why Greece should not have two thirds of the island and Turkey the remainder, solving everyone's interests and removing any communist threat. Many observers did expect him to move against the archbishop at some point once he had consolidated his authority, which he duly started planning in spring 1974. He had already boasted to the Americans shortly after seizing power the previous November that he could remove the archbishop whenever he pleased within twenty-four hours.

Chapter 6

AN INCOMPLETE PICTURE: JANUARY TO JUNE 1974

At the start of the year there was a sense that something was about to happen in Cyprus, but there was always sense that something was about to happen in Cyprus. And against the other international matters of the day across *détente*, improved relations with China and the overriding need to stabilise the Middle East after the Yom Kippur War, Cyprus did not attract the attention of world leaders. Diplomatic reporting, intelligence reports and warnings by individuals created a continually incomplete and sometimes contradictory picture that reached points of tension, which then abated as happened so often in the past.

Increasing violence across Cyprus in early 1974 sufficiently worried the Department of State's experts, Bob Dillon, Tom Boyatt (Cyprus), John Day (Greece) and Harmon Kirby (Turkey), to think a climax of sorts was coming. These experts, the equivalent civilian rank of colonel and recently transferred to the new EUR branch in the reorganisation of the Department of State, found themselves with greater authority and access to senior diplomats and Henry Kissinger than would otherwise have been normal. Tom Boyatt played the most prominent role. An Ohio born Princeton University graduate first commissioned in the United States Air Force, he was an ambitious desk officer, strong willed, earning rapid promotion and one of the most knowledgeable officers about Cyprus having served there between 1967 and 1970, alongside a record of bravery surviving one of the early plane hijackings by Palestinian terrorists in 1969.

Boyatt and his colleagues had already concluded something was stirring given Grivas's increasingly well-planned raids using EOKA-B and the seizure of power in Athens by Ioannidis whose hatred of

Makarios was well known. But they could not be sure, for, alongside this increased violence, community talks though continuing in fits and starts looked strong and well, supported by Greece and Turkey and grudgingly by Makarios.

An uneasy silence then spread across the island when Grivas died on 27 January 1974. Would there be a power struggle for control of EOKA-B or violence threatening Turkish Cypriots? Rumours proliferated about possible consequences, which heightened when nothing immediate happened.

Makarios seized the opportunity to diminish EOKA-B by offering an amnesty, releasing 124 members from prison and proposing to release more for those turning their weapons and themselves into police. No one came forward. Instead, thousands attended the general's funeral on 31 January 1974 under the wet skies of Nicosia, including the Greek ambassador, Greek soldiers and the Cypriot National Guard with Makarios and his government staying away. On the crowded steps of the church, a handful of EOKA types shouted defiantly they would continue the *enosis* struggle.

This they did by appointing the former deputy of Grivas, Major George Karousos, as their new leader. However, Karousos promptly disappointed their ambitions, for despite a reputation for toughness he surprisingly accepted Makarios's olive branch and ordered them to pursue non-violent means. This led to another power struggle for control giving Dimitrios Ioannidis chance to intervene from Athens and cement Greek authority over the organisation.

During this process and with the temporary ceasefire still holding, speculation flourished about what was really happening inside EOKA-B. Makarios's supporters threw out names as possible successors, including a former head of the National Guard commandos linked to the 1970 assassination plot against the archbishop, who turned out to be contentedly working at his desk in the Greek Pools Football Agency in Athens – though this may have been a front organisation channelling funds to the organisation. Colourful theories arose and even the pro-Western Cypriot Foreign Minister Ioannis Christophides stubbornly thought the Americans were supporting EOKA-B either directly or through Athens.

A theft in early February 1974 of weapons from a National Guard centre in Famagusta, allegedly with the unit's complicity, exacerbated rumours that something big was afoot. Makarios even claimed his own intelligence network spotted former CIA station chief, Eric Neff, speaking to the EOKA-B hardman and Cypriot politician, Nikos Sampson, in Athens in the second week of February. Neff was Cyprus station chief from 1969 to 1971 until Makarios complained to the Americans about the agent working against him causing his recall. In reality, Neff had made indiscreet comments about removing a man seen by some in Washington as the obstacle to community talks, which he was, and as a supporter of communism, which he was not, as no bad thing.

Ioannidis completed his control of EOKA-B in the second week of February 1974 when Greek officers of the National Guard nabbed Karousos and smuggled him back to Greece aboard a British-registered yacht where he was placed under house arrest in Athens. EOKA-B issued a dry explanatory statement saying, that retired Greek army officer, Major George Karousos, had returned to the mainland as a necessary measure for the organisation and to avert complications after the death of General Grivas.

Athens also increased the number of Greek officers and non-commissioned officer ranks in the National Guard and passed over weapons and money with Makarios watching these developments closely.

So did Tom Boyatt in Washington who drafted a strongly worded cable for the American ambassador in Greece, Henry Tasca, to warn Ioannidis that the American government, the only Western government on friendly terms with Greece, opposed any overt or clandestine efforts to interfere in Cyprus, overthrow Makarios or install a pro-Greek government. He drafted supporting cables for American ambassadors in Nicosia and Ankara.

Wells Stabler, deputy assistant secretary of EUR, questioned Boyatt about his reasoning for such strong wording saying,

'Nobody in this town wants to alienate the Greek government.'
[Tom] Boyatt replied, 'You would prefer a war?'
Anyway, we argued back and forth, he refused to clear the cable. So I went back and I redrafted it, and I toned it down but with essentially the same message, and I came back with another try.
This time he said, 'Okay.'
So we went to the Assistant Secretary [Art Hartman], and the Assistant Secretary said, 'We can't do that. Nobody in this town wants to hear this sort of thing.'
And I said, 'We have to do it. As responsible people we just have to.'[41]

Hartman and Stabler also rejected using the CIA channel insisting that formal messages go through the recognised government to government route, so the internal 'battle went back and forth, and up and down' for the next two months.

In March 1974, perplexed Department of State officials also pondered how to deal with the new Greek regime of Ioannidis, which they did not expect to last long but could not be sure what might follow, perhaps an even more radical group of extremist soldiers. When American Ambassador Henry Tasca returned to Washington on 20 March 1974 to brief Congress and the secretary of state, Kissinger notably laid down American policy towards Greece. He dismissed the approach of his predecessor, Secretary of State William Rogers, who supported the junta while making public noises edging it towards a return to democracy. In Kissinger's realpolitik theorising, Greece must decide its own regime free of American interference: if Ioannidis were so weak and easily replaceable by other disaffected officers or political grouping, the United States should not interfere for fear of damaging long-term interests by gambling on which group might win.

Kissinger told Tasca that the Department of State is not a 'Political Science Division. It conducts the foreign policy of the United States. It deals with any government – communist or non-communist – within the context of the foreign-policy objectives of the United States.'[42] And he set out the United States' approach as giving 'priority to mutual US-UK Greek security interests and to leave it to the Greeks themselves to determine what kind of government they have'.[43] This advice framed the mentality of senior Department of State staff, though not without dissent by some middle rank officers, against issuing strong warnings to the junta or interfering in Greek internal affairs.

Britain's interest in Cyprus at this time focused on the costs of maintaining its large bases on the island while suffering perpetual financial worries at home made worse by an unaffordable defence budget. Following Labour's surprise election victory in February, Prime Minister Harold Wilson announced another defence review on 21 March 1974 forewarning of major cuts. This sent shivers down Turkish spines when the BBC prematurely reported the closing of the Cyprus bases, which Ankara thought provided stability in the Eastern Mediterranean and potentially protected Turkish communities if violence broke out. The Turkish ambassador told Foreign Minister Roy Hattersley that Britain should not regard the bases simply as a relic of the British Empire.

What no policy makers could know in the distant offices of London and Washington was that Ioannidis had already started plotting the downfall of Makarios. Between February and May 1974, he met with his prime minister, Adamantios Androutsopoulos, his president, Phaedon Gizikis, and the top soldier, General Grigorios Bonanos, to discuss the details. Tentative plans were made for April, then May and then postponed further because of tension over the Aegean Islands and a visit by Makarios to China.

Left-wing agents in Cyprus, who suspected such moves, appealed to the Soviets for help. Moscow as much to keep them happy as anything else had its ambassadors spread the warning in London, Ankara, Athens and Washington, and made announcements on Radio Moscow and in the Soviet state-owned newspaper, *Pravda*, which added its own flourish alleging that the junta and NATO were acting in collusion. The Cypriot communist party, AKEL, even publicly pronounced that Ioannidis planned a coup. Much of this sounded like the usual propaganda and warnings to American and British ears with officials in both countries concerned about the trends in Cyprus, but not finding anything specific in the Soviets' claims.

On 25 March 1974, a puzzled Foreign Secretary Jim Callaghan questioned his diplomats about Soviet motivation. The British ambassador in Greece, Robin William John Hooper, checked with his contacts who, outside of Ioannidis's narrow circle of influence, said they did not think there was much in it but admitted the junta had favourable links with EOKA-B. Local contacts of the British high commissioner in Cyprus, Stephen Olver, similarly denied the rumours though also admitted the link. In words that would come back to haunt him, Olver told London that 'I dismiss as nonsense the present wave of rumours ... I am sure that the present silly season will pass over, and that those who are now prophesying a *coup d'état* (either through conviction or malice) will be proved wrong.'[44]

London concluded that Russia did not know anything, probably believed the stories about a new hard-line leader taking over EOKA-B and was likely trying to keep in with the archbishop and his supporters. Curiously, and a mystery to this day, is why Makarios himself disregarded the threat despite assorted signals from his own sources.

Britain and the United States were anyway distracted by deteriorating relations between Turkey and Greece over oil rights and ownership of the Aegean Islands, which had more prospect of causing trouble than Cyprus. Turkey granted exploration rights to one of its oil companies despite Ioannidis's declaration of an extended exclusion zone but did offer to negotiate with Athens over competing claims. When Ioannidis did not reply, Turkish Prime Minister Bülent Ecevit licensed drilling operations, which provoked Greece, causing Turkey to fly over contested Aegean Islands areas during a NATO exercise at the end of the month and Athens then to reinforce troops along its northern border.

Harmon Kirby on the Department of State's Turkish desk was in the middle of American efforts to calm the situation. There were 'major high-level intercessions in Ankara, we had an almost daily dialogue with the Turks at the time … we told them not to be provocative themselves, and not to be overly sensitive to what they considered provocation from the Greek side.'[45] For the time being this was mostly posturing with each side trying to upstage the other, though Kirby realised 'that where Greek and Turkish national pride were involved, even the smallest acts often, unfortunately, took on high symbolic significance'.[46]

A more compelling drama meanwhile gripped Washington as the net moved closer to the truth behind the 1972 attempted burglary in the Democratic Party's headquarters. An American grand jury indicted seven senior aides to Richard Nixon, including his attorney general, John H. Mitchell, and closest of advisers, Harry Robbins 'Bob' Haldeman and John Ehrlichman. In perhaps the most astounding development in American legal and political history, Richard Nixon was named as a co-conspirator though not at this stage indicted.

Cyprus community talks broke down again on 2 April 1974. A perfect circle was reached of Greek Cypriots opposing too much autonomy in case the door to federalism was opened and Turkish Cypriots insisting on these freedoms to guarantee their status as junior partners not an underclass. Ecevit caused a brief shock when saying over a lunch with Turkish-Cypriot leader Rauf Denktaş in Ankara that he wanted a federal approach, which, if true, suggested a sudden change in Turkish thinking from letting local leaders find a solution.

However, Ankara, while tiring of endless local talks, had at this time no intention of interfering politically or militarily in Cyprus. Ecevit's fragile coalition government faced more pressing concerns at home grappling with a weak economy, reviewing an amnesty law for political prisoners and competing with Greece over the Aegean Islands. Ecevit's comments nonetheless gave Makarios, who consistently tried to stymie the talks, a pretext for Clerides, his chief negotiator, to challenge the Turkish position and walk out. No immediate consequences followed, for while there was bound to be a natural limit to Turkish patience Ankara had no reason to intervene provided Turkish communities were not threatened.

On 5 April 1974, the American deputy ambassador in Nicosia, Lindsey Grant, was concerned enough about Greek developments to recommend Washington warn Ioannidis off any action against

Makarios. This did not happen. However, an American intelligence assessment in Washington on 18 April 1974 noted that the junta of Ioannidis was 'more adventurous than its predecessor in regard to Cyprus and Turkey, and is more narrowly nationalistic in dealing with the US'.[47]

Tension increased between Makarios and EOKA-B, now controlled by Ioannidis from Athens. The archbishop outlawed the organisation on 25 April 1974 and expanded his own private police force, the Tactical Reserve Unit, which was still outmatched by the 10,000-strong Cypriot National Guard. Innocent people got caught in the middle of this friction, such as 32-year-old British citizen Michael Howe who was driving with his wife and two companions near Limassol when the Tactical Reserve Unit tragically mistook his Land Rover, recently bought from a Turkish Cypriot, for a threat and shot dead all four occupants.

From his desk in Washington Tom Boyatt had another crack at his bosses Hartman and Stabler, who this time passed the matter to the newly appointed undersecretary for political affairs, Joe Sisco. Boyatt had worked for Sisco over Vietnam and the Middle East and told him frankly, 'God damn it, Joe, we have to do something.' Joe replied, 'Look, this is very difficult. Nobody in Washington wants to do this, particularly they don't want to hear anything anti-Greek in the White House. Don't ask me why. I don't know why, but I know that's how they feel over there.'[48] Sisco knew that Nixon's administration wanted stable relations with Greece and that Kissinger resisted any private disapproving messages to Athens. So started another merry go round of discussions and arguments about what to do.

President Richard Nixon's own worries increased in mid-April 1974 when the special Watergate prosecutor subpoenaed him to hand over all tape recordings made in the Oval Office. On 30 April 1974, his offer for 1,200 pages of edited scripts was rejected by the investigating House of Representatives' Judiciary Committee, which demanded he hand them over unedited. This kicked off a legal contest about the boundaries of executive privilege.

Greek-Turkish tension worsened throughout April and into May 1974 with Ioannidis sabre rattling over various hotspots on the Aegean Islands. Both countries made minor military preparations for show, raising the potential for incidents to spark a wider clash. NATO Secretary General Dr Joseph Luns tried reconciling them with little effect, for the Greek puppet prime minister, Adamantios Androutsopoulos, declared on 8 May 1974 that the Greeks would protect their rights and sovereignty.

Underneath this international tension a slow burning fuse was lit in May between Makarios and Ioannidis over who ruled the Greek officers of the National Guard in Cyprus. When EOKA-B guerrillas stole more arms from another National Guard armoury with the probable connivance of its officers, Makarios ordered EOKA-B members to surrender unregistered arms or face prosecution. When none did, Cypriot police arrested some in the organisation and Makarios complained to Greek Foreign Minister Spyridon Tetenes about National Guard activities against him.

Coincidently, Henry Kissinger visited Cyprus on 7 May 1974 to discuss the disengagement of Israeli and Syrian forces with his Soviet counterpart, Andrei Andreyevich Gromyko. He briefly met Makarios as the welcoming head of state, who said that after solving the Middle East the secretary should turn his attention to Cyprus. Kissinger ruefully replied there were two problems he never intended to touch; one was Cyprus and the other Northern Ireland.

Meanwhile his anxious Cyprus desk officer Tom Boyatt, trying to change the Department of State's way of thinking, co-wrote a notable paper on 6 May 1974 outlining six likely scenarios in Cyprus. One was the possibility of Athens-backed *enosis* forces launching a coup against Makarios. He argued for international diplomatic intervention in Greece and Turkey before the situation degenerated or, if that was not possible, for unilateral American intervention. Slowly the paper's analysis and recommendations rose upwards through the departmental hierarchy.

Three days later, the House of Representatives started impeachment proceedings against a sitting American president, which had not happened for 100 years.

On 12 May 1974, British newspaper *The Observer* ran a story claiming that the junta was seriously considering conflict to protect the Aegean Islands from Turkish interests.

Art Hartman, head of the EUR, on a visit to London told Foreign Minister Roy Hattersley that the Greek regime was as about as bad as it could be but that the United States would not interfere in other countries and Kissinger did not want to say anything about promoting democracy in Greece. Hartman thought Ioannidis was looking for a conflict such as oil rights to divert attention from internal worries and Cyprus could be next. He confided that the United States was considering contacting disaffected military people in Athens, before realising he had said too much and worriedly telephoned the Foreign Office when returning to Washington to ask that his views not be reported back – Kissinger would have gone berserk to learn his staff was considering any type of intervention against his own policy.

While this was going on, Kissinger resumed his shuttle diplomacy to negotiate a disengagement between Syria and Israel spending nearly the whole month in the air travelling some 24,000 miles, the longest period out of the country since Secretary of State Robert Lancing in 1919. His plane became a mobile centre for American foreign policy, managing the world's affairs from 30,000 feet. Among the many papers in his pile of international issues sat Tom Boyatt's recommendations. For whatever reason, possibly because he had resisted criticism of the Greek regime and did not want to worsen the Middle East situation or become entangled in the Aegean Islands dispute, Kissinger did not respond to Boyatt's paper or the request for an expression of concern to Greece.

On 17 May 1974, Boyatt and his colleagues, Day and Dillon, nonetheless persuaded their immediate masters to send Ambassador Henry Tasca in Athens watered down instructions warning Ioannidis that if Makarios was overthrown, conflict between Greece and Turkey would likely follow. These instructions started a remarkable tug of war between the Department of State and Tasca who refused on 24 May 1974, saying that such a message might anger Ioannidis and damage American security interests. He pointed out that Greek Foreign Minister Spyridon Tetenes had already condemned the arms theft in Cyprus and the junta was anyway reviewing the role of the Cypriot National Guard, adding that Ioannidis could not be expected to rein in the Guard or EOKA-B unless Makarios reduced his own armed groups. Tasca was of the opinion that Makarios knew how to take care of himself.

Ioannidis meanwhile took some heat out of the Aegean Islands dispute, informing Ankara on 24 May 1974 that he might be prepared to discuss the matter informally.

This easing did not allay the anxiety of American diplomats in Cyprus about the internal Greek situation. On 29 May 1974, they agreed with Boyatt and his fourth-floor colleagues that Greece should be warned about the consequences of any move against the archbishop.

In the absence of any formal contact between Tasca's embassy and Ioannidis, CIA number two in Athens, Ron Estes, accompanied by head of operations, Gust Avrakotos, was sent in to probe the brigadier general's intentions. They met him quietly on 29 May, as usual in an office of the Greek Pentagon for Ioannidis was paranoid that his internal enemies might think him under Washington's influence and unseat him.

Quite remarkably Ioannidis repeated his November 1973 threat of removing Makarios in twenty-four hours with little bloodshed and Turkish acquiescence if he wanted, but said the archbishop was currently in Greece's national interest. He added, however, that he was still deciding on what to do about Cyprus, saying that Makarios's irrevocable tilt towards the Soviets did not serve Greece: Ioannidis could either pull Greek troops out of Cyprus and let Makarios fend for himself or remove him once and for all and let Greece deal directly with Turkey. Both options, Ioannidis claimed, were distasteful and extremely dangerous.

This was a statement designed to test American reaction of his plans for a coup. Would Washington oppose him? Or would Kissinger make a play of protesting while otherwise quietly accepting the removal of the archbishop who supposedly favoured communism? Was not the removal of Makarios in the interest of the United States and the West?

When Estes reported back to CIA headquarters in Langley, the agency's chief of the Bureau of Near Eastern Affairs, John A. Waller, contacted his Department of State counterpart, Bob Dillon, and asked if he had seen the report. No said Dillon, so Waller in an unusual move for the CIA went over to discuss the report that Ioannidis might be planning a coup. Dillon subsequently reviewed the evidence with John Day and Tom Boyatt. Day, the expert on Greece, was sure that Ioannidis was testing American opinion. The three experts again concluded the junta leader must be sent a strong warning.

Greek-Turkish escalation over the Aegean Islands, though slightly abating, still prevailed over any concerns about Cyprus in Washington and London. In the last week of May 1974, Turkey sent an exploration ship to the disputed waters accompanied by warships. Athens again increased troop numbers on its northern border and in the Dodecanese causing Turkey's general staff to issue another military alert.

On 31 May 1974, Ambassador Henry Tasca continued to resist any formal warning to Ioannidis over Cyprus, repeating his views that there were more important matters in American-Greek relations. He reckoned that Ioannidis would not risk dangerous escalation and, in any event, thought that the co-guarantor powers Britain and Turkey should lead on any worries over the island.

For its part, Britain was concerned about the damage done to NATO by the Greek-Turkish dispute over the Aegean Islands. Harold Wilson's government, which was considering Art Hartman's request for a joint British-American initiative over the junta, asked Washington about what was really happening on the Aegean Islands.

By the end of the month, the Washington machine was again fixated on Watergate as the House of Representatives' Judiciary Committee started impeachment hearings against President Richard Nixon with the special prosecutor appealing to the Supreme Court for access to the tapes.

Greece toned down its rhetoric over the Aegean Islands in June 1974, partly because its navy could not stop the Turkish exploration ships without dangerous consequence and repeated an offer for talks.

Makarios was not calming tension in Cyprus though, when he undermined community talks about to restart under UN auspices. On 2 June 1974, in Paphos, he declared there was no more room for concessions to Turkish Cypriots and threatened to withdraw all offers made should talks fail again. Greek Cypriots, he announced, 'would accept neither partnerships nor cantons nor regional self-government nor federation', adding they would not submit to blackmail, intimidation or threats of Turkish intervention and 'with this determination would continue their struggle until its happy conclusion'.[49] Ankara took his denouncement of partnership badly, especially his description of Turkish Cypriots as a privileged minority.

On 4 June 1974, British Ambassador Peter Ramsbottom in Washington followed up with Art Hartman and his deputy, Wells Stabler, following the London visit. Hartman told him that Kissinger remained steadfast over not interfering in Greece and was sceptical about proposals from the Department of State's experts to send even private signals of concern to the Greeks. The secretary of state, he added, did not want any more problems in the Eastern Mediterranean.

That very country team of experts, Boyatt, Day and Dillon, balancing their growing alarm with Kissinger's stand-off policy convinced their chiefs to send American Ambassador Henry Tasca another message on 8 June 1974. They were duly allowed to advise him to make a low-key expression of US concern to the Greeks in the way he thought most suitable.

Their views coincided with more beatings and shootings in Cyprus on top of the recent weapons theft, causing Makarios to denounce the perpetrators of high treason and vow the end to an intolerable and unacceptable situation. The archbishop remained surprisingly unconcerned about his personal safety despite increasing warnings of a threat to his life; possibly reasoning that rumours had peaked in February 1974 without substance and, having always been a target and survived several assassination attempts, from complacency.

He then sensed a weakness in the junta when it backed down from dispute with Turkey over the Aegean Islands. Thus, in defiance of all warnings of threats to his life, Makarios deliberately antagonised the junta on 10 June 1974 by announcing a purge of the 1,500 Greek officers commanding the Cypriot National Guard who sympathised with EOKA-B. His declaration unsettled many Greek Cypriots and the military in Athens who regarded the National Guard as a necessary counterweight to strong left-wing forces on the island and as indispensable in any confrontation with Turkey.

Intercommunal talks restarted on Tuesday, 11 June 1974, though without much expectation of progress given the Turkish-Cypriot demand for more autonomy grating against Makarios's obstinacy and exacerbated by personal animosity between Rauf Denktaş and the archbishop. High Commissioner Stephen Olver thought its usefulness 'as a safety valve is wearing thin, and the talks now hang mainly in the slender thread of unwillingness on each side to incur responsibility for the final breakdown'.[50]

On 13 June 1974, Henry Tasca told the Department of State's experts that he had raised their concerns of 17 May 1974 with Athens. In fact, he had avoided upsetting Ioannidis by passing on American disquiet only to a middle-ranking desk officer in the Greek Foreign Ministry.

Tasca also used an intermediary, either someone arranged by the American Embassy's Defense Attaché Office or head of the Greek Orthodox Church, Archbishop Seraphim, who knew Ioannidis from their days together fighting the Nazis, to probe Ioannidis's thinking without issuing warnings. Ioannidis consequently told this middleman that Cyprus will either

> slowly drift left and become a Cuba of the Mediterranean (this drift will be caused by the Communist propaganda which is being taught in the school system), or the 80 per cent Greek majority will achieve union with Greece. The one thing that cannot happen is union with Turkey.[51]

Ioannidis was again likely testing Washington's reaction to his plans, but Tasca thought his comments showed nothing to suspect imminent moves against Makarios.

Deputy ambassador in Cyprus, Lindsey Grant, awaiting the arrival of the new American Ambassador Rodger Davies, was not so easily persuaded. On 17 June 1974, he wanted Athens warned against toppling Makarios though in a way that did not help the archbishop gain control of the National Guard.

Ioannidis continued playing his game when he met with local CIA officers, Ron Estes and Gust Avrakotos, on Wednesday, 19 June 1974 and speculated about his intentions. He claimed to be undecided on pulling out of Cyprus completely or removing Makarios and dealing directly with Turkey over the island's future. Ioannidis said Makarios was exploiting Greek-Turkish tension over the Aegean Islands to build power over the National Guard and destroy Greek influence in Cyprus. Again, probing American reaction, he declared that Turkey would agree to the removal of their archfoe, Makarios, but, if not, he proposed an all-encompassing agreement with Turkey over the whole Aegean Islands, a statement Estes read as meaning Turkish capitulation in Cyprus. Ioannidis thought only an uncertain Soviet reaction might be a problem, and, possibly sending another signal to Washington, said the United States would favour a Greek-Turkish agreement that removed friction in the region.

Two days later, on 21 June 1974, a joint CIA and DIA assessment judged the prospects of Greek-Turkish conflict over oil and territory on the Aegean Islands as unlikely, advising that both countries might go through the motions without wanting or affording conflict. If hostilities did break out, both American agencies, which were in the dark about Ioannidis's impending coup, thought the island would escape involvement.

By now even Tasca, similarly unaware of scheming by Ioannidis, realised that Makarios's gauntlet over the National Guard was creating a show down with the junta when he reported to Washington on 24 June 1974. This, however, did not dent his insistence against warning Ioannidis formally, for he still preferred any initiative on Cyprus to come from the UN, NATO or the guarantor powers keeping the United States out of the affair.

On 25 June 1974, Ambassador Bill Macomber in Turkey reported that Ankara was closely watching the growing tension of Greek versus Greek with no intention of intervening provided Greece did not win control of Cyprus or threaten Turkish communities. Unhelpfully for the Department of State's experts, he agreed with Tasca's suggestion of involving the UN and NATO before the situation became uncontrollable – and accepted Tasca's view that a formal message to Ioannidis was not desirable at this time.

In the last week of June 1974, Tasca stressed to Archbishop Seraphim that the United States supported a peaceful community solution in Cyprus, confident that the priest would pass this message on to Ioannidis.

On 27 June 1974, Lindsey Grant in Nicosia also endorsed Tasca's idea about working through NATO and the UN while doubting the effectiveness but disagreed vehemently over not warning Ioannidis. He emphasised that Makarios's complaint with the junta risked encompassing Turkey and urged that American Ambassador Rodger Davies, shortly to take up post in Cyprus, tell Makarios not to escalate the affair. Grant also wanted Ioannidis informally told that if the junta had the National Guard drop its anti-Makarios campaign and reduce its role in selecting cadet officers, 'we think Makarios (probably already shaken) would be glad to defer any larger plans for asserting control over [the] NG [National Guard]'.[52]

All these uneven messages from American embassies trying to avoid any contradiction of their fellow diplomats frustrated Tom Boyatt and his colleagues on the fourth floor trying to get backing for strong action.

On the 27 or 28 June 1974, two CIA officers based in Athens again met Ioannidis who told them he would continue thwarting Makarios over the National Guard and develop a contingency plan should the archbishop force a showdown. Once again, Ioannidis appeared to test American resolve over Cyprus.

Intelligence assessments missed the meaning of his words and proved as unbalanced as the reporting from American embassies. That same day the CIA desk team in Washington used its daily government intelligence reports to both repeat Ioannidis's earlier speculation about removing Makarios and, confusingly, repeat his statement that such a move had dangerous consequences and he was unlikely to attempt it soon unless Makarios went too far over the National Guard. CIA officers were no closer to understanding Ioannidis's intentions than anyone else.

By now a resilient Tom Boyatt and his expert colleagues managed to get Joe Sisco's approval for a watered-down version of their draft encouraging Ambassador Henry Tasca to express concerns. Boyatt, Dillon and Day were forced to go with this version after Sisco, mindful of Kissinger's bidding not to interfere in Greek matters, talked them out of a stronger written text. Dillon thought the result too general saying only that '"we were opposed to violence". What news! "Could we have taken any other position?" We argued that this was not nearly strong enough and that the Greeks would never "get the message".'[53] But that was all they could get agreed.

Sisco duly told Henry Tasca, on 29 June 1974, to inform Ioannidis through whatever channel he thought appropriate of disastrous consequences for Greece, Turkey and Cyprus if Makarios was removed, and instructed Lindsey Grant in Nicosia to hold fast until Tasca reported back.

Bob Dillon wanted the message sent through CIA channels given the agents' relationship with Ioannidis, but the department's principals overruled the idea.

> They said that the US government doesn't communicate that way with foreign officials and we don't communicate through low level CIA officials. What a pompous position! It was sacrilege that we would even consider communicating with a one star general! Of course, the fact that he was the power behind the throne did not seem to impress [them].[54]

These concerns proved correct as that month Ioannidis and his chief of staff, Grigorios Bonanos, briefed a select group of army commanders to plan the coup for 15 July 1974. These included former chief of the National Guard, Pavlos Papadakis, head of the Greek forces in Cyprus, Brigadier General Michalis Georgitsis, and his deputy, Colonel Constantinos Kombokis. Georgitsis was made leader of the operation with Kombokis his deputy.

Diplomats, soldiers and intelligence experts in Washington completely unaware of this development were, like other government officials, preoccupied with Watergate, which in the middle of the month saw *The Washington Post* reporters, Carl Bernstein and Richard 'Bob' Woodward, publish *All the President's Men* (1974), describing their reporting of the burglary of 1972 and the revelations that the paranoid Richard Nixon had taped conversations in the Oval Office.

On 1 July 1974, Henry Tasca rejected his latest instructions from Joe Sisco. Tom Boyatt paraphrased Tasca's response as 'Those are terrible instructions that you've given me. I can't possibly do that. If I do that it's going to alienate the Greek government, and we won't have any influence with the Greek government. I reject these instructions. You've got to change them.'[55] Tasca wanted to wait until the new American ambassador, Rodger Davies, spoke to Makarios and other Cypriot leaders for a picture of the situation in Cyprus. As far as he was concerned, Ioannidis fully understood the United States' opposition to any attack and its support for a peaceful solution.

So, Boyatt and his colleagues had to rethink other ways of getting the message across, though now they were attracting the attention of the CIA and the United States Department of Defense, which did not want important relations with the Greeks disturbed. Months had now passed since these experts first wanted Ioannidis warned against sponsoring action in Cyprus, and four weeks had elapsed since John Day thought that Ioannidis was testing American reactions. The absence of any official American message very likely persuaded Ioannidis that the United States would not cause too much trouble.

On Tuesday, 2 July 1974, 53-year-old Rodger Davies arrived in Cyprus with his teenage daughter and son to start their new lives away from Washington and the memories of a lost wife and mother to illness. He would formally present his credentials as the United States' accredited ambassador to Makarios eight days later.

That same day in Athens, American Ambassador Henry Tasca spoke with Greek President Phaedon Gizikis, a general but still an Ioannidis appointee, who assured him of Greek support for community talks in Cyprus and opposition to violence. Tasca reported back his satisfaction that the junta was not about to do anything stupid and left for his annual holiday.

Makarios then threw caution to the wind by directly challenging the authority of the junta over control of the Greek officers in the National Guard. He wrote to President Phaedon Gizikis accusing the junta of trying to assassinate him and seize power, and demanded Athens recall the Greek officer corps, saying,

> The root of the evil is very deep, reaching as far as Athens ... I state that members of the military regime of Greece support and direct the activities of the terrorist organisation 'EOKA-B'. This explains the involvement of Greek officers of the National Guard in the illegal actions, conspiracies and other unacceptable situations.[56]

Here was a public challenge to Greek authority, which the Department of State's Intelligence and Research Bureau advised in its daily summary opened up a direct confrontation with Ioannidis.

Everyone in Cyprus knew about the Makarios letter. Lindsey Grant in Nicosia was leaving a meeting about Davies's arrival with Cypriot foreign affairs director general, Chris Veniamin, when the official turned to him and said, 'We sent it'. Grant knew exactly what he meant and 'he knew I knew it. "It" was a letter that had been kicking around among the archbishop's closest advisors, the one that insulted Ioannidis and said, "I'm going to run my show." I said, "I hope you get away with it." And he said, "It'll work."'[57]

Unlike Greece, information in Cyprus was easily obtained and Grant had even seen the text of the letter, 'That's how transparent it was. In this case, we really did know it was going to happen.'[58]

On Wednesday, 3 July 1974, the CIA team in Athens reported information either from Ioannidis or from a source close to him that he had, for the moment, decided against removing the archbishop because of uncertain Soviet reaction and a fear that Turkey might misinterpret the move. In reality, Ioannidis, having tested American reaction, was now throwing them off the scent of his operation only two weeks away.

Makarios's letter far from adding greater pressure gave Ioannidis cause to confirm the date and execute his long-held desire to remove the priest. Many in the military with no love for Ioannidis saw the archbishop's letter as an attack on mainland Greece, forcing the removal of Greek soldiers who countered any Turkish designs and were a bulwark against communist forces. This was the support Ioannidis and his flagging authority needed.

On 5 July 1974, the CIA's Ron Estes and Gust Avrakotos met Prime Minister Adamantios Androutsopoulos, the civilian stooge installed by Ioannidis, who suggested the junta was adopting a conciliatory tone towards Makarios's demands. Others either knew or suspected better. The Greek foreign minister, Spyridon Tetenes, and two of his senior officials resigned that very day in protest at the military taking control of foreign affairs. The junta announced Tetenes's resignation on health grounds three days later.

This ambiguous statement from Androutsopoulos, which the CIA passed on to Washington did not assuage Tom Boyatt, John Day and Bob Dillon in the Department of State who insisted the Greeks were still not getting the message from their instructions to Tasca on 29 June 1974. Dismayed by Tasca's stubbornness, they kept telephoning the American Embassy in Athens to find out what else was being done and were told that messages had been passed to the Greek government at different levels.

Boyatt finally convinced Joe Sisco to send further instructions to the embassy in Athens on 5 July 1974. With Tasca on leave, Sisco telephoned the embassy to speak to a friend, the political counsellor Elizabeth 'Ann' Brown, about developments. Brown said the instructions had been passed to her and she had carried them out. But as Dillon recalled, 'Joe turned to us indicating that the matter had been taken care of'. However, 'it was quite clear from the conversation, which we could hear over the speaker phone, that Brown, who was a very good officer, did not have the faintest idea what Sisco was talking about. She did not indicate that she had understood that the issue was a very serious one that required special attention and care.'[59]

In fact, this capable but not high-ranking officer had passed on the message to the head of the Greek Orthodox Church, Archbishop Seraphim, rather than anyone in Ioannidis's junta contravening the instructions from Washington. For Tom Boyatt, this meant they had passed on 'the message of the United States government to this religious figure ... It became clear that the instructions had been carried out in a half-hearted manner at best by the embassy in Athens.'[60] Bob Dillon was similarly kicking himself that they had not been allowed to use the CIA, 'The General had to be told directly that the US had received his message and that we were unalterably opposed to any coup on Cyprus'.[61]

Whether or not such a message might have forestalled him, Ioannidis acted out a public ruse of reconciliation with Makarios by having Greek ambassador in Nicosia, Efstathios Lagakos, invite Makarios to Athens without preconditions. The archbishop rejected the invitation saying Athens must first accept his demands over the National Guard. The American Embassy in Nicosia moved into a state of alarm. James Williams helped draft a cable round about 7 July 1974 saying,

> we really need to get Athens to step back or call off the dogs or tone it down, words to that effect. We didn't know what we were asking for concretely except that the tensions were getting a little higher. I remember using the phrase that Makarios was challenging the self-esteem of [President Phaedon] Gizikis and by extension of Ioannidis by slapping them in the face by the publication of these letters ... high stakes poker.[62]

Lindsey Grant also remembers drafting the very cable that summarised the situation as 'We think they're going to try to kill Makarios'.[63] However, newly settled-in American Ambassador Rodger Davies felt uneasy about such a bold statement. He told Grant that 'We can't say that people are going to kill a foreign head of state just like that, in the summary',[64] so they took it out but left it in the body of the message. By good fortune, Grant, who was about to leave Cyprus for his next diplomatic appointment had already sent his wife home. The family cat was booked out on a flight for the 15 July 1974.

Writing the daily intelligence summary for Henry Kissinger on 7 July 1974, the Department of State's Intelligence and Research Bureau reckoned Makarios would treat any prevarication by the junta to his demands as its intention to keep Greek officers on the island. Officials across the Nixon administration read this briefing while waiting to hear about the latest developments in the Supreme Court where the Watergate special prosecutor presented his case to access the president's tapes.

A day later, Cypriot Ambassador Nikos Dimitriou in Washington warned the EUR's deputy, Wells Stabler, that Athens would not take this lying down. Greece's own ambassador in Cyprus also told Rodger Davies that his Foreign Ministry had recommended Athens accept Makarios's demands while admitting that the junta favoured either confrontation or complete withdrawal from Cyprus.

When Athens duly delayed a response, Makarios pushed what he thought was his advantage. On Wednesday, 10 July 1974, he announced his intention to sack the Greek officers commanding the National Guard in the middle of the week, virtually spitting in the face of the junta.

Despite this ultimatum, two of the local CIA staff in Athens, most likely Ron Estes and Gust Avrakotos, reported the next day, on Thursday, 11 July 1974, a source telling them that Prime Minister Adamantios Androutsopoulos still wanted compromise. The CIA branch chief in Washington was not so sure, for that day's national intelligence briefing argued that a Greek move against Makarios could not now be ruled out.

In reply to Joe Sisco's instructions on 29 June 1974, the American Embassy in Athens reported on 11 July 1974 that aside from Tasca's contacts with President Phaedon Gizikis and Archbishop Seraphim other staff had used their own channels to convey the US position against any resort to violence. What these were and their significance is unclear.

British diplomats were none the wiser. In Cyprus, High Commissioner Stephen Olver met a rather shocked Greek Ambassador Efstathios Lagakos also on 11 July 1974, who, annoyed at developments and suspecting the junta of some form of plotting had asked to be recalled, was complaining that his efforts over the last two years were wasted. However, Lagakos did not think a last-ditch confrontation had been reached as EOKA-B or the junta could have assassinated Makarios any time during the last six months. Both he and Olver, therefore, dismissed talk of a coup and Olver advised London that Makarios was unwise in refusing to visit Athens, though he did not rule out any assassination attempt.

Olver was wise to hedge his bets for that same Thursday the Greek Cabinet discussed Makarios's letter and decided to hold another meeting on Saturday supposedly to consider withdrawing Greek officers from the National Guard in Cyprus. In fact, it was to give final approval for Monday's coup.

Boyatt, Day and Dillon in Washington instructed Ambassador Rodger Davies to have Makarios calm the situation. Davies duly met

Makarios in the Presidential Palace the next day, Friday, 12 July 1974, telling him that Athens knew that the United States wanted stability in the Eastern Mediterranean and suggested he also try and reduce tension. This was a point of much contention for it was not clear if Ioannidis had got the message with sufficient force: an opaque conversation with President Phaedon Gizikis and Archbishop Seraphim and conversations through the CIA were far from a formal government communication. Moreover, Davies's message may have inadvertently fortified Makarios into thinking the Americans were restraining Ioannidis and making him even more complacent about any threat.

While Davies met the archbishop, Washington was concerned enough to have CIA chief Stacy Hulse in Athens relay the United States' formal views to Ioannidis through an emissary. There is some doubt over this person's identity. William Crawford, the temporary American deputy ambassador in Nicosia from August 1974, recalled this person was 'a longstanding asset who was very close to [Brigadier] General Dimitrios Ioannidis'.[65]

Only two people fit this bill, either local CIA agent Gust Avrakotos, who knew Ioannidis well and had previously been used as an official emissary when Papadopoulos led the junta, or Peter Koromilas, another former Greek-American CIA agent previously stationed in Greece, who had a good relationship with Ioannidis before his posting to another role outside the country in 1973. A Department of State official supposedly confirmed that Koromilas was the agent though this was denied by CIA boss Stacy Hulse.

Whether it was Avrakotos or Koromilas, Ioannidis was days away from launching his plan and fed this man a story wrong-footing American intelligence. He denied any intention to move against the archbishop or damage stability in the Eastern Mediterranean, saying he felt the cost of action too explosive to ensure success and that he was reducing 100 mainland officers from the National Guard that very day. And on top of other incomplete information, the US intelligence community fell for the ruse.

From the perspective of diplomat William Crawford who knew Cyprus from his own tour there, the CIA asset came back and said

'No, there's nothing to it, I can assure you'.
    Of course, this was believed, because he, in turn, had worked so long and faithfully for the United States. But nobody ever considered the possibility that he might still be loyal to his boss and reporting to him, Ioannidis, the whole time he was also working for the United States.[66]

Neither the CIA nor DIA officers foresaw the coup that sparked the whole July and August crisis. The CIA had reported on 29 May 1974 that Makarios was planning a move but then on 3 July 1974 reported he would not; then on 11 July 1974 that this could not be ruled out, which they then contradicted on Friday, 12 July 1974, when their emissary met the brigadier general. Ioannidis had outplayed them. Tom Boyatt was exasperated:

> There we were, sitting there with the entire intelligence establishment of the United States in all of its majesty, having been conned by a piss-ant Greek Brigadier General, on the one hand; and on the other hand the disaster which I had been trying to avert, and avoid, coming true like your worst nightmare.[67]

Ioannidis himself had read into the public messages from Kissinger and the Department of State about not interfering in Greek matters that he was free to move. He was likely reinforced in this view by the informal and ambiguous nature of American warnings, which suggested Washington cared only about ethnic strife escalating into a Greek-Turkish conflict not about fighting between Greeks.

For all the seriousness of these developments, Cyprus was nonetheless but one and far from the most pressing foreign affairs issues among the many from East Germany to South America facing Kissinger and the Department of State. Peace in the Middle East between Israel and Syria and Egypt, and constant chess board movements in the Cold War against the Soviet Union, which centred on mind-bogglingly complex strategic arms reduction talks, preoccupied most of the Department of State's time. Nixon, though assailed by Watergate, had even continued his *détente* agenda travelling in late June and early July 1974 to Moscow for another nuclear test ban treaty.

An accompanying Kissinger, tired from his many burdens, including the Arab-Israeli peace shuttles, stopped off in London and briefed the British foreign secretary about the *détente* talks. He and Jim Callaghan discussed every pressing matter from the Middle East to the failing health of Spanish dictator, General Francisco Franco, but at no time did they talk about Cyprus, which simply did not attract their interest. As Callaghan admitted, he did not expect every 'Mediterranean rumble to lead to disaster'.[68] Even the issues they did discuss were eclipsed by the imminent collapse of the Nixon administration gripping the Western world.

On Friday evening, 12 July 1974, American bureaucrats left the capital to start their weekend in some comfort following the CIA message suggesting nothing was imminent – and doubtless to watch the latest television news analysis on Nixon. As Tom Boyatt recalled,

> That same day we received a raw intelligence cable from the station in Athens which said, in effect, 'We have been in touch with [Brigadier] General [Dimitrios] Ioannidis, and we have been assured by [Brigadier] General Ioannidis that the Greek government is not, and will not be involved in any clandestine activity designed to overthrow Archbishop Makarios, and to damage the situation in the Eastern Mediterranean.'
>
> That was a weekend, so all right, we'd had it from the horse's mouth. I went home.[69]

This position was reflected the next day, Saturday, 13 July 1974, in the equivocating summary of the Department of State's Intelligence and Research Bureau for Kissinger advising that Athens was now reacting moderately to Makarios's demands but remained capable of an attempt to remove him.

On that second point they were correct for 5,000 miles away in Athens, President Phaedon Gizikis accompanied by the Greek general staff briefed the Cabinet, including the commander of the National Guard, Georgios Denissis summoned from Cyprus, of the plan to kill Makarios. The archbishop and most observers knew about the meeting though not the subject for it was billed as discussing a peaceful outcome and expected to last for two days resuming on 15 July 1974 to create the impression of compromise. Denissis refused to carry out the order and resigned so coup planner Michalis Georgitsis took command of the Cyprus National Guard.

This drama was a world apart from normal life in the towns and villages of Cyprus in peak summer, which though awash with routine speculation saw community talks resume and a reduction in Greek-Turkish tensions over the Aegean Islands. British newspaper reports covering the worsening crisis ironically created a surge in holiday demand as hopeful tourists rushed to visit an island where history was unfolding irrespective of the dangers. Britannia Airways running out of Luton Airport enjoyed a healthy boost in profits. Despite having to clear flights with the government, Foreign and Commonwealth Office approval came through to the astonishment of ground staff technicians in the airline's engineering department who wondered if the diplomats were watching the same news they were on television.

A blissful social scene meanwhile continued on the British bases. On 13 July 1974, 56 (Lightnings) Squadron held a formal cocktail party of starch laden dress uniform in number 2 officers' mess before the liberating revelry of a beach party at Dreamer's Bay. The do-it-yourself barbeque was supported by a mobile operations room generator tapped to power a stereo system blaring out the latest 1970s hits.

This life came to a shattering halt on Monday, 15 July 1974. An officer in the Department of State's operations centre woke up Tom Boyatt early in the morning saying, 'You better get in here. There's fighting in Nicosia, and something is going on and it doesn't look good.'[70] So, Boyatt rushed over where he was told,

'Here's what we've got.'
        And he put two pieces of paper in front of me. On the left-hand side was the Daily Intelligence Summary, which is done by the entire intelligence community for the President and the Vice President, the Secretary of State, and the highest officers.
        And it said, in its lead item, 'We have been assured by [Brigadier] General [Dimitrios] Ioannidis that Greece will not move its forces on Cyprus against Makarios. To the right was a cable from Embassy Nicosia describing the fighting between Cypriots loyal to Makarios and Cypriots and Greeks trying to overthrow him. The Presidential Palace was in flames the Cypriot force has been decimated. We don't know where Archbishop Makarios is. We presume he's dead. A government has been installed in Cyprus, and the new leader is Nikos Sampson.'[71]

The coup had started.

Chapter 7

AN UNEXPECTED COUP: MONDAY, 15 JULY 1974

Early in the morning on Monday, 15 July 1974, Greek soldiers of the Hellenic Force in Cyprus, Ελληνική Δύναμη Κύπρου (Elliniki Dynami Kyprou or abbreviated to ELDYK) – a unit of the Hellenic Army and stationed in Cyprus under the independence arrangements of 1960 – together with the Cypriot National Guard began their action against democratically elected president, Archbishop Makarios III. Officers who refused to participate were either kept in barracks or sent off to exercises to keep them out of the way.

After spending the weekend at a lodge in Mount Troodos, Makarios made the usual journey to his Presidential Palace with his car even passing the ELDYK barracks at Waynes Keep and no one noticing anything out of the ordinary. Ironically, Makarios had stationed some of his presidential guards to watch the barracks who left when daylight broke; others who saw the tanks leaving Waynes Keep thought the Greek soldiers were on exercise. He arrived at his official residence at 7.45 am local time and settled into the week's work moving into the reception room to receive thirty school children from Cairo.

A bodyguard then walked briskly into the room and told him about tanks moving towards the front of the palace, with shooting already audible as the presidential guards began returning fire. Makarios and his aides moved to a corridor where they stayed for fifteen minutes. Fortunately, the tanks took their time on the frontal assault and those covering the western wing at the back were delayed when the lead tank broke down providing a crucial window to get away.

His aides believing Makarios was the target said he must escape. The archbishop disrobed and accompanied by his four bodyguards, one of them his nephew, escaped through a secret passage to the back of the palace crossing a dry riverbed in the back garden and then, outside the palace grounds, flagged down a passing driver who recognised him.

They abandoned this car when fuel ran out minutes later and flagged down another driver, remarkably a disabled man driving with two wooden legs, who handed over his vehicle. A second stroke of luck fell upon the archbishop, for his fleeing party intended making for a local branch of the Kykkos Monastery about 1 kilometre north but turned around after a loyal reserve officer of the National Guard – there were some – warned him about encroaching tanks. That building was surrounded fifteen minutes later. They dashed instead to a police station in a village called Klirou, 20 kilometres south-west of Nicosia, before the capital was cut off, with the reserve officer driving ahead to warn them of more roadblocks.

They changed cars again in Klirou using a vehicle of an off-duty presidential guardsman living there and drove through hair-raising mountain roads to reach Kykkos Monastery in the Troodos Mountains arriving at 1.00 pm. Makarios, relieved at reaching his spiritual home, went in and prayed.

His escape went unnoticed during the inept frontal assault by the National Guard who thought him dead when tank shells destroyed his official car. Within a few hours they had badly damaged the Presidential Palace. Makarios's Tactical Reserve Unit rushing to the scene were cut off by regular Greek troops and its commander, Major Andreas Pantazis, was captured and persuaded to surrender his forces to avoid bloodshed. Palace staff were taken out unharmed though some of the former, including Justice Minister Christos Vakis, the very man previously kidnapped by EOKA-B, did not receive good treatment.

As these events unfolded 3,500 British servicemen and their families, many living outside the RAF bases, particularly in Limassol, awoke to another blue summer sky and routinely started their journey into work. High Commissioner Stephen Olver hurriedly told London about fighting in Nicosia believed to be around the Presidential Palace and Supreme Court. Within an hour, Britain's Near East Joint Intelligence staff at RAF Dhekelia reported to Air Marshal Sir John Alexander Carlisle Aiken, a Belfast born RAF pilot flying Spitfires in the Second World War who commanded British forces on the island, that a coup was underway. An hour later, Olver discussed the situation with Aiken, who raised the station security alert and put in motion a Near East operations centre.

The National Guard sealed off the airport, formerly RAF Nicosia, and seized the island's communication network, including the radio station, Cyprus Broadcasting Corporation. Cypriots tuning in were perplexed by unusual military music and then astounded by a message around 10.00 am announcing 'Makarios *ina necrosa*' ('Makarios is dead'), repeated every hour. Shortly afterwards, the coupists announced a government of the National Salvation Party to restore unity between Greek Cypriots, harmony in the Cypriot Church and stop the armed forces from falling into the hands of what they called anarchy and criminal elements. They justified this action on the grounds of stopping Greek infighting and, doubtless using a scripted message from Athens to assure Ankara that Turkish Cypriots were safe, stressed this is an internal matter. For good measure they added that anyone trying to interfere will be immediately executed.

A senior Soviet diplomat, Beliaev, heard the shooting from the Soviet Embassy and took his military attaché to the Presidential Palace to investigate until a bullet pierced the windscreen barely missing them causing his hasty return. (He and his colleagues then remained holed up in the embassy until 18 July 1974 surrounded by the National Guard until Brigadier Francis 'Frank' Henn, commanding British forces of UNFICYP, persuaded the Cypriot soldiers to withdraw.)

In the middle of fierce fighting in Limassol stood the British International School where young pupils had begun their lessons unaware of the very grown-up dangers around them. Their exceptional teachers took a huge risk walking out into the hot street with the National Guard and Makarios supporters shooting at each other only yards away, raised a white flag and escorted anxious children in a crocodile line to safety the far side of the road.

In London, Foreign Secretary Jim Callaghan received a flash message about the coup and summoned his senior staff, including Permanent Secretary Sir Thomas Brimelow and Foreign Minister Roy Hattersley. A bullish Callaghan decided that Britain's special role as a guarantor power with sovereign bases on the island meant he must take the initiative with Greece and Turkey; and he also had to worry about the safety of British personnel, their families and UK nationals holidaying in Cyprus. Stopping a Turkish military reaction was the priority, so Callaghan told Greece and Turkey to keep wise heads and stressed their mutual roles guaranteeing the territorial integrity and sovereignty of Cyprus.

Turkey was caught unawares. Turkish Foreign Minister Turan Güneş was in China, the chief of the general staff, Semih Sancar, was in Istanbul and the Turkish ambassador to Greece was sailing in the Mediterranean. Prime Minister Bülent Ecevit and his government, like everyone else, was trying to grasp what was going on without making hasty decisions as Turkish communities did not appear under immediate threat. His chief concern was whether the coup presaged *enosis*, exposing the Turkish mainland to a strategic threat which he would not countenance. Major General Bedrettin Demirel's 39th Infantry Division – the unit long planned for reacting to problems in Cyprus – was placed on alert just in case with Ecevit planning to review the situation with Turkey's generals later in the day.

Turkish-Cypriot leader Rauf Denktaş had long anticipated a coup but thought this likely when the tourist season wound down in October 1974. Turkish Cypriots for the time being heeded his direction to stay calm and not get involved in what seemed a Greek only affair. Meanwhile, the National Guard hunted down and settled scores with prominent Makarios supporters as rumours of executions started to flow in. Vassos Lyssarides, as head of the AKEL communist party, fled to the Syrian Embassy for safety.

Almost immediately the plans of the coupists started crumbling as two men they had approached to become interim president refused. Glafcos Clerides – as parliament's speaker who normally became acting president when Makarios was absent – wanted nothing to do with the conspiracy. First choice, Chief Justice Michael Triantafyllides, happened to be in Strasbourg, France, and second choice, Health Minister Zenon Severis, feigned a heart condition. Instead, the coup organisers settled as a desperate third choice on the thug and killer Nikos Sampson, the man most likely to excite Turkish opinion. On hearing the news, Ioannidis in Athens reportedly exclaimed they could have chosen anyone on the island other than Sampson.

Probably a psychotic killer, Sampson was the man who had burnished his credentials killing Turks, Cypriot police officers, civilians and British soldiers during the 1950s struggle for *enosis*. Alongside him, right wingers and EOKA-B nationalists replaced Makarios's ministers in a quickly stitched together Cabinet. His appointment as president was announced at noon on Cyprus Broadcasting Corporation, when he read out a script written by his Greek masters wanting to forestall any Turkish reaction by announcing community talks as the way forward, dismissing talk of *enosis* and emphasising the independence of Cyprus.

Undermining these messages were reports filtering through that Makarios was alive and given credibility when one of the archbishop's bodyguards tipped off Paphos Free Radio. Word also passed to the Bishop of Paphos, who, in turn, telephoned the British High Commission to request UN intervention and asked the nearest local UN commander, Major Richard McFarlane of the Coldstream Guards, to forward a request from the archbishop for an urgent meeting of the Security Council.

At RAF Akrotiri, Wing Commander Ken Watson, in charge of the nuclear armed Vulcan squadron, soon learnt something was wrong after he settled into work. Watson was an experienced officer who had decided the RAF was a good gig during his national service and stayed on to become a respected heavy bomber pilot and was now on his second tour of Cyprus. His co-pilot was friendly with local Greek-Cypriot kitchen staff in the officers' mess who provided an inkling of the coup in motion. This was confirmed by their RAF bosses when preparing for the day's flying programme.

As part of the undeclared nuclear force to NATO, Vulcans had to maintain a round-the-clock flying operation. Watson checked with the flight operations officer whether it was wise for a highly visible aircraft to fly over the island during such instability. Carry on regardless he was told, this was a remote affair not to worry about. Still not sure this was correct, Watson fired up the engines, moved the large aircraft into position and prepared for take-off. Only 20 yards before the runway, he slammed on the brakes when the command 'stop'[72] bellowed down from the flight operations officer who clearly had second thoughts.

Around noon, RAF Akrotiri's Security Committee reviewed the position of stranded families in Limassol, especially given reports of sporadic shooting close to their quarters. Security officer Wing Commander David was sent out with the deputy head of the base police and an armed Land Rover escort to find someone in charge in Limassol. Amid all the confusion, David located a National Guard district officer who agreed a safe passage to get worried servicemen back to their families. David rushed back to set the plan in action.

The British ambassador to Turkey, Sir Horace Hyman Phillips, was driving back to London across Europe from his summer holiday in Venice, Italy, and heard about the coup when stopping off in Monte Carlo. He promptly telephoned the Foreign and Commonwealth Office and was told to fly back to Ankara, so he left his car with the consul general in Nice, France.

Early afternoon in London, Callaghan told the Greeks of his grave concern, requesting their comments and for even handedness told them he was sending a similar message to the Turks. He urged Turkey to observe 'exemplary patience'[73] on the grounds this was an intra-Greek problem. Henry Kissinger was told of the messages and asked for American views. NATO Secretary General Joseph Luns sent similar messages to Turkey and Greece. London also wanted the UN Secretary General Kurt Waldheim to intervene, but he declined for the time being knowing that Washington would resist any efforts to internationalise the situation until more was known.

A flurry of cables passed between the British embassies in Greece, Turkey, Cyprus and London. What were the implications of the coup? Was the junta involved? How should the dispersed British community be protected? And what Turkey might do? Athens maintained a pretence of ignorance: Greek Foreign Minister Konstantinos Kypraios (the replacement for Spyridon Tetenes who had resigned when realising that military action was imminent) told British Ambassador Robin Hooper that Greece 'was not fully informed about the situation'[74] in Cyprus, and its support for intercommunal talks had not changed.

The American defence attaché, Colonel Frank Athanason, working as a NATO liaison officer was attending a passing out parade at the Greek Naval Academy near Piraeus. Athanason was a second-generation Greek-American artillery officer from Augusta, Georgia, attached to the Greek military since 1972 helping them order new equipment and improve their working conditions, including accepting women into the armed forces. He saw cadets all neatly lined up on a parade field ready for inspection, but everyone appeared to be waiting for someone else. Fifteen or twenty minutes passed when the entourage of Greek President Phaedon Gizikis arrived. Athanason had known Gizikis when the Greek general was a corps commander in Salonika, Greece. Gizikis's car continued passed the reviewing stand to the far end of the parade field.

> He got out and summoned the chiefs of the army, navy, and air force to come down and they had a pow wow. While they were down there talking, someone came and said, 'Your office wants you on the phone. Come upstairs.'
>
> I went there. They said, 'Something happened in Cyprus. You've got to come back to the office.'[75]

Three years later, Athanason spoke to those same three chiefs, saying

> 'What did you guys go down there and talk about?'
> They said that general [Phaedon] Gizikis told us there was a coup in Cyprus. The chief of the navy said that it caught [him] by complete surprise. The chief of the air force said that it was the first he'd ever heard of it. The army told me the same thing. Not the three together, they were separate conversations. All three denied that they knew anything about the coup in Cyprus until that very moment. I found out later that the army guy was lying, he knew about it. But, the other two still stuck with their stories.[76]

In Washington, Tom Boyatt realised the junta was behind the coup and quickly pulled together an assessment for his bosses. Thinking Makarios dead, he outlined the risks of drawing in the Turkish Cypriots, Soviet intervention and a Turkish military reaction. He thought it crucial Washington denounce Ioannidis's actions, try to restore the status quo and have Athens withdraw Greek forces.

Kissinger, briefed about developments for the first time that Monday morning, convened at 10.18 am in Washington the Special Actions Group of National Security Council staff, military chiefs, the head of the CIA and senior Department of State staff from the EUR, including Sisco and the fourth-floor experts, such as Boyatt. In these early hours of the unfolding drama with confusion all around no one could say what was happening and whether Makarios was alive. Only Boyatt had even heard of Sampson when Kissinger asked who he was. Boyatt replied, 'He is a killer. He has already got twelve notches on his gun. I've known him personally for several years.'[77] Kissinger's priority was clear:

> it seems to me that our immediate objective is to keep this thing from becoming internationalized, the Greek-Turk problem, the Soviet angle. There is really nothing we can do at this time internally but we can keep it from becoming an international issue.[78]

He wanted an even-handed approach without blaming the Greeks. Ankara was to be advised against internationalising the problem and told that the United States supported Turkish-Cypriot rights and opposed any change to the existing political structure but without 'picking a fight'. The carrier USS *America*, scheduled for return, was ordered to remain at port in Rota, Spain.

American Ambassador Henry Tasca, back from holiday in time for the coup, cabled in from Athens naming Ioannidis as the likely culprit behind the coup. As if to distract attention from the embassy's mixed record of reporting and the misjudgement over 12 July 1974, he drew attention to the dangerous and unreliable nature of the brigadier general's character in his own assessment in November 1973: 'once again how dangerous and unreliable [Brigadier] General Ioannidis can really be – a concern which my reporting and analysis of the November 25 coup clearly reflected'.[79] Remarkably, Tasca continued arguing against a tough reaction fearing that the irrational brigadier general might well take stronger action over the Aegean Islands. Therefore, a 'negative substantive reaction on our part will likely lead to negative substantive reaction from them'.[80]

Kissinger still told him to find out the Greek position and to convey the United States' opinion that 'we wish [the] GOG [government of Greece] to know that the United States continues to regard Cyprus as a single, sovereign and independent state and our actions in this matter will be governed by this continuing fundamental tenet'.[81] Tasca was to say that the United States did not condone any Greek action in Cyprus and supported a peaceful resolution. Similar instructions were issued to Prime Minister Bülent Ecevit in Turkey to show American even-handedness – a point made to both countries.

Over the next few hours Kissinger learnt that Makarios was alive affecting his handling of the crisis. Rather than immediately support the deposed democratically elected president, he decided not to intervene in fast moving events in case the United States ended up supporting a faction that did not win power.

In Cyprus, other quandaries presented themselves on the ground as Wing Commander David and his team implemented a plan to rescue stranded service families. They assembled every reachable service and private vehicle on which were tied every recoverable Union Jack in highly visible positions to prove British credentials against trigger happy gunman. Then in the mid-afternoon heat he ordered the assembled vehicles over the armed forces' radio network, the British Forces Broadcasting Service, to form a long convoy at the eastern end of the long road on the RAF Akrotiri estate called the M1. They just started to move off when the order came to halt as fresh reports came in of more fighting in Limassol.

They tried again at 5.00 pm when conditions appeared less threatening but did not get far before congestion forced them to pull up. By unlucky coincidence, 1,000 Makarios supporters on their way to oppose the National Guard drew up alongside in a parallel convoy. This motley crew of irregulars encompassed everyone from defiant police Tactical Reserve Unit officers to members of the Communist Party, all armed with every type of historic weapon from rifles to Second World War Japanese field guns. Stuck in this traffic jam the British soldiers had no option but to stay put as the gunmen slowly drove past and shouted 'Makarios eh?'[82] testing or perhaps hoping that both sides were on the same mission. Nervous servicemen smiled back with forced enthusiasm, enough to allay the suspicion of the irregulars.

Continued fighting gave the British convoy little hope of breaking through so exposed service families and civilians trapped in the Limassol fighting had to prepare for a night of violence alone and unprotected.

Makarios had, meanwhile, lunched with monks at the Kykkos Monastery, borrowed a cassock and a hat and travelled onwards over more tough mountain roads, reaching a warm welcome at the Bishop of Paphos' palace around 6.30 pm. He confirmed his survival over Paphos Free Radio, saying the junta had failed to kill him and asked Greek Cypriots to ignore the new Sampson regime. This promptly stopped the Cyprus Broadcasting Corporation from announcing his demise – National Guard soldiers were still looking for his remains at the Presidential Palace.

Local UN commander Richard McFarlane drove in from St Patrick's camp on the edge of Paphos to see if the archbishop really was alive. Makarios, unaware his forces were being defeated in Limassol, told McFarlane that he intended visiting Limassol the next day where he hoped to lead a fightback, repeated his request for Security Council condemnation of the coup and wanted UN envoy Dr Luis Jesús Weckmann-Muñoz and UN commander Lieutenant General Dewan Prem Chand to visit him, all of which McFarlane passed on.

Ominous developments unfolded in Ankara. Chief of the general staff General Semih Sancar and senior commanders met with Turkish Prime Minister Bülent Ecevit and Turkish President Fahri Korutürk around 9.50 pm. Ecevit had now decided the coup represented *enosis* in all but name not only threatening Turkish Cypriots but giving Greece chance to create a base on Cyprus and station bombers threatening Turkey. Sancar told them the military could intervene in five days using the plan developed and rehearsed since 1964. Ecevit agreed and approved a two-phase operation, starting with a secure bridgehead giving Turkey a seaport, which became his unbending requirement.

They set Saturday, 20 July 1974, for the assault knowing the UN would inevitably ask for a ceasefire once shooting started but would be hampered by weekend working. Military chiefs thought they could achieve all objectives within forty-eight hours.

In Washington, confusing reports that a Soviet diplomat in Cyprus had raised with Britain the prospect of Soviet troops reestablishing order reached Kissinger's ear. At 5.30 pm local time, he telephoned Soviet Ambassador Anatoly Dobrynin, his principal Soviet contact, and, despite finding him on holiday, told him over the telephone, 'I can't believe this'. Dobrynin, whether he knew or not, expressed disbelief in his imperfect English, 'I have no information. I have no telegram telling me this. I doubt that very much ... The second man come to the British ... to me it sounds unbelievable.'[83] Satisfied, Kissinger warned him that 'I don't want to start a crisis to keep you here. I don't want anything to interfere with your vacation.'[84] Keeping the Soviets out of Cyprus was a crucial consideration.

Dobrynin went off to check that no such action was intended and telephoned back an hour later when they briefly discussed the news that Makarios was alive in Paphos, which Kissinger said was 'a new complexion on the situation'.[85] Kissinger told Dobrynin about his messages to Ankara and Athens and assured the Soviet ambassador they would talk before taking actions, emphasising that the United States had no 'unilateral interests'[86] in Cyprus and supported the existing constitution.

That was all he could do while he and the rest of the world struggled to understand what was going on in this extraordinary day in Cyprus.

Chapter 8

TURKEY GOES THROUGH THE MOTIONS: TUESDAY, 16 JULY 1974

Despite their passion, supporters of Makarios proved no match for the better armed and larger National Guard, who overcame their resistance during night fighting in Limassol and Larnaca and otherwise controlled most major cities. By 7.00 am, beaten and weary supporters fled in a seventy-vehicle convoy for a final defence in Paphos with National Guardsmen not far behind.

Dr Luis Weckmann-Muñoz and Lieutenant General Dewan Prem Chand flew to Paphos by helicopter at 10.00 am to meet the archbishop, who thinking a fightback was possible, declined protection of the British bases and repeated his request for a Security Council meeting. He changed his mind several hours later after making another broadcast on Paphos Free Radio to appeal to all freedom loving nations, when National Guard forces moved nearer supported by a gunboat, which shortly after noon fired on the bishop's residence.

Weckmann-Muñoz and Chand returned to UN headquarters in Nicosia at 12.30 pm to find Makarios's request for evacuation by helicopter, which they passed on to the British High Commission. Stephen Olver liaised with the base commander, John Aiken, who agreed on condition that once at Akrotiri the RAF immediately flew Makarios to Britain before the National Guard or EOKA-B types discovered his whereabouts and turned on the bases or threatened service families. With the gunboat now pounding the radio station to stop further broadcasts, Makarios agreed, and permission was sought from London.

Having decided on military intervention the previous evening, Prime Minister Bülent Ecevit went through the required 1960 consultation process summoning British Ambassador Horace Phillips for discussions. Would Britain join Turkey in military action to reverse the coup and restore the constitution he asked? Phillips politely suggested not as any British action exposed its troops and thousands of civilians to danger on top of the associated problems of interfering in relations between Greece and Turkey. Undeterred, Ecevit requested a meeting with Harold Wilson and Jim Callaghan in London, which Phillips set in motion. Ecevit meanwhile called a special meeting of the Turkish Parliament for two days' time on 18 July 1974.

Before London received the request, Callaghan worked out a new position taking into account that Makarios was now alive but still removing any cause for Turkey to intervene and the Soviet Union to interfere. He advised the Greek government to recognise Makarios as the legitimate president, withdraw Greek officers from the National Guard and preserve Cypriot independence, territorial integrity and security. British Ambassador Robin Hooper found Greek Foreign Minister Konstantinos Kypraios receptive though fretted that 'as we have learnt from experience, making representations to civilian Ministers is one thing and getting them translated into action is another'.[87]

Callaghan told both Turkey and the United States of his actions and publicly repeated this position in the early afternoon at the House of Commons, affirming that 'President Makarios was elected, and is now the elected leader of the people of Cyprus'.[88] Western European countries followed suit, irritating Ankara, which could not see why its allies took an even-handed approach to an obvious Greek sponsored coup, and creating a difference with Kissinger who wanted to see which faction emerged in Cyprus before supporting any particular side – though he was adamant Sampson was not to be recognised.

With frightened families still isolated in Limassol, the RAF launched another rescue initiative contacting the National Guard's area commander, a weary but helpful Colonel Sirmopolous who appointed one of his majors as a liaison officer, who proved rather efficient in arranging plans. An afternoon lull in the fighting provided the chance, so two convoys from each RAF station again formed up on the main highway leading to Limassol, this time under escort by the National Guard liaison major to avoid incidents.

National Guard efficiency did not mean control of the assorted gunmen fighting alongside them, some taking it on themselves to form picket posts around the perimeter of RAF Akrotiri patrolled by the Royal Scots army regiment. In an incident not widely reported the Royal Scots came under fire from one of the vigilante groups who shot a soldier in the backside, fortunately causing no lasting harm. Unfortunately for the trigger-happy thugs, the Royal Scots boasted a crack shot boasting medals at the British Army's firing range in Bisley, Surrey, who despatched the would-be assassins in return fire.

Meanwhile Turkey's land forces' commander, General Eşref Akinci, summoned fellow officers for a secret briefing at army headquarters in the Turkish city of Adana about the 20 July 1974 operation.

Restless British commanders in Cyprus still awaiting London's permission to rescue Makarios prepared Operation Skylark, a plan rehearsed since 1968 to evacuate the archbishop in an emergency. A problem arose over aircraft markings as John Aiken, wanting to keep Britain's involvement secret to avoid retaliation, gave the mission to 84 Squadron, a Whirlwind helicopter unit on UN duties at Nicosia. Frank Henn, commanding the British contingent of UNFICYP, protested fearing retaliation against the UN but had to relent as Aiken controlled the aircraft. Ground crew did, however, try and disguise the helicopter from any obvious UN associations.

Whitehall finally gave approval at 3.45 pm relieving frayed nerves in RAF Akrotiri's operations centre where staff were charting National Guard advances on Paphos. The Whirlwind flew a meandering route pretending to come from Nicosia, an established flight path to avoid suspicion, landed at the UN camp near Paphos for twenty-five minutes and took off with one deposed Cypriot president and three bodyguards arriving in Akrotiri at 4.50 pm. Three hours later, the National Guard surrounded the Paphos compound and overcame all resistance, the fighters capitulating when learning of Makarios's departure. John Aiken realised how close this was for 'had the National Guard followed up its earlier successes more quickly, it is probable that we would not have saved Makarios and indeed we might have lost a helicopter and crew in the attempt'.[89] The British rescue operation saved Makarios from the second likely assassination attempt within forty-eight hours.

Shortly before the archbishop arrived at Akrotiri, American Ambassador Henry Tasca asked one of his intermediaries to tell Ioannidis about the United States' position in what proved a meeting of extraordinary theatre. Ioannidis, his nerves beginning to show, told the emissary he was wasting his time in repeating the same points given to his foreign minister. Undeterred, the emissary continued to set out Kissinger's view causing Ioannidis to jump up, knock over a table, smashing a glass in the process and swear. One day Kissinger made public statements against interfering in Greek internal affairs, he shouted, and then weeks later threatened interference:

> No matter what happened in Cyprus [Ioannidis] will be blamed. If I had pulled the troops out the former politicians would have blamed me for turning the island over to the Communists. Someday USG [United States government] will realize that on 15 July 1974 Cyprus was saved from falling into the hands of the Communists.[90]

Ioannidis then said it was irrelevant whether or not he had supported the coupists and, showing his lack of grasp on the situation, claimed that Turkey accepted there was no *enosis* and the matter was one of Greek internal affairs. He denounced the archbishop as a corrupt 'priest, a homosexual, who was perverted, a torturer, a sexual deviant and the owner of half the hotels on the island'.[91] And he asserted that Greek nationalists in the National Guard realised that Makarios was sacrificing Cyprus to communism and begged him to help. What else could he do when presented with such a *fait accompli*?

The emissary replied that it was implausible, causing Ioannidis to explode again, throw his arms around, knock over the same table and swear some more while ineffectively denying he plotted the coup. They planned it and came to me on 13 July 1974, he declared unconvincingly. Besides, he added, Makarios is finished and no one cares if he is still alive, 'he now has no power and no one, if he believes in principle of non-interference in internal affairs of sovereign nation will assist him – not even the Russians unless Turks ask them to do so and the Turks just don't care'.[92] Ioannidis even thought that Greece and Turkey could now settle their differences and joked that Turkey might sell its stake in Cyprus for oil rights. At the peak of his performance, the brigadier general said he acted honourably by not abandoning an island for the Americans to sort out but protected national identity against anti-communism. Sampson was 'crazy' he admitted but the nationalists chose him. He then shook the emissary's hands adding,

> Remember we too believe in a free, independent and sovereign Cyprus, we too believe in non-interference, along with Turks and especially with [Henry] Kissinger. We too believe that the Cypriots should be free to solve their own problems, be they Greek Cypriots, Turk Cypriots or both.[93]

Turkey belied Ioannidis's calculation by readying for action while performing a diplomatic ruse for the West in pursuing consultation with London. British Ambassador Horace Phillips thought Ankara was reacting calmly and would only send in troops if *enosis* were pursued or Turkish Cypriots threatened, a sentiment shared by American Ambassador Henry Tasca who erroneously suggested to Washington that Turkey's relaxed attitude meant Ioannidis had forewarned them through a private channel.

Callaghan duly offered Turkey talks for the following day in London without agreeing to joint military action. As he did so, British Secretary of Defence Roy Mason and chief of the defence staff Sir Michael 'Mike' Carver in the afternoon diverted HMS *Hermes*, en route to Malta with forty-one Royal Marine commandos, to Cyprus. (The United States kept two task forces in the region including the USS *Forrestal* ready to move if the Soviet fleet moved nearer to Cyprus.)

Back in Akrotiri, John Aiken worrying that Greek-Cypriot nationalists might attack the bases if they learnt of the archbishop's presence had his own Argosy aircraft fuelled and ready to fly Makarios out, while Callaghan and his diplomats pondered over the destination. Annoyed at the delay, an agitated Aiken then complained that London's dithering risked an incident. When this had no effect, he made up his own mind and chose Malta, which was close enough for the Argosy's flying range and from where another RAF plane could fly Makarios to London. He told vice chief of the defence staff, Air Chief Marshal Sir Peter de Lacy Le Cheminant, about his plan and got on with it, flying out a bewildered Makarios and his bodyguards just after 5.00 pm. Callaghan's staff were furious at Aiken's disobedience, but they provided no instruction to his cheeky return cable asking whether he should recall the flight.

Callaghan told Kissinger, now mid-morning in the United States, that Makarios was asking for British help and there was a plan to take him to Malta but did not know where after that. Kissinger had no idea either but Makarios's departure from the island disturbed him as he now thought the archbishop would lead an outside opposition movement relying on Soviet support. Callaghan urged him not to recognise Sampson, which Kissinger agreed, but he kept quiet about Makarios, not wanting to formally recognise anyone until the prospects of who was coming out on top were clearer.

Kissinger repeated this point ten minutes later at 11.20 am when telling his Special Actions Group that American priorities were to stop the situation becoming an international matter and, if civil war developed, manoeuvre to keep the keep the Soviets out. This meant decoupling the Greeks from the situation – a rather unrealistic aim given Ioannidis's role – and stop the Turks from intervening. He was dumbfounded when the CIA director, William Colby, said that Ecevit's convening of a special parliamentary meeting on 18 July 1974 might presage a Turkish invasion. 'I just can't believe that. I just can't believe they want Makarios back in power.'[94] He was similarly baffled by Makarios's decision to leave the island giving no chance to organise resistance among his forces, which left even Tom Boyatt bewildered. In the fog of poor information, they did not appreciate how quickly the National Guard had overcome Makarios's disparate forces, surprising even the archbishop himself.

The Cyprus Task Force was created under EUR's chief, Art Hartman, as the coordinating point for all information pulling in staff from every government department in a day and night shift, and comprising many junior officers enthralled by the prospect of working under Henry Kissinger, who had developed celebrity status.

All was not smooth, however, across the Department of State where policy differences emerged with one body of opinion wanting strong action against Ioannidis to forestall a Turkish intervention. Tom Boyatt pressed for this course arguing for the reinstatement of Makarios, which was now Britain's position, but treading carefully recognising that he was a desk officer subject to the policy of his masters. Others in the Department of State were not overly concerned about the demise of the archbishop and wondered whether the new circumstances allow NATO to station a base in Cyprus. Boyatt's colleague and fellow expert Bob Dillon saw that a

lot of Americans, and I was one of them, didn't like Makarios; he was a hypocrite, full of humbug, very much anti-West, but Boyatt was right. When I was asked whether the Turks would accept the return of Makarios, I said that I thought that if it were done quickly, they would accede. If time passed, then the Turks might well raise objections.[95]

When the Department of State's press spokesman, Robert Anderson, did not condemn Greek actions or recognise Makarios at the daily press briefing on Tuesday, 16 July 1974, some newspapers reported American satisfaction over the removal of the 'Fidel Castro of the Mediterranean'. This sowed a seed for Greek conspiracy fantasists believing tales about American complicity in the coup; yet at no time did Anderson or the Department of State recognise Sampson as few thought he would last.

Makarios, now airborne in Aiken's Argosy with his bodyguards en route to Malta, certainly did not think he would, while thinking about how to make it to London. An RAF wing commander who only forty minutes earlier had learnt he was to escort the deposed president received a message from the Foreign and Commonwealth Office asking Makarios where he really wanted to go. Makarios replied he had no concrete plans but wanted his final destination to be London. Another message came through, this time from the unique personality of Maltese prime minister, Dom Mintoff, inviting the archbishop to stay in Malta until he made further plans. Makarios politely declined.

When they landed at Luqa airport shortly gone 9.00 pm Greenwich Mean Time (GMT), Makarios, now impatient to reach London, spotted an RAF Comet on the runway and asked whether this could be used. The wing commander duly checked and was told the aircraft was being repaired. Prime Minister Dom Mintoff suddenly appeared on the Argosy and persuaded Makarios to stay overnight. An exhausted archbishop with no money or clothes though as composed as always offered little resistance and went off with the governor general who had also boarded the now busy stationary aircraft.

UN Secretary General Kurt Waldheim briefed the Security Council at 3.00 pm in New York. Cypriot Ambassador Zenon Rossides, an old hand who had represented Cyprus since independence, denounced Athens for organising the coup, a claim which the Greek Ambassador Constantine Panayotacos forcefully rebutted – he may genuinely not have known about his own government's complicity though most of the West, including Waldheim, had by now worked out Ioannidis was the culprit. The session acted as a steam valve without agreeing any measures to the relief of Washington. The Soviet Union condemned outside interference and pushed for urgent action but only enough to satisfy public consumption for it was not going to disturb the waters. Both Britain and the United States avoided apportioning blame while condemning violence and recognising Cypriot independence.

Chapter 9

TONES OF DIFFERENCE EMERGE: WEDNESDAY, 17 JULY 1974

By the third day of the coup, the National Guard had more or less secured the Greek parts of the island and mopped up remaining fragments of opposition in Larnaca, Famagusta and Limassol, which provided generally quieter though eerie conditions with British servicemen moving cautiously between their homes and RAF stations. Thuggish and heavily armed young hotheads still roamed the streets firing their weapons in the air and Turkish Cypriots erected make-shift barriers around their enclaves. Sampson's regime doubtless under direction from Athens continued to reassure them, announcing that Glafcos Clerides remained as the Greek-Cypriot negotiator for community talks.

Most Cypriots had not yet formed a common view about the whole affair. Stephen Olver found them inconvenienced, annoyed at the interruption, damage and danger to their lives with mixed views about the archbishop. With 'scepticism at the new regime and dislike of a veiled military dictatorship, relief that the slide to the left has been stemmed: for many (but not all) grieve at Makarios's departure mixed with relief at his survival'.[96]

Their relief came to fruition when a refreshed Makarios and his men flew into RAF Lyneham in Wiltshire at 9.00 am. The archbishop stood at the top of the parked aircraft gangway calm and dignified in his black garments blowing gently in a breeze, before being greeted by Foreign Minister David Hedley Ennals, the Cypriot high commissioner and a protective avenue of British soldiers.

He gave an impromptu press conference at the airport, saying, 'They tried to kill me by attacking the palace with mortars and other weapons ... They thought that I was killed and indeed they said over the radio I was dead. As you can see, I am alive!'[97] Ennals replied, 'We greet you not as the former President of Cyprus but as the elected President of Cyprus',[98] a statement that unknowingly defined a growing difference with the United States with Kissinger prevaricating over who to back.

During the car journey to London, Makarios recounted his story of the last forty-eight hours telling Ennals that he wanted to fly to New York for a UN resolution calling on the Greeks to withdraw their officers and recognise him as president. He also needed provisions, having arrived with no possessions and no money. Ennals took him and his three aides to the Cypriot High Commission in St James's for fresh clothes and travel documents: a member of the commission went shopping to buy underwear and a bishop's crook. A room was also found at a top London hotel, Clarridges, in Mayfair. Some 3,000 Greeks and Greek Cypriots gathered outside it to express their support.

In Ankara, Turkish Prime Minister Bülent Ecevit prepared to fly out to London. He had agreed with his generals to intervene on Saturday unless three demands were met: the return of Makarios or a successor through the constitutional process, the ejection of Greek officers in the National Guard, and, fundamentally, a sea corridor in Cyprus giving Turkey swift access for long-term security interests. Legal process mattered to Turkey and Ecevit's government had a slight hope that Britain as a fellow guarantor power might agree joint action, but, if not, he considered the 1960 treaty granted the right of unilateral action after consultation.

Unaware of Ecevit's real intentions, Jim Callaghan wanted to persuade Turkey there was no cause for intervention though he had few levers other than argument, dinner and sympathy. He did not know whether Turkey would intervene, for there were convincing reports of Turkish military movements in the naval stations of Mersin and İskenderun and at air bases Adana and Antalya but this could be part of a diplomatic bluff.

Callaghan reviewed the position with his senior staff, including Anthony Ackland, his principal private secretary, and Sir John Edward Killick, number two at the Foreign and Commonwealth Office, in the morning. Dom Mintoff had already briefed him by telephone, passing on a request from the archbishop to rescue some of his supporters, which he was amenable to, though wiser heads around him argued against. Callaghan asked if British forces could restore Makarios by force. Probably yes said the Ministry of Defence, but only if facing the National Guard and no Greek forces, and not without reinforcements and much depended on how Cypriots reacted and how far bases and civilians were threatened. Defence officials were told to get an assessment ready before Turkey's delegation arrived as he wanted to know how bloody it might be. He preferred an operation of surprise but realised there were political realities, including the necessity of acting under UN authority, which would take time, and winning American approval.

Any such action raised a dilemma for Britain, which needed to work with the new Sampson regime to maintain operations on the sovereign bases. Both the British high commissioner, Stephen Olver, and the new American ambassador, Rodger Davies, had already met new Sampson-appointed Foreign Minister Dimis Demetriou to open up a line of communication for practical reasons.

Defence officials were hurriedly reinforcing the bases against potential violence and substituting 6,000 essential Cypriots, including cleaners, cooks, mechanics and clerks, no longer turning up for work. Fortunately, Operation Ablaut, for reinforcements of an infantry battalion, the Royal Marines commandos and a Royal Armoured Corps squadron, was developed in 1973; and by coincidence 19 Brigade and a battalion of the 12 Light Air Defence Brigade were already training on the island as other units prepared to fly out. And another planned operation, Platypus, got ready civilian and military nurses, mechanics, clerks and kitchen hands, including army sappers to maintain sewage plants. These staff were transferred discreetly for Stephen Olver was alarmist about Cypriots misinterpreting the arrival of new personnel as a British operation to reinstate the archbishop.

Another essential task required defence staff to hurriedly gather stranded children across Britain on boarding school sponsorships, one of the perks of military life, who had broken up from term with air tickets booked to visit their parents in Cyprus.

An overwhelmed Southern European Department in the Foreign and Commonwealth Office set up an emergency crisis unit, the first ever created to deal with a prospective war situation, mirroring the Cyprus Task Force in Washington. It was staffed by junior officers, such as Peter John Goulden, Oliver Miles and Roger Tomkys, who all later became prominent ambassadors, working in a nucleus to Alan Goodison, the principal adviser to Jim Callaghan.

At noon in Turkey, Bill Macomber grabbed ninety minutes with Prime Minister Bülent Ecevit and Defence Minister (later acting foreign minister) Hasan Esat Işik before they left for London finding them set on intervention if their conditions were not met. Macomber suspected this tough stance was designed to force American pressure on Greece, with Ecevit saying the longer any intervention was delayed, the 'bloodier' it would get, and he would wait no more than a 'few days'.

'How will you achieve this if Wilson agrees to help this evening?', probed Macomber knowing that British action let alone any by the United States was improbable.

Ecevit replied, 'They have bases there. If they do not use them now what are they for? We will see what the British think. We will explore all peaceful solutions before considering others.'[99]

Back in Britain an anti-Greek mood prevailed in the House of Commons when the foreign secretary briefed parliamentarians alleging Greek complicity saying the country 'bears a heavy responsibility for the situation'.

He reaffirmed support for Makarios as the legitimate president, adding, 'I have no doubt that it would be in the best interests of stability in the Middle East – and moreover, would restore the legal position – if Archbishop Makarios was recognised and returned to the island in his full capacity and with his full powers'.[100]

His stance won support, with the European Community similarly telling Greece they supported Makarios as the lawful president, widening a split with the United States. American press spokesman Robert Anderson prevaricated at the Department of State's press conference saying, 'We rest on the question of recognition as of this moment of either' Makarios or Sampson because the 'political situation remains unclear and therefore in our view, the question of recognition does not arise now'.[101]

A Kissinger aide told *The New York Times* reporter that 'We think he is finished politically ... He can't go back to Cyprus unless [Brigadier] General [Dimitrios] Ioannidis is thrown out in Athens and, even though the junta has problems, that doesn't seem likely now.'[102]

An agreed position had not actually been decided in the Department of State when Kissinger's Special Actions Group met mid-morning in Washington. Director of Central Intelligence William Colby told the group Turkey was on the move in the south and pointed to a map showing the north-east corner of Cyprus as the likely objective. Though neither he nor Deputy Secretary of Defense William 'Bill' Perry Clements Jr, thought Turkey would move without first trying diplomacy and only if necessary – and that military preparation could still be a ruse to gain support. Kissinger decided it was too late for cables so had Sisco leave the room and forestall Turkish action by telling Ankara that Greece was not sending in troops and Washington shared its concerns.

Washington's conundrum was what to do about Makarios. Kissinger continued resisting some departmental views to recognise him. Press outlets had already criticised his failure to recognise the archbishop publicly with *The New York Times* calling it disgraceful. And Turkey's apparent desire to restore Makarios continued to baffle him. He reasoned that Ankara did not understand the United States' assessment: if the archbishop were restored by force in the short-term, he would in the longer term rely on the Soviets thereby reducing Western influence across the region.

Everyone agreed that Sampson was unacceptable, including Kissinger who thought the man 'a most unattractive guy. It's not in our interest to have him.' He pondered whether Glafcos Clerides, the speaker of the Cypriot Parliament, was better for American interests. Undersecretary Joe Sisco thought Makarios 'has had it' and agreed on Clerides, as did Ambassador Bob McCloskey. In contrast, Director of Central Intelligence William Colby did not see any alternative to the archbishop and Tom Boyatt saw Makarios as 'best for stability, Clerides better for the Turks' suggesting a diplomatic initiative to restore him and have Ioannidis withdraw the Greek officers.

Kissinger challenged Boyatt, 'Yes, but what if Greece doesn't agree? It might be tough to do. We all love to conduct these grand stand plays, but where do we go after that? What do we want after that?'[103]

There was no clear answer, so Kissinger decided that 'constitutional continuity is what we want. We want to keep the Turks from interfering and the London talks from collapsing'.[104] He did not want the Turks running loose in London without knowing where the United States stood so went off to call Nixon about sending an emissary. Sisco shortly learnt it was to be him.

In Cyprus, Stephen Olver got wind of Jim Callaghan's desire to rescue Makarios supporters and, aghast at any such operation, warned the foreign secretary in the early afternoon about possible repercussions against British citizens and the functioning of the bases. He was already worried that the Ministry of Defence was about to make public the despatch of HMS *Hermes* which together with the BBC's reports of HMS *Devonshire* and HMS *Rhyl* sailing towards Cyprus suggested British action. 'If any such suggestion is allowed to gain currency it would gravely affect the whole future of Anglo-Cypriot relations. It would also have highly dangerous consequences for the large British community and tourist population here.'[105] He also had a dig at London claiming there was a 'lack of guidance on British aims and intentions'.[106]

John Aiken similarly complained about the rescue operation to the vice chief of the defence staff, Peter de Lacy Le Cheminant, saying London did not grasp the reality of power on the island. 'Let us be absolutely clear that the new regimes exercise full control over the island ... They are the masters now and we should not misunderstand that this is the case.' From his perspective Makarios requested too much, 'Not to put too fine a point on it, his Beatitude was extremely fortunate in the bread he was given and now he is asking for cake'.[107]

In London, his 'Beatitude' was starting to organise international support meeting first with Harold Wilson at 2.30 pm, arriving at Downing Street to cheering crowds, heavy security and the world's press. Wilson played safe, assured him of support and listened while Makarios condemned Greek statements about respecting Cypriot independence because Athens had organised the coup. Wilson then waved him off in a public gesture of support, with Whitehall rather unsure how the archbishop could possibly return to Cyprus without armed force.

A couple of hours later Makarios met with Jim Callaghan and senior diplomats to argue that Britain must refuse to recognise Sampson and press Ioannidis to withdraw Greek officers. Callaghan, conscious of needing to work with the new regime over the bases, skirted the issue by reaffirming recognition of Makarios as the elected head of Cyprus. The archbishop also criticised American leniency towards the anti-communist junta but was realistic about not returning quickly to Cyprus and about military action, which might cause intervention by the Turks, who he correctly foresaw would not leave when they got there. His main aims were stopping any recognition of Sampson, winning international support for restoring the status quo and removing Greek National Guard officers.

When he left, the Foreign and Commonwealth Office began drafting a UN Security Council resolution requesting that Greece observe its international obligations in Cyprus and withdraw its officers.

Makarios rested at Clarridges before his trip to New York by reading his obituaries, finding particular pleasure in a radio tribute by former Cypriot governor general, Sir Hugh Foot. Lord Caradon, as Foot was otherwise known, also visited him at his hotel suite and explained he had revised the tribute when learning the archbishop was still alive; saying he had written much nicer things when thinking him dead.

Before the Turks arrived for dinner at Downing Steet, Callaghan and Kissinger spoke around 7.50 pm, the foreign secretary saying he favoured diplomatic means to restore Makarios as did the European Community. Kissinger did not protest but floated Clerides as an alternative. 'He couldn't hold it ... But the compromise might be an election in 3 months with Makarios back on the Island', said Callaghan. Kissinger knowingly asked Callaghan how he proposed achieving this 'diplomatic solution'. The foreign secretary replied, 'Well, hopefully you would exert your influence on the Greek Government about the national guard officers', most likely causing a furrowed brow on the secretary of state's face who was scathing about Britain expecting American pressure on the Greeks at the expense of the United States' own national interests, describing it as reminiscent of a bad Second World War joke.[108]

Kissinger dodged any recognition of Makarios for time to devise a strategy, saying he 'did not want to give the Russians an excuse for intervention by going too far in declaring the illegitimacy of the Sampson regime.' Instead, Kissinger said he was sending someone over to explain the United States'. Callaghan replied, 'Well, send somebody, but I don't think we can afford to lose much time to begin pressuring the Greeks.'[109]

Prime Minister Bülent Ecevit arrived in London in the evening with two generals and a clutch of ministers hoping for rather than expecting support. As British diplomat Richard Fyjis-Walker wrote from Ankara, they were 'sceptical on achieving worthwhile results by political means, especially as they saw it the Americans continued to take a neutral position'.[110]

A polite conversation over dinner in the state dining room between the twenty politicians, soldiers and civil servants could not bridge the divide. The poet-journalist Bülent Ecevit elegantly explained that Greece had achieved *enosis* in all but name and merely postponed the threat to the Turkish community. Britain and Turkey must jointly or separately refuse to recognise Sampson, Greek forces must withdraw under UN supervision and the balance of forces evened out with more Turkish forces, he argued.

Then came the big moment when Ecevit requested Turkish troops enter through the British bases, catching Wilson and Callaghan off guard for use of their facilities was not something they had considered. Ecevit said although it was strange that Turkey was 'almost weeping' over Makarios, now was the time for discussion with him and an historic moment for a peaceful solution, otherwise Tukey would act unilaterally, 'which he felt would be inevitable later if not earlier – later would be worse and bloodier'.[111] Wilson and Callaghan had no option other than to decline his request, and instead offer consultation with Greece to put the junta under pressure.

While the Turks and British dined and disagreed, Kissinger updated President Richard Nixon, holed up in his San Clemente compound in California thinking through his next moves over Watergate. Kissinger criticised the Europeans for wanting the return of Makarios and pressure on Greece without the means to do so, recommending that 'we work for a compromise in which neither Makarios or the other guy take over ... [the Europeans] want us to rake the Greeks but if they get overthrown then that will jeopardize our whole position.' He foresaw Greece becoming a rogue state like Colonel Muammar Gaddafi's Libya.

Nixon said, 'I get it ... Too bad he has to come back.'[112] Forty-five minutes later Kissinger told Joe Sisco to pack his bags for London.

An after-dinner break around 10.00 pm during which the Turkish and British sides assessed each other's position gave Callaghan chance to catch up with Kissinger, explaining that Ecevit wanted a joint British-American statement condemning the Sampson regime and calling for the restoration of Makarios, which they both agreed went too far.

A resumption in Downing Street's Cabinet room made no progress. The opposite occurred, for Ecevit had received word that three Turks were killed by the National Guard with Greek forces reportedly landing in Paphos, saying his fears were realised sooner than anticipated and he must protect Turkish Cypriots. Britain, he continued, must decide how to use its bases, adding that he did not look favourably on American intervention – a clear reference to 1963/1964 and 1967 – as this usually strengthened Greece.

Wilson said he thought Ecevit meant Britain should not blockade Turkish troops but might interfere with any Greek intervention, which Callaghan, reacting rather too quickly as was his want, said this was not impossible. More efforts to encourage diplomacy got nowhere so the meeting finished without agreement. Neither side could agree on a joint communiqué for the press so they settled on separate statements. Ecevit and his colleagues then left Downing Street half an hour after midnight considering their treaty obligation fulfilled.

Shortly before the Turks left, British Ambassador Peter Ramsbottom in Washington updated Jim Callaghan about his own conversation with Kissinger earlier that evening. The foreign secretary thought Britain was moving too quickly, risked involvement in a civil war and might end up strengthening the communist presence. Why move so fast and why so absolutely Kissinger questioned when the archbishop's return was not certain and there were other options. Sampson was clearly unacceptable and he would not mind if the junta collapsed of its own accord, but he did not like Britain's draft UN resolution removing the Greek officers who from his perspective held off communist infiltration and changed the island's balance of power. Sisco will explain the United States' thinking in person was the message.

Ramsbottom also made an unusual request of Callaghan's private secretary, Anthony Ackland, asking to be informed about every conversation between Callaghan and Kissinger. He learnt that Kissinger had not recorded their own conversation as practice required and, at the Department of State's own request, had updated Joe Sisco so that American diplomats knew what their own boss was doing, otherwise 'improbable though it may seem, I fear there will be a danger of both the State Dept., and this Embassy working in the dark with all the resultant risks of confusion and misunderstanding'.[113]

That evening senior diplomat Wells Stabler confided to a British diplomat in Washington that the United States was thinking of a similarly worded UN draft but wanted to avoid any public commitment to Makarios. Referring to Ecevit's three objectives, Stabler said they were looking at alternatives to Sampson, excluding Makarios who needed force to restore him and Clerides was the ideal person to emerge, adding that 'if such a solution could be worked out, Makarios's retirement would be the price, and the problem would be how to achieve that'.[114] Stabler was being polite for the Department of State, like Kissinger, thought London was trying to decide the United States' own policy, with Britain 'unwilling' to restore Makarios as 'They wanted to leave that to us'.[115]

Writing from Athens, Ambassador Henry Tasca also protested against any idea of forcing Athens to withdraw the Greek officers, which would be regarded as tantamount to causing the junta's downfall.

Ecevit returned to his embassy in London's Belgravia ten minutes after leaving Downing Street and telephoned the Turkish general staff, telling them to continue with the plan and had the Grand National Assembly meeting moved to Saturday, creating the impression that no action would be taken until after its deliberations.

Kissinger briefed Sisco before his top diplomat left for London in a meeting that fell into Department of State folklore. Tom Boyatt, Bob Dillon and Sisco's assistant, Robert 'Bob' Bigger Oakley, who were all to accompany him alongside staff from the newly formed Cyprus Task Force went to Kissinger's office. Here the CIA told them that Turkish aircraft were on a five-minute standby with the 39th Infantry Division, the unit long marked for action in Cyprus, ready to move, which was expected within twenty to forty-eight hours. Dillon remembers the meeting starting 'with a lecture by Henry Kissinger on history which was totally irrelevant to the issue that we were to address. Kissinger asked whether anyone had any questions. I asked a couple, which went essentially unanswered.'[116] Kissinger then told Sisco the mission was to stop Cyprus moving to the international stage and to avoid pressure on Turkey with no repeat of the 1964 Johnson letter. In other words, Sisco was going empty handed.

Boyatt and others argued for a hard line against Ankara, including a threat to cut off military aid. Dillon asked several questions about what he believed was a flawed plan:

> I thought that our only chance of getting the Turks' attention would have been to threaten to cut off aid. The Turks were never going to take us seriously unless we threatened to suspend aid immediately. I knew that that was the only language the Turks would understand.[117]

When Dillon's exhortations failed, Boyatt, no stranger to speaking his mind, also disagreed with Kissinger. The secretary of state just looked at him and turned away. 'Nothing further was said and we all got up and left the office, went to the airport and took off'.[118]

In the same way he resisted action against Greece, so Kissinger did likewise with Turkey. He was not about to threaten a vital strategic relationship that upset the Eastern Mediterranean balance of forces affecting the Middle East. Boyatt thought Kissinger was sending Sisco and not going himself because the mission was an impossible one: 'He knew that there was no hope, and he didn't want to have a loser identified with himself. So he sacrificed Under Secretary Sisco [sic], and his staff, of which I was one. I mean it's a clear bureaucratic signal that you're not going to win.'[119] Kissinger, though, was sucked into the Watergate quagmire, which was building to a denouement with a predictable outcome.

Chapter 10

DON'T LEGITIMISE MAKARIOS: THURSDAY, 18 JULY 1974

A peculiar peace descended over the island on the fourth day of the coup. Wary Turkish-Cypriot fighters patrolled their isolated enclaves with UNFICYP providing occasional grain supplies. Nicosia airport reopened with customs and immigration officers in post though all portraits of Makarios removed, allowing thousands of stranded tourists to depart and met the other way by foreign journalists arriving to cover the story. More sinister was the arrival of high numbers of young men from Greece whom observing UNFICYP officers suspected of being National Guard reinforcements.

A semblance of normal life had otherwise returned with 70 per cent of local Cypriots showing up for work at the RAF bases. Sampson's regime relaxed a night-time curfew allowing soldiers and airman to move fairly freely between home and work, and their families to go shopping. For safety's sake John Aiken had families return home by 2.00 pm each day and service personnel by 4.00 pm, with convoys protecting both travelling families and NAAFI (Navy, Army and Air Force Institutes) supply vans moving between RAF stations.

HMS *Hermes* had now reached its anchor point off the coast, though far enough away to satisfy High Commissioner Stephen Olver so as not to be seen off the horizon, from which the Royal Marines could make it to Cyprus within twenty-four hours. HMS *Devonshire* with HMS *Rhyl* were en route. This added to a very busy Eastern Mediterranean with the Sixth Fleet anchored at sea, another American amphibious force in the south-west, the USS *Forrestal* and other ships sailing between Crete and Cyprus, and Soviet vessels monitoring activity.

In the morning, six Turkish Phantom aircraft flew over Kyrenia beachhead creating a temporary panic on the island and RAF stations until the flights were dismissed as only a demonstration of support for Turkish Cypriots. These were, in fact, on reconnaissance for the risky amphibious landing.

A BBC bulletin misleadingly reported a picture of continuing resistance by left-wing forces supporting Makarios. This annoyed both Stephen Olver and John Aiken who saw no evidence of any fighting apart from occasional misfiring in the air and thought the report risked the fragile peace. Olver rebuked the news organisation and requested a correction, but the damage was done as suspecting Greek Cypriots began thinking Britain planned to help them by restoring Makarios using force. Pent-up feelings led to an RAF airman being dragged from his car at a National Guard roadblock and harangued about British treachery. The same happened to a flight lieutenant.

International tension added to the situation as the world's press rounded on the Greek government. Egged on by Makarios and the UN secretary general who argued that getting the Greeks to withdraw their officers would force the junta's collapse, Callaghan made ever stronger statements, now calling for withdrawal of Greek officers of the National Guard.

Olver complained that such public statements threatened a necessary relationship with Sampson's regime and with the National Guard, which had not yet let resentment over the RAF saving Makarios affect British citizens. Newly installed Cypriot Foreign Minister Dimis Dimitriou had already warned him about British actions. Olver also thought that withdrawing Greek officers might affect the balance of power between Greek and Turkish military contingents and tempt Turkey to act. Not for first time, he said there was confusion in London's policy.

British Ambassador Robin Hooper wrote in the same vein from Athens, suggesting that forcing the withdrawal issue to topple the junta might produce an even worse replacement. He questioned support for the archbishop saying he thought Britain was going too far out on a limb for Makarios. Such views aligned with American thinking and presaged strong disagreement with fellow British Ambassador Horace Phillips in Ankara.

Harold Wilson's Cabinet tried to pin down its policy eventually deciding on the priority of stopping Turkey from acting alone – though sympathies around the table, which were not yet affected by Greek-Cypriot community wrath – broadly sided with the Turks. Wilson even had the Ministry of Defence explore prospects for a naval blockade against Greek reinforcements under UN auspices, which even the contemplation of such an intention would have caused Henry Kissinger's immediate reprimand. Otherwise, the Cabinet agreed to push three-way talks with Athens and Ankara in London, which the United States supported though the foreign secretary explained his disagreements with Washington over both Makarios and the Greek officers.

Callaghan then broke out of Cabinet to see Joe Sisco who arrived with his staff from Heathrow Airport for a tough meeting of minds. Sisco, in his no-nonsense Italian-American style, repeated Kissinger's discomfort about British policy saying Makarios must not be legitimised by the UN for fear of strengthening the Soviets, as international legitimacy gave him a free hand to let in the Soviets. Kissinger supported trilateral talks to buy time though without pushing for Greek withdrawal, which might create an imbalance of forces in Cyprus, and time was needed to work out a package solution incorporating all Greek-Turkish issues. He denied the United States had done anything to 'de-recognise'[120] Makarios.

Callaghan disagreed. He liked the idea of a package, but the United States must push the Greeks hard to stop Turkish action, though he confessed that British public pressure partly informed his stance on Makarios. He also told Sisco about tentative ideas for a naval blockade knowing that American backing was vital for any military operation.

Both men failed to convince the other. Sisco reported back that he could not shake Callaghan from his public wicket of supporting the legitimacy and restoration of Makarios. They did agree about the talks, so Callaghan had Ambassador Robin Hooper in Athens duly invite the Greeks to London stressing they must send people who actually had power. They then both went off for separate meetings to work on the Turks.

Prime Minister Bülent Ecevit delayed his return so he could see Sisco at noon, who, in his robust manner said that any military assault in Cyprus risked relations with the United States. An unshrinking Ecevit replied more elegantly but no less firmly that the United States had repeatedly obstructed Turkey's efforts, which had hardened Turkish public opinion against them, and if they interfered again, reaction in his country might get out of hand.

'What will stop you?' asked Sisco. Ecevit repeated his three objectives of Greeks out, Turkish troops in with a seaport and equal rights for Turkish Cypriots. Sisco thought Ecevit's strong opinion partly reflected problems managing Turkish hardliners at home and there might be a way to satisfy these demands, so he agreed to present these to Athens and visit Ankara on Saturday. Ecevit cleverly persuaded him to come back earlier on Friday, 19 July 1974, so that Turkey did not embarrass the United States' envoy arriving the same day as the planned assault.

As the working day started in Washington, Kissinger repeated his anxiety about British policy to Peter Ramsbottom warning about excessive zeal. Get the Greeks and Turks to thrash out a constitutional solution he urged Ramsbottom, who reported how Kissinger was 'clearly troubled that we might be committing ourselves too far without being able to calculate the longer-term consequences'.[121]

These ideas were outdated for Callaghan's afternoon meeting with Turkish Acting Foreign Minister Hasan Işik bore no more fruit than Sisco's session with Ecevit. Işik presented a five-point plan attributing blame on Greece and permitting a military response, which Callaghan swiftly ruled out warning that any British-Turkish action was 'quite out of the question' and Greek consultation was the way forward. Işik replied with a cryptic message that 'the decision to intervene might be forced on the Turkish government if something could not be done immediately to reverse present trends, and if the situation in Cyprus continued to deteriorate'.[122]

Makarios flew into New York with high hopes of strong UN support, arriving at Kennedy airport courtesy of British Airways and greeted by supporters waving placards, one reading 'Nixon arms the Killers'. He was whisked over to another swish hotel, The Carlyle on 5th Avenue, amid more placard waving advocates and then waltzed into UN headquarters three hours later. UN Secretary General Kurt Waldheim expecting him twenty minutes later had to rush down to greet the archbishop in the foyer. Makarios had arrived with the Cypriot ambassador to the UN, Zenon Rossides, whom the Sampson regime tried to replace with its own man whom Waldheim rejected. The UN Security Council agreed to receive the archbishop as head of state and hear his address the following day.

In Cyprus, the scheduled rotation of Greek soldiers permitted under the 1960 arrangements passed without incident under UN, British and Turkish observation – Ioannidis wanted to reassure Ankara and Turkish Cypriots the coup did not affect them.

This smooth transition contrasted with the chaotic first press conference of new Cypriot President Nikos Sampson held in the afternoon at the government information office. Sampson walked downstairs from the first floor trying to look presidential in suit and tie, which was somewhat belied by his stocky frame and toughened face embellished by thick black sideburns and accompanied by four armed guards. He sat behind a make-shift table with four colleagues and justified his actions using props of various looking truncheons and clubs to explain how the government of Makarios had tortured political opponents. For good effect a number of these supposed victims of tyranny'[123] were seated for the press wearing clean and neat bandages mostly on their legs, the occasional crutch leaning against a wall. A Cypriot newspaper reporter whispered to a colleague that he had seen one of them walking perfectly normally days earlier.

Sampson followed his script from Athens to remove reasons for Turkish concerns. No assistance for the coup came from Athens he said lying. His reason for acting was to prevent civil war: 'I see no reason why Turkey should intervene militarily in Cyprus in view of the fact that the Turkish community is in no danger whatsoever'.[124] For good measure, he announced that the dead and wounded numbered only dozens. Scepticism from the audience about his own selection as president caused an outburst of patriotic modesty when he replied that the youth of the Cypriot National Guard had turned to him.

In Athens, British Ambassador Robin Hooper became the first foreign diplomat to meet with Ioannidis and invite him to the London talks. Hooper found the brigadier general defiant over the National Guard, having signed orders to replace but not withdraw them, which he would not countenance, and 'would bitterly resent it, if no similar request were made to the Turks'[125] to replace their men. Ioannidis also refused the invitation, for he still assumed that the United States would restrain Turkey.

Despite Hooper's feat in meeting Ioannidis, American diplomat Henry Tasca rather astoundingly advised Joe Sisco, who was still in London, not to try and meet the brigadier general when arriving in Athens. Tasca had told the Greek acting foreign minister of Sisco's visit but not the request to meet with Ioannidis; and cabled Sisco that, because of the brigadier general's reluctance to meet with American representatives, he will be particularly anxious not to talk with you about the Cyprus crisis.

Back in London, Callaghan and Sisco exchanged impressions about their separate meetings before the American diplomat left for Athens. Callaghan now warmed to Sisco's idea of a package solution that included a flexible political solution in Cyprus, Turkish access to the sea under UN supervision, replacement of the Greek officers, closer UN supervision of troop rotation and a strengthened Turkish presence on the island. But he still disagreed over Makarios and had not completely ruled out military force.

Both men did mistakenly agree that Turkish action was not imminent. Nonetheless, Whitehall prepared for a possible Turkish move at the weekend with chief of the defence staff, Field Marshal Sir Mike Carver, placing further provisional reinforcements on a seventy-two-hour alert. And Callaghan still felt sore enough at the United States' pressure over a draft UN resolution to vent his annoyance through Peter Ramsbottom, who diplomatically passed on British dismay to Washington.

Sisco found Prime Minister Bülent Ecevit more bullish then ever when returning to the Turkish Embassy and now insisting on a government for Turkish Cypriots besides a seaport, and adamant about not talking to the Greeks. While Sisco thought these ideas 'tantamount to partition'[126] and designed to satisfy his hardliners, he still read something in Ecevit's manner wanting peace. Deliver this message to the Greeks, said Ecevit, and fly back to Ankara with the response tomorrow, Friday.

In Washington, Kissinger was struggling to keep his divided Department of State in line. Later that morning, he told the Special Actions Group that 'I know some of my colleagues believe we are advocating the overthrow of the Ioannidis government, but that is not our policy ... Our first objective is to avoid a Greek-Turkish war and Soviet intervention.' Director of Central Intelligence William Colby replied that they could not avoid taking a position on the archbishop for long. 'Well let's see', said Kissinger, 'It's fine to say that everybody is behind Makarios – that is easy to proclaim. But the problem still remains of how to bring him back.'[127]

His concern was American strategy rather than the archbishop's legitimacy. If Makarios was the answer, Kissinger wanted him back though only through American support and without interfering in Greece unless this benefitted the United States. He told his staff,

I'm not worried about [Dimitrios] Ioannidis. If he falls, fine. That doesn't worry me. Let him fall because of his own incompetence. Getting rid of Ioannidis is no more a worry than keeping Ioannidis; it's no factor. Preventing a Greek-Turkish war and a shift in the balance of power are factors. I don't think Ioannidis is going to survive very long anyway.[128]

So, they decided to wait for the results of Sisco's toughest mission to date.

More criticism in various Western newspapers particularly the left-leaning *The New York Times* claiming uncertainty and drift in American foreign policy added to Kissinger's concerns. Washington's equivocation over Makarios already stood apart from London, the European Community and other NATO leaders. This irked the secretary of state who wanted it known that the United States did not have doubts and wanted matters to settle before following the 'howling mob'.[129] He had his senior staff of Stabler, McCloskey, William 'Bill' Buffum and his assistant Lawrence 'Larry' Eagleburger draw up internal guidance to explain 'we are not drifting and our ambassadors should understand that we want the situation to crystallize'.[130]

They tried their best to explain American prevarication in a cable distributed to American embassies. Washington was not currently supporting Makarios for fear of letting in the Soviets, and the archbishop was not completely ruled out though British plans to restore him were unrealistic.

> It is important that our friends and allies understand that any course of action relating to Cyprus which results in the overthrow of the Greek regime, opens up the Eastern Mediterranean to Soviet meddling and exploitation, and invites active Turkish intervention would initiate a course of events which would be unpredictable, difficult if not impossible to control, and which would have seriously damaging effects on Western interests.[131]

Otherwise, 'The thrust of our position at this time, therefore, is to avoid assuming a public posture which commits us to any particular course of action'.[132]

Time did not support Kissinger's thinking, for he wanted Sisco to push the Clerides option with Turkey and have Britain push the Greeks for talks on Sunday 'where everyone needs us and comes to us. At that point we can deliver the Greeks'.[133] But Sunday was the day after Ankara's planned assault.

Prime Minister Bülent Ecevit got back to Turkey and told the military to proceed so that troops could start embarking the next morning, Friday, 19 July 1974. If the Americans or British somehow secured his sea corridor for Turkish troops, he might hold off but otherwise he and his generals were determined to avoid any repeat of the 1960s American restraint. Opinion backed him across the Turkish-speaking world.

Joe Sisco and his staff duly left for Athens with nothing to offer but their wits. Turkish demands were clearly unacceptable to Ioannidis who intended to replace not remove his Greek officers in the National Guard and Henry Tasca continued to argue that any pressure was counterproductive. This mission would test the hard talking Italian American to the full.

Callaghan updated his own diplomatic community with a message at variance to Kissinger's guidance: 'In a dangerous and fast-moving situation, and one on which there is no unanimity of view among the governments most concerned, I cannot yet be too specific'.[134] He maintained that Makarios must be restored by all means short of force for which the United States was the tool in providing maximum diplomatic pressure but he was astute enough not to refuse recognising Sampson in all circumstances and likewise recognise Makarios completely. He and the Americans still thought diplomacy the answer while Turkish troops enjoyed an evening meal before boarding their vessels.

Chapter 11

THE SISCO MISSION: FRIDAY, 19 JULY 1974

Prime Minister Bülent Ecevit and his chief of general staff Semih Sancar gave the green light even while Joe Sisco was flying to Athens. Three thousand troops in the first landing party set sail to make the Saturday schedule on the tourist beaches of Kyrenia. Aware of these movements but not the intentions, Callaghan and Wilson arrived in Paris, France, to discuss British entry to the common market and Henry Kissinger went to Richard Nixon's so-called second White House in San Clemente, California.

Lieutenant General Nurettin Ersin, the 56-year-old commander of the 6th Corps and a former head of Turkish national intelligence, commanded Turkey's operation. He was using plans actually informed by President Lyndon Johnson's terse warning to the Turks in 1964, for their intention to intervene then revealed stark shortcomings in equipment and training, which were corrected over time by creating an amphibious and airborne landing capability. Ersin had fine-tuned this plan as recently as May 1974 when tension flared over the Aegean Islands.

Phase one established a bridgehead at Kyrenia in a risky amphibious operation not tried by any country since the Suez Crisis in 1956 and in awkward terrain inhibiting easy landings and a mountain pass separating airborne and seaborne troops after landing. Once the bridgehead is secured in three days, phase two intended occupying the northern third of Cyprus where many Turkish Cypriots were concentrated. Turkish generals originally intended to land in the east on the long beaches of Famagusta until learning in 1971 of a Greek counter plan, so settled on Kyrenia hoping that the surprise element compensated for the constraints of geography and a small port.

Sisco arrived in Athens accompanied by Tom Boyatt, Bob Dillon and experienced career officer Bob Oakley, a Texan who had spent time in navy intelligence during the Korean War and had worked for Sisco on Middle Eastern affairs. Oakley found the talks unforgettable. What first shocked them was not the situation in Greece but the one in Tasca's embassy where they dashed for a briefing. They found Tasca and his political staff in the dark about the junta's intentions and an American ambassador under the influence of the CIA station chief not the other way around; not that station chief Stacy Hulse and his staff knew much more for the intelligence staff were already 'shaken'[135] by events, and doubtless by their failure to foresee the coup having fallen uncritically for the false assurances of Ioannidis.

Tasca, 'ashen faced'[136] according to Tom Boyatt, proved of little help and was excitable over the likelihood of Greece attacking Turkey. He and Hulse wanted the Sixth Fleet to deter Turkish intervention arguing that if American military power was not brought to bear Greece would start a war. Sisco and Oakley looked at Tasca in disbelief. They thought that even Ioannidis was not stupid enough to attack a vastly more powerful country. Tasca stuck to his guns insisting that the Sixth Fleet be brought offshore, which 'was the Station's [station chief's] line and Tasca had bought it lock, stock and barrel'.[137] Oakley knew that there was no way Washington would countenance such action.

They then discussed getting access to Ioannidis. Tasca still argued that Sisco should meet only with the civilian government, saying that any approach to the brigadier general was inappropriate as the Greeks officially denied involvement in Cyprus. When Tasca said he had arranged for them to meet the Greek acting foreign minister, Sisco snapped back that he was leaving if it was not Ioannidis.

So Sisco and his colleagues spent much of the morning tracking down the brigadier general, the junta fobbing them off with offers to meet civilian leaders, including the foreign minister and Prime Minister Adamantios Androutsopoulos. Sisco insisted on Ioannidis until they

were finally escorted through a large crowd of security people into the principal government building in downtown Athens. That building was guarded not only by uniformed personnel, but cops and security people in civilian clothing. We were taken to the basement of the building. There we began to talk again with the nominal leadership. After about half an hour, Ioannidis walked in with general [Grigorios] Bonanos, the top Greek general.[138]

American appeals for Ioannidis to make concessions had little effect. All the brigadier general offered were minor measures, such as strengthening UNFICYP to control ports and airports against the clandestine importation of troops and weapons, though he did now agree to send representatives to the London talks.

Sisco refrained from presenting Ecevit's proposals but pushed the Greeks for more, warning the brigadier general about Turkish landings in Cyprus. Ioannidis, wrecked by his hubris in thinking that Kissinger would stop this intervention, dismissed Turkish intentions as showboating. Sisco protested, 'If you don't do something we're going to have a war, and you're going to lose the war. Now give me some elements of compromise that I can take to Ankara that we can work with.'[139] This demand, recalls Tom Boyatt, caused Ioannidis to launch

> into an emotional, weird, surreal, description of Byzantine history, and the struggle against the Osmanli Turks, and Constantinople, not Istanbul. We were clearly in real trouble because this guy had disconnected from the world, and he had all the power. And he didn't give us anything.[140]

That is as far as they got. Meagre pickings to offer Ecevit, which Sisco had no other option but to try. Off they went on a wing and prayer to Ankara with Sisco cabling Washington, 'I have the distinct impression that no matter what is done in this situation, the Turks see it as an ideal time to achieve by military intervention a longstanding objective, namely, double *enosis*'.[141]

Sorting out domestic arrangements before they left had proved almost as problematic, for Sisco and his party found Henry Tasca generally unhelpful, which extended to matters of hospitality. John Wolf, Tasca's staff assistant later to become an ambassador, realised the Department of State was not 'enamored [*sic*] with its Ambassador in Athens and vice versa',[142] a point highlighted by a lack of consideration given to Sisco's sleeping arrangements when Tasca denied him any rooms in the ambassador's residence claiming to have house guests. Sisco instead bunked down in the deputy chief of mission's office: 'So I remember we had a little sign that said Joseph J. Sisco, Undersecretary, on Mr Brandon's door. And Sisco came in, looked around and inquired, from me: "Son, the name on the door is Joe Sisco and if this is my room where's my bottle of scotch?"'[143]

Tourists in Cyprus received mixed advice on whether to leave or stay on the island depending on their nationality. While many had rushed out when Nicosia airport reopened, others continued their holidays after fighting stopped, some unfortunately deciding to stay in the popular holiday spots of Kyrenia and Famagusta. (Although landing in Kyrenia, the Turks still intended to gain control of Famagusta.) Sweden's government advised its 4,000 holidaymakers to leave, which contrasted with Olver's High Commission telling sunning Britons not to worry and even announce over the British forces' radio there was no reason to believe Turkish invasion rumours. Gossip still spread across the island about a Turkish task force heading for Cypriot waters, with fears tempered by hopes of a Turkish feint to pull back at the last moment, which was very much the thinking in Western governments.

British bases went to a state of Defcon Charlie, the third highest alert, particularly due to increasing flights by Turkish aircraft. UNFICYP devised a makeshift plan to destroy the Czech weapons they guarded rather than let them fall into combatants' hands. The United States' amphibious task force moved to within ten hours sailing time for evacuation purposes.

Turkey's large naval flotilla set sail from Mersin at 11.30 am local time already behind schedule to meet daybreak on Saturday. British and American military intelligence watching the Turkish build up over the last few days tracked its movements through radar. RAF Avro Vulcan marine reconnaissance bombers and then Nimrods from Malta followed the naval convoy until it split into one force of twenty-seven craft and another of six – a decoy convoy making for Famagusta, pursuing the larger into the night. Turkey's naval task force commander, Rear Admiral Emin Goksan, had to push the vessels to their top speed, risking break downs, to make up time – he was blessed by perfect sea conditions. Turkish soldiers in Cyprus and irregulars from the TMT Turkish resistance movement were briefed at 12.30 pm.

Uncertainty reigned in the Department of State as Kissinger struggled to get control from the claustrophobia of San Clemente. Sisco's briefing cable about his meeting in Athens had proved confusing. Watergate and the Middle East weighed on him as did splits in the department and leaks to the press from, he suspected, the Cyprus Task Force. Henry Tasca was also making a nuisance of himself rallying support for the Greeks.

Kissinger had it out with his top team of Bob McCloskey, a former ambassador to Cyprus whom Kissinger brought back for general duties, including liaison with Congress, Deputy Secretary of State Robert 'Bob' Ingersoll, a political appointment and business executive of a major automotive parts company, Wells Stabler from EUR, and experienced diplomat Bill Buffum who headed the International Affairs Division responsible for the UN. 'Any of you disagree with me?'

he asked them firmly. Even more stressed in the afternoon, he vented his feelings when reviewing Sisco's progress, telling his senior staff that things would be done how he wanted them as long as he was in charge. And staff were not independent emissaries but worked under his instruction, which he stressed, included Sisco who was not to move until he said so.

At 2.30 pm in London, the British Joint Intelligence Committee assessed likely Turkish plans, forecasting a parachute drop and an amphibious landing at Famagusta and a small airfield south-west of Nicosia. Similar reporting came from the DIA and CIA but the Department of State complained there was not enough information to determine whether the assault would actually proceed.

British Ambassador Horace Phillips issued similar warnings from Ankara claiming Turkish military leaders sensed they must move now or the situation would consolidate against them with Greece eventually winning complete control of Cyprus. He noted the heady atmosphere in Turkish society with even moderates 'coming round to the view that, cost Turkey what it may to act on its own, and whatever the Greek relations in Thrace or the Aegean [Islands] coast, better now than later'.[144] Phillips, though, expected action after Sisco's visit and the meeting of the Grand National Assembly.

At 6.00 pm in Cyprus, Frank Henn of UNFICYP attended a briefing by John Aiken in the British Near Eastern command. Henn looked at a map and saw for himself the positions of four navies close to Cyprus with the Turks moving in. Aiken was not sure whether the convoy was a Turkish bluff to force diplomatic action and suspected Turkey would wait until Sunday, 21 July 1974, before landing and concentrate on Famagusta.

A perturbed Callaghan in Paris drafted Kissinger a personal message at the end of the afternoon pushing for a common approach. He suggested a policy that affirmed Makarios, removed Sampson and appointed a temporary replacement until elections, and revised both the Greek and Turkish military presence and provided safeguards for Turkish Cypriots. He wanted substance which 'will satisfy the Turks and sufficient pressure must be put on the Greek Government to ensure that it moves in the right direction'.[145] Even before the draft was finished, he learnt about Turkish movements stiffening his view that the United States must work on Greece.

British Ambassador Peter Ramsbottom in Washington doubted the wisdom of Callaghan's message. Kissinger had not budged from concerns that Britain prematurely favoured Makarios and viewed Cyprus through the prism of the Middle East and possible Soviet gains.

'As is his habit', wrote the ambassador ruefully, 'he has expressed his anxieties fairly widely, to others as well as to us, and they are beginning to creep into the press'.[146] Ramsbottom nonetheless sent on the message and telephoned Kissinger at 2.05 pm local time to talk it through. Kissinger concealed his true feelings about British action when denying any 'real differences'[147] of approach and blaming press rumours for reporting a British-American split.

In Kissinger's absence in California, Ingersoll chaired the early afternoon meeting of top diplomats who decided they must stay Ecevit's hand for one or two days with Director of Central Intelligence William Colby expecting the Turkish move on 21 or 22 July 1974. But apart from preparing evacuations for American personnel and tourists, little could be done until Joe Sisco reported back from Ankara. Kissinger kept interrupting them by telephone – making some thirty-four calls to both his staff and foreign leaders from France and Britain to delay Turkish action, and insisted the department publicly deny any American intention to intervene other than through diplomacy – rumours were circulating about American action that risked a Soviet response.

Horace Phillips telegrammed Jim Callaghan just before 8.00 pm that Turkey might well resort to force if Sisco arrived empty handed.

By mid-afternoon in New York, Makarios was sitting in the green chairs of the round-tabled Security Council accusing the Greek government of callously violating Cyprus. He pleaded for the Security Council to 'call upon the military regime of Greece to withdraw from Cyprus the Greek officers serving in the national guard, and to put an end to its invasion of Cyprus'.[148] Inevitably, the Greek representative, Constantine Panayotacos, condemned the archbishop, attacked Soviet criticism and, as a distraction, drew attention to Turkish air strikes on Cyprus in 1964. This caused Turkey's Osman Olcay to joke that everything which had been said was predictable and he could easily have said 'we told you so'.

The Soviet Union's representative was measured but not without a dig at the West, claiming that the coup was planned within NATO as the alliance could not, he alleged, tolerate an independent Cyprus. American Ambassador John Scali explained played it safe, maintaining the United States' line of non-interference saying without attributing blame or pushing for withdrawal of the Greek officers. (Scali's accidental description of Makarios as 'president' later infuriated Kissinger.) And Callaghan, although piqued by American pressure, had British representative, Ivor Richards, recognise Makarios; though, mindful of American opinion, told him not to commit to continued recognition indefinitely.

Kissinger telephoned Ramsbottom again in the evening to talk through Callaghan's six ideas, saying the analysis was right and he did not want Sampson, 'the least desirable outcome',[149] but the United States would only apply pressure on the Greeks when there was a clear American objective and he still did not like the proposed draft UN resolution. He emphasised the point in a telegram seeking close British-American cooperation but stressing they do not precipitate the downfall of the current regime in Cyprus without having a viable alternative. Shortly after sending the cable, he learnt that Turkish movements now suggested a landing in Cyprus.

Kissinger's reply did not impress Callaghan who wanted immediate pressure on Greece to withdraw their officers. As he later wrote,

> This was no immediate assistance to me, for constitutional discussions would obviously stretch into the future, whereas pressure on the Greek government to withdraw their officers was needed without a moment's delay if the Turks were to be denied an excuse for acting.[150]

At 11.00 pm in Cyprus, John Aiken and Stephen Olver debated by teleprinter whether to return families to the safety of the bases. They decided against this unless there was an imminent threat: like much of the thinking in the West, Turkey's intentions remained ambiguous and still might be a gambit. And they wanted to avoid premature actions arousing Greek suspicions about British and Turkish collusion. It was also unwise to break a night-time curfew policed by the edgy National Guard.

British Ambassador Horace Phillips met Turkish Foreign Minister Turan Güneş, now back from China, shortly after midnight in Ankara. Güneş had left his Cabinet meeting, which was preparing for Sisco, to tell Phillips that Turkish ships had not yet been told to land. Ecevit and his government waited to see if Sisco came bearing dramatic Greek offers to satisfy them.

Sisco, Boyatt, Dillon and Oakley landed around the same time with largely 'empty bags' in Oakley's words. They met up with American Ambassador Bill Macomber, a likeable, loquacious and well-educated educated diplomat (having attended both Yale and Harvard universities) who despite starting in the CIA became a political appointee in the Department of State with a keen interest in Ottoman history. With him was the embassy's public affairs officer, Paul Julian

Hare, whose father Raymond Hare had been ambassador to Turkey in 1963/1964. They all went on to meet Ecevit and Güneş.

But they were too late. Ecevit walked into his room where they were waiting and said Turkey had already decided on intervention: 'I have just been to our National Security Council meeting where we agreed that we have no choice except to go to the assistance of our brothers on Cyprus. Our ships will land on the Cyprus beaches in three hours.'[151] He continued, saying that they must look to the future and once a military presence gave them bargaining power, they would negotiate with anyone.

As American diplomats worked hard to persuade him otherwise, Ecevit stayed firm though graceful talking for what seemed like hours thought Tom Boyatt. To every proposal, the Turkish prime minister shook his head. Joe Sisco made the strongest case arguing that the junta realised it had gone too and agreed to talks (which was not quiet the view of the embattled but obstinate Ioannidis). He appealed for a forty-eight-hour delay, which did not work so the tough Italian-American diplomat got rougher saying the Greeks were ready to fight. Finally, he said Washington would not support Turkey and floated the Clerides idea, which even Jim Callaghan had mistakenly believed might work.

Ecevit replied that Turks would not repeat the mistake of adhering to the 1967 Vance mission. He turned to Paul Hare,

> I remember your father was involved in a prior similar situation. At that time, the US assured us that it would take care of the interests of the Turkish minority on Cyprus if we refrained from military action. There was a second situation when the same promise was made. In both cases, you did nothing. Now the situation for our people on Cyprus is even worse; so this time we will go our way, not yours![152]

Joe Sisco looked over to Bill Macomber and asked if he could say anything, prompting the elegant ambassador to deliver the speech of his life.

> Mr Prime Minister, you're a teacher and a poet. You're not a military man, and there are kids all over the world who are not going to forgive you if you let this happen ... you are a man known for peace. If you give the word to go in a few hours a lot of people will be dead ... Greeks, Cypriots and Turks. It is not clear that's necessary to protect your interests. In a week's time there is no way the Greeks can reinforce their position. You don't lose any option you don't have today and maybe we can pull something off in a way of a more peaceful solution. Give us a chance to try.[153]

Words spoken with sincerity visibly moved Ecevit but not enough. The plan was minutes away from execution. Ecevit said he was a humanitarian, but, thinking of the military operation underway, added that there was momentum which has reached a point of no return, and concluded, 'Mr Ambassador, it's out of my hands'.[154] Ecevit did though agree to consult with his council of ministers one more time but told them not to raise their hopes.

Sisco and the American delegation returned in the early hours to Macomber's embassy to wait, realising the improbability of changing Turkey's position. Bob Dillon, who knew Ecevit best, realised 'what he would do, he loved the opportunity presented to him. He couldn't have cared less about American position: he was going to invade Cyprus.'[155]

Sure enough Sisco was called back to meet Ecevit at 2.00 am GMT who said nothing had changed and no delay was possible and intervention was irrevocable. Turkish troops were already landing, though he gave no details. American appeals proved fruitless. Ecevit asked Sisco to instruct the Greeks that Turkish troops would not fire on them unless fired upon. A message that the United States duly passed on in a vain effort to limit any conflict, and which, ever since, conspiracy fabulists have misinterpreted as evidence of American collaboration with Turkey.

Sisco reported back to Washington shortly afterwards, having several conversations with Bob McCloskey in Washington over a poor-quality open line. He declined returning to Athens because Ioannidis would not accept Turkey's conditions or the Clerides proposition and the Turks had already rejected paltry Greek suggestions and equally had no interest in Clerides. Sisco said he was instead returning to London as agreed with Callaghan to take stock there. McCloskey could not get all the information on this creaky line and passed on incomplete messages to Kissinger in California.

Macomber also reported events to Washington and then went to his personal quarters to sit quietly on the front porch by himself, reflecting on the historic moment which had just passed. He saw that night,

how the next big war will start where a rational state will be convinced that it is totally right and the enemy is totally wrong and they have no choice but to go to war. There is no logic anymore. That was very scary. That could happen with not just another Turkey but with the great powers and result in another world war. It is a scary thing to see something like that.[156]

Chapter 12

THE FIRST ASSAULT: SATURDAY, 20 JULY 1974

Britain's Near East Operations centre at RAF Akrotiri spent a tense night tracking Turkish progress towards the Cypriot northern coast as did the Americans. Turkey's main fleet suddenly steered north-west when only 7 miles from the coast causing further uncertainty and giving Henry Kissinger and the Department of State a brief hope Ankara was bluffing – and then a briefer moment of alarm in case the ships were heading to the Greek mainland at Thessaloniki. The ships had, in fact, likely made up lost time and, arriving early, tacked to make the coordinated air and land assault on schedule.

An RAF Nimrod reported the fleet's sudden change of course back towards Kyrenia and traced a smaller force moving towards Famagusta as 280 Signals Unit observed large-scale take-offs from southern Turkish air bases. Nimrods continued tracking Turkish ships right up to the Cypriot coast and were withdrawn only a minute or so before the first wave of Turkish aircraft arrived to avoid mistakes or possible engagement.

At 4.40 am local time on Saturday, 20 July 1974, Turkish military chiefs ordered their forces to commence a sea and parachute landing under cover of air power. (Advance parties had already arrived on the beaches near Kyrenia to mark out landing strips.) They activated the Turkish-Cypriot fighters, TMT, and their own forces stationed on the island and then, forgetting the summer hour difference with Cyprus, told civilian leader Rauf Denktaş to announce the operation over Turkish-Cypriot radio. Denktaş dutifully warned everyone to stay at home at 5.00 am instead of 6.00 am. Fortunately, prevailing anxiety on Cyprus since the coup caused most Greek Cypriots to dismiss the message as propaganda.

British diplomat Derek Day, asleep in Nicosia, was woken around 5.00 am with a warning of the impending Turkish landings. He dashed over to the commission where he remained for three days unable to risk the bullets to get back, his house even nearer to the fighting.

American political officer James Williams was sleeping in his office in the residence, spending virtually all his time there. Families still had not been evacuated, so his wife, Ann, pregnant but with the threat of miscarriage, stayed in bed at home. Day woke him by telephone to say the Turks were on their way. Planes arrived shortly afterwards, Williams watched

> all those parachutes coming down; it was like watching butterflies descend. Quite surreal. I'd never seen something like that before. Once in a while you'd see a parachute collapse and its occupant fall like a stone to the ground and you knew what had happened, but again it was just as if I was detached from it, watching it on a large, wide-angle screen.[157]

John Aiken warned service families to stay inside their homes and servicemen not to report for duty when explaining the situation on the British forces' radio network. In typical British understatement, he did his best to provide assurances in an unfolding conflict:

> Finally, there is no cause for alarm. Obviously, it may prove necessary at some time to bring you into the SBAs [sovereign base areas] just to be on the safe side. We hope it won't be but it will be as well to think of putting a few things in a bag just in case but we must emphasis this: the best thing you can do is remain calm and act sensibly.[158]

Kissinger was confused about Sisco's progress from a series of calls with McCloskey, Ingersoll and Stabler in Washington. McCloskey had passed on Sisco's intention to return to London, which confounded him as he mistakenly thought Ecevit was up for the Clerides solution. Sisco should push for a constitutional deal with the junta and suggest Clerides to stop an all-out war, he demanded. But an exhausted Sisco waiting to get out of Turkey saw no point in going to Athens and refused again when McCloskey passed on the secretary of state's instruction over another bad telephone line.

Working out of San Clemente frustrated Kissinger, but he had little choice. An embattled President Richard Nixon awaiting the Supreme Court's judgement over his tape recordings was planning how to muster a working majority against impeachment if Congress moved against him. There were so many documents about Watergate sent through to Nixon that Kissinger had to secure special priority for ones related to Cyprus. For his own political safety, he also trod a fine line between assisting the president in building his defence and keeping enough distance to avoid implication.

Confusion did not help. He yelled at Ingersoll and McCloskey over the telephone that Sisco is going to Athens or he would clean out the whole stinking department, and insisted his undersecretary tell Bülent Ecevit about the Clerides plan and then hot foot over to Athens for instructions. Kissinger also ranted about Sisco using an open line, moaning that everybody from Yugoslavia and beyond now knows American plans.

Ecevit announced his country's objectives at 6.10 am in Ankara, warning civilians including tourists to avoid the area, especially the Pentemille (Five Mile) Beach road in Kyrenia. He explained that Turkish armed forces were landing in Cyprus for the good of the nation, Cypriots and humanity and in doing so rendering a great service to humanity and to peace. He also reassured the Greeks and Western governments of his intentions saying Turkey was going to the island for peace not war for the Turks and the Greeks, a decision, he added, which was made after the political and diplomatic routes had failed.

Even while he spoke, Turkish naval guns destroyed a Greek-Cypriot artillery unit firing cannons against its landing craft and sank two attacking Greek-Cypriot torpedo boats vainly sent out to tackle the task force. Within the hour Turkey's French-purchased Sabre aircraft bombed Greek-Cypriot targets and helicopters and transport aircraft neared their destinations to drop parachutists.

BBC foreign correspondent John Sergeant caught the action from the Ledra Palace Hotel in Nicosia, where he bought a room after the coup. Shouting woke him up around 5.00 am, when he and other journalists ran to the roof to see Turkey parachutists floating down and flames in the distant Kyrenia hills. Sergeant was exasperated in watching the biggest story of his life unfold without any means to file it. Luckily, he survived to make contact later in the day.

Thirty or so Greek-Cypriot soldiers stationed in the hotel fired at the Turks with heavy machine gun blasts from the roof. In response, Turkish planes were sent to bomb the hotel but called back en route when the Turks decided against bombing a hotel with 200 international journalists and used guns instead. One Greek-Cypriot soldier was killed within an hour and another injured. Three mortar shells did hit the hotel. Clouds of cement dust fell from the cellar roof onto sheltering women and children with others making to the stairwell for safety.

Badly shaken, Sergeant broke his own rule on smoking and lit up for comfort, having never smoked since – and while fighting continued outside, he and fellow Britons listened to *Round the Horne* on the *BBC World Service* to pass the time.

Kissinger working late into the night on the west coast of the United States made a flurry of calls starting with Secretary of Defense Dr James 'Jim' Schlesinger to coordinate actions. He intended pushing Ankara quickly towards negotiation and promote the Clerides option even though 'We don't think this will really fly but at least it's a slender thread'. Schlesinger offered a more realistic understanding that Turkey wanted a third of the island. Kissinger, muddled by Watergate, disagreed and clung to the idea of replacing Sampson with Clerides, saying 'the Turks have said that they are willing to stabilize their forces and that they are willing to keep the existing structure and they will accept any president other than Sampson.' This master of grand diplomacy saw only two options, 'either double *enosis* or Clerides'.[159]

Jim Callaghan was woken by Henry Kissinger at 3.22 am GMT to learn of the landings and to agree that Sisco should go to Athens. The foreign secretary telephoned his office for a car that had not arrived when he dressed, so he dashed into the street and, finding no taxis around that early, flagged down a delivery van en route to start his rounds, asking if he could be dropped at Downing Street. The driver, recognising him, agreed and 'a few minutes later the delivery van and I drove in style down Whitehall'.[160] (Prime Minister Harold Wilson also abandoned his later attendance at the Durham miners' annual gala to get back to London.)

Sisco and his party could do no more in Ankara. Dispirited and desperately tired, none of them having slept much since leaving the United States, they rushed back to the airport and boarded the aircraft disagreeing between themselves about where to go next. Should they return to Athens to stop the Greeks responding? Or wait in Spain and see what happens? Bob Dillon had no idea except that they should leave Ankara.

Horace Phillips met with Turan Güneş who, observing protocol, told him Turkish troops were landing under Article Four of the Treaty of Guarantee 1960, saying after 'Mr Sisco had brought no concrete proposals for resolving it. Turkey regretfully had no alternative but to intervene militarily on her own.'[161] Ecevit later told Phillips that a movement inside and outside his party had for years wanted action to help the repressed Turks in Cyprus, which he had resisted by supporting negotiation despite the endless time they took. But the coup against Makarios and the installation of Sampson changed the balance and risked the annexation of Cyprus to Greece, giving a life-time opportunity to save Turkish communities.

Having agreed a course of action with Callaghan, Kissinger gave McCloskey new instructions for Sisco to return to Ankara, express American objection and formally propose the Clerides solution by saying 'we expect the Turks to go along with us'. What, he demanded of McCloskey, did Sisco think he could achieve in London? An exposed McCloskey tried to explain what he had learnt from his bad line with Sisco, that Greece would not accept Clerides, and Ecevit did not care. 'Now, what in the hell does that mean?' barked Kissinger. McCloskey retreated and tried again to reach Sisco before going back to his boss, who insisted that Sisco go to Athens and 'stay there'.[162] McCloskey's admission that they were still trying reach Tasca did not help the mood.

McCloskey's instructions arrived too late, for the exhausted Sisco and his colleagues were already on the plane set for Athens pursuing Kissinger's first instructions. Just before they took off, Turkish air traffic controllers refused permission to leave claiming the airport was now closed to civilian traffic. Sisco turned to the pilot and told him to take-off anyway. After a moment of tension, they flew off without trouble. With Sisco in the air, McCloskey instead told Bill Macomber in Ankara to speak with Ecevit.

At 7.00 am in Cyprus, Stephen Olver and John Aiken decided to start evacuating. Aiken told servicemen and their families over the forces' network to

stay put and prepare for your move: one or two suggestions – pack a bag for a day or so – we hope it won't be longer. Turn off gas, electricity and water, and secure your belongings in the house as best you can. It would be a good idea to bring your easily eatable food with you if possible.[163]

'Don't flap', he added 'and continue to follow instructions'.[164]

Hundreds of service families and civilians in Famagusta had every reason to flap, however, when fighting broke out between National Guard forces and Turkish troops. In the crossfire stood the British military quay housing a Royal Corps of Transport unit, which the Dhekelia operations centre ordered out after several mortars hit the harbour. The commanding officer, Major D.G. Hammett, rounded up his small staff who packed up classified material and salvaged as much equipment as they could fit into their 18-foot-long landing craft and a harbour launch, including the unit's Land Rover and mini, and motored off. The crews of fifteen vessels had the same idea, their ships jostling with each other in a panic to escape. The National Guard fired at the two transport unit vessels as they left the harbour walls despite flying large Union Jacks causing a quick change of course for deep sea to escape the mortars' range. Further shells fell short but close enough to spray them with salt water. Evacuation had proved a wise course as subsequent shells hit the unit's accommodation block and bullets pocketed other buildings when the National Guard advanced.

Similar problems affected 11 Marine Craft Unit in the other large dormitory city of Limassol, which escaped bullets and mortars by a whisker when the National Guard and irregular Greek Cypriots attacked the Turkish quarter.

Turkey's 1st and 2nd airborne troops under the command of Brigadier General Sabri Evren parachuted down on two main drop zones, one 8 miles from the beach landings on the other side of the Pentadáktylos Mountains and another 2 miles north of Nicosia. Empty transport planes returned to collect the waiting 3rd and 4th airborne troops.

Watching on the ground were a collection of reporters including ITN journalist Michael Nicholson, later famed for counting off British aircraft during the Falklands conflict, who achieved a journalist scoop by filming their landing in the dry field where he stood. In a somewhat surreal picture of relative calm with Turkish Cypriots clapping to welcome the paratroopers, the descending troops exuded more an image of a display team than an attacking force.

Nicholson even greeted one of them as he took off a parachute harness, 'I'm Michael Nicholson. How do you do'[165] and shook his hand. His crew filmed a sergeant waving a Turkish standard as the troops casually assembled and took up position in a large, reaped corn field to secure the landing spot, seemingly easy prey for the Greek artillery gunners the other side of the road. Turkish-Cypriot children helped carry some of their machine guns. The RAF obligingly flew Nicholson home that evening armed with his newsreel for a big splash on British television.

Helicopters made the third assault landing at the Krini air strip in the north. So many helicopters were used during the day that Michael Nicholson thought this the largest assault by helicopters there had ever been. Turkey's overall commander, Nurettin Ersin, arrived in a second wave at 11.00 am and established his command post at a nearby village at Bogazköy where he somehow appropriated a BBC Land Rover, possibly for a return favour of letting them interview command staff before their press rivals.

Director of Central Intelligence William Colby told Henry Kissinger at 4.35 am GMT that Turkey probably wanted a line between Famagusta and Kyrenia. He thought local Greeks would fight but not with mainland Greek forces, which were too far away, and which, he feared, might instead start conflict along the northern border with Turkey where Greece stationed most of its 100,000 strong army. 'I think the biggest thing is to get the Greeks not to fight',[166] he told Kissinger.

Turkish ambassador to Cyprus, Asaf Inhan, told General Dewan Prem Chand, a much-respected Indian officer commanding UNFICYP since 1970, of his country's action under Article Four of the 1960 Treaty of Guarantee. Inhan repeated the message that Turkish troops would not fire unless fired upon, which Chand passed on to Michalis Georgitsis, the National Guard commander who led the coup against Makarios. By this time Turkey had already broken its own mandate with air strikes on Nicosia, pummelling the airport to stop Greek reinforcements, and National Guard positions in Kyrenia, causing later accusations of duplicity by UNFICYP. Georgitsis said he would respond unless Turkey stopped immediately but did not wait for an answer before mobilising his troops, who he had allowed to sleep through the early signs of a Turkish landing.

At 5.06 am GMT, Kissinger briefed President Richard Nixon, who amazingly had the mental faculty to compartmentalise a likely impeachment from world affairs. The president asked if he should go back to Washington but Kissinger said there was no need to unless Greece attacked Turkey: 'There is still a 10% chance that this thing will be settled by Monday ... if the Greeks accept Clerides as a solution and if they – and if the Greeks and Turks then meet in London, I think we could get a ceasefire.' Nixon intrinsically realised the United States would be blamed for events: 'We got to posture needless to say in a way that we are not – that we aren't responsible for the damn thing. I don't think – except for a few nuts – that what, that we could have saved this fellow [Makarios] – how could we have saved him'.[167]

Jim Callaghan interrupted their conversation with a telephone call, which the president left Henry Kissinger to take. Now arrived at his office in King Charles Street the foreign secretary wanted to assess joint action. They agreed that Britain take the lead and convene an immediate meeting in London with Athens and Ankara as the three guarantor powers. Sisco, said the American secretary of state, was flying to Athens to get the Greeks to abandon Sampson and send representatives to London. And Richard Nixon sent supporting messages telling Greece and Turkey that the United States backed London talks for the 'restoration of a just and stable peace in Cyprus'.[168]

Turkey's first landing craft hit the Pentemille (Five Mile) Beach west of Kyrenia around 5.30 am GMT, releasing two battalions of marines and engineers to secure the area for tanks and vehicles. Three subsequent waves landed once every hour disembarking with minimal resistance by the National Guard and the Greek regiment, ELDYK, both caught off guard by the event and the location. A defence plan first drawn up by Georgios Grivas in 1964 called Aphrodite had been updated over the years but relied on fighter support and reinforcements from far away Greece. Without these, the result was slow and disjointed, and like many Western intelligence agencies, the National Guard and Greek forces fell for the Turkish feint of landing at Famagusta not Kyrenia. Greek forces were, however, more efficient in attacking Turkish-Cypriot enclaves, especially in the west and south.

Joe Sisco heard about Turkish bombing runs in Cyprus while en route to Athens and, fearing anti-American hostility, asked if the Greek prime minister and foreign minister could meet him at the airport.

Brigadier Dimitrios Ioannidis started to tip over the edge when facing up to his dreadful miscalculation. Greek intelligence, the KYP, had tracked Turkey's naval convoy during the night and, like Western governments, did not know whether this was a bluff, an exercise or a real assault. Even in the morning Greek intelligence and military figures in Cyprus were not sure whether the Turks would land at Kyrenia or might suddenly change course for Famagusta.

Military staff officer Charalambos Palainis broke the news telling him, 'The Turks are landing'. 'What are you on about? Have the Turks really landed on Cyprus?' questioned the bewildered brigadier. Another aide Georgios Stavrou saw how 'when Ioannidis found out that the Turks had invaded [Cyprus] he was in a state of shock. He was at a loss. His eyes had turned red and he was not speaking.'[169] Slowly recovering, Ioannidis summoned a war council at the Greek Pentagon of the heads of the armed forces, including top general, Grigorios Bonanos, his puppet, Prime Minister Adamantios Androutsopoulos, President Phaedon Gizikis and a senior minister, Konstantinos Rallis.

Sisco, now arrived in Athens with Kissinger's latest orders to threaten an immediate cessation of aid if the junta moved against Turkey, rounded up Tasca and met with Greek military leaders as they assembled for the war council. The generals presented a strong front with Ioannidis appearing 'extremely hawkish'.[170] Sisco and Tasca tried to reason with them, saying they would do everything in their power to stop Turkey's advances adding ominously that Greece would lose in any conflict. An angry Ioannidis argued for war and shouted at Sisco that the Americans had cheated them. Although his generals appeared less enthusiastic and, despite their bravado, Sisco sensed growing divisions between these military leaders so held back from issuing Kissinger's ultimatum in case he united them in favour of conflict.

He and Tasca, therefore, left with no offer for Turkey but had made clear the United States' position to the war council, which subsequently resumed in an atmosphere of disbelief as military chiefs came to terms with their predicament and struggled for a suitable response. Ioannidis, unaffected by Sisco's words though likely still expecting American restraint on Turkey, gambled by calling for aggression: 'We should call Sampson and tell them to convene a Cabinet meeting and declare unification with Greece. We will accept it and war will break out. We shall see what happens from there.'[171]

Wiser military heads around the table who were generals outside of Ioannidis's circle realised the nonsense of this course. Even Grigorios Bonanos, who helped instigate the coup against Makarios, realised its implausibility. Demoralised Greek forces shaken up several times since 1967 and littered with competing loyalties and resentments stood no chance against an army three times its size. So Greece's general staff, including Bonanos, and civilian members of the junta found ways to thwart Ioannidis's delusions for an all-out conflict. No decision to counterattack was, therefore, given but to keep the Turks guessing they ordered a general mobilisation, which started at noon and, worryingly for the Americans, moved an army division to the border with Turkey. They also called for a UN Security Council meeting and recalled the Greek ambassador from NATO.

In London, Callaghan decided on Britain's response to events. First and foremost, protect British lives and property besides the bases; pressure Turkey to limit hostilities and agree a ceasefire; encourage Ankara to support the restoration of constitutional government in Cyprus; stop the Greeks from escalating and get them to eject Sampson; and get both countries to London for talks. Aware of Kissinger's concerns, he instructed British diplomats to keep the situation in London and away from the UN Security Council.

Callaghan told the Greek chargé not to make any statement or take any action which made relations with Turkey worse, causing the Greek diplomat to reply that Greece was now unwilling to meet in London and intended declaring war unless Turkey withdrew from Cyprus.

Kissinger got a similar message from the Greeks that if Turkey did not immediately ceasefire and withdraw, they would declare war on Turkey and *enosis* with Cyprus. He fumed when Sisco reported back a similar message saying that no threat had been made to cut off Greek aid. Go straight back and tell them in person, the secretary demanded, that all American military aid would stop immediately. He then updated Callaghan who, in turn, had British Ambassador Robin Hooper pressure the Greeks not to escalate the situation.

Turkish navy commander, Emin Goksan, who had taken such a risk in speeding along the convoy, signalled Colonel İbrahim Karaoğlanoğlu in charge of the 50th Infantry Regiment, part of the 39th Infantry Division, around 1.00 pm that the first part of the naval mission was complete. Karaoğlanoğlu, safely on shore, replied with a request to send over beans and rice for lunch.

To try and buy Sisco time, the American Embassy in Athens sent in American defence attaché Frank Athanason to appeal to Grigorios Bonanos. Tasca's embassy staff called Athanason into their lively office discussions about what steps to take with the junta, where he heard Tasca talking to Kissinger on the telephone:

> You could hear him almost all the way down the hall, talking loudly. Then they called me in and said, 'Get on the phone. You know those guys over there. Get on the phone and get the General Bonanos, who was head of the armed forces, (similar to our joint chiefs), to agree to declare Athens an open city.' If the Turks will declare İzmir [a Turkish coastal city] an open city... İzmir was the only one they could have done any [d]amage to.[172]

Athanason pushed back thinking his Greek was not good enough to do that over the telephone. So Tasca said, 'Just go on over there and talk to him'.

> So I went over and I sat in this general's office for several hours. My mission was to keep him from giving the go ahead to strike back. It was touch-and-go there. All the Greeks could realistically do would be attack İzmir causing a heavy reprisal, so the US idea was to get both sides to declare Athens and İzmir as 'open cities'.[173]

His task proved uncomfortable sitting in the general's office for a few tense hours with no result. Bonanos demanded to know what Athanason would do in these circumstances:

> I couldn't give him any advice. The only thing the Greeks could have done to bloody the Turks' nose right there would have been a surprise strike on İzmir. And then hope to hell we stopped the retaliation. But, they couldn't strike in Cyprus; they didn't have the means to go all the way there.[174]

Athanason tried to reason with him about consequences to which the general answered that Athanason 'didn't really understand the Greeks'. He said that they were 'willing to burn their house down to get rid of the bed bugs', meaning that he did not care what happened and was 'was ready to go'.[175] Bonanos, however, was posturing to put pressure on the United States for he was not taking Greece to war.

Sisco and Tasca duly went back to the junta but this time could only meet Foreign Minister Constantine Kypriaos to whom they passed on Kissinger's threat in courteous but unequivocal terms and not quite as robustly as the secretary might have wanted. They said Greece bore a 'certain responsibility',[176] was isolated and neither Athens nor Washington wanted the Soviet Union fishing in the area. Kypriaos, in turn, read a script from the war council's meeting demanding that Turkey immediately cease action and withdraw its troops to Turkish enclaves by 2.00 pm or face war and *enosis*, a threat he backed up by pointing to the call-up now underway.

Sisco read into this threat the basis for a negotiated ceasefire and worked up with the Greeks and Kissinger a text incorporating Kypriaos's two points, with both countries to attend London talks under the 1959 / 1960 London and Zürich agreements.

When done and before dashing back to Ankara, he wanted to finalise the details with Kissinger, who after another long night was driving back from San Clemente to accommodation in Newport Beach. Tasca's assistant John Wolf telephoned through the American air base in Turkey reaching the White House. Wolf told the staff that Joe Sisco needed to speak with Kissinger urgently, so they put him through to San Clemente, from where the sergeant managing the telephone said the secretary of state had already left. Sisco yelled over to Wolf that he must speak now, so the White House Communications Agency said they could have Kissinger's motorcade pull into a gas station to use a pay telephone. Wolf passed this on to Sisco who hit the roof and threw a pencil close to his head in 'volcanic' frustration. Wolf, a relatively young foreign service officer, did not mind at all for he was relishing this experience at the heart of world affairs.

Kissinger eventually called in from somewhere over an open telephone. Wolf saw Sisco at work, 'really sharp, really focused. He said, "Henry, this is the situation. This is what I'm going to do. If that doesn't work I'll fall back to this, and if that doesn't work I'll fall back to that."'[177] As much as he was enjoying the experience, Wolf worried this highly sensitive conversation was happening over an open line. Sisco reassured him afterwards, saying,

Not to worry, there is some little guy in the basement of the [Cypriot] Ministry of Interior who has now copied down everything that I said. He's going to translate it into Greek and then he's going to go and take it to the [Cypriot] navy chief of staff. By then I'll be, I'll be long gone.[178]

Sisco told Washington that he could get Greece to agree a ceasefire if the Turks withdrew into the Turkish-Cypriot enclaves providing the basis for talks in London. Kissinger, worried about irrational Greek action and facing prospects of a possible Greek-Turkish war, overcame his inhibitions about causing a 1964-type reaction from the Turks. He told Sisco to be brutal with Ecevit and, if needed, threaten to withhold aid if war broke out. He also told Art Hartman, the head of EUR, to give the same warning, as personal opinion not as government policy, to Turkish Ambassador Melih Esenbel in Washington, if the Turks refused Sisco's proposal. Kissinger also updated Jim Callaghan who likewise directed Ambassador Horace Phillips to press Ecevit to accept these terms.

Sisco, Dillon and the American party dashed off to Athens airport but were again delayed from taking off by Turkish authorities who refused clearance to enter their air space. An angry Sisco told Bill Macomber from the airport that he wanted to see Turan Güneş immediately on arrival and to tell Turkey's top general, Semih Sancar, that the United States would not tolerate any more stalling; he was taking off immediately, entering Turkish airspace in an hour and it was up to the Turks if they wanted to shoot down the personal representative of the president of the United States.

For the second time, Sisco and the American party risked personal danger. His nervous pilots wanted to know what to do when nearing Turkish airspace without clearance. He told them to circle when nearing the perimeter. Much to their relief, the clearance came in a short time later when Turkish fighters escorted them to Ankara.

As they flew out, the Greek mobilisation took effect with unintended consequences. Rather than readying a country for war it began restoring the proper military chain of command, which undermined Ioannidis's pockets of influence in the middle ranks. Senior generals and admirals, including the naval chief of staff Petros Arapakis, no friend to the regime of Ioannidis, regained their full powers of authority from his coterie of captains and majors.

Back in Cyprus, John Aiken and his commanders faced hard decisions over timings of the rescue operation. By a miracle, no service family caught up in the fighting in Limassol had yet been harmed but defending everyone in dormitory towns from further risk was impossible. He, therefore, planned their transfer to the safety of RAF bases in three operations from 20 to 23 July 1974, starting with dormitory towns that Saturday and Sunday. These went well in Famagusta, Larnaca and Platres but fighting in Limassol caused problems. Any chance of safe extraction depended on a ceasefire, which British officers tried to negotiate, the leading officer reporting that 'to their credit the NG [National Guard] extended their ceasefire until it was completed, thus delaying their assault on the Turkish quarter by two hours'.[179]

Aiken had announced over the forces' radio that all friendly nationals could join, which more or less meant every tourist and civilian. And in they poured alongside Cypriot refugees of both sides seeking sanctuary. Every form of accommodation was appropriated to house them, including mixed quarters, churches, schools and social clubs. What to do with everybody was solved the next day when the largest air evacuation operation since the Berlin Airlift in 1948 began.

Confusion reigned in London over the results of Sisco's morning meeting with the Greeks. Given Kissinger's information to Callaghan, the Foreign and Commonwealth Office expected Sisco to threaten Athens with withdrawal of American nuclear assistance. Yet a different picture emerged when British Ambassador Robin Hooper found Greek Foreign Minister Konstantinos Kypraios not cowing under any American threat – Sisco and Tasca having downplayed the point – but talking of 'war on all fronts'[180] unless the ultimatum was met. Hooper told him that Greek chest beating would not influence Turkey and what 'we were discussing around the table might well prove to be the preliminaries to another world war'.[181]

A crumbling junta now thrashing around for help in a helpless world began mustering popular support by claiming that British military movements were part of a conspiracy with Turkey to divide Cyprus. The Greek foreign minister claimed British warships were assisting Turkish ones and British helicopters supplying a Turkish village in the north near Cape Apostolos Andreas. Conversely, elements of Turkey's popular press had earlier accused Britain of being in cahoots with Greece to unseat Makarios.

Greek allegations started this new big lie about British and American scheming with Turkey. Criticism until this point been limited to general mutterings about Washington's involvement in the 1967 and 1973 Greek coups and recent condemnation by some Greek Cypriots over not restoring Makarios – though significant numbers lost no sleep over the archbishop's removal. Now, however, a coherent narrative began emerging, one which soon harmonised the Greek speaking world, especially Greek Americans, as never before. Even local Cyprus

FM radio accused British warships of abetting Turkey's landing, which John Aiken countered with public denials on the forces' radio. Identifying himself and his right to speak for Britain, he said, 'I want to make it absolutely clear to you of whatever nationality that Britain is not involved in any way in the action which began in the Republic of Cyprus at dawn today'.[182]

Turkish air strikes over Limassol close to RAF Akrotiri gave him another headache in deciding the practical and moral issues of engaging a fellow NATO country. Any intervention by British planes might exacerbate the confused fighting and bring retribution on unprotected civilians or the bases and raise the prospect of air collision or even accidental attacks. In the late morning, London told him not to open fire on any Turkish aircraft over Limassol, but planes should, however, intercept Turkish aircraft intruding on sovereign airspace and, if needed, apply agreed military rules of engagement. RAF pilots subsequently intercepted twenty Turkish aircraft, fortunately all in safe operations with temperate Turkish pilots making off when issued with internationally recognised warning signs.

This still did not alleviate John Aiken's concerns about intense fighting in the dormitory towns with Turkish aircraft supporting Turkish-Cypriot fighters. When Turkish bombing got perilously close to the Greek part of Limassol and family living quarters, he warned the Turkish general staff about protecting civilian lives. By a miracle, Turkish aircraft left the area alone sparing him his 'appalling dilemma'[183] over orders to fire.

Clifford 'Cliff' Spink, a 28-year-old flying officer of 56 (Lightnings) Squadron, experienced his first fighter interception in Cyprus. Born a farmer's son in Suffolk, Spink's own story was one of remarkable colour, rising through the ranks from sergeant aircraft apprentice in 1966 at RAF Halton in Buckinghamshire to become a fighter pilot – and later air marshal himself. Brimming with excitement at his first real engagement he was still apprehensive when preparing to warn off six Turkish aircraft until he saw his boss, Clive Mitchell, strapping into the second Lightning as his wing man.

Spink received another morale boost when airborne instructions were issued from flight operations. That voice sounds familiar he thought, before recognising that his girlfriend Catherine was speaking. She was by coincidence was the radio communications officer on duty at Mount Olympus and would later become his wife.

He soon intercepted a Turkish Phantom taking photographs through the camera bay, noticing that the foreign pilot was more nervous than him and who compliantly heeded all warnings. In one of those incongruous junctions in life Spink met his potential adversary through sheer chance twenty years later. As a group captain posted at Mons in NATO, he sat down next to a Turkish colonel who described himself as a pilot seeing action in the Turkish campaign in a reconnaissance mission. To which Spink replied, 'I know, I was the man who escorted you around the entire island'.[184]

Additional British troops arrived at Akrotiri throughout the day under the reinforcement operations Ablaut and Platypus, including a second marine commando, and some 2,700 troops besides Puma helicopters and Scorpion tanks. Naval vessels now included the submarine HMS *Onslaught*, the carriers HMS *Hermes*, HMS *Devonshire* and HMS *Andromeda*, and the frigate HMS *Rhyl* with HMS *Brighton* en route, arriving on the Monday, and supported by the Royal Fleet Auxiliary (RFA) ships RFA *Gold*, RFA *Rover*, RFA *Regent*, RFA *Olna* and RFA *Olwen*. Every occupation was flown out to cover the shortage of local labour, including nurses, technicians, mechanics, clerks, kitchen hands, Royal Corps of Transport drivers and Royal Pioneer Corps staff.

In the afternoon with Joe Sisco en route to Ankara, British Ambassador Horace Phillips received nothing but cold water when discussing Greek ceasefire demands with Turkish Foreign Minister Turan Güneş, who was trying to buy his military forty-eight hours. Withdrawal to the enclaves simply made Turkish troops vulnerable argued Güneş and relinquished their advantage to no benefit – and he doubted attendance at the London talks as this 'could only be negotiation from weakness'.[185]

An increasingly isolated Athens, under pressure from the United States, backed off from demanding a Turkish withdrawal to the enclaves by 2.00 pm to one completed within forty-eight hours, and then without specifying a time limit or any conditions about how long they should stay there.

Evacuation of civilians from Limassol still looked dangerous with British airman and soldiers pinned down by small arms fire, so contact was made with the National Guard area commander Colonel Sirmopolous and a three and half-hour truce negotiated in concert with UNFICYP. Aiken even had UNFICYP tell the Turks he would launch Lightning fighters if they attacked Limassol during the evacuation. This truce let tired and nerve-racked servicemen and their families walk tentatively to a by-pass for collection by a waiting convoy of lorries, cars and coaches or else drove themselves, in either case making inch by inch progress along a now busy road to the base. Progress was so slow that the National Guard extended the ceasefire for a further two hours before resuming attack.

Fighting prevented any evacuation in Nicosia but plans were drawn up for a UN controlled operation if a ceasefire occurred. By the end of the afternoon, the Larnaca operation had finished and was continuing in Famagusta, where collecting and accounting for everyone in hotels was slow going. John and Dana Davies, the two children of American Ambassador Rodger Davies, were in the convoy that went south to Akrotiri and flown out to Beirut with other family members of the American staff.

Large numbers of evacuees soon choked the quickly formed RAF base reception centres. Yet despite the oppressive July heat, there was air of gentle excitement at the novel situation as service families stood patiently awaiting the allocation of rooms from already occupied quarters, comforted by tunes from the Royal Scots pipers and airmen and soldiers handing out Quality Street chocolates.

With ever sparse accommodation to cater for the extra thousands, service families were squashed into whatever free space was available, some sleeping on pavilions or sleeping six or more to a bedroom. Men were ordered to sleep in squadron headquarters.

Helen Watson, wife to wing commander Ken Watson in charge of 35 Squadron, was at the forefront of ferrying wives to new quarters. Watson telephoned his wife from his squadron office asking her to pack him a sponge bag and spare shoes for collection by his driver, not knowing when they would next meet. Helen Watson remained unflappable: she was an experienced squadron wife who came from a military family herself, having been a young girl in Egypt when the Suez Crisis unfolded.

All squadron wives were told to attend the sergeants' mess, which Helen Watson dutifully complied with taking her 8-year-old daughter on half term through a huge base traffic jam, which an overwhelmed Royal Military Police officer struggled to manage with sweat dripping from his elbows. Greeting her at the mess was the unforgettable scene of endlessly queueing families and in front of cars hurriedly parked everywhere.

Helen Watson spent the day ferrying bewildered wives and children to their new temporary homes, sometimes with unsuspecting landlords unaware they were taking tenants. She drew up outside the married quarters of one warrant officer and his wife enjoying the afternoon sun on their veranda dreamily gazing at the Troodos Mountains, and deposited a mother with young girls departing quickly before any airing of opinion.

At 7.00 pm, a somewhat tired Helen Watson then heard a knock at her front door to receive her own house guests, ten strong, including children and one baby. She found sleeping quarters in all parts of the house, with two pregnant women sleeping in the cooler night temperature of the patio.

American Ambassador Rodger Davies also granted safety to Cypriots in the American compound. James Williams saw how such people

> were deathly afraid of what might happen to them if the Turks should get them, and they moved in. They sort of arrived at the gate with an aide or a family member. These weren't large numbers, but the Ambassador made the decision to let them in [and] put them in [a] ground floor office somewhere which unfortunately had a telephone in it, which they started using. So, we had to restrict their phone privileges [and] establish rules of conduct for them while they were in this anomalous situation on the ground.[186]

While waiting for Henry Kissinger to return from San Clemente, senior aide Bob Ingersoll reviewed American evacuation procedures with the Special Actions Group in Washington. An amphibious evacuation task force with 14 helicopters and 1,800 marines was moved 40 miles south of Cyprus with a second task force under USS *Forrestal* positioned in support. Planes and men in Greece, Italy and Turkey were discreetly made ready, along with destroyers in the American naval port at Rota, Spain, and the carrier, USS *America*. If things went wrong, 54,000 military personnel in Greece alongside some 26,000 staff in Turkey needed evacuation with untold thousands of civilians and tourists, and American assets, including nuclear material.

In the sometimes uncoordinated nature of the United States federal government, the Department of Defense told Ingersoll that military aid supplies to both Greece and Turkey had been suspended, flying in the face of Kissinger's insistence that aid continue so he did not lose influence. American generals were unsure about the status of supplies already en route, including F-14 fighter aircraft. They did know that Greece had mischievously stolen a consignment of bombs and rockets intended for Turkey when American barges carrying supplies for both countries docked in Greece. General Amos Jordan complained that this 'business of the Greeks commandeering our vessels is something else again, it seems to me. Ever since this crisis began the Greeks have been obstreperous. I am wondering if we shouldn't be increasing our distance from the Greeks.'[187] They agreed to protest through Tasca.

Joe Sisco finally arrived in Ankara to face several hours of delays fighting Turkish officialdom before eventually getting to Prime

Minister Bülent Ecevit. He handed over the Greek ceasefire proposal and argued that Turkey's conditions for starting talks had been met; Turkey self-evidently having won a military presence on the island with the Greeks already agreeing to replace their officers and to remove Sampson after a period of time. Then, 'raising the tone of my voice and put on a display of controlled anger',[188] Sisco emphasised that prolonged conflict risked badly damaging American-Turkish relations and issued the brutal threat to stop military aid. (President Richard Nixon, at Kissinger's request, backed this up with a personal message to Turkey's head of state, President Fahri Korutürk, saying he regretted Turkey's military actions, urged Ankara not to escalate and attend London talks.)

Ecevit, playing for time, agreed to speak with his military and Cabinet as soon as possible and get back to Sisco, which was not going to be this evening, and parried any further American request for meetings. He pointed out that military operations could not be easily stopped as certain objectives must first be achieved before a ceasefire. Sisco reported to Washington that he thought Ankara did not take the Greek war threat war seriously but noticed that Ecevit was taken aback by the sanctions warning.

As evening progressed in Cyprus, Kissinger, balancing many issues, struggled to control the situation before leaving San Clemente in the afternoon. When learning the Department of Defense had apparently cut off aid to both countries, he quickly called Secretary of Defense Jim Schlesinger who assured him this was only a threat. He then told Ingersoll to sort out the confusion and keep the supplies in a nether land of neither stopped nor delivered, fearing that if formally stopped he might not get them restarted without congressional approval depriving him of bargaining levers: 'It doesn't make a G. [god] D. [damn] difference Bob [Ingersoll]. You're in charge of this operation until I get back. You just tell them what I agreed with [Jim] Schlesinger.'[189]

He fumed when then learning that Art Hartman, head of the European department, had been softer on the Turkish ambassador in Washington than instructed and not passed on the threat to stop aid, just as Sisco had not first threatened the Greeks. Hartman had decided that the Turkish ambassador to the United States was not the right person to receive the threat. 'Well, it's going to be a lonely department when I get back', snapped Kissinger to Bob Ingersoll, 'You get Hartman to call the Turkish Ambassador and you tell Hartman that the next time he doesn't carry out instructions I want his resignation. I do not accept the principle that Assistant Secretaries have a judgment when they're given an order.'[190] Ingersoll reassured him within the hour that Hartman had made the call, causing Kissinger to quip that the message was supposed to be made as Hartman's personal opinion, 'I will bet my bottom dollar he didn't do it that way'.[191]

Turkey had by night more or less achieved its landing objectives in a remarkable tricky amphibious operation, beating back limited counterattacks though badly behind schedule and in terribly exposed positions with its disparate forces not yet connected.

Henry Kissinger gave an impromptu press briefing before flying to Washington, partly to cover up a spontaneous decision by an American general to put the Italy based 509th Airborne Infantry on alert as part of prospective evacuation procedures. He passed these movements off as a routine precaution not an alert to avoid any Soviet knee jerk reaction, saying that the United States was not in a posture of confrontation with the Soviet Union. Privately he moaned, 'That G. [god] D. [damn] General Goodpath that just went ahead and alerted for 509th Air Force [509th Airborne Infantry] without telling anybody'.[192]

Two hours later, at 8.15 pm GMT, when furnished with Sisco's update, Kissinger briefed President Richard Nixon: 'They [the Turks] will have to decide by midnight this time. The proposals are placed for a ceasefire and the Turks to go into enclaves that they have there and the Turks are gaining a strong barging position.'[193] For the first time in a week Kissinger felt sufficiently in control to tell Nixon that 'If the Greeks don't go to war in the a.m., I think we are all right'.[194]

Nixon decided to stay in San Clemente working out options and jostling for political support before the Supreme Court issued its judgement over the full release of his tapes.

After three and a half hours of debate the UN Security Council unanimously passed Resolution 353 calling for all states to recognise the sovereignty of Cyprus, agree an immediate ceasefire and end foreign military intervention, exercise restraint and cooperate with UNFICYP – and Greece, Turkey and the United Kingdom were to negotiate a peaceful solution.

American Ambassador John Scali, a former *ABC News* journalist and go-between during the Cuban Missile Crisis of 1962, kept his own comments brief, regretting Turkey's failure to follow diplomacy then criticising Greece and impressing on all the importance of the London talks (Kissinger, worried about war, was now prepared to publicly admonish both countries). The Soviet Union and China did not object but subtly exploited the situation, with Soviet Ambassador Vasily Stepanovich Safronchuk criticising the absence of any reference to Makarios, which the United States and Britain had sought to prevent so that the archbishop was not included in the talks. The Soviet state newspaper, *Pravda*, had already condemned Greek militarists for aggressive action against an independent.

At the end of this tumultuous day few in Washington or London grappling with the prospect of war between fellow NATO allies suspected the junta might collapse. A young deposed Greek king did. King Constantine II, living with his family in London, sensed an opportunity and began manoeuvring by contacting the CIA and the Department of State. Washington, rightly, felt that Constantine commanded little authority among the Greek public though at this stage did not consider the alternative, elder Greek statesman, Konstantinos Karamanlis, who was exiled in Paris since 1963, as a likely replacement. This Macedonian born lawyer, who as a previous Greek prime minister had renounced *enosis* and agreed the 1959/1960 London and Zürich agreements before leaving his country after the political crisis of 1963, watched events closely. His time was coming.

Chapter 13

TURKISH PREVARICATION: SUNDAY, 21 JULY 1974

Turkey's exposed position had been highlighted overnight when National Guard commandos in fierce hand-to-hand fighting contested control of the Agirda mountain area, a crucial vantage point needed to join Turkish paratroopers with the Kyrenia beachhead landings. Another blow occurred at 3.00 am when a mortar, most likely from its own forces, landed on 50th Infantry Regiment's command post killing Colonel İbrahim Karaoğlanoğlu and an air controller with the air force, and badly injured the regiment's second in command. Troops had also failed to seize the airport in Nicosia or damage it enough to stop Greek planes flying in supplies. And they were behind schedule and heavily outnumbered while pressure was building for a ceasefire.

They also could not protect the enclaves, which suffered terrible onslaught with most in the south overrun displacing some 60,000 Turkish Cypriots, and only the larger ones in the north and east able to resist. At least the effect was to divert Greek-Cypriot forces from otherwise concentrating attacks on the Turkish landings.

Remnants of Turkish-Cypriot fighters around Paphos then reported that Greek reinforcements were landing in the port alarming Ecevit's government. This information came on top of confusion about a supposed Greek naval convoy, which the Turks thought they were tracking from Rhodes since the early hours, causing intense debate between army and air force commanders in the task force operations centre in Ankara.

Bülent Ecevit told American Ambassador Bill Macomber these ships risked attack if sailing into Cypriot waters, so the United States had better stop them. He even telephoned Kissinger overnight to complain about the Greeks disguising their ships as other nationalities, to which a grumpy Nancy Kissinger allegedly said, 'Why don't you tell him to shut up and sink the god-damned thing?'[195] Even without her advice, this was a course the Turks intended following. By 7.50 am GMT, Foreign Minister Turan Güneş told Macomber that Ankara could not hold off attacks on the supposed convoy beyond late morning.

There were, in fact, so many ships in the areas, no one could tell which ships belonged to which navy with even the CIA unsure. A confusing canvass covered the waters west of Cyprus comprising ships of six nationalities including British pleasure craft and a Messalina cruise liner. American reconnaissance planes later found thirteen ships reasonably close together, five were Soviet, four American and another four unidentified. Greece had, in fact, despatched some ships – though had called them back – and was landing some reinforcements for the National Guard possibly under ruse of another country's flag, though not in large numbers. Ambassadors to Britain and the United States in Turkey tried reassuring Ecevit, who insisted the Greeks were deceiving them all.

Aside from these concerns, daylight gave Turkey the edge allowing its aircraft full control of the skies and its navy of the seas – with ships rushing back to reload the next wave. On what had been thronged tourist resorts along the Cyprus north coast at the height of summer now appeared a landing strip. Turkish warships pounded Kyrenia while American-made A4 Skyhawks attacked from the sky. Bodies were littered along the roadside.

Ten thousand Cypriot National Guardsmen supported by 30,000 reserves provided more resistance than Turkey had expected, but overall, their response was chaotic, exacerbated by a delay in responding to the invasion and the absence of any air support from Greece.

Heads of the Greek armed services who thought the current Cypriot and Greek forces strong enough to pin the Turks down for two days initiated some reinforcements without escalating the situation too far. Two diesel submarines were sent to intercept further Turkish landings and an operation to fly in commandos overnight was finalised with other reinforcements sent to Rhodes. Most worrying for Washington, Greek forces on the northern border with Turkey were increased, causing the Turks to do likewise.

Yet Greek movements and threats were intended to apply pressure on Turkey and get others to do the same rather than risk war. Greek Prime Minister Adamantios Androutsopoulos demanded ceasefires times, which were then allowed to slip and told Ambassador Henry Tasca that Greek ships – which ones was not clear – would not turn around without a ceasefire while hinting there was time to manoeuvre them away. President Phaedon Gizikis again threatened a Greek withdrawal from NATO causing surprised Greek staff officers in Brussels to foil the order. Henry Kissinger had Richard Nixon warn him against a step that might cause causing irrevocable and disastrous effects.

Joe Sisco was still knocking on Turkish doors early in the morning to get a ceasefire from Ecevit's government, which teased out every minute to win time for its military. Ecevit had even stalled Kissinger, his former professor at Harvard University, in three other overnight calls causing the secretary to wonder, 'If their generals are as bad as their leaders, what can their captains and majors be like!'[196]

Sisco and his colleagues talked with Macomber at the embassy about what to do as even the ambassador's repeated calls received no answer and time was running out. While the embassy staff sat in a large circle discussing options, an impatient Sisco took his assistant Bob Oakley aside and told him of a senior contact in the Turkish foreign ministry, Ümit Haluk Bayülken, from his UN days. Sisco said to telephone him, which Oakley duly did, using as strong a language as possible by a professional diplomat, saying that Turkish prevarication threatened the entire American and NATO relationship simply for the sake of gaining a few more metres on the ground.

This almost worked. Bayülken called back twenty minutes later and said that Turan Güneş would meet Joe Sisco at 8.15 am but would not relent when Oakley demanded it must be Ecevit, though implied the meeting would work. So off they went to Güneş's office at the agreed time. Ecevit, as Bayülken had alluded to, entered through a side door as he did not want to be seen meeting Americans. Sisco was handed Ecevit's handwritten acceptance of the UN ceasefire resolution on condition that the United States got Greek acceptance to the ceasefire, which meant stopping any reinforcements. On this basis, Turkey would attend London talks.

In referring to reinforcements, Güneş had in mind the supposed Greek flotilla about which the Turks were developing a paranoia, claiming to have spotted thirteen disguised ships off the Cypriot coast which he said must be stopped. Their request gave Sisco cause to berate them saying this was the reason he had tried to talk with them all night. Thinking the Turks about to announce the ceasefire, Sisco then dashed off to the airport for a major selling job with the Greeks and to stop their ghost fleet.

Back in Athens, Ioannidis called in Grigorios Bonanos, Adamantios Androutsopoulos, Phaedon Gizikis and his defence minister telling them of his decision to attack Turkey on all fronts from Cyprus to Thrace. The brigadier general mistakenly hoped to unite Greeks behind a common cause against a longstanding enemy, miscalculating that this unity was greater than the consequences of war – and probably gambling on American intervention to stop matters going too far. General Bonanos prevaricated saying he wanted to confirm any decision with the heads of the armed forces, who with their deputies he duly summoned to his room at the defence ministry after Ioannidis left.

Instead of treating this as a rallying cry, these military chiefs, who all outranked Ioannidis, pushed back against the madness. Army chief of staff Lieutenant General Andreas Galatsanos said that he was ready for a defensive war not one of aggression, with air force chief Lieutenant General Alexandros Papanikolaou adding, 'The Air Force is ready to carry out its duty ... but an air attack would be unwise and have no decisive results.'[197] One after one they said no. Grigorios Bonanos agreed.

Afterwards, the three heads of the forces stayed on for another meeting to plot insurrection against the man who had brought them to this untenable position and return power to the politicians. To back up the point, they ordered back the two diesel submarines heading for Cyprus.

By late morning, Sisco and his party arrived in Athens to find a junta slowly disintegrating but uncertain what might come next with rumours of different groups in the military plotting another coup. British intelligence suspected a Soviet backed coup. There was even talk of a fresh move by Ioannidis with his nationalistic group of captains and majors bringing back the exiled Konstantinos Karamanlis and have him sign a humiliating peace treaty which they could then denounce. In any event, these conditions hindered Sisco in his search for a Greek government representative.

He managed to get hold of Bonanos who along with navy chief, Petros Arapakis, rejected Ecevit's terms until Turkey declared an immediate ceasefire. Nonetheless, Bonanos, with little intention of permitting war, encouraged Sisco to keep working on his efforts.

By 11.45 am GMT with still nothing coming from Ecevit, Kissinger and Callaghan stepped up their diplomatic activity to support Sisco, who himself returned to the embassy and worked the telephones with his Greek and Turkish contacts. The foreign secretary urged Ecevit early in the afternoon to agree an immediate ceasefire in accordance with the UN resolution, which the Turkish prime minister evaded preferring to put the matter to his National Security Council later that day, though giving the impression it would be accepted. When Callaghan asked about the London talks, Ecevit replied he must stay close to Ankara causing the foreign secretary to think Vienna a suitable alternative.

Half an hour later, Callaghan warmed up Austrian Chancellor Bruno Kreisky to use the Hofburg Palace in Vienna the following day, a request that aggravated Kissinger who thought London the better location for Callaghan to control the Greeks and Turks.

After consulting Kissinger, Sisco then worked again on the civilian ministers taking Ambassador Henry Tasca with him at noon GMT to meet Greek Prime Minister Adamantios Androutsopoulos and Foreign Minister Constantine Kypriaos. He used a softer line, appealing to the Greeks as their only friend saying that he was not bullying them as he was Turkey, which had some effect in an emotional discussion with Androutsopoulos who even quoted American President Abraham Lincoln. Sisco read out Ecevit's handwritten copy of a ceasefire proposal, which both ministers mistrusted, Androutsopoulos alleging Turkish duplicity as Greece had called back its ships without Turkey reciprocating with a ceasefire. Sisco tried harder, offering full American support for the London talks, even participating if requested, which eventually encouraged Androutsopoulos to recommend the junta agree a UN ceasefire at 3.00 pm – a time Sisco pulled out of the hat.

This was not certain to be accepted. Androutsopoulos admitted his government was likely to change within the next twenty-four hours claiming that captains in the army were going to take over – and as neither he nor Kypriaos expected to be part of any new regime, no decision could be made about going to London. Despite this, Sisco thought a ceasefire was in the bag and prematurely told British Ambassador Robin Hooper it could happen within half-an hour even if the Greek government collapses.

Away from international politics, Air Marshal John Aiken continued the assorted rescue missions of stranded civilians. Not a single person was lost among the thousands of tourists gathered up in tough circumstances dodging crossfire and trigger-happy irregulars. Cooperation from the National Guard and the Turkish military all assisted by UNFICYP, sometimes as interlocutor, proved indispensable, though the principal role played by the British armed services, which had already saved the life of Makarios, has not yet been fully appreciated. Among the rescued were forty-one supposed Soviet tourists, which caused a sceptical raising of eyebrows in the Foreign and Commonwealth Office with deputy head John Killick exclaiming about what might such sightseers being doing in Cyprus as they were unlikely to be deserving railway-workers on holiday.

Nicosia was still a problem with fierce fighting in the north and air attacks over the airport pinning down British soldiers whenever they got near. However, fearing the situation might worsen, an evacuation order was given at 10.50 am local time. High Commissioner Stephen Olver, working from the basement of his Nicosia office as battle raged outside, patiently negotiated with his contacts for the convoy's safe passage, but not without 'a harassing time on the Nicosia by-pass when heavy fire was directed over their heads but they suffered no casualties convoy'.[198]

BBC journalist John Sergeant travelled in the convoy when rescued with other reporters and tourists from the besieged Ledra Palace Hotel by Canadian soldiers of UNFICYP. 'Ceasefire, ceasefire'[199] shouted the UN commander over a loud hailer when preparing to take out the hotel residents, even though the shooting continued. Nonetheless, they all made it into an armoured personnel carrier without injury. Sergeant used his influence at RAF Dhekelia to jump the long telephone queue and file his story on a bad telephone line for the BBC 6.00 pm news.

Meanwhile staff at RAF Akrotiri began the largest air evacuation of civilians since Berlin in 1948, returning, by Saturday, 10 August 1974, thousands of service families and 12,000 tourists of all nationalities. The RAF accommodated American and Canadian aircraft flown in to rescue their own citizens, France and Soviet Union had their nationals transported to Larnaca for a boat rescue and Britain took care of everyone else, taking them back to the United Kingdom for onward travel.

Flight Sergeant John 'Taff' Lee was a logistics specialist of 70 Squadron flown to Kingsfield at Dhekelia to pick up civilians. Lee knew from his previous posting about the problems of landing on the short Kingsfield runway and the stress on the aircraft tyres: spare wheels were loaded but it was agreed that unless a punctured happened Lee would approve the plane as fit to fly. His first load of civilians was a large number of Scandinavian ladies, who had been trapped on Famagusta Beach when Turkish shells dropped, and who to Lee's great delight turned up in minimal clothing.

Flying out all the civilians again overwhelmed the hastily developed reception centres with day and night flight processing to cater for the vast numbers. Last into the camp and first out was the applied rule of thumb with young mothers given preference. Helen Watson was aghast at the situation she found of endless lines of families with minimal belongings standing for hours, occasionally overnight, in Cyprus's fatiguing summer heat with little to eat or drink. She had Ken Watson's driver meet her at home, where they manoeuvred a barrel of iced water into the car and grabbed every biscuit and sweet in sight, and then set about arranging refreshments back at the processing centre. Commandeering a trolley, she and other helpers made coffee, the simplest drink to arrange, which they handed out to appreciative families along the isles. One evacuee, mistaking her for NAAFI canteen staff, shouted out, 'I don't drink coffee. Got any tea love?'[200]

Overcrowding caused other discomforts across the camps, including blocked sewers and limited water supplies. Food was not such a problem; in fact, military rations helped Watson understand why many supposedly fit troops had such large stomachs. Every thronging household was issued with plentiful campo rations, normally given to troops for their rucksacks, packed with goodies from tinned beef to chicken, vegetables, much prized Tic Tok biscuits with coloured icing on one side, cream crackers, jelly, margarine, rice pudding and even Christmas pudding, as well as menu suggestions on how to mix ingredients for the tastiest meals. Everyone put on weight. By good fortune, the local orange trees were ripe, and troops who picked them while passing the large nearby Fatima plantation threw the citrus delights into households they passed. Aircrews from the United Kingdom brought ready supplies of toilet rolls and bread hastily purchased at supermarkets.

One unacceptable consequence of the departure of the wives became the inappropriate roving eyes of the now lonely and sometimes bored servicemen in summer conditions. Helen Watson, wife to a wing commander, now avoided the mess as improper wandering male hands proved a very unwanted feature of her visits.

Back in Athens, Sisco's optimism following his meeting with the Greek prime minister had receded. Kissinger told Callaghan at 12.30 pm GMT about his confidence of a ceasefire, after which Callaghan could publicise the talks. He telephoned back fifteen minutes later to say that the Greek government is weak and should not be asked to make more decisions than it can handle, and the Turks are not ready for a ceasefire.

Turkey's prime minister also refused to believe Greek denials over the supposed Greek flotilla passed on by Kissinger and Macomber. They are duping you claimed Ecevit, saying that Greek ships were fanning out to land at different points on Cyprus and would be attacked by Turkish planes. Bill Macomber frantically worked with Kissinger, Tasca and Sisco to reassure him. Prime Minister Adamantios

Androutsopoulos had privately told Sisco there were no ships, which the undersecretary passed on with an accompanying Greek message saying said that the Turks could sink any Greek ships they spotted in the area.

Ecevit claiming that his military was tracking three destroyers and seven troop carriers was not for persuading. 'Well,' he said, 'you may find this useful after all. You will discover that the Greeks never tell the truth. They can't. You will see this proved when those ships cross into Cypriot waters and we sink them!'[201] Turkish High Command alerted its three destroyers, TCG *Kocatepe*, TCG *Adatepe* and TCG *Maresal Fevzi Çakmak*, which were being used to support the landings.

It also checked with the Royal Navy attaché in Ankara whether the approaching convoy might be British ships. The attaché checked with John Aiken, who knew they were not but could not otherwise work it out as intense Turkish fighter plane activity over the area stopped a Nimrod from getting close enough for identification. Nervous Turkish fighter pilots had already forced the Royal Navy to take defensive action.

Confusion reigned everywhere, especially in Turkey where miscommunication caused the worried Turks to mistake their own destroyers for Greek ones. A sortie by Turkish F104 fighter jets just before 3.00 pm reported no sightings of foreign ships but Ankara did not receive the message in time and took its own intercepting vessels for the enemy. Turkey's navy had recently taken delivery of several second-hand American destroyers, including the TCG *Kocatepe*, which were not yet equipped for Turkish air-to-sea recognition and were identical to those bought by Greece.

Shortly after 3.00 pm the 111th Squadron of the Turkish air force attacked the ships in a three-hour battle as identifying signals sent from sea did not match air codes and were ignored and large Turkish flying flags were assumed a ruse. Fifty-two assaults were made on the TCG *Kocatepe* with the TCG *Maresal Fevzi Çakmak* also drawing heavy fire. One pilot made a direct hit with a 750-bomb down TCG *Kocatepe*'s funnel sinking it within twenty-four hours. The two other ships limped back to Mersin for repairs. Staff at the operations centre in Ankara fell silent when realising what had happened. The tragedy was compounded by the fate of the pilot, who after learning the truth on his way back, crashed into a hillside, possibly because of a shortage of fuel or possibly in remorse.

An hour later, the Turkish Foreign Ministry asked Britain for search and rescue assistance. Aiken's operations centre sent up a Nimrod after Turkey guaranteed its safety, which after searches in the area found only an empty dinghy and some dead sheep and cattle before dusk. The operation centre passed on these findings and requested permission to resume searching the next morning.

In Washington, Kissinger, back from San Clemente, tried to stop the Greeks from leaving NATO and his own government from kicking them out during an early afternoon meeting of his Special Actions Group. Still irked by leaked stories of aid embargoes, he suspected the Department of Defense of stopping aid against his wishes. Tough-talking Secretary of Defense Jim Schlesinger openly expressed his concerns about the reputational damage to NATO and the United States of having a Greek dictator as an ally, a view shared by some in the Department of State. Schlesinger pushed to end the regime, saying 'other European countries have said that we have gone beyond the point of no return regarding Greece ... we are viewed throughout the world as supporting the Greek regime.'[202]

This was the moment Kissinger stopped the American government ejecting Greece from NATO. He replied, 'Well, we can't settle the NATO problem today. Cyprus is our problem today. I don't like overthrowing governments. I'm not sure the Greek government will last out the week, anyway. It seems to me there is no way it will survive.' If it did fall, Director of Central Intelligence William Colby thought that replacements would come from the lower military ranks, and in a short-sighted judgement dismissed the former Greek prime minister, Konstantinos Karamanlis, in Paris as 'not being around' while commenting about King Constantine II: 'as you know, has already made some moves. He would probably command more popular support than anybody else.' Kissinger was not persuaded, 'That's dangerous business in the middle of a war. I'll talk to the President about it.'[203]

Callaghan interrupted the meeting at 3.15 pm GMT with news that the European Community did not support the United States' position and that a coup against Ioannidis was expected early next morning. You must try to get a ceasefire today and I will focus on getting talks started said Callaghan. Kissinger agreed. Sisco, continuing to work on both the Greeks and the Turks, had already interrupted the meeting to tell Kissinger that Turkey now wanted the evening to consider the ceasefire; and Kissinger already knew from his own calls that Ecevit wanted a 4.00 pm meeting of his National Security Council and then a 6.00 pm meeting of his Cabinet.

He turned to his colleagues and readied them for a change towards Turkey, which he had resisted since the coup against Makarios. He would threaten to remove nuclear weapons, the very threat President

A young Makarios, who in 1960 combined the roles of president of Cyprus, *ethnarch* and archbishop.

Founder of the Cypriot paramilitary organisations EOKA and EOKA-B, General Georgios Grivas.

Archbishop Makarios III alongside speaker of the Cypriot Parliament and chief negotiator for the Greek Cypriots, Glafcos Ioannou Clerides.

Rauf Raif Denktaş, leader of the Turkish Cypriots.

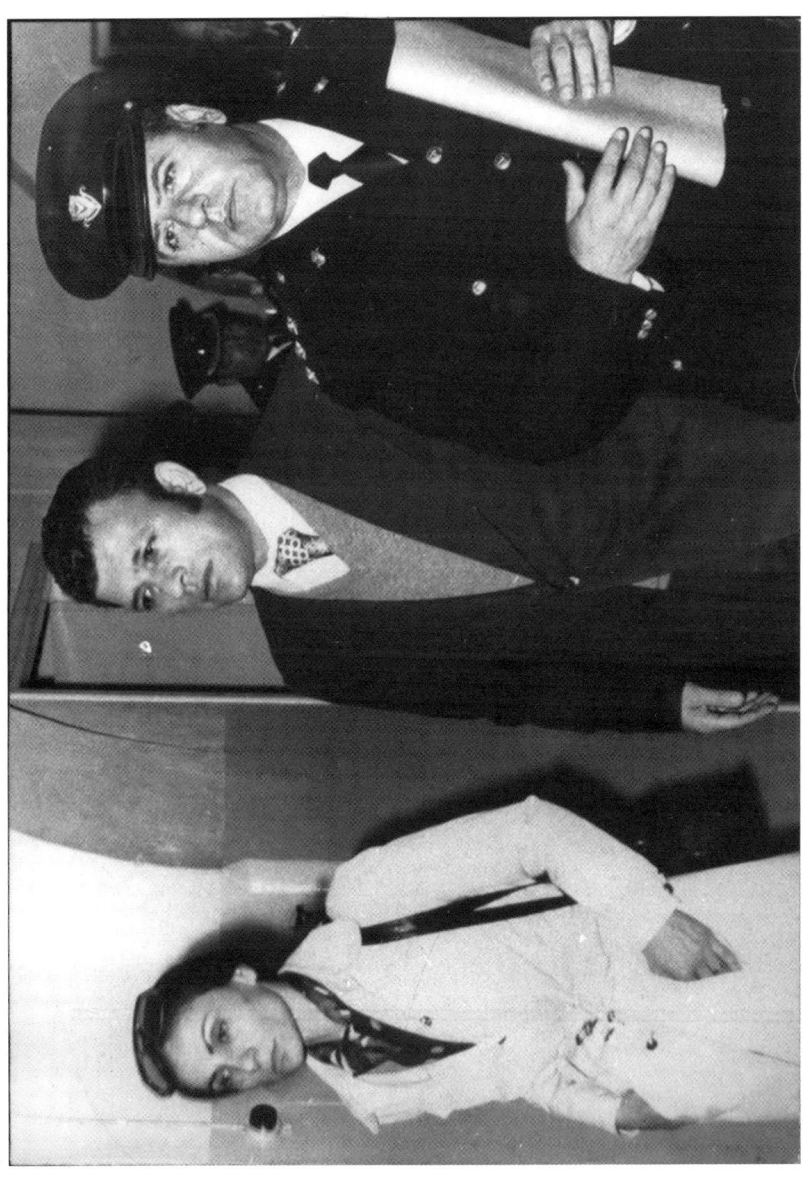

Nikos Sampson who briefly became president of Cyprus after Makarios was deposed during the July 1974 coup.

British Foreign Secretary James Callaghan.

Turkish poet and prime minister, Bülent Ecevit.

Turkish Foreign Minister Turan Güneş.

Foreign ministers James Callaghan, Turan Güneş and George Mavros at the Geneva peace conference.

American Secretary of State Dr Henry Kissinger, American President Richard Milhous Nixon and American Vice President Gerald Rudolph Ford Jr.

Top American diplomat Joe Sisco meeting Turkish Prime Minister Bülent Ecevit in Ankara 1974.

Georgios Papadopoulos, head of the Greek junta from 1967 to 1973.

General Dimitrios Ioannidis, centre, at the trial of the junta in 1975.

Turkish naval ships supporting the landing in Cyprus July 1974.

Turkish soldiers on Cypriot territory 1974.

A Royal Navy Westland helicopter rescuing civilians identifying themselves with a large Union Jack.

Rescued civilians fast filling up the flight deck of HMS *Hermes*.

Constantine Karamanlis who became president of Greece on 24 July 1974.

James Callaghan, Turan Güneş and George Mavros at the second Geneva conference before the arrival of the Cypriot community leaders.

Turkish bombing run of Nicosia, Cyprus.

American President Richard Nixon resigns from office on 8 August 1974.

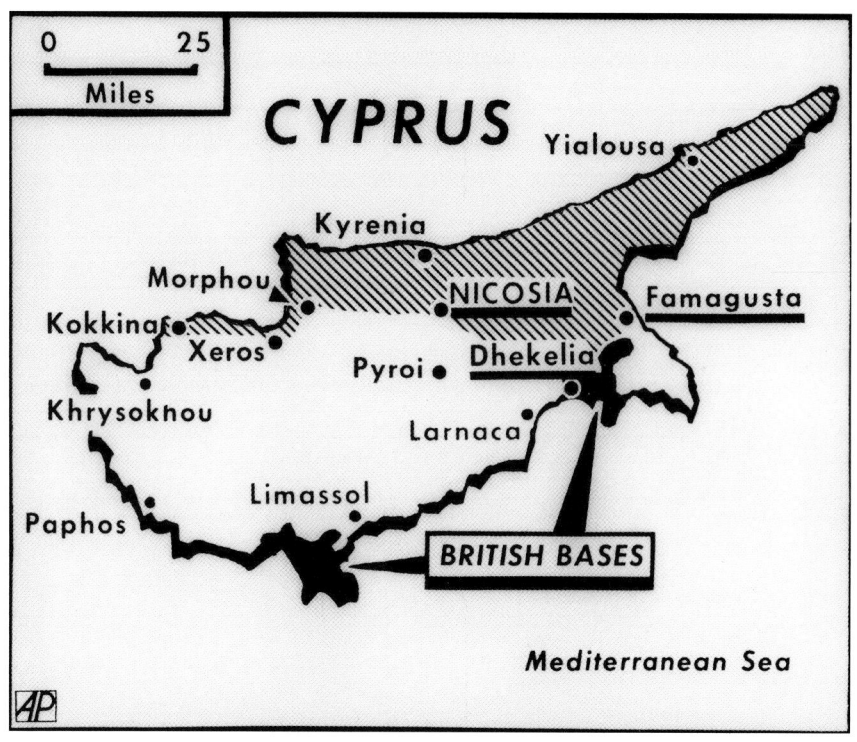

A divided Cyprus after the second Turkish assault on 15 August 1974.

Lyndon Johnson had made ten years earlier. 'I want you all to consider very carefully what we are doing here. I would propose to call Ecevit and insist on a ceasefire. Callaghan and Sisco are going to insist on talks – in Vienna. We don't have any other choice. Are there no objections?' Only William Colby thought this placed Ecevit in an untenable position, and they should give Turkish generals something in exchange. Kissinger disagreed, 'Our policy is to get rid of Sampson. What replaces him is no concern to us. The only issue is whether Makarios or Clerides or somebody else comes in.'[204]

After the meeting finished, Kissinger complained several hours later to the White House chief of staff, General Alexander Haig, about being 'outflanked on the left' and there being a 'massive insurrection in Defense'. He confessed to Haig that 'Al [Alexander], we can never go through another crisis like this. It has been too bad.'[205]

In the evening, Greek military leaders met Ioannidis, against whom they were plotting but not had yet administered the fateful blow, to decide on reinforcements, against a background of another Turkish wave preparing to land in the morning. General Grigorios Bonanos had decided from the time of Turkey's first assault that Greece was not going to war, so the chiefs again thwarted significant reinforcements efforts with excuses about security. Instead, limited measures were given the green light, including that evening's ill-fated commando raid and sending a regiment by car ferry from Piraeus to Cyprus.

However, to the outside world, Greece appeared ready to attack Turkey on the northern border, a ruse that had some effect for the CIA reported that Greek movements in Thrace were complete. Sisco and Kissinger kept working on both countries to get the ceasefire.

Both Kissinger and Callaghan also kept the Soviets informed about developments, without giving away too much detail. This stopped any nervous Soviet over-reaction and kept its interference to calibrated statements by *Pravda* alleging that certain NATO countries 'had practically started on the road towards helping the putschists'.[206] Senior Foreign and Commonwealth Office mandarin John Killick was delighted to brief the Soviet Ambassador Nikolai Lunkov on the day's event: when Lunkov mischievously alleged NATO involvement, Killick recounted how Britain's rescue of the forty-one supposed Soviet tourists would not have been possible without British bases on the island.

Having got President Richard Nixon's approval to threaten Turkey with the removal of nuclear weapons, Kissinger called Prime Minister Bülent Ecevit during mid-afternoon in the United States. Ecevit prevaricated even more when Kissinger first told him about a possible coup in Greece saying replacement leaders for the junta might not observe any agreement. Kissinger then issued his ultimate threat. Although this was as strong as 1967, the punch was cushioned for Turkey now had troops in Cyprus and some form of a sea access though all terribly exposed to counterattack. Ecevit replied, 'Well, that is very important ... Our Chief of General Staff is here. I'll speak with him. We will leave the other subjects and then telephone you say within a half an hour.'[207]

At the same time an emotional Greek foreign minister, Kyprianos, told Callaghan that Turkey is bombing Greek Cypriots and without an immediate ceasefire his country will declare war. Callaghan passed on the warning thirty minutes later when Kissinger told him of the threat made to Ecevit.

Turkish reflection moved in a way Kissinger did not expect for the news of Ioannidis's possible demise reinforced their intention to strengthen the exposed bridgehead in Kyrenia. Ecevit called Callaghan at 3.55 pm GMT to say he was postponing the ceasefire because the Greek colonels might resign and a pro-Soviet government emerge in its place. He accepted the principle of a ceasefire giving Callaghan confidence to think he would eventually accept it but first wanted a Cabinet meeting on Monday morning to discuss procedures. He repeated this message to Kissinger.

Even though Greece and Turkey had accepted the UN resolution, Athens would not attend talks without a ceasefire and Ecevit wanted to agree the process before accepting one. And with an actual ceasefire now unlikely until the next day, Callaghan and Kissinger feared the Greeks might act recklessly.

Sisco kept working on both governments from Athens though getting hold of anyone with remaining authority proved problematic as the Greek government started dissolving. He told British Ambassador Robin Hooper at 5.40 pm GMT that the Turks were stalling, and warned that any British pressure on the Greeks would not help as Athens regarded the United States as their 'only friend' and was 'terrified' it might desert Greece.[208] Kissinger then told Callaghan ten minutes later that if the junta did not agree Ecevit's ceasefire in principle for effect the next day, they must both work on Ecevit again.

With time eroding and no progress, Callaghan told Kissinger at 7.40 pm GMT a ceasefire must be in place by morning to get talks started in Vienna. Tell Ecevit, said Kissinger, who did the same with both governments. They spoke again an hour later at when the American secretary admitted the Greeks were fobbing off Sisco even though Turkey is promising an effective ceasefire tomorrow – and that Athens insists on American not British assurances.

Greece then suffered its own military disaster. Service chiefs had approved Operation Niki, for twenty twin-engine Nord Noratlas military transport planes to fly a commando battalion into the bombed but still functioning Nicosia airport. Delays reduced the Noratlas fleet to fifteen aircraft when taking off around 9.00 pm with two more ducking out with mechanical problems en route. Worse happened when a Cypriot National Guard anti-aircraft battalion at Nicosia airport, unaware of the plan, shot down one plane killing all but one person aboard and damaged another killing two crew before the plane landed. Only nine aircraft made the return flight after offloading the commandos.

When Operation Niki began, Sisco and Hooper were in despair. There was still no ceasefire in place, no confirmation from Ecevit's government and no progress with the Greeks. So poor did prospects seem that Callaghan told his ambassador in Paris efforts for a 'ceasefire seem temporarily at least to have failed'.[209] He and Kissinger, who had now returned home to the temporary residence of wealthy friend Wiley T. Buchanan while looking for a house with newlywed Nancy, worked on a backup plan readying NATO and the European Community to push for a Monday 2.00 pm ceasefire.

Sisco persevered in Athens and was now equipped to make the same threat issued to Turkey that 'in the event of a refusal the US would consider the whole of her relationship in this area'[210] implying aid and nuclear cover. Civilian ministers ignored his calls as did Ioannidis, now having his own problems in holding power, so he worked on the military first with Grigorios Bonanos and Petros Arapakis. The top Greek general looked tired though composed when complaining about the constant movement of proposed ceasefires, four already, implying that he could not hold back his troops without affecting their readiness. This was for effect as Bonanos was not going to issue the order. Sisco, more exhausted than the general, summoned all his diplomatic wiliness to counter the general's suspicion of the United States not controlling Ankara. Petros Arapakis chipped in, rather accurately, saying Turkey did not believe the Greek threat of war but that history proves the opposite, which is why the situation is tragic. In that case, let's stop it being so replied Sisco, who thought he had persuaded Bonanos not to escalate the situation overnight.

A mini drama then played out. At 11.30 pm GMT, Sisco learned that Ecevit agreed to announce a ceasefire at 3.00 am. He had Tasca inform Greek Foreign Minister Constantine Kypriaos who said he would report back but did not, so Sisco tried the Greek prime minister and other ministers who ignored him and eventually contacted Grigorios Bonanos again, who told him not to worry and he could contact ministers in the morning.

Sisco's assistant Bob Oakley then learnt that one of the embassy's local employees was a nephew of Arapakis, who, when asked, took them to his uncle's house in the dark of the night. Sisco briefed the admiral and asked whether the Greek government would announce the ceasefire at 3.00 am for effect at 4.00 pm. Arapakis said he wanted to help and would consult his colleagues.

This consultation proved unhelpful as Prime Minister Adamantios Androutsopoulos thought the Americans were fooling them and General Bonanos wanted to wait until morning as did Foreign Minister Constantine Kypriaos. So, Arapakis took matters into his own hands and telephoned Sisco to say yes. The undersecretary asked whether he spoke for the Greek government and with the agreement of Ioannidis. Arapakis, lying, said yes, but on condition that Kissinger not Turkey made the announcement as they did not trust the Turks.

Not entirely convinced the helpful admiral had authority, Sisco got through to the Greek foreign minister. Can the admiral really speak for Greece given that no one else wanted to speak about the proposal asked Sisco. 'Go ahead',[211] replied Kypriaos. So Sisco did. He and Oakley called the Department of State duty officer to track down Kissinger, now having a Chinese dinner with his wife and Winston and Bette Lord at the Empress Restaurant in Washington. Sisco linked him up on the telephone with Arapakis to ask whether Greece would publicly confirm the ceasefire once made. When Arapakis said that they would after an 8.00 am Cabinet meeting, Kissinger agreed the United States would take the risk of announcing the ceasefire at 6.00 am with the Greek confirmation at 9.00 am for a 4.00 pm start. Arapakis agreed.

Kissinger got Ecevit's agreement, so Sisco called the admiral back at 12.40 am GMT on Monday saying both governments now accepted a ceasefire and the United States was working for full agreement on a 6.00 am, 9.00 am and 4.00 pm sequence. Meanwhile, Joe Sisco worked with Art Hartman and a colleague, James G. Lowenstein, to draft the announcement keeping rigidly to the Security Council formula, which he checked with Petros Arapakis just as Kissinger checked with Ecevit. The admiral gave final agreement at 3.10 am.

Sisco and Kissinger had finally achieved their breakthrough for a ceasefire, even while Greece's limited air reinforcement operation was ending in disaster and Turkey about to land to another wave of troops. Top American official Bob McCloskey issued the press notice in Washington that brought their diplomacy to the first conclusion after forty-eight hours of intensive negotiation:

> The United States Government announces that the Governments of Greece and Turkey agree to the cease-fire as provided in the Security Council resolution of Saturday, July 20 [1974]. This announcement will be confirmed by the Greek and Turkish Governments at 3[.00] AM EDT [Eastern Daylight Time] – 9[.00] AM Athens and 10[.00] AM Ankara time.[212]

Sisco had to wait for the Greek announcement before he could sleep.

Chapter 14

RELIEF: MONDAY, 22 JULY 1974

Early in the morning, Callaghan seized on the momentum and repeated his offer for three-way talks in Vienna at 10.00 am the following day, Tuesday, 23 July 1974. An ever-weakening government in Athens doubted being ready to attend in one day and preferred Geneva. Turkish Foreign Minister Turan Güneş accepted in principle but initially wanted to delay for a day or two before relenting.

Little remained of the Greek commando raid at Nicosia airport. On the runway lay the burnt-out carcases of three aircraft, two through damage and one for lack of fuel blown up by Greek Cypriots on orders from the Greek air force. The British 280 Signals Unit had tracked the doomed Greek reinforcement mission the previous night as it had trespassed on RAF Akrotiri's flight corridor. The operations centre complained to the Greek embassy about the violation and John Aiken also informed the Turkish air commander at İzmir in case the Turks suspected British acquiescence in the operation.

Fighting continued as both sides exploited the remaining hours before the anticipated cessation of hostilities. British soldiers were lucky to escape Turkish fighters dropping napalm bombs on Famagusta that morning, which demolished the Salmina Towers hotel and badly damaged the Golden Marina used by the National Guard. Turkish aircraft strafed a Coldstream Guards patrol car scouring the city for remaining British citizens close to the services' NAAFI club injuring two men, one seriously. The Foreign and Commonwealth Office thought this a genuine mistake and made only a cursory protest to the Turks for the record. Britain flew out badly burnt National Guard officers to Athens for treatment.

High Commissioner Stephen Olver, holed up in Nicosia, observed that 'Somewhat to our surprise, the Greek-Cypriot forces have held their ground and maintained pressure. The general picture is one of Turkish confusion. They have failed to take advantage of their opportunities and have, until this morning, shown no real drive.'[213] And British Ambassador Horace Phillips in Ankara noted, 'Turkey appears to have overestimated their own ability and underestimated their enemy'.[214]

Despite these setbacks Prime Minister Bülent Ecevit, needing to patch over the problems, declared the military objectives achieved. At a press conference he announced, 'the Turkish presence on the island is now irrevocably established' and the 10-mile corridor Kyrenia beachhead to Nicosia 'will be a permanent base of strength for the Turkish people on the island', even though Turkish soldiers were fighting to win control of the coastal city.[215]

Turkey's next landings provided enough force to push through National Guard resistance. Major General Bedrettin Demirel, commanding 39th Infantry Division, arrived with his reinforcements at 9.00 am on Platoni Beach at Kyrenia to survey the situation for himself. Like many fellow officers, he could not fathom why politicians had agreed a ceasefire given exposed Turkish lines and he certainly was not going to observe it until his forces were consolidated. He took command of the beachhead and ordered the tired and demoralised troops landing in the first and second waves, few having slept for two days, to completely take Kyrenia. They broke through to the harbour at noon.

Near to that location, Britain was beginning the third evacuation operation, this time by sea using the Royal Navy, which Stephen Olver and John Aiken had judged least risk given fighting on the roads. Using the *BBC World Service* and the forces' radio network, the Foreign and Commonwealth Office had advised British and foreign civilians to make their way north to Kyrenia for evacuation at dawn. Royal Navy carrier HMS *Andromeda* and frigate HMS *Rhyl* and Royal Fleet Auxiliary vessels were readied for the operation.

Turkish and Greek cooperation was vital. Although Ecevit readily gave his approval, Olver had to negotiate with local Turkish commanders for, as happened many times, whatever politicians in Ankara agreed, the military had their own ideas. Turkish commanders needed time to complete their Kyrenia reinforcement and consolidate their bridgehead before the ceasefire. Without this assurance, London postponed the rescue because of too much fighting – leaving 2,000 British and foreign nationals exposed on Kyrenia beaches – and pushed to try for Turkish agreement the next morning, Tuesday.

In the meantime, RAF Flight Sergeant John 'Taff' Lee and his fellow servicemen worked around the clock on logistics to fly out civilians and service families. A steady pattern had developed with inbound flights from RAF Lyneham delivering essential supplies and reinforcements and returning loaded with evacuees. He and his colleagues had already relinquished their bedrooms and then faced local calamity when the mess ran out of beer, as the shelling of Limassol hit the Cypriot Keo Brewery. Lee asked his wing commander whether RAF Lyneham could send over vital replacement drinks. A Britannia aircraft obliged two days later, 'the army lads (I think it was the [Royal] Anglians) who were dug in along the SBA [sovereign base area] perimeter were very appreciative. My boss did well'.[216]

A Nimrod resumed the search for sailors from the sinking Turkish destroyer with little information about casualties. A nearby Israeli training ship had already picked up forty-two survivors taking them to Tel Aviv. Crew aboard RFA *Gold* soon realised the location they had been given did not account for the Southeastern Mediterranean drift, so a Nimrod and HMS *Andromeda* moved to a new area where they found Turkish tracker aircraft and the Turkish destroyer *Berk* already searching. Survivors were soon spotted. Britain despatched two Sea King helicopters, a Whirlwind from 84 Squadron and two launches from the RAF Akrotiri quayside.

By 5.00 pm they had picked up seventy-two men, some badly burned, transferring them to the base hospital, Princess Mary, at RAF Akrotiri, which was fast filling up with other casualties. John Aiken asked Ankara about survivor numbers to which the Turkish naval command confirmed that sixty were still missing. The British military continued searching until 28 July 1974 only recovering nine bodies.

Ambassador Horace Phillips later asked Bülent Ecevit what to do about the casualties when prompted by Aiken, who brutally wanted them off the British bases before Greek Cypriots discovered their whereabouts. Ecevit confided that Turkey had sunk one of its own ships, which was not yet public, and asked for the survivors to be repatriated. Phillips diplomatically decided not to remind him of British and American assurances about the phantom convoy.

After catching some sleep when Turkey and Greece issued their public agreement to the 4.00 pm ceasefire, Joe Sisco learnt that his next destination was the then planned Vienna peace talks. As he got ready, an embassy resources officer asked to speak with him privately about an internal problem, most likely about conditions under the ambassador. Tasca's embassy had not impressed Sisco with the ambassador, in turn, making clear his disapproval of the undersecretary's presence. Sisco's assistant, Bob Oakley, did not see much of Tasca over the weekend who 'entertained his guests, while Sisco and his delegation ran around Athens looking for any member of the junta to stop the war'.[217] Sisco, who had no idea how bad the situation had been at the embassy, decided that Tasca must go and told Oakley on the overnight plane to Washington – when the Vienna talks were subsequently delayed – they must first find a deputy for continuity and then replace Tasca. When back in Washington, he duly informed Kissinger 'about Tasca's political naivete [naïveté] as well as his behavior [sic]',[218] which the secretary of state, who had come to regard the ambassador as a spokesman for the junta, agreed and started the search for two new senior diplomats.

Tom Boyatt, also back in Washington, began penning his reflection on what had happened and whether the United States could have prevented Turkey's intervention. In an official memorandum he set down 'what I had tried to do, where I had been blocked, what the intelligence community had said and done, what the Defense Department had said and done, what had had [sic] happened'.[219] He also advocated a tough line to keep Turkey inside the Kyrenia bridgehead, 'because if they break, and drive to both coasts, they will divide Cyprus in half, and Greece and Turkey will have another boundary over which they can fight until the end of time'.[220] And he championed a military embargo on both Turkey and Greece, a weapon which Kissinger had threatened but was reluctant to employ fearing the long-term effects on relations with both countries and interference by Congress.

Greek drama dwarfed these matters as military chiefs in Athens moved to defy their paper subordinate, Ioannidis, who had opposed the ceasefire. A powerful field commander, Lieutenant General Ianos Davos, in charge of the third army corps in Thrace and a former chief of staff to the Greek Cypriot National Guard, decided enough was enough. He threatened to intervene in Athens unless the government changed leaders, with support from forty of his officers who petitioned for a return to civilian rule. A German newswire got wind of events fuelling a rumour, briefly reported in American intelligence circles, of a rebellion by Davos in the north.

Davos had certainly issued an ultimatum giving backbone to the Greek military chiefs assembling in Grigorios Bonanos's office in the morning. They finally told Greek President Phaedon Gizikis, himself an Ioannidis appointee and a general, that things could not go on and that a new civilian government must be formed. Ioannidis learnt about the meeting and made his way over to tell them they were all wrong and they must stop the second Turkish landing.

This provided the moment to take back control. Chief of the Greek air force Alexandros Papanikolaou declared, 'In the name of my country and my children, I don't accept here a decision on such an important matter by a subordinate of ours. We must not accept it.' Ioannidis slammed the table and said menacingly, 'It seems that General Papanikalaou doesn't know me'. Papanikalaou shot back quickly, 'It is clear that you don't know me. If you think you can act, then remember, General, that I also have the means to act'.[221] President Phaedon Gizikis, who realised the time had come for a new government, tried calming tempers.

Faced with a united front Ioannidis had no option but to acquiesce. He went off screaming, later telling his followers of betrayal by the organs of government and that 'We have been betrayed in Cyprus and now here.'[222] By 1.00 pm, even before the ceasefire had started, civilian leaders were invited to Athens to discuss a new government. Ioannidis did not go quickly though for he was not dismissed, and his well-placed military followers did their best to have reinforcements sent to Cyprus, which Grigorios Bonanos had to rescind; the commandeered car ferry filled with commandos en route to Cyprus was diverted.

In expectation of the afternoon ceasefire, Jim Callaghan told the British Cabinet he did not know where this left Makarios vis-à-vis the Greeks, Turks and Cypriots and whether Clerides might now be appointed, though he would forge ahead with negotiations. He diplomatically noted how the 'Americans had been slow to appreciate the prime importance of the situation in Cyprus itself'[223] and were preoccupied with keeping Greece in NATO, though they had worked closely to get the ceasefire. From his perspective, the United States had the power to bring Greece and Turkey around, which, as Kissinger and Sisco sharply discovered, was far from true.

Guns did not stop when the ceasefire took effect but Greece and Turkey loosely complied to their commitments, having assented to talks, which all agreed should now be held in Geneva. Turkey had pulled off an incredibly risky sea and air landing overcoming the constraints of a small beach area and the bisection of their forces by a mountain to establish a secure bridgehead and connect with their paratroopers. Greek and Greek-Cypriot soldiers without any air cover and limited artillery support had surprised them with tenacity, denying them many tactical positions most notably Nicosia airport; though ultimately the National Guard could not defeat a larger, well-armed and coordinated force. Even the coupist and now Cypriot President Nikos Sampson, who had started the day expecting Greek reinforcements and intending to declare *enosis*, broadcast on the radio for all Greek Cypriots to respect the ceasefire.

Prime Minister Bülent Ecevit proclaimed the establishment of a permanent presence contributing to an overall solution in Cyprus. Making peace would be hard he said and accused the Greek Cypriots of genocide in Famagusta, Chatos, Kokkina and Paphos. In answering journalists' questions, he credited the United States' role while denying Washington strong-arm tactics had forced his hand. Instead, he noted the United States had 'contributed greatly to establishment of a cease-fire [sic]'[224] and thanked Britain and the UN, comments that were again misinterpreted by suspicious Greeks as evidence of collusion between Washington and Turkey.

Ecevit also complained to Callaghan about the alleged atrocities in overrun enclaves. Both sides made accusations with old scores settled and new ones made: UNFICYP had the mandate to separate fighting between Cypriot communities but not the manpower to cover the whole island and had lost the trust of Ankara. The United States had no information of mass executions though did not rule out executions of individuals – and UNFICYP investigators claimed to see find no evidence even though people from both sides were disappearing.

Meanwhile, Henry Kissinger prepared for the following day's negotiation in Geneva and his first meeting with the deposed Makarios that afternoon when chairing the Special Actions Group mid-morning in Washington.

He continued resisting any military embargo on Greece apart from fighter aircraft as he did not want its isolated and wounded leaders, whoever they were, 'to feel that we have contributed to their rape'. And he still prevaricated over Makarios until outcomes were clearer: 'I want to make it clear that we are not disassociating ourselves from Makarios, but by the same token, we have no incentive to push him. We'll wait to see what emerges from the negotiations.' From his perspective, war between two NATO countries had been averted, Greece remained in the alliance and the Soviet Union had been unable to exert any influence which would be noted in the Arab world. In these calmer waters, he thought this 'has been a well-coordinated and well-run crisis. I want to congratulate you all', little knowing worse was to come.[225]

He then called Jim Callaghan, who was in the House of Commons, over a crackling telephone line at 3.25 pm GMT about how to handle Makarios. British practicality gently clashed with American grand strategy as Kissinger said he would 'be non-committal though he would be friendly' towards the archbishop. 'Don't be too cool', stressed Callaghan, 'You must recognize, he's the legitimate President until any other arrangements are made' and avoid becoming isolated for not supporting him – and be 'absolutely filthy to Sampson'.[226] Kissinger, who was more than happy to see Sampson gone, preferred a slower route to see who emerged before backing any horse. (They also agreed to postpone the Geneva talks until Wednesday given what they thought, mistakenly, might be a possible coup by Ianos Davos in Greece.)

Another telephone call between them at 4.00 pm GMT highlighted this continuing difference when Kissinger said he did not want Sampson but before turning on him wanted to see the general package. He would keep Makarios in play but not go overboard. Callaghan, by contrast, thought Sampson should be replaced by Clerides as a temporary solution until elections were held with Makarios having chance to stand. Kissinger, full of caution, said he supported the procedure and probably the outcome causing Callaghan's retort that he expected support for both.

This time Kissinger decided to send out Bill Buffum, a career official and head of the Department of State's UN section who had earned his spurs in Lebanon surviving several assassination attempts, as observer to Callaghan's talks. Sisco, having had his fill of excitement and danger, preferred Washington.

Turks and Greeks continued making minor movements, the Turks particularly trying to grab the airport and stop further Greek reinforcement. Their assault imperilled the nearby UNFICYP camp, from where John Aiken had already removed the RAF from its residual responsibilities annoying Brigadier Frank Henn, commanding the British contingent of UN troops, who thought this exposed his soldiers to any Turkish assault. By good fortune, the Whirlwind helicopters of 84 Squadron assigned to UNFICYP had already moved to another UN camp three quarters of a mile away, avoiding a subsequent direct hit by Turkish aircraft on the squadron hanger.

Callaghan raised Turkey's actions with Kissinger at 5.15 pm GMT asking him to warn Ecevit, whom he could not raise, against bombing the UNFICYP camp. The foreign secretary, bullish and passionate in having to deal with reality on the ground, declared that if 'this happened we (the British) would stop them',[227] irritating Kissinger who privately derided such sabre rattling.

As UN peacekeepers dug in around the airport, the United States evacuated their remaining nationals, including archaeologists working in Kyrenia and 150 CIA staff of the Foreign Broadcast Information Service who intercepted messages in the Middle East, and, obligingly, eighty stranded Lebanese citizens. They were all escorted by the UN to RAF Dhekelia, helicopters then taking them to the waiting task force for transfer to Beirut. No one was shot or harassed apart from assaults by sandflies on a miserable night on the beach waiting to be flown out.

American political officer James Williams decided not to ship out his 4-year-old son, Ben, and his expecting wife, Ann, for fear of miscarriage – her obstetrician ruling out the rough trip to the RAF base. Ambassador Rodger Davies reluctantly agreed on condition they take a guest room in the embassy residence as no other diplomats' families had stayed and, for safety, he did not want them staying in their own home. Williams walked up the five flights of stairs whenever he could, seeing Ben enjoy this big adventure shooting at overflying planes with a bow and arrow – with Ann, annoyed about having to leave her house, confined to bed.

In the calm of Washington, much publicity surrounded the arrival of Makarios to the capital with the Department of State tiptoeing around whether he was being received as president, archbishop or a private citizen. British Ambassador Peter Ramsbottom met him in the morning when Makarios handed over a six-point solution for Cyprus, which included proposals for outlawing the National Guard and retaining the permitted Greek and Turkish contingents alongside a mixed force of UN military police. Ramsbottom thought these points sensible though doubted whether an international police force could protect Turkish Cypriots.

Henry Kissinger then greeted him outside the Department of State amid vociferous supporters for an hour-long meeting in which he found the archbishop impressive, though naïve in thinking Washington had the ability to force Turkey and Greece to restore him or that the United States would act under pressure.

Makarios told him the United States had caused the mess either through what it did or failed to do. Kissinger admitted the United States had suspicions about a coup but not when this might happen, and explained American efforts to stop Turkish intervention. Makarios then presented his six-point plan and posited that Kissinger wanted him to stay away for the time being, which the secretary quickly denied, saying he wanted the Cypriots to work it out themselves. We do not oppose you, Kissinger told him. To which the archbishop protested this was not enough for he needed American support to return. That depends on who else you ask, said Kissinger, cautioning him against going to the Soviets.

A worldly archbishop played the game when afterwards appearing before the world's press with Kissinger. He said that the secretary of state assured him that he favoured the return of constitutional order. When asked by a reporter whether this meant restoring him to office, he replied carefully that the consequences of constitutional order were fully understood.

Joe Sisco, thinking his mission done in Athens, sat on Washington-bound aircraft that started taxiing to the runway before suddenly turning around. Tasca had called him back because Prime Minister Adamantios Androutsopoulos demanded to speak with him about continued Turkish advances. Sisco tried reassuring the prime minister from an airport telephone that such incidents might be expected and he would have Washington check the situation, and would personally speak to the UN secretary general – and even gave Androutsopoulos his personal number.

Ambassador Henry Tasca subsequently met with the prime minister and foreign minister to assuage their anger by offering further assurances. When back at the embassy he pushed Washington to get full Turkish observance. Kissinger duly impressed this on Ecevit but Turkish generals on the ground had other ideas.

London instructed John Aiken at 7.15 pm to proceed with the delayed naval rescue at dawn the next day despite the continued absence of Turkish consent and dispatched HMS *Hermes* and HMS *Devonshire* to boost the flotilla. Callaghan told his diplomats to make sure Ankara got the message not to interfere and 'indeed, we expect their support for it'.[228] Still no reassuring message came from the Turkish military, so as a precaution London told Aiken to fly combat aircraft over the very area Turkey had declared as a danger zone. Back in Washington, Kissinger compared notes about Makarios with British Ambassador Peter Ramsbottom without changing his opinion.

> We do not mind jettisoning Sampson, but not before we know who will take his place ... I object to him [Makarios] because he is ambitious, able and strong; with the present balance of forces in Cyprus he must get the Turks out, and this can only be done with Soviet help.[229]

Ramsbottom protested, 'I think you are wrong on that. I hold no brief for him; indeed, he has caused the UK a lot more difficulties than he has the United States, but he has handled that lot on Cyprus successfully for 14 years without outsiders like the Russians coming in'. Unmoved, Kissinger kept his options open saying that he wanted to see how the balance of forces developed following the 'excellent British example of the 19th century'.[230]

Early rumours of a coup by Ianos Davos evaporated by the end of the day in Athens as had the Greek threat to pull out of NATO. Prime Minister Adamantios Androutsopoulos was still in post and Britain thought the current junta shaky but capable of governing. Nonetheless, young King Constantine II sensing his moment arriving issued a statement from London denying that he would return to power as the result of yet another coup, while secretly hoping for that very return, all a forlorn expectation.

Rumours about a coup were not unfounded, however, as later that night Ambassador Henry Tasca met with the Greek generals who had now effectively sidelined Ioannidis and wanted to form a new government. At their request, Tasca telephoned Kissinger with them all sitting in President Phaedon Gizikis's office wanting the secretary's assurance that American-Greek relations remained intact and for him to urge Turkey to show the greatest restraint. Kissinger gave them the necessary undertakings setting the scene for the next act.

Chapter 15

GREEK FALL: TUESDAY, 23 JULY 1974

Skirmishes continued overnight with Turkey strengthening control of the road from Kyrenia to Nicosia, trying to seize Nicosia airport and sort out some pockets of resistance. Both sides took care not to escalate enough to break the ceasefire convincingly.

Continued fighting created dilemmas for Britain's morning naval rescue with a Royal Navy frigate sent to a well-known Kyrenia beach where the *BBC World Service* had told people to gather. John Aiken's staff woke him at 2.05 am to say the Turkish military had not yet approved the dawn operation and refused to accept responsibility for any ship that entered what they called an 'advertised, forbidden and dangerous zone'; and, equally, the Cypriot National Guard said they could not guarantee the operation's safety.

Jim Callaghan had Ambassador Horace Phillips obtain Prime Minister Bülent Ecevit's personal assurance. At 2.00 am in Ankara, Phillips duly visited Ecevit's town apartment escorted by a guard. Ecevit's wife, awakened by the call, answered the door, recognised the ambassador and brushed aside his apologies saying that an important matter must be at stake. Despite Phillips offering to wait, she insisted on waking her husband who had returned from his office only two hours earlier. 'She invited me in and went to rouse him. After a short time Mr [Bülent] Ecevit appeared, wide awake, freshly dressed and spruce, he greeted me affably and assured me there was no need for apologies at so critical a juncture for our two governments.'[231]

When Phillips informed him of the operation, Ecevit said, 'He perfectly understood London's concern over the evacuation of its citizens and lifted the telephone there and then to waken the chief of the defence staff and ask him to instruct all Turkish units in the area appropriately'.[232] However, not knowing about the operation himself and with his government plagued by continued poor communication, he also advised Phillips to postpone by a day.

Delay, however, that exposed vulnerable civilians to more danger was not an option so an hour later John Aiken made the call. He told them to carry on and review the situation with him at 4.00 am. Callaghan sent Ecevit a personal message saying the rescue was on and he expected the full cooperation from Turkey and would them to account for any incident involving Turkish forces.

Against the odds with no confirmation received from the Turkish military, Aiken consulted his naval and air force commanders and decided to proceed despite protests from Ambassador Horace Phillips in Ankara. He instructed the task force to move 2 miles off Kyrenia and reconnoitre the beach; and then, if clear, proceed to the port with the biggest Union Jacks hanging over the side of the ships and extra ensigns. He advised the Royal Navy, 'appreciate considerable risks are entailed in operation and must exercise care and restraint but mercy mission has highest priority. Kyrenia is most touchy and decision to start there must be weighed most carefully depending on situation.'[233]

Turkish aircraft spotted over Kyrenia forty minutes later did not deter Aiken who had sent out the defence rules of engagement to the task force: Lightning patrol aircraft should only be summoned if actively threatened and they must engage only when a foreign aircraft had committed a hostile act directly on British forces.

London and the base operations centre girded their loins. Ambassador Horace Phillips repeated his warning to the Turks at 5.50 am. Ecevit, getting up to speed, still wanted a delay, but it was too late. Two Wasps and a Wessex helicopter took off from HMS *Devonshire* to begin their reconnaissance mission making contact at Kyrenia with UN contact Major Gill, a British Army Air Corps officer, and flew him to HMS *Hermes*, where he briefed the task force commander, Captain Cecil Robert Peter Charles Branson. Aiken warned Branson at 6.45 am: 'You should know that gloomy noises keep coming from Ankara to the effect that the Turks are not ready for us to begin. Your operation has strong support at highest level in London. We are gritting our teeth: you play it cool.'[234]

Aiken also used his interim communications method, a Vulcan aircraft relaying messages to the Turkish military through the United States Air Force station in Adana, to send the Turks another warning. Down that same line Turkish High Command replied that 'unless the operation was called off, Turkish authorities would take appropriate action'.[235] This worried Aiken enough to suspend the helicopter evacuation, move all ships 23 miles off of Kyrenia and ask the chief of defence staff Mike Carver in London for help.

Several replies were rattled off to the Turks with Aiken sending personal messages to the Turkish general staff urging them not to interfere with a humanitarian operation: 'Please inform Turkish tactical commanders that I rely on them to ensure that these British ships are not in any way harmed whilst on this mission of mercy. I do not want to have to take the decision to order my air force to protect these vessels against attack from a NATO ally.'[236] High Commissioner Stephen Olver did the same in softer language: 'People in distress and in need of medical attention. Proceeding. Kindly do not interfere in this purely humanitarian operation. 2,500 people of all nations known to need my help.'[237] Vice chief of the defence staff, Peter de Lacy Le Cheminant, sent the Turkish chief of the general staff Semih Sancar, whom he knew personally, a gently ironic missive:

> I am assuming that this message (the Turkish order to hold off) was signed at low level without your knowledge or approval. CBFNE is proceeding with the operation. Grateful for your urgent instructions to your commanders that the operation is not to be interfered with.[238]

Placing all his faith in the replies, Aiken ordered the evacuation to continue at 7.25 am with HMS *Andromeda* moving close to Kyrenia. Helicopters picked up civilians from the nearby Six Mile Beach and both helicopters and landing craft collected people from the port town itself. HMS *Rhyl* did the same further west, with HMS *Hermes* and RFA *Olna* close to Kyrenia in support. An inspiring view of flag waving British naval ships lined up to rescue exhausted though heartened civilians.

Turkish authorities interrupted this exhilaration with a sudden message insisting that one ship, HMS *Devonshire*, leave the area immediately, which a strong-willed captain ignored and continued to rescue citizens along the shoreline. For good measure, he had the ship's radio operators regularly issue a weapons free signal on the open frequency for a 20-mile radius to any approaching vessels.

Tension also affected the situation on land. A rogue Turkish tank drove up the harbour at 11.05 am with its commander threatening to shoot everyone in sight and at the anchored ships if he were stopped from entering the old fort where he believed there was a National Guard tank. UN officers resolved the situation, but HMS *Hermes* and RFA *Olna* were moved back towards Six Mile Beach as a precaution.

With 800 people airlifted by noon, evacuation in the east finished first. The operation in the west continued against a silhouette of fighting. HMS *Devonshire* had collected another group of so-called 'Russians', who turned out to be a Ukrainian folk-dancing group causing much debate at the operations centre about whether to let them aboard a Royal Naval ship. This reservation was overcome on condition they always remain on the flight deck before being handed over to a Soviet ship in Limassol, and which resulted in morale boosting displays of dancing given for beleaguered civilians on the journey back. HMS *Hermes* and HMS *Rhyl* swept the coastline at the end of the operation for any stragglers waving Union Jacks from the shoreline.

As the British task force returned to port, a Turkish naval force approached from the north-east towards Kyrenia causing Aiken to have them turn west for safety. When HMS *Hermes* attempted to make contact, the Turkish force appeared surprised to find British ships present and itself turned quickly northwards.

By the operation's close, 1,522 tired and hungry civilians of 23 nationalities were rescued by the 5 ships. Radio operators aboard the vessels blistered their hands sending some 400 telegrams a day to inform relatives and friends of safe arrivals. Even Athens asked if Aiken could rescue some stranded families of National Guard officers from Kyrenia: thankfully he was saved from this dilemma, as the force was already well on the way back to Akrotiri when the request was received.

Then another signal followed, this one from Ambassador Horace Phillips in Ankara still insisting the operation be postponed for forty-eight hours. Instead of replying, John Aiken sent a note of appreciation to the Turkish military on a completed effort without casualties, 'Many thanks for your co-operation in facilitating a conduct of life-saving naval evacuation North Cyprus coast today. It has been a complete success and up to 2,000 innocent people have been evacuated.'[239]

While this rescue operation was underway, a similarly successful political operation unfolded in Greece and Cyprus changing leaders in both countries. A weakening hold by Athens spelled the end of Nikos Sampson whose Cabinet decided to appoint, seemingly with his acquiescence, Glafcos Clerides, the speaker of the Cypriot Parliament, as acting president. Cyprus radio announced this appointment late morning causing some reflection in Washington and London on what basis this happened, who supported Clerides and whether he could carry Athens or Turkey.

Makarios quickly stamped his authority on the development telling Clerides, 'I have just heard the news that Sampson has resigned and you have assumed the duties of acting president according to the constitution. Until I return to Cyprus, you shall preside over my council of ministers.'[240] The old president wanted to make clear who was in charge and that he was passing power to his deputy for a limited period only.

Clerides, the chief negotiator in the intercommunal talks since 1968 and co-leader of a political party, the centre-right Unified Party, had clout with politicians and businessmen but did not boast the political sway Makarios had over the island. For this moderate man, a London trained barrister and former wartime RAF pilot, had to balance the Sampson type extremists, the centre and the left without the same authority Makarios had enjoyed in the 1960 London-Zürich talks. Threats surrounded him: Makarios's supporters criticised him for being sworn in by the very bishop, Bishop Yennadios, whom Makarios had defrocked in 1973 and were suspicious when he stayed in contact with the coup perpetrators.

Clerides, therefore, moved cautiously retaining nearly all of Sampson's ministers. He also set himself up against his undeclared political rival Makarios, announcing that he did not see himself as a caretaker president, advised that the archbishop should not return in current circumstances and the UN should decide who spoke for Cyprus. But bold words that he would not act on the orders of anyone, implying Makarios, soon found boundaries.

Ankara welcomed the appointment of this political moderate though Ecevit, who now had his eyes firmly set on a changed political status for Turkish Cypriots, had doubts. He bashed out a note to Henry Kissinger on his own typewriter in front of the summoned Ambassador Bill Macomber saying that Clerides had still followed the previous Makarios policy of Greek-Cypriot domination. The fact was Turkey wanted a political change and federation in some form, which made the post holder of president a side issue.

In Athens, Greek generals began their political operation to install a civilian government in a white coup, one without force, that simply sucked power away from Ioannidis. Heads of the air force Alexandros Papanicolaou, navy Petros Arapakis and the army head Andreas Galatsanos met with Grigorios Bonanos and agreed the transition to civilian authority. They then all met with President Phaedon Gizikis to break the news to the brigadier general who was duly summoned. Ioannidis protested but recognising his obvious lack of power over the last twenty-hours and faced with another united front reluctantly agreed to withdraw and requested a two-day leave of absence from the head of the army, nominally his boss. He received such permission on condition he did not cause trouble in the army, which he agreed allowing him to fade into the background.

His removal paved the way for an early afternoon meeting without precedent in Greek history when the generals under President Phaedon Gizikis summoned a glitter of political leaders previously exiled or imprisoned, except from the extreme left, to decide who should form a civilian government. Four former prime ministers attended, including intellectual Panayiotis Kanellopoulos, the caretaker prime minister deposed by the junta in 1967, and a collection of former ministers, including George Mavros, head of the EDEK, whom the junta had exiled for a short period, and former foreign minister, Evangelos Averoff.

Gizikis assured them that Ioannidis had been dismissed and the military would return to barracks, which facilitated nearly four hours of discussion about a successor. Tasca monitored the situation and thought the runes foretold a Panayotis Kanellopoulos premiership. His assessment was correct as the attendees agreed on Kanellopoulos and set a confirmation meeting for 8.00 pm. However, prominent politician Averoff had other ideas and stayed behind to convince Arapakis and the other generals that conservative elder statesman sitting in Paris, Konstantinos Karamanlis, possibly the most respected political figure in Greece, was the man to get them out of their mess. They consented, revoked their earlier decision and Averoff made the call to Karamanlis.

Although Washington had been slow to recognise his appeal, Karamanlis was a man who was ready, having kept in touch with events. He reached an understanding with the Greek generals by telephone giving them immunity from any future prosecution in return for their support.

British Ambassador Robin Hooper kept Jim Callaghan informed about the drama in Athens as the foreign secretary and his diplomats examined how to manage the next day's peace talks. They eventually decided the conference should let the Turks and Greeks get their grievances off their chests, make the ceasefire stick and agree procedures for a follow-on conference. The 1960 arrangements were, they realised, a dead duck and 'practicability and acceptability'[241] should be the order of the day, which rubbed up against the ideas of Makarios, who was the unresolvable dilemma simultaneously holding both the key and creating a stumbling block to a long-term solution; and whom, they assumed, Kissinger wanted gone.

With expectations of a return to a civilian rule in Greece, Callaghan wanted the talks to proceed whether Athens was ready or not to attend as he thought it better to work on the Turks and stop further Greek humiliation. Prime Minister Bülent Ecevit agreed and said Foreign Minister Turan Güneş would attend regardless but neither he nor Callaghan had consulted Kissinger about only the Turks turning up.

In Cyprus, the immediate concerns of new Acting President Glafcos Clerides during the afternoon was a report of Turkish heavy armour getting ready for another dawn offensive. He quickly appealed to the United States and Athens for help. Two old political hands in Athens, Mavros and Kanellopoulos, telephoned Kissinger, introduced themselves as the new government and complained about the imminent Turkish attack. The secretary passed the message as fact, not threat, to Ecevit who dismissed any intention of a fresh assault. Turkish commanders were not preparing any major transgression but they did push ahead to achieve phase one objectives, including an assault to seize the airport, but without realising UNFICYP had taken control with National Guard forces close by.

Turkey's continued violations also put American Ambassador Henry Tasca in a tough spot, for there was a limit to how many times he could urge patience on fretting Greeks. He became even more unpopular in the Department of State, acting alone to advocate the Sixth Fleet cordon off the island, contacting NATO, contacting ambassadorial contacts in France, Germany and Britain and even had his staff bypass the standard departmental machinery to solicit help through the Pentagon's National Military Command Centre. These activities enraged Kissinger and astounded fellow diplomats who were trying to restrain Turkey without losing the confidence of either Ankara or Athens.

Tasca was already on his way out without knowing it, Kissinger having already chosen a deputy ambassador to sideline Tasca in Athens before a new ambassador took over. Monteagle Stearns, known as 'Monty', a career officer from a New England family whose forebears had started an upmarket department store and who had previously worked for the secretary over Vietnam, was the nomination. The secretary of state spotted his name on a list of prospective candidates and was delighted to discover 'his Indochina man'[242] spoke Greek. No one else was needed. Stearns had also served in Athens in the 1950s when he ended up marrying the ambassador's daughter Toni Riddleburger – a rumour at the time was that rather than transfer Stearns, the Department of State kept him on and transferred the ambassador instead And not only had Stearns formed a close relationship with left-leaning Andreas Papandreou, son of the former Greek prime minister, Georgios Papandreou, his wife, Toni, once babysat for Andreas.

Stearns was enjoying a family holiday in Cape Cod when the Department of State telephoned twice. One caller told him to get to Washington on a Vietnam issue, the second said Kissinger wanted him back pronto for another reason. Stearns protested saying he had another week of holiday left. No chance came the reply, Kissinger wanted him in another country within a week. Learning about his new appointment in Washington, Stearns felt uncomfortable about bypassing Tasca when the ambassador did not know about his own demise. Kissinger told him not to worry and that he would liaise through a back channel causing further protest, 'Mr Secretary, it won't work if we have two embassies'.[243] Kissinger assured him he had consulted President Richard Nixon, so Stearns agreed. He broke the news delicately to Toni as they had both expected a desk job in Washington for three years and now had to shift the family to another foreign destination.

Karamanlis prepared to fly out from Paris that evening causing speculation to flood the evening streets of Athens about the junta's demise. Hopes were confirmed when President Phaedon Gizikis publicly announced the end of military rule at 7.15 pm leading to the immediate restoration of a free press. Crowds thronged Constitution Square shouting 'Tonight fascism dies!', 'No more blood' and 'Hang Ioannidis' with one person telling *The New York Times*, 'For the first time we can thank the Turks for something'.[244] Police commanders scolded their officers for being too friendly with the crowds and reminded them to concentrate on moving people away from government buildings. The British defence attaché reported champagne flowing around the city and Robin Hooper described the atmosphere as Greece having won the World Cup.

Greeks in the street did not notice that Ioannidis was neither removed nor arrested but retained his position as head of the military police, with, for the time being, other members of the junta retaining theirs. Grigorios Bonanos and his fellow armed forces chiefs even told Ioannidis of developments to make sure his network of loyal officers did not cause trouble.

Washington welcomed the idea of Karamanlis for his pro-Western credentials while realising there were bridges to build with the man largely snubbed during his Paris exile and his ministers likely to be 'critical of our failure to dissociate ourselves from the Papadopoulos and Ioannidis regimes'.[245] Turkey cautiously welcomed him and his new Defence Minister (former foreign minister) Evangelos Averoff, men known well to them not the least as negotiators of the 1960 Cyprus independence arrangements. King Constantine II again thought the elder statesman's return augured well for him personally and telephoned around to win allies, meeting with Harold Wilson and Jim Callaghan at Downing Street and talking with Karamanlis, leading him to dream naïvely of a royal restoration.

Prospects of a Greek civilian government also affected London's outlook. Wilson's minority government with a perennial eye to another general election and mindful of the influential British-Greek voice in the Labour Party, had to appear protective of this nascent Greek civilian government from another coup or further humiliation. As Callaghan saw the situation, 'With the arrival of a democratic government in Greece, British policy acquired a new element. It was important for the Greek people and for international relations that Greek democracy should be strengthened.'[246]

Henry Kissinger felt satisfaction at the fall of Ioannidis without American interference when he reviewed developments in the afternoon with his senior diplomats: 'If we had overthrown that government last week, we would be in deep trouble. There would have been no restraints on Turkey. We would have been blamed in Greece. This government fell on the basis of its own incompetence.'[247]

Such satisfaction was offset by worries that Greece would turn left in his balance of power prism. Kissinger feared that Karamanlis would have to rely on the left as the right was downtrodden, which made the Mediterranean ever more fragile for NATO with the prospect of Turkey turning rogue and similar worries about Portugal and even Spain where an aging Francisco Franco neared his end. He, therefore, wanted matters to settle and to understand the position of the new Greek prime minister towards the archbishop and Cyprus. Senior aide Bob McCloskey thought 'Karamanlis will be more receptive to Makarios initially. We may have to think differently about Makarios.' This did not disturb Kissinger, who replied 'If that's the case, that's it, but let's not rush in'.[248]

Callaghan's decision to start talks in Geneva with or without Greeks very much seemed to be rushing in and set Kissinger's pulse racing when Joe Sisco, now in Washington, told him of the plan. 'Get me Peter Ramsbottom on the phone', he snapped, seconds later telling the British ambassador that we will hold off recognising Clerides and would like you to do the same. In a second call, he told Ramsbottom that under

no circumstance will we support a conference on Cyprus without the Greeks, and we will have no one there under such conditions. Let us separate two problems: (a) we strongly support a conference on Cyprus with Greek representation; (b) you cannot count on our support for a conference which excludes the Greeks. The day after a *coup d'état* is not the day you should have a conference.[249]

Such was his worry about one-sided talks that Kissinger even telephoned Callaghan's private secretary, Michael Alexander, insisting Greece be given forty-eight hours saying he did not fear any imminent Turkish action. And later dictated a note for the foreign secretary. As far as he was concerned,

> It will look like the raping of the Greeks and will only reinforce the myth of a US-UK-Turkish rape of Greece. It would undermine any civilian group coming to power in Greece. We made no move without checking it with the British. We are astonished at this decision and we think it is a horrible idea. In sum, until we have official word from the Greeks, there will be no US representative in Geneva.[250]

Sisco blamed Callaghan for this difference of approach between London and Washington:

> This is an attempted pre-emptive move by Callaghan. He wants to display assertive leadership. He says he has Parliament behind him and he thinks he can force the Greek hand. He is mistaken. The UK could play such a leadership role only if they maintain their credibility with the Greeks and the Turks.[251]

Kissinger anyway decided that

> We cannot impose Clerides or, for that matter, back Makarios before the Turks and the Greeks have either acquiesced to Makarios or decide to oppose Makarios. If both the Turks and Greeks acquiesce to Makarios, it is okay. If both oppose Makarios, then we should go for Clerides. What we cannot have is a conference between the UK and Turkey opting for Makarios. The Greek Government could then blame it on us.[252]

Larry Eagleburger disappeared to repeat the message to Alexander, returning a few minutes later to say he gave them hell, convincing Britain to postpone the conference for twenty-four hours if Athens had not agreed by the evening.

In Cyprus, Turkish soldiers continued to move on Nicosia airport from the north-west causing General Dewan Prem Chand to strengthen UNFICYP forces as a deterrent. UN Secretary General Kurt Waldheim appealed to Prime Minister Bülent Ecevit who said that his military had strict instructions not to contest UNFICYP's control of the airport only to prevent Greek reinforcements. A concerned Acting President Glafcos Clerides still ordered the National Guard to take up position around the airport, which created confusion as Greek diplomats in Cyprus feared that UNFICYP had surrendered the airport to attacking Turkish forces.

High Commissioner Stephen Olver reassured them at 8.35 pm this was not so. Chand reinforced this message late at night announcing that 'UNFICYP has taken over the Nicosia International Airport temporarily, after a new and earlier breach of the ceasefire earlier this morning in the vicinity of the airport. The airport thus becomes a United Nations internationally protected area.'[253]

By the close of the day a fall of two governments – one in Cyprus and one in Athens – had not deterred Turkish generals from achieving phase one of the ground operation. They may have kept Ecevit in the dark about falling behind plan though there was no division about the principal objective: Turkish troops were there to stay. And Ecevit was not overly concerned about violations as he was about starting the talks to maximise Turkey's new bargaining power.

New regimes in the Greek speaking world did, however, mark one significant development for Ecevit, as Western opinion now began transferring sympathy from the Turks to a new civilian government in Athens.

Chapter 16

KARAMANLIS RETURNS: WEDNESDAY, 24 JULY 1974

A relatively quiet night passed to the fifth day until sunrise saw the Turks consolidate their positions with territorial incursions between Kyrenia and Nicosia. Greek-Cypriot forces dug in as best they could.

Konstantinos Karamanlis flew back to Greece early that morning in the French presidential jet for a welcome by massed crowds. Thousands, many with white candles signifying the resurrection of Christ, lined the streets throwing flowers on his passing car from the airport to the Greek Parliament. Then, standing adjacent to President Phaedon Gizikis, who wore his distinguishable dark-lensed glasses, and surrounded by hundreds of jostling onlookers, he was sworn in by Archbishop Seraphim at 4.15 am. New Prime Minister Karamanlis told the Greek people that he was here to contribute with all his forces to return the country to normalcy.

Not to be lost in the limelight, Makarios publicly expressed his hopes of returning to Cyprus in two or three weeks sparking alarm across the island and raising the prospect of renewed violence between Greek Cypriots. The archbishop's statement also undermined the authority of Clerides who, trying to consolidate his power and with a view to his own political fortune, needed time to bring order to Cyprus and explore opportunities with Turkish Cypriots and their leader Rauf Denktaş. Clerides telephoned around his new book of world leaders. He urged Karamanlis, whom he thought could control the archbishop, to stop him returning for three months, beseeched Washington and London to do likewise and held his own press conference saying Makarios's return should be decided later through elections.

In the south of the island, the British task force started offloaded relieved nationals, which took until the following morning given the number with most processed and taken to the airport for flights back to the United Kingdom.

Turkey asked that survivors from the sunken TCG *Kocatepe* be transferred at sea using a jackstay, a wire between two vessels. Helicopters duly transferred them to RFA *Olna* in preparation until the Turkish navy decided the operation too risky. Instead, naval pilot Lieutenant Ian McKenzie transferred Turkish seventy-two sailors over four hours in tricky flying conditions with his Wasp helicopter from HMS *Andromeda*. Prime Minister Bülent Ecevit passed his gratitude and admiration for British efforts (and a year later Turkey awarded McKenzie the Turkish Distinguished Service Medal for his mission). That evening Turkey's general staff publicly admitted the loss of their own ship but not the reasons for it.

Another British concern was the prospect of an imminent Turkish assault on Nicosia airport risking the lives of UN soldiers, many of them British. Turkey panicked the UN into action after a confusing conversation between Dewan Prem Chand and the UN's special representative for Cyprus Luis Weckmann-Muñoz with Turkish Ambassador Asaf Inhan. The ambassador told them that on day one Turkey intended to land troops, day two secure a bridgehead and day three take the airport, which Chand and Weckmann-Muñoz interpreted as Turkey's intention to finish the third step.

Inhan's message was actually meant to reassure the UN that no action was imminent. He was reading a message from Ankara, which, through crossed wires with the military, mistakenly thought Turkish soldiers already controlled the airport. However, Chand, whose UN forces were actually controlling the airport, read it as a planned Turkish assault and defiantly dug in to deter them.

Brigadier Frank Henn commanding Britain's UN troops and High Commissioner Stephen Olver agreed that UNFICYP must stop any Turkish assault. The airport was not only crucial for Cyprus but also housed the Czech weapons relinquished by Makarios in 1972 and the UNFICYP base – and nearby Greeks-Cypriot forces would fight back at terrible human cost. Knowing that UNFICYP could last only four hours against this superior force, they hatched a plan on the bluff of deterrence expecting an international outcry to restrain the Turks. Chand told Inhan that UNFICYP would oppose them knowing full well that Foreign Secretary Callaghan would not standby and that RAF air cover could dramatically affect Turkish thinking. This was a high-risk plan.

Olver had London inform Ankara about the consequences of its actions and convince Ecevit 'against the disastrous road down which the Turkish military leadership would seem to be leading him and his country and the whole Western alliance'.[254] UN Secretary General Kurt Waldheim also worked on Ecevit, explaining that Greek reinforcements could not land on bomb-damaged runways anyway and that he had no evidence of Turkish-Cypriot persecution to justify continued ceasefire violations.

Callaghan told Ecevit at lunchtime about reports of a proposed Turkish attack on the airport. The Turkish prime minister again thought London susceptible to false Greek allegations and replied that neither he nor his generals had any information about these intentions. In the confused communications between Turkish bureaucrats and the military, Ecevit was unaware that Turkey did not control the airport.

Renewed threats to UN troops prompted Callaghan into action. He threatened Ecevit and Güneş again at 6.55 pm with a military response, raising the real prospect of British and Turkish troops fighting each other. 'If the Turks were to carry out Inhan's threat, they would come up against the UN and British contingent, who were at present in control of the airport. HMG [Her Majesty's government] would not stand by if our forces were attacked; we would not allow them to be slaughtered'.[255] Güneş claimed the UN had vacated the airport and Ecevit declined to assert publicly that the UN controlled it, causing London to interpret this confusion as Turkey's intention to attack. Callaghan told the Turks that peace talks were off if they tried and called Kissinger for help.

He also sought UN permission to reinforce UNFICYP, though UN Secretary General Kurt Waldheim was already on the case making his own request twenty minutes later, which the Security Council granted. A squadron of Phantom fighter jets flew out overnight from Britain. John Aiken spoke to Stephen Olver, Frank Henn and Dewan Prem Chand about whether the American task force could participate – a point that was not followed up and with good cause, for Kissinger had no intention of supporting any military action against a vital NATO ally.

Kissinger did though warn Ecevit in a brief evening call when the Turkish prime minister explained the airport was either in UN hands and surrounded by Turkish forces or Turkey held all but one corner of the airfield where British troops were flying a UN flag. In either case, he assured Kissinger that Turkey would not act. Listening to all this, the doubtful secretary of state wondered if the Turks even knew what an airport was. He told Ecevit he did not want to get into a debate, but the airport must not change hands, and Turks must not attack UN troops to which Ecevit pledged agreement. Kissinger relayed the message to Callaghan admitting that on any rational basis the Turks would not attack but there were too many irrational people around. With this lingering worry, he called on NATO military chief General Andrew Goodpaster to apply pressure on the Turkish High Command.

When completed, Kissinger thought there was little more to be done as Ecevit would either keep his word or not. Ambassador Bill Macomber reached a similar conclusion in Ankara because Ecevit had dismissed reports of Turkish action as absurd and assured him that the Turkish general staff ordered local commanders not to attack Britain or the UN under any circumstances. Macomber, therefore, decided against contacting the Turkish military reckoning that if the generals were bamboozling Ecevit, they were hardly likely to comply with American appeals. It was clear to him though that Ecevit thought Turkey controlled the airport. Kissinger's patience was anyway wearing thin about excitable positions in London, telling Kurt Waldheim that last week the British were ready to go to war with Greece and this week they are ready to fight Turkey.

John Aiken's operations centre surged into activity trying to assess sundry sometimes conflicting signals about Turkish intentions. A fearful Dewan Prem Chand wanted immediate British reinforcements, so Aiken asked the vice chief in London for permission. When approval arrived ten minutes later, he sent over shortly before 10.00 pm an advance party of soldiers from RAF Dhekelia letting the local National Guard commanders know of their route to avoid any mistakes. The six Phantom fighters were due to arrive by 2.00 am.

Calming diplomacy continued between London and Ankara with Prime Minister Harold Wilson now warning Ecevit against action. The Turkish prime minister gave the same assurance he had to Kissinger that his forces already controlled the airport, had strict instructions not to attack it and no operation was planned for that night. Turan Güneş told the Foreign and Commonwealth Office that the affair was all a misunderstanding of technicalities.

This did not alleviate tension as a Turkish battalion continued advancing, possibly unaware of the UN presence, and soon only a few yards away. Clocks ticked loudly moving towards midnight in the operations centres in Cyprus and London with fears about hostilities breaking out between two fellow European democracies. Fortunately, Ankara got control just in time and halted the advance. An explosive situation was averted.

A different type of drama unfolded in Washington when President Richard Nixon learnt that after two weeks of arguments the Supreme Court judged the presidential office did not have an unfettered right to withhold information and he must hand over his unedited tape recordings to a federal court. This landmark precedent not only set the boundaries for the power of his office, but it also surely sealed the end of his political life. His enemies seized the moment with the House of Representatives' Judiciary Committee starting two days of deliberations to develop articles of impeachment, all watched by millions of spellbound Americans who could not believe what was happening. Although Nixon complied with the ruling without any public appearance, the born fighter in him did not know how to surrender, so onward he strode calculating how to assemble enough Republican votes to defeat impeachment despite support dwindling by the day.

All this spelt trouble for an overworked Kissinger who, while managing the continued disengagement of Israeli and Arab forces besides the *détente* process, was thrown into managing Cyprus and propping up the American government. He prospectively faced a collapse of the administration affording enemies around the world chance to exploit the situation. For the moment, he comforted himself in bringing the Cypriot crisis under control without foreseeing how Watergate and Cyprus would collide in spectacular fashion.

Chapter 17

THE FIRST CONFERENCE

A new phase emerged as Britain took the reins to make the ceasefire last. A dramatic ten days since the coup against Makarios had created a new political landscape against which to make it work. Makarios had been deposed, replaced first by a thug and then by a constitutionally appointed deputy, Glafcos Clerides, and was manipulating events from London; civilian leaders had replaced a military dictatorship in Greece; and Turkey had a significant body of soldiers in Cyprus fulfilling a long-held objective to win a sea access on the island.

All these developments were fluid. Clerides feared for his life from right-wing extremists who declared, even now, they would rather serve under the Turks than a returned Makarios: a situation about over which he had no influence for the left was equally determined to restore the archbishop who was, anyway, too popular to be denounced. Military purists in Athens carefully watched new Prime Minister Konstantinos Karamanlis. Turkey's military forces were vulnerable in the long term, and Prime Minister Bülent Ecevit had to manage demanding Turkish generals and a coalition of tough right-wing politicians pushing for more in Cyprus.

Dawn revealed clearer details of the positions around Nicosia airport. Turkey's claim to control the airport in some ways looked justified with tanks and guns dominating the approach road and able to destroy approaching enemy aircraft. Opposite them sat a thousand UN troops, mostly British and Finnish, their number bolstered with further reinforcements throughout the day from the Coldstream Guards, including light tanks and armoured patrol carriers. High Commissioner Stephen Olver had worked out the problem:

Having announced publicly and through diplomatic approaches that they were in possession of the airport, the Turks were faced with a cruel dilemma when they realised that this was not the case. They had either to good their declarations by taking over, even if this meant a war with UN; or they had to find some way to make a graceful retreat.[256]

Fortunately, tensions had lowered by 9.00 am though UN forces stayed on high alert. John Aiken increased security measures around the bases and sent up a Vulcan patrol over northern Cyprus in case a frustrated Turkey turned on Britain. RAF staff faced their own problem when trying to arm the twelve recently arrived Phantom jets for the new deterrence role. They only had cluster and 1,000-pound bombs, which were pointless when UN and Turkish forces faced each so closely, so had to ask London for more precision-firing rockets.

Turkey's airport climbdown seemingly against the threat of credible force injected Jim Callaghan with a terribly flawed understanding of what had happened overnight. He assumed that good old-fashioned British gunboat diplomacy halted Turkish action without appreciating the complexity and confusion in Turkish communication. This resort to threat bedevilled his approach to handling the Turks in the following two Geneva peace conferences. Other diplomatic consequences also followed Britain's threat of force: Callaghan's pressure on Turkey caused rancour in Ankara, which saw it as an attempt to humiliate Ecevit's government and started to colour Turkish attitudes regarding Britain as an unreliable mediator.

Aside from these developments, eyes now turned to the first peace conference starting in Geneva later that day, to make the ceasefire work and agree the machinery for a long-term solution in a second conference two weeks later.

Ecevit wanted to exploit his advantage and turn this conference into a long-term political settlement for two autonomous administrations under one Cypriot government with a permanent Turkish military presence on the island. He feared Greek prevarication at the talks just as Makarios had done for a decade. He had also to keep his fragile coalition together with a far-right Islamist party besides generals and opposition parties watching carefully to make sure once in a generation gains were not squandered – any sense of retreat in Cyprus would finish him. This meant a tight rein over his Turkish delegation and Foreign Minister Turan Güneş, an academic and close political ally, who consequently was told to avoid endless talks without results, given no room to manoeuvre and not breathe any word about withdrawal.

Greek aims were complex. New Prime Minister Konstantinos Karamanlis, managing a thousand problems in steering his country back to democracy while restoring Greek pride, wanted to resolve outstanding Greek-Turkish problems but faced pressure from his military and various purist factions not to capitulate to Turkish demands. Ioannidis still sat at his desk in the Greek Pentagon holding his same position and armed with supporters across the military. Karamanlis also had to a steer a national unity government comprising experienced politicians of differing views, principally Foreign Minister George Mavros, an academic lawyer, who disliked ceding Turkish Cypriots their own administration and who, unlike Karamanlis, looked favourably on Makarios. The prime minister, therefore, had to pull off a face-saving agreement to survive, starting with the minimal position of continued Cypriot independence and ideally a return to the status quo without Makarios and without Turkish troops.

Callaghan, with his eye on Labour's party politics that now favoured the new Greek government, was well disposed to the newly appointed Greek Foreign Minister George Mavros. Here was a fellow left-wing politician and Western-minded diplomat Callaghan liked. Harold Wilson's decision to cancel the planned royal naval visit earlier in the year had caused Mavros's banishment to Kos for supporting British action, so when Callaghan met the new Greek minister later that day Mavros told him jokingly that the Foreign Secretary had taken the action for which he had paid the price. His plan for the talks was to encourage Turkish concessions and persuade Greece to lower its expectations.

This was a hard task as Turkey's continued sea reinforcements tarnished the opening atmosphere of the conference, which was also attended by Henry Kissinger's emissary Bill Buffum and a former senior Argentinian diplomat Dr Roberto Guyer for the UN. Acting President Glafcos Clerides in Cyprus telephoned around everyone for help. Callaghan, in bullish mood thinking that a show of British force had once stopped the Turks, asked his generals for an assessment of possible action and enquired whether Washington might entertain joint naval action under UN auspices – an answer to which there was only going to be one very vocal reply.

General Dewan Prem Chand, likewise, persuaded by the overnight precedent, went a step further requesting Security Council authority to place his UN forces between the Turks and Greeks and Greek Cypriots. Fast moving activity in New York brought him down to earth. Top British diplomat Ivor Richards suggested his proposal be discussed in Geneva rather than New York; and the secretary general's private office doubted that contributing nations to UNFICYP wanted to risk their troops. The Canadian defence minister had already removed its soldiers asserting they should surrender if attacked as it was not their job to constitute a third army fighting combatants.

John Aiken, also in the same frame of mind as Callaghan, proposed a naval blockade along the northern coast preventing further Turkish reinforcements and even despatched four ships in anticipation of London's consent. New Greek Prime Minister Konstantinos Karamanlis requested similar action arguing that Britain's guarantor role obliged it to stop Turkish seaborne reinforcements.

Proceedings nonetheless went ahead in Geneva's Palais de Nations at 8.30 pm with a first meeting between Callaghan and the foreign ministers of Greece and Turkey setting the tone for a heavy-going event. Neither Güneş nor Mavros gave way on their opening positions over a declaration, with the former wanting to refer to the Guarantee Treaty of 1960 and his Greek counterpart only to the UN Security Council resolution. Mavros became excitable and Callaghan thought him likely to walk out if things went badly, while Güneş soon got under Callaghan's skin, for he could not understand from the inscrutable Turk what Ecevit's government really wanted. He found their endless discussions worse than any national executive meeting of the Labour Party.

As the day ended, the Ministry of Defence in London preparing Callaghan's military assessment asked John Aiken what Britain could offer UNFICYP. Even though he had spiritedly despatched ships, Aiken said not much apart from the recently arrived Phantoms. Whitehall thought the blockade gambit unwise in any event with the vice chief of the defence staff, Peter de Lacy Le Cheminant, telling Aiken that using the navy was 'too grave a step at this stage, would have serious consequences and might not affect the ground situation'.[257]

In the early morning of day two, 26 July 1974, military chiefs, therefore, poured cold water on Callaghan's reinforcement hopes, saying Britain had enough ships and airpower for a deterrent but using force needed more ships and certainly more planes to assure local air superiority. This idea stood little chance without at least tacit approval from the United States, which was inconceivable. Aiken, therefore, recalled his ships and, after reflecting on the Nicosia airport precedent, concluded that using 'UN forces on a much wider timescale to interpose between resolute combatants is unlikely to be acceptable politically or be practicable in a short timescale'.[258]

In truth, no Western nation and very few in the UN Security Council, which boasted many Muslim countries had the appetite. UN Secretary General Kurt Waldheim wanted to intervene but wavered without UN authority, admitting that he was no former Dag Hammarskjöld, who, as a former secretary general, had on his own shoulders imposed a UN force to resolve the Suez Crisis in 1956. French and British diplomats also pointed to the many sided political problem of winning a new mandate from Security Council members. And Washington firmly told Waldheim that the United States would in no circumstances use force or the threat of force to deter Turkey.

With Callaghan's well intended though hopeless idea of force fallen by the wayside, he fell back to diplomacy in another day of fruitless conversations in Geneva. Güneş refused any notion of UNFICYP supervision restricting Turkish movement and Mavros insisted on Turkey's withdrawal to a 22 July 1974 ceasefire line. Continuing reports of Turkish reinforcements did not help the mood with warlike noises coming from Prime Minister Konstantinos Karamanlis in Greece who had few cards left to play.

After much discussion, accusations and checking of positions in capital cities, Güneş produced a draft text refusing withdrawal to 22 July ceasefire position but accepting a role for UNFICYP to monitor a buffer zone and proposing political changes in Cyprus. Mavros rejected this so both ministers threatened the fall of their governments if pushed too far. Güneş, who had no choice but to defend continuing military action, tartly told Callaghan, 'It might be preferable therefore to have war with Greece because the alternative would be Turkey detached from the West'. [259] He had a tough job: Turkish generals were close to meeting their objectives to the frustration of their diplomats in Geneva who saw the souring effect on the conference and world opinion. Callaghan ruefully summarised,

> the principal achievement of the day has been that Mavros has been dissuaded from leaving the Conference and returning to Athens as he had regularly threatened to do. It is not impossible that provided the overnight news from Cyprus is not too bad, we may be able to agree on a text before we leave.[260]

Surely enough, officials started what turned into a fourteen-hour-long effort to thrash out a communiqué on Saturday, 27 July 1974, a day increasingly coloured by Turkey's growing sense of Britain bending towards the Greek camp. A point of view that bore some truth with the principal Foreign and Commonwealth Office expert Alan Goodison admitting there was no alternative but to side with the Greeks as Athens needed a ceasefire more than Ankara, and the Turks should therefore be manoeuvred into an agreement.

Events on the island were quieter but fragile as the Turkish army mostly concentrated on getting supplies ashore for phase two, to take a third of the island in the north. Diplomatically, both sides maintained their positions with Mavros playing for time, saying he could not settle all matters now and Güneş pushing for swift agreement saying that 'having reached the age of 50 he felt that he had spent too much of his life talking about Cyprus. Never again in his life did he wish to discuss it. He was an optimist and felt that it should be possible to get it out of the way.'[261] The truth was Ankara sensed world sympathy moving away and wanted to agree the basis of a political settlement to avoid another decade of debate.

Tired officials drew up a broad declaration containing the wishes of both sides with few concessions by either. Callaghan frustrated at the end of another long day thought seriously about continuing British involvement in the island, which would have delighted Treasury mandarins in London pushing to save money. He sent the frights up the United States when confiding these views to Kissinger's emissary Bill Buffum, for Washington saw the island as vital for Mediterranean defence stability, its own intelligence capability and peace in the Middle East. Callaghan told him the bases had declined in importance and suggested Britain and the United States reassess them – and initiated yet another Whitehall study. Buffum, taken aback by the idea, quickly made the opposite case though also had Washington assess the bases' significance principally to prove their worth to the West.

In Athens, Monty Stearns arrived as the new deputy ambassador to a cold reception from Henry Tasca. An administrative officer met him at the airport and drove him to a hotel as his official residence was being renovated. Finding the hotel room ridiculously small, he went back down to the officer and said that he was jolly well staying in the residence during the redecorations as he needed to entertain and talk privately to guests. Ambassador Henry Tasca did not receive him for three to four days later and when they did meet, the ambassador made his unhappiness clear, pulling out a load of books from the bookshelf saying, 'You haven't been around here for a long time so I think you should spend the next couple of weeks reading'.[262] That relations between them were strained did not matter for Stearns knew Tasca's days were numbered and he himself had the authority of Kissinger.

In Washington, the House of Representatives' Judiciary Committee began impeachment proceedings accusing President Richard Nixon of an obstruction of office, misuse of power and contempt of Congress. The president clung to power trying to canvass support but senior Republicans knew he did not have the numbers.

Impasse continued in Geneva on day four, Sunday, 28 July 1974, with Greek pressure to stop Turkey's expansion, further allegations of atrocities by both sides and Callaghan struggling to bridge the divide.

Realising the implausibility of getting an immediate Turkish retreat, Callaghan pushed for a compromise of withdrawal 'with the least possible delay'and 'after consideration of the constitutional problems'.[263] Mavros threatened to walk out and attend the following day's UN session in New York sponsored by the Soviets. The foreign secretary did not fall for this crude tactic, saying that if they could not fix the problem here today, the UN was unlikely to do so, telling Mavros, 'There was a prospect of war between Greece and Turkey. They had to make up their minds what they wanted to happen.'[264] He pushed on despite gloom about ever reaching an agreement and urged Kissinger, through Buffum, to apply pressure from afar.

On day five, Monday, 29 July 1974, Callaghan moved for showdown with the Turks after they came close to a breakthrough at 4.30 am when Foreign Minister Turan Güneş dropped a bombshell declaring he needed approval from Ankara despite staying in touch with Ecevit throughout the night. Taking him aside, Callaghan learnt from the nervous minister that Ecevit was having trouble getting agreement from his military. Güneş appeared so hesitant that when Ecevit disagreed with wording he had already approved, the Turkish foreign minister 'had not dared to tell us he wanted to go back on it'.[265] Callaghan telephoned Ecevit himself at 7.00 am, his passion overcoming any diplomatic polish by accusing the Turkish prime minister of deliberate delay. Ecevit replied with a list of objections from the role of the vice presidency to the treatment of Turkish villagers.

Proceedings at the conference remained tortuous for the rest of the day with repeated objections to different texts. Güneş earnestly strung together a new formula until Ankara again revised his work. An incensed Callaghan then gave the Turks another ultimatum, either agree to his compromise text on withdrawal by 9.30 pm tonight or he was handing the whole mess over to the UN and would make clear in public where the fault lay.

Henry Kissinger briefed about developments from a Watergate-laden administration was left incredulous thinking the foreign secretary was 'operating like a madman. If Callaghan stops screaming, the issues can be settled.'[266] He was aghast at a proposed formula, sponsored by Callaghan, of the idea of demilitarisation – having all forces including British ones leave the island – and set about proposing a new text and applying pressure on Ecevit to accept it.

At the end of the afternoon in Geneva, senior Turkish diplomat Coşkun Kirca confided that problems arose in Ankara not only because of the military, but also Ecevit's own eccentricities and his fragile coalition. This experienced official suggested leaving Güneş, alone he thought was shattered, and instead apply pressure on Ecevit himself saying that British threats in the Security Council and pressure by Kissinger would probably cause him to give in to the Güneş-Callaghan formula. Callaghan, however, thought it best not to telephone Ecevit given their previous bruising conversation and left this to the Americans.

In the meantime, the Ministry of Defence produced a complicated fudge when responding to Callaghan's request to assess the worth of Britain's bases and explore the idea of demilitarisation. Against a background of Britain's continuing defence review with the three service chiefs defending their own patch, the assessment trod carefully saying there might be merit in pursing the idea, but it was complex, could not happen quickly and depended on the defence review and the Americans. This paper, which annoyed RAF chief, Andrew Humphrey, argued that 'Cyprus in common with all other Mediterranean and non-NATO commitments, was not so strategically vital to the UK, despite its importance to the cohesion of NATO'.[267]

Makarios, still in New York and keeping abreast of developments, again tried to get action from Kissinger when they held their second meeting at the Department of State. 'I am not satisfied with the position of the United States. It is in your interest to stop the Turkish invasion',[268] he asserted in wanting to know why the United States could not repeat the tough talking that brought about the ceasefire.

Kissinger did not take well to Makarios dictating American foreign policy. He supported Britain's two-stage conferences approach, was satisfied Turkey had stopped advancing and was not going to impose a solution on unclear waters:

> Right now there are too many cooks. Callaghan needs a quick success. The Soviets have their own motives. The Government in Greece has its problems. And, [Bülent] Ecevit … We have been encouraging a settlement. We have not been all out active. We can't be the only country to produce a settlement, but this may change. In this phase of the Geneva talks the prospects are good. In the next phase Turkey will have to change its position. There are still too many cooks.[269]

Kissinger offered only silent diplomacy though one in an 'increasingly constructive role' for he was not about to make the United States the fall guy until the way forward was clearer. Makarios left dissatisfied.

Kissinger did, though, argue it out with Ecevit in the evening and over the morning of Tuesday, 30 July 1974, to pull off an agreed conference text. This draft incorporated Security Council Resolution 353 and, to pacify the Greeks, a watered-down reference to reduce forces when 'peace, security and confidence are established'. Ecevit agreed but would not propose it himself fearing internal backlash, so Sisco asked Callaghan, who said yes on two conditions: the United States guaranteed Turkey's acceptance – he had plenty of egg on his face from texts submitted by Güneş, which Ankara then overruled; and the text must refer to withdrawal 'with the shortest possible delay' to sell it to Greece. Sisco said they would get Ecevit's consent and call back if this were a problem.

This worked for at 8.45 am Turkey's permanent representative in Geneva, Kirca, mentioning Kissinger's involvement, offered up the text from Ankara. He did so with theatre, complaining about Callaghan's ultimatum as Güneş had acted in good faith to find a solution. Kirca then admitted his complaint was to save Turkish face. He also privately warned Britain not to be brutal with Ecevit, a man he knew well, who was 'a mixture of good and bad and at the moment he was in a strange frame of mind. It would be better the tone soft however firm the substance.'[270] This all proved unnecessary as Callaghan decided against any further contact with Ecevit, leaving Kissinger to push the Turkish prime minister on final changes.

When the text came through Callaghan and his staff worked on Mavros and his colleague Dimitrios Bitsios telling them to be realistic as there would be no withdrawal until a full solution was agreed and the text was not negotiable. This did the job. The foreign ministers of Greece, Turkey and Britain agreed the draft shortly after noon leaving aside until later in the day the matter of buffer zones, demarcation and civilian prisoners. They also agreed to a second conference on 8 August 1974 to include Glafcos Clerides and Rauf Denktaş representing the two Cypriot communities. Callaghan thanked them for their cooperation and apologised for his occasional 'roughness'.

It was not quite over yet. Another meeting started at 3.15 pm to thrash out demarcation zones with Güneş insisting on 10-kilometres to protect Turkey's position as 'they should recognise they were all Mediterranean, and hence hot-headed people'[271] and Mavros 1 kilometre. An angry Callaghan said he was not ready for another two hours of this and, apart from agreeing some detail, had them postpone these issues to the next stage. Overburdened civil servants hurriedly worked out what had been agreed for a final declaration in French and English.

They cracked it. At 10.00 pm Mavros, Güneş and Callaghan signed the Geneva Declaration, calling for a ceasefire line at the time of signature, a buffer zone managed by UNFICYP to be agreed and implementation of Security Council Resolution 353 in 'the shortest possible timeframe'. Greek Cypriots would also leave Turkish controlled enclaves with both sides releasing prisoners. Callaghan provided the champagne.

Everyone provided their own interpretation of the declaration. Greek Prime Minister Konstantinos Karamanlis describing it as the start of a settlement while privately regarding it as the opening point for the next negotiations. Ecevit hailed the deal as laying the foundations for a healthy new status for Cyprus though he had already publicly said Turkish troops would stay until Turkey's long-term security was achieved. And Güneş received a hero's reception in Ankara.

Washington publicly praised Callaghan's skill and persistence while expressing private doubts about his style, which Kissinger described as taking negotiations to a certain point, issuing an ultimatum and then expecting the United States to pull his chestnuts out of the fire. He opined that the United States had twice saved Callaghan from himself and did not want to repeat the experience. Callaghan himself was simply pleased to leave and get some sleep. Above all Washington and London thought the corner had been turned and while not naïve about tough conditions on the ground did not expect tension between Greece and Turkey to reappear. Kissinger even wound down the department's Cyprus Task Force.

Events would overtake them at the worst possible time for news of the Geneva Declaration received less publicity in the United States than the Democratic-led House of Representatives' Judiciary Committee passing three articles of impeachment against a sitting president. A vote in both houses of Congress (House of Representatives and Senate) looked certain to go against Nixon leading to a trial in the United States Senate with damming evidence awaiting. What was the president going to do?

While people across the world wondered, service families in Cyprus breathed a sigh of relief. A quieter situation across the island and the Geneva Declaration gave the green light for Operation Homestead on 31 July 1974 letting those who had decided to stay on the island return to dormitory towns, relieving the overcrowding, blurring of ranks, six-hour volunteer shifts on the commercial steam-plate washing machine and intense boredom in the summer heat nearing 40°C. The worst seemed over to everyone.

Chapter 18

FALL OF A PRESIDENT

Attention now turned to stopping any further conflict before stage two in nine days' time. This second-round conference had the herculean task of finding a workable political solution for Cyprus, which had defied everyone who had studied the problem since the island's independence in 1960.

The Soviet Union continued making a nuisance of itself without going too far by vetoing Security Council Resolution 355, which adopted the Geneva Declaration. It had annoyingly taken over presidency of the council with, as Britain thought, a secretary general who scares easily, so London and Washington worked hard to stop any changes to UNFICYP's mandate in case a new contingent was formed of Soviet soldiers.

Makarios, having returned to London, loomed over the preparations, though to the relief of the Foreign and Commonwealth Office was not demanding to attend the Geneva talks. The archbishop told Foreign Secretary Jim Callaghan he was keeping his options open, seeking neither to undermine Clerides nor embarrass the new Greek government. Callaghan suspected the wily cleric was biding his time, waiting to see what Clerides did and whether to accept or denounce it, 'I fear ... it is the latter course which he may have in mind.'[272]

On the island a messy process settled the method for mapping out Turkish and Greek-Cypriot demarcation positions. Neither the Turks nor the Greeks agreed on their own 1:15,000 scale maps so their respective views were transferred to a British map, showing stark differences in overlapping lines and the huge task of visiting all these areas to verify positions. Colonel J.J.G. Hunter, Britain's defence attaché, a Turkish colonel and a Greek major together with Colonel C.E. Beattie of UNFICYP began the process in Puma helicopter flights starting on 4 August 1974. On one occasion, they had to return to a location as Turkish soldiers had advanced from the eastern side of an enclave mapped out three days earlier.

UNFICYP tried policing the buffer zone causing friction with Turkey. Prime Minister Bülent Ecevit complained to UN Secretary General Kurt Waldheim that UN forces had no right to act in an area controlled by a guarantor power.

An improved security situation let Britain release reinforcements with the Royal Marines commandos setting sail for Malta. Large numbers of Cypriot refugees were, however, a continuing problem living in hastily erected tent cities on RAF land. Turkish generals transferred Greek Cypriots out of Kyrenia allegedly telling them they will never return, causing High Commissioner Stephen Olver to request formal protests from London, which he caveated by noting that a Turkish Kyrenia with the rest of the island Greek might offer a stable situation.

In Washington, Henry Kissinger chose his moment to dispense with Ambassador Henry Tasca, as Richard Nixon was preoccupied and Monty Stearns had settled into Athens as deputy ambassador. Local political counsellor Elizabeth Brown had the unenviable task:

> Early one morning, about 2:00 AM, when I was the Acting DCM [deputy chief of mission], the communications people called me up and said that they had received a cable for the Ambassador and would I come into the office. So I went to the Embassy at around 4:00 AM and took this cable to Ambassador Henry Tasca. He opened it up, read it, and threw it at me. The cable recalled him as Ambassador to Greece.[273]

(Tasca left his post on Monday, 16 September 1974.)

Significant protests started across the United States as the Greek speaking community searched for scapegoats to explain the Greek tragedy. For the time being, these were balanced by welcome news of a restored civilian government without left-wing credentials.

Meanwhile, the United States' domestic political saga reached a denouement on 5 August 1974 when President Richard Nixon reluctantly handed over missing tapes with the smoking gun transcripts revealing his attempt to cover up the 1972 theft at the Democratic Party headquarters. Not even this innate political animal could escape the inevitable disgrace of a trial and likely impeachment given the evidence. What would he do and when would he go became the frenzied talk on television and in newspapers. Might the government collapse? Would chaos ensue? How would the Soviet Union react?

Kissinger had little time for Cyprus under this cloud, which led to hurried and incomplete preparation. In place of Sisco and Buffum, he sent out Art Hartman, the quietly spoken cultivated head of the European department who had only recently taken over the Eastern Mediterranean desk, to assess thinking in Greece, Cyprus and Turkey. Kissinger expressly told him to avoid any criticism of Turkey, unlike other Western nations, which appeared to be jumping on the Greek bandwagon.

Career diplomat Bob Oakley who had already been on the Sisco and Buffum missions found out he was off a third time with Hartman. Before leaving, Kissinger told them something usual, which Oakley did not quite appreciate at the time that

'some things may happen in Washington while you are gone.' He never said or hinted what that was. But he said that we were to tell each and every foreign official we saw that regardless of what might be happening in Washington or what they may be perceiving as happening in Washington, the US would react very strongly to any provocation or interference with our goals.[274]

Out they went, meeting Ecevit on 5 August 1974 whom Hartman found loquacious and interesting, listening for hours while the Turkish prime minister gave them a complete history of the Turkish-Greek relationship. Hartman pressed the importance of avoiding further military action and tried persuading him that Washington was not leaning towards Greece unlike some European countries. (An annoyed Ambassador Horace Phillips heard about this comment and, taking this to imply Britain, complained to London that about an unfair over-simplification undermining London's honest broker role. Diplomats at the Foreign and Commonwealth Office were similarly furious when they read the report.) Ecevit did not anyway yield to what he thought was American pressure and told Hartman about his ambitions for a federal political system in Cyprus, which could be one or several zones encompassing 30 per cent of the island though without partition. He made clear an intention to occupy the whole of the Kyrenia mountain range giving Hartman a sense Turkey would go no farther.

Hartman and Oakley then flew to Cyprus where they caught up with Ambassador Rodger Davies bearing a searing message from Kissinger. The secretary of state had misinterpreted Hartman's report on his meeting with Ecevit and had assumed his top diplomat had criticised Turkey. Kissinger's zinger of a message read along the lines of 'You disobeyed me! You go back to Ankara and you correct the impression you left there.'[275] Davies just shook his head and Hartman, who had no intention of returning and was accustomed to the moods and methods of his boss, drafted a reply explaining the misunderstanding.

He and Oakley then spent a three-hour dinner with Clerides who gave his version of events and predicted that Athens would not accept Ecevit's proposals, though he himself was ready to discuss a cantonal system, and repeated his concerns that Makarios should not return as president. Hartman subsequently met Rauf Denktaş for the Turkish-Cypriot view to be even handed, though left the island generally sensing the Greek side felt the United States favoured Turkey.

Finally, Hartman ventured to Athens for another history lesson from Prime Minister Konstantinos Karamanlis who said he wanted to be 'sure you understand what this problem is' and brought in Foreign Minister George Mavros, telling him, 'Now you just take the ambassador in hand and give him a little whisper of what this problem is all about',[276] which Mavros did for the next five hours. At the end, Karamanlis, just as Clerides had predicted, refused Ecevit's ideas while conceding that Greece would protest publicly about Turkey's violations though not privately because he wanted a long-term solution if the Turks showed willing. He also did not want Makarios back.

Hartman flew out with these competing Mediterranean demands to brief Foreign Secretary Jim Callaghan whom he knew from an earlier posting in the United Kingdom.

At his end, Callaghan and his diplomats were grappling with how to play stage two. The foreign secretary admitted to Kissinger that 'I don't have much feel on how to play the second round. I think I shall need to see the whites of their eyes before I shoot. If you have any thoughts, I hope you will let me know.'[277] They eventually decided the aims should be making the ceasefire and buffer zone stick and agreeing a framework to discuss new political arrangements for Cyprus. Also, from the Foreign and Commonwealth Office perspective, try and escape from British long-term political and defence responsibilities for the island, which meant being flexible about retaining the RAF bases. Callaghan also wanted a tougher position on the Turks because the 'Turkish government, despite its new found [sic] popularity, may still lack real authority to make concessions needed to keep the Greek side talking and to impose sufficient restraints on the Turkish forces in Cyprus'.[278]

High Commissioner Stephen Olver argued from Cyprus that a federal solution represented the only plausible scenario and urged for momentum in the talks to avoid 'a dangerous increase in intercommunal tension which on each side remains only just beneath the surface'.[279]

Thinking speed an important factor, London pressed Turkey for a 9 August 1974 start date when neither Ankara nor Athens was ready. Ecevit's coalition was considering a new general election and preferred 12 or 14 August and Greece favoured 14 August. A forced pace also stood against Kissinger's desire for both countries to find common ground themselves, however long that took.

Domestic affairs affected Callaghan's rationale as Cyprus was but one of the pressures bearing down on Harold Wilson's government and a less important one than the country's financial troubles. Even leading diplomats recognised that while the island offered opportunities 'to play a leading and exciting role on the world stage', it diverted attention away from 'more pressing problems, particularly economic and domestic on which national survival (to which Cyprus [was] irrelevant) depend'.[280] Britain was also stung by the exposure of its service personnel and tourists and its limited influence over Athens or Ankara, which pushed many in the Foreign and Commonwealth Office and the Treasury to get out – with the service chiefs playing games to protect their own turfs from defence cuts. The Cabinet Defence Committee even wanted to announce an intention in principle to wind up all commitments outside of NATO, which on paper meant Cyprus.

A mid-morning meeting with Hartman on 8 August brought out these internal conflicts and further British-American differences especially over Turkish ceasefire violations. Callaghan questioned whether talks could even proceed given continued Turkish transgressions. Keep them talking in all circumstances to find common ground advised Hartman, urging Callaghan to be a patient referee as 'the important thing was to keep the process going. As long as there was talking, there was hope'.[281] Hartman also warned Callaghan, who had one eye on Greek lobby influence for a forthcoming general election and another on his role as Labour Party chairman, not to push for Turkish withdrawals as Kissinger did not want the Turks alienated.

On the eve of stage two, Prime Minister Bülent Ecevit had a clear view on conference aims. Turkish advantage must not be squandered in fruitless talks leading to another decade of community discussions. Flushed with success and a supportive public opinion, he had no reason to offer concessions, for while he did not want partition, he did want a political federation in Cyprus and a seaport. British Ambassador Horace Phillips realised Turkey would not mind the talks breaking down as freed 'of the constraint of negotiation, they will simply continue to consolidate their position on the island – justifying any continued military activity by the Greek refusal to sit down and talk'.[282]

Turkish generals were indeed set on phase two, to seize the northern third of Cyprus in an operation called Drop Star 4, for Ecevit's approval if Greece showed no willingness to agree a 30 per cent land transfer to a Turkish-Cypriot community under a federal system. Ecevit briefed trusted Foreign Minister Turan Güneş that military preparations would be ready in several days, and, if at this point, you present our ultimatum and the Greeks refuse, we will send you a secret message to break up the conference. As your daughter Ayse is planning a holiday, we will use the code that 'Ayse is going on vacation'.[283]

In Greece, Konstantinos Karamanlis faced divided views from his Cabinet including Foreign Minister George Mavros, from forces loyal to Brigadier Ioannidis and from a country seemingly humiliated by continued albeit minor Turkish encroachments. He wanted to compromise but had little ground to achieve it, so his unelected civilian government of many personalities steering the country back to democracy after a seven-year military dictatorship had to appear strong. He did, however, make a remarkable offer to back whatever the Acting Cypriot President Glafcos Clerides agreed at the conference. But Clerides was similarly trapped for while he accepted some form of autonomy for the Turkish Cypriots, a federation on a geographical basis went too far. Makarios was still the principal political power in the land and would disown any such agreement. An opportunity was lost to posterity.

Chapter 19

SECOND ASSAULT

Evening talks at the opening of stage two on Thursday, 8 August 1974, again started in an atmosphere of distrust, Turkey having violated the Geneva Declaration within a day of its signature and Turkish Cypriots alleging more atrocities against their enclaves.

Dangers across the island were highlighted when tragedy struck ten journalists taken in a four-car convoy to the Kyrenia front line. The front driver pulled up after noticing freshly covered holes as a sure sign of mines recently laid by Turkish soldiers. BBC sound engineer Ted Stoddart walked out of the car unsuspectingly onto one that exploded and staggered a few yards before falling to the ground where he sadly died. Fellow BBC journalist Simon Dring ran over to him causing another mine to explode badly wounding his own legs. Three others were injured.

Journalist John Sergeant, now returned to Britain, was woken by a telephone call to his Ealing home when the BBC told him about these terrible events and asked if he would return. With a deep breath he said yes. He flew over in a nearly empty VC10 with a *BBC News* editor sent to repatriate Stoddart, listening intently to the Watergate coverage on the flight. When in Cyprus, Sergeant checked into the Hilton hotel, walked up to his room, entered, saw clothes lying around and quickly closed the door thinking the previous occupant had not checked out. He returned to reception where he was told the room was Stoddart's. Nausea swept over him.

In contrast, a more relaxed Air Marshal John Aiken felt confident enough to enjoy a delayed holiday in Rome, with the crisis operations centre closed and the naval task force reduced to HMS *Devonshire* and HMS *Rhyl*.

Jim Callaghan accompanied by his wife, Audrey, arrived in Geneva and booked into the splendid Hotel La Reserve overlooking Lake

Geneva. He carried with him the baggage of domestic politics for that very day a pugnacious Chancellor of the Exchequer, Denis Healey, reminded Harold Wilson of the government's decision to relinquish all non-NATO responsibilities, which meant cutting troops in Cyprus. This, Healey argued, was essential for Cabinet and Labour Party unity on public spending and was good for Labour Party politics and the declining economy. Mischievously, he thought Callaghan 'might find it useful to keep the planned rundown of forces in Cyprus as one of his objectives in the ongoing negotiations with Greece and Turkey'.[284]

Callaghan, already scarred by events, had this very much in mind for the talks, which he opened with a press conference at 3.45 pm expressing disappointment that the Geneva Declaration had not been carried out, rather tarnishing his impartial credentials to the Turks. His concern, he said, was the future of the Cypriot people and he was not here to lay blame, giving Turkey reason to suspect the contrary.

Opening positions set the scene for a weary five days. An emotional Greek Foreign Minister George Mavros demanded that Turks holster their weapons and return to 30 July 1974 ceasefire position or he would work through the UN instead. Callaghan did not disagree and assured him he would not let Greece be humiliated but results from the UN were unlikely. Turan Güneş defended continuing Turkish infringements on the failure of the Greek National Guard to leave Turkish villages, and maintained a right to carry on until Greece fulfilled all aspects of the declaration. A 7.00 pm photoshoot was held in silence.

Callaghan held the first day together by suggesting they produce reports on all matters by 6.00 pm the following day and letting everyone air their grievances 'but at least they managed to say it without anyone walking out, and we are to meet again tomorrow. I did not hope for much more.'[285]

News outlets had more colourful headlines to concentrate on in the United States. Republican Richard Nixon, a mainstay of American political life in his second presidential term having served as vice president for eight years under President Dwight D. Eisenhower and first winning election to the House of Representatives in 1947, was about to resign. He was making a live announcement from the White House at 8.00 pm, six hours behind Geneva.

Television chiefs across the world scrabbled to get their crews and equipment to the Oval Office for an address by the forlorn looking 60-year-old politician, the first president to resign while in office. He told his audience that 'I have never been a quitter. To leave office before my term is completed is abhorrent to every instinct in my body. But as President, I must put the interest of America first.'

Signals went out from the Department of State to foes across the world against causing mischief. James Lowenstein, a second deputy to Art Hartman, recalled,

[Henry] Kissinger called all the assistant secretaries and I think all the deputy assistant secretaries ... to tell us what was going to happen so that we could get started on the messages. I remember he made one of his famous 'this is a test of the discipline of the Foreign Service whether they can keep this to themselves, etc.' I think that was done. So that was another wild night because all these messages had to go out to chiefs of state saying that the American policy would remain exactly as before.[286]

On top of this drama, American sources detected increased Turkish mainland activity, including a prospective air mobilisation. Assurances were sought from the Turkish Defence Ministry that no further military action was planned. Kissinger, overwhelmed by Watergate not to mention the Middle East, did not have a fixed view on what to do. Noise came from within the Department of State not the least from Tom Boyatt about using the Sixth Fleet, which he had no intention of permitting.

Friday, 9 August 1974, dawned in Geneva against this dramatic news from the United States and anticipation of a new American president being sworn into office, though without affecting the slow progress at the conference.

UN Secretary General Kurt Waldheim, holidaying in his nearby Austrian homeland, flew in and met Callaghan at noon, discussing what they felt was a standoffish approach from the United States and an obstinate attitude from Turkey. When Waldheim said that Kissinger was not putting enough pressure on Ankara, Callaghan admitted to differences with Washington. The foreign secretary also wanted him to publicise any information correcting what he thought were obsessive Turkish fears about atrocities, which Waldheim himself thought were exaggerated.

Later in the afternoon, Callaghan vented his opinion about the need for American pressure to Kissinger's emissary Art Hartman. He also explained an idea to win the Greeks over to an autonomous Turkish-Cypriot administration in return for phased Turkish troop withdrawals with both communities working through the details themselves. Callaghan admitted this approach was designed partly to meet his political needs at home, where he must not be seen as selling out the new Greek government.

Hartman thought him perpetually gloomy and saw himself becoming the professional 'optimist' among these 'gloomy Joes'. He reported back that

> After listening to Callaghan in London express his righteous indignation about even sitting down with fellows who break their word (read Turkey), I gradually nursed him (with no great opposition on his part since he was really letting off steam) to the point where he began to see his role as impartial chairman and not a moral arbiter of equities.[287]

Ankara saw only Greek prevarication at the conference. Güneş, knowing swift agreement alone could postpone Operation Drop Star 4, told Callaghan that Greece must quickly accept the principle of a federal solution of two regions, the Turkish one accounting for 30 per cent in the north, in return for troop reductions. The foreign secretary agreed to consult Clerides, who had now arrived in Geneva along with Rauf Denktaş, on condition of Güneş's personal assurance that Turkey had no intention of enlarging its presence on Cyprus. Callaghan left thinking this given.

Güneş's demands predictably hit the skids. Not by the Greeks, as to Callaghan's surprise Mavros proved receptive provided 'he could sell the idea to Makarios' – the Greek foreign minister looking done in as if 'he wanted to get rid of the Cyprus problem at almost any price provided Greek face could be saved'.[288] It was Clerides who over dinner said he could not sell autonomous regions and the ensuing large population transfers to Cypriots: he could instead consider autonomy to Turkish-Cypriot enclaves linked together in a Turkish-Cypriot administration.

Intelligence filtered through about Turkey's planned second assault extending east of Morphou through Nicosia and to the port of Famagusta in an eighteen-hour operation before 20 August 1974. The British Joint Intelligence Committee thought this more likely a contingency plan, which the Turks would execute if they failed to make progress at Geneva. An angry Callaghan called Hartman back in saying he thought the United States had access to the same information and let rip about Güneş's duplicity after his supposed assurance. More worrying to Hartman, Callaghan, blinded by the apparent success of the Nicosia airport precedent, for a third time threatened a military response to deter Turkey, saying he thought UN secretary general Kurt Waldheim would back him and 'Wilson liked to play with soldiers'.[289]

Such intervention was improbable for British chiefs had already ruled out action when considering whether to restore Makarios and then whether to stop further Turkish naval reinforcements. Hartman calmed him, suggesting they get an accurate intelligence picture and mused this might be Turkish bluff – he asked for instructions from Washington, especially 'since this report will obviously color [sic] Callaghan's attitude in the crucial hours of negotiation this weekend'.[290] A bullish Callaghan nonetheless had the Phantom fighter jets scheduled for return stay at RAF Akrotiri and stopped any further wind down of troops.

Hartman's assistant, Bob Oakley, saw Washington's reply that American intelligence did not find the British report credible, which Ambassador Bill Macomber in Ankara most certainly did. Hartman told Washington the report was plausible, 'Time passed and we could not get a reply, despite Hartman's pleadings. He called [Larry] Eagleburger and told him that something had to be done. Larry told him that he didn't understand what was going in Washington at the moment.'[291]

What was going on was immense anxiety as Americans fretted over whether the nation could hold together waiting for Richard Nixon to leave the White House. On that Friday morning his chief of staff, Alexander Haig, brought him a paper containing one line to sign, which read, 'I hereby resign the office of president of the United States'. Nixon signed, resigning to Secretary of State Henry Kissinger at 11.35 am.

Thirty minutes later American chief justice Warren Burger swore in Gerald R. Ford Jr, a long-term congressman from Michigan, as the thirty-eighth president of the United States. Ford gave a brief address saying, 'fellow Americans, our long national nightmare is over'. Then just after midday the former president, Richard Nixon, gave an impromptu speech in the East Wing thanking his staff, who saw him drop his guard for the first time when notably saying 'only when you have been in the deepest valley can you ever know how magnificent it is to be on the highest mountain'.

David M. Evans, a 34-young-old diplomat from an old Philadelphian family working on economic policy in the vice president's office, witnessed the event:

We got a call to come over to the East Wing, because there was going to be a very dramatic statement by the President [Richard Nixon]. I raced over, knowing instinctively that this was going to be very important. It was [Richard] Nixon's famous farewell address to the staff, which was probably one of the finest speeches Nixon gave ... It was a very dramatic statement, relatively free of accusation and rancour, looking back over his years, and how he had tried to serve the country. If I had to list the 10 most momentous moments in my life, I think I would include that. It was a spellbinding performance.[292]

Richard Nixon walked down to the diplomatic reception room to wish President Gerald Ford well and stepped out with his wife, Pat, arm in arm with Ford and his wife, Betty, on the south side of the White House to possibly the largest gathering that lawn had ever seen. He turned at the top of the short steps to the helicopter entrance, gave a victory sign with two extended arms and flew out bound for San Clemente. Hartman and Oakley watched Nixon's departure from Geneva, realising why they had such a hard time getting meaningful responses from Washington, and what Kissinger had meant in his pep talk before their shuttle diplomacy.

On advice from Kissinger who was responding to anxiety about an imminent second assault in Cyprus, one of Ford's first presidential actions was to caution Turkish President Fahri Korutürk against humiliating Greece. Another was appointing the new ambassador, Jack B. Kubisch, a 52-year-old Missourian and experienced diplomat who knew Greek Prime Minister Konstantinos Karamanlis, to replace Henry Tasca in Athens. Kubisch was at the White House privately with the new president and Henry Kissinger talking about the Greek-Turkish problem;

> President [Gerald] Ford, whom I had known fairly well as a congressman and as Vice President, called me by my first name, 'Jack, Henry tells me that you're willing to go to Athens as our ambassador. Is that right?' And I said, 'Yes, I would welcome the assignment.' He said, 'All right, that settles it. You can go.'[293]

These dramatic developments did not budge diplomacy in Geneva, as by the end of the day Güneş was still demanding swift Greek agreement to the principle of autonomy and two separate regions.

Saturday, 10 August 1974, therefore, became about applying pressure to stop Turkish moves, which Turkey's general staff had now finalised in Operation Drop Star 4 to start on Wednesday, 14 August 1974.

Even before formal meetings began, Turkish-Cypriot leader Rauf Denktaş repeated warnings to Callaghan of a Turkish move unless the Greeks agreed in principle to two regions saying that troops were not on the island to play football. In turn, Clerides said only functional federation was acceptable even while recognising this did not satisfy

Turkey – a Turkish newspaper had that morning printed the 30 per cent land being sought between Famagusta and Lefka. George Mavros asserted that if Turkey attacked, Greece would send a whole division to Cyprus. Callaghan, again thinking of the airport precedent, encouraged Waldheim, who had stayed overnight, to think about UN resistance, which surprisingly the secretary general agreed might now be possible without a new Security Council mandate.

Back in the formal Geneva sessions, a farce ensured over name cards when the conference was formally extended to incorporate Clerides and Denktaş. Güneş wanted the Cypriot cards to show who came from the Greek community and who from Turkish one, with Mavros insisting the cards simply read, Republic of Cyprus. An overheated Güneş walked out with Denktaş following until persuaded back at 1.15 pm when everyone agreed to place cards that read Greek Community of Cyprus and Turkish Community of Cyprus.

Callaghan, determined to avoid Greek humiliation, told a stupefied Hartman at 2.30 pm of his intention to reinforce UNFICYP, saying he was for deterrence not bluff and was not going to let Turkey break the ceasefire, adding Turkish soldiers must decide how to deal with British troops wearing blue berets with anti-tank weapons and heavy artillery. Hartman who could not believe what he was hearing calmed the foreign secretary's indignation. Let's assess the situation of Turkish forces, do not give them reason for leaving the talks and do not close down options, he urged. Callaghan agreed but still insisted on preparation to forestall any Turkish move. Hartman agreed to consult Kissinger but warned that the secretary was mindful of Turkish sentiment. Callaghan, unmoved, insisted that Britain and the United States plan for Turkish action before it happened.

Once again military reality tempered Callaghan's bravado. The Ministry of Defence pointed out that UNFICYP was not strong enough to even hinder a main Turkish advance let alone deter one, and Britain did not have 5,000 troops to bolster it without affecting German or Northern Ireland commitments, which would anyway take two weeks and require air defence.

With his passion once again dimmed Callaghan kicked off a sombre 5.00 pm meeting of the five parties without photographs or without place cards, listening to an hour and a half of obvious comments. Even when they got to constitutional matters, the two accomplished barristers Denktaş and Clerides gave oratorical performances about their separate views of Cypriot history 'with no grievance left unaired'.[294] Clerides insisted on using the 1960 constitution and the Treaty of Guarantee before anything else and Denktaş insisted on two autonomous geographical regions. Their only point of agreement was to talk together in the morning.

Kissinger, settling in Ford's administration, intervened from Washington warning his former student, Prime Minister Bülent Ecevit, against unilateral military action in the first forty-eight hours of a new American presidency. Ecevit agreed to stay his hand for twenty-four hours giving Kissinger time to write back with ideas.

Five minutes later Kissinger briefed his new political master, Gerald Ford, criticising Britain for thinking about domestic elections and, therefore, 'looking for a quick success and they are a bit like a bull in a china shop'. Callaghan's backing for Greece and threat of force is 'one of the stupidest things I have heard ... It is purely a political thing. They could not pull it off. They want to get a crisis started and we would then have to settle it and they would claim credit.'[295] Kissinger instead wanted to work for compromise, having Athens accept two or three autonomous Turkish areas rather than a straightforward division of the island and being tough on the Turks to stop them moving but without giving reason to blame the United States as happened in 1964 and 1967.

He wrote to Ecevit suggesting areas for flexibility based on several cantons. A nervous Turkish government did not want to be seen presenting concessions even though Ecevit himself was thinking in terms of cantons, so turned these ideas around to be a so-called 'American plan'. Kissinger insisted these suggestions were not an American proposal and that any such ideas must be Turkish ones, at which point Ecevit confirmed no moves would happen before talks concluded. Based on these two points, Kissinger had Hartman and Macomber, in Ankara, develop ideas for Turkish Cypriots to have several areas equating to around 30 per cent of the island.

Athens meanwhile thought Turkey intended to resume activity the next day on Sunday, 11 August 1974, but could not be sure whether this was pretence. However, when it came, the day was occupied not with a fresh Turkish assault, as Ecevit stood by his commitment to Kissinger, and the Turkish generals anyway planned for 14 August, but by the so-called American plan.

First of all, reality dampened Callaghan's enthusiasm for UN deterrence when Secretary General Kurt Waldheim buckled. Waldheim's senior adviser, the much-respected British Brian Urquhart, doubted whether the current UN mandate gave sufficient authority or could happen at all given Washington's opposition and refusal to criticise Turkey – and he feared the Soviet Union's reaction when learning that reinforcements were to be British. In addition, non-aligned countries in the Security Council were split with many Muslim countries, including Iraq and Indonesia, favouring Turkey. Then British diplomats in New York also advised Callaghan that Waldheim 'can be unpredictable' and 'it might not be wholly wise to rely totally on the line he took with you'.[296]

In Ankara, Ecevit's Cabinet started an all-day meeting on whether to proceed with Operation Drop Star 4 or see if Geneva might yet fulfil Turkish needs, an unlikely prospect after three days. Güneş in Geneva had to play for time until the decision came through and spent the day making himself unavailable – Callaghan suspected him of touring local casinos.

Incredibly, the foreign secretary was undeterred by the news from the UN and privately briefed journalists about British troop movements and retention of the Phantoms, saying that soldiers were ready to open fire to protect UNFICYP. This caused a frosty noon meeting with Art Hartman, who was stunned not only by the consideration of force but publicising it as the impartial chairman of a peace conference. Kissinger 'was not happy', he said. The secretary of state was satisfied with Ecevit's overnight assurances, disagreed with Callaghan's ideas and will 'react very strongly against another public announcement of British military activities'[297] as such threats undermined him and entrenched the Turks. Hartman beseeched him to keep the talks going as to Kissinger's mind there was a real possibility of moving Ankara away from a single region proposal.

Callaghan was having none of it. What was Kissinger going to do if the Turks expanded? Hartman told him to focus on diplomatic not military efforts, causing an outburst that he was not going to sit here forever especially without Kissinger's support. The tougher you were with the Turks, the more they would listen he claimed, adding that Kissinger did not understand this and he, himself, must consider service personnel and their families. In a veiled warning, Callaghan suggested Britain might renounce the Treaty of Guarantee of 1960 and withdraw from Cyprus. He nonetheless agreed to talk to Kissinger before taking any action, and duly sent a telegram to the secretary of state stressing they use convincing diplomatic and military means against Turkey – and that he did not care for American complaints.

Relations took another hit when Callaghan inadvertently learnt from the Turkish senior diplomat Coşkun Kirka that Ecevit's Cabinet was discussing what were called 'American proposals' for a canton-based settlement. Finding out about this proposal from Turkish sources, which was actually Kissinger's attempt to find compromise and intervene with Ecevit just as Callaghan wanted, caused fury in the British camp and Callaghan to claim he was not being consulted and there was a failure in British-American communication.

Henry Kissinger was tied up, so Joe Sisco called him at 5.20 pm to smooth his feathers and explain the background behind the so-called plan. There were no American proposals, he said, instead Kissinger was testing with Ecevit whether the Turks wanted cantons or a regional split. Callaghan still grumbled about not being informed, saying he was not prepared to be a 'dummy in the middle' and still did not know the United States' position if Turkey moved. He agreed to stay on the diplomatic track, but we must all keep 'in mind the darker possibilities', which Sisco agreed to think about and reply. Following the call, Callaghan moaned that he welcomed this assurance. However, it seems inevitable that Kissinger must have put forward some ideas.[298]

Callaghan's displeasure had little effect on a Washington in no mood for a long-term rupture with NATO ally Turkey especially while reeling from the second most tumultuous period in American politics. In support of compromise and hoping to ward off Turkish action, the Department of State publicly called for greater Turkish-Cypriot autonomy in Cyprus. Greek minds mistook this as American support for Ankara, especially when Ecevit greeted it warmly in public and thanked the United States for its understanding.

Having cleared the air with Washington, Callaghan tried repairing relations with Güneş in the late afternoon. He explained that Britain's attitude was coloured by reports of Turkish military moves and that time was needed to bring the Greek Cypriots round to a cantonal solution. Turkey would not act without compelling reason, replied Güneş, which the foreign secretary took to be a second assurance but which, for Güneş, meant if the Greeks did not quickly agree to Turkish proposals. The Turkish foreign minister also hinted that Ecevit would accept cantons and not a geographical split if the Greeks quickly and formally agreed the principle of federation.

Later meetings and an apparent softer attitude from Güneş, who, still awaiting Ankara's instructions, briefly gave Callaghan reason to think 'there is just a chance that we can reach at least an oral understanding which might open the way to constitutional arrangements acceptable to all the parties'.[299] In fact with the clock ticking away, Turkey wanted the principle of federation fast: all it saw from afar was Mavros and Clerides prevaricating, which strengthened its determination that Turkish Cypriots must never again be second-class citizens.

Kissinger telephoned Ecevit a number of times to keep negotiations going and buy another thirty-six hours telling the Turkish prime minister that he would do everything to stop them through the Security Council.

Against everyone's fears of a Turkish move, Monday, 12 August 1974 instead became a day of ultimatum. Ecevit needed a solid agreement on federation lest Turkey lose its advantage, for delay weakened the bridgehead giving the Greeks chance to reinforce and transfer the problem to the UN.

At 10.30 am, Hartman told the still angry Callaghan about Kissinger's efforts to restrain Turkey and his disappointment over the term 'American proposal', adding that the secretary supported British diplomatic activity but not unhelpful military threats. This was still not enough for an irate Callaghan, who had British Ambassador Peter Ramsbottom in Washington complain about a 'family quarrel', saying that 'in the last 48 hours mutual confidence has been somewhat impaired ... you should make the point, in whatever terms you see fit, that if we and the Americans are to work together on this I must know exactly what is in [Henry] Kissinger's mind.'[300]

Putting differences with the United States aside, Callaghan worked his damnedest to tease out a diplomatic solution with nothing up his sleeve to reconcile opposing positions. Young British diplomat Peter Goulden felt the demanding nature of the whole event: 'a very exhausting conference, round the clock all the time. It was unremitting, I lost a stone in weight, and I wasn't fat at the time'. And he saw the efforts of his diligent and tactile foreign secretary trying to find answers, particularly when Callaghan once sent

> the Greek Cypriot out of the room to ring Nicosia again for permission to make yet more concessions. Callaghan leapt to his feet and walked out with him and put his arm round him saying, 'I know what it's like having to take these difficult decisions but you and I are paid to take the right decisions. If I can help in any way.'[301]

Callaghan's touch had limits, though, when dealing with the Turkish foreign minister. Goulden saw that when Güneş

> was making an awful filibustering type speech. I remember Callaghan saying out of the corner of his mouth 'I think I'm going to lose my temper. Yes I feel I'm going to lose my temper', and he slammed his fist down on the table and did a real temper tantrum which shut the Turk up, and changed the subject and stopped what was going to be a

very undesirable development. He did it in a purely theatrical way and within a minute he was back to his normal affable, cuddly Jim mode. But his ability to act that part was, I think, part of his political skill.[302]

With growing urgency Callaghan decided community leaders should work out the answer over Cyprus and sent Clerides a draft formula of 'two autonomous administrations within suitable boundaries, united under a central government' for him and Denktaş to report back to the foreign ministers in September 1974. This earnest effort lost Turkish interest for Ankara wanted the principle of federation agreed now, with domestic Turkish opinion increasingly seeing Geneva as a stalling device giving Greek Cypriots chance to lay mines around Turkish enclaves. A member of Turkey's delegation warned Peter Goulden that Britian was onto a loser, as he could not control Turkish generals, so British diplomats stood no chance.

Clerides could not, in any event, agree two regions but offered to take the proposals back to Nicosia on condition that acceptance of any framework resulted in Turkish troop withdrawals. His opposite number, Rauf Denktaş, who was himself upset to learn that Turan Güneş was even contemplating a cantonal solution as well as two regions, said he must speak with his side and the Turks before agreeing any draft, though he thought agreement with Clerides was possible if there were backing from Athens. Callaghan, therefore, pushed for that support from George Mavros who, in turn, said he needed time to consult with Prime Minister Konstantinos Karamanlis.

Despite all Callaghan's preparation the local leaders could not agree on any draft along these lines when he joined their afternoon meeting at 4.40 pm. Rauf Denktaş still opposed a cantonal solution and even submitted his own draft for 34 per cent of land in a northeast triangle. Clerides continued to refuse two regions under a single government though would consider groupings of villages.

Then at 6.30 pm, Turan Güneş issued his ultimatum. Armed with new instructions to get agreement or stop the conference, he told Callaghan that the Turkish Cabinet had examined the cantonal ideas but decided the best solution was two main regions with further Turkish cantons in the Greek area and handed over a United Kingdom map showing the detail. Unless Clerides accepted these two zones now, he was off. Callaghan remonstrated saying Clerides would be overthrown to which Güneş retorted he would be overthrown if no solution were agreed tonight. The foreign secretary acquiesced and arranged another meeting.

A flurry of conversations followed to test the waters. At 7.35 pm, Callaghan pushed Clerides to accept a cantonal system with counter proposals to steal the Turks' thunder and keep them talking. Denktaş then told him Turkey had lost patience: newspaper reports of being hemmed in by Greek forces had enraged the army and they were ready to shoot through the UN, adding that Güneş was told to finish the talks tonight, which the foreign secretary read as a dawn attack.

'After my call to Ecevit has failed, what do we do?' asked Kissinger of his senior diplomats at 2.45 pm in Washington, including British Ambassador Peter Ramsbottom who had been patiently waiting to see him. His dilemma was stopping Turkey without damaging the United States' long-term relationship, which meant agreeing a UN resolution of condemnation but not cutting military aid when suggested by some of his staff. 'We are throwing the threat of military assistance around like it is charity. What is the long-range advantage to the US?', he questioned before stamping down on Ramsbottom's comment that Germany was reviewing its own aid: 'We did that after the Suez Crisis in '56 – a grandstand play and look where it got us'.[303] With no obvious answers Joe Sisco went off to draw up options while Kissinger continued working on Ecevit over the canton ideas.

He then telephoned Callaghan to soothe the still aggrieved foreign secretary saying Watergate had put him 'virtually out of touch' with Cyprus and that writing to Ecevit about cantons was not an American proposal but the right thing to do and Britain would get a copy. In any event, the United States was not about to incur hostility from Athens or Ankara and weaken NATO by pushing them too far. Speaking frankly, he 'cared less about events in Cyprus itself'.[304]

Kissinger called Ecevit at 4.15 pm in Washington who agreed to waive the deadline Güneş was insisting on and give the Greeks time for counter proposals the next day, Tuesday, 13 August 1974. He updated Callaghan, before speaking again to Ecevit, now early morning in Ankara, who admitted Turkey's deadline came from the military and he promised to do what he could to control them.

At 10.40 pm in Geneva, Callaghan met with Güneş who, desperate to forestall the generals, responded angrily when told that Clerides wanted to make further proposals. He insisted the Greeks accept a Turkish northern region and five other districts or the conference finishes. Kissinger interrupted their conversation to inform Callaghan about Ecevit's agreement to delay – Güneş unaware of the concession rambled on about the non-negotiable condition until Ecevit himself interrupted to give his foreign minister new instructions.

Güneş duly told Callaghan they should all meet at 10.00 am next day giving Greece chance to review the proposals and then reconvene at 6.00 pm to either accept or reject them. Callaghan's protests for a longer postponement got nowhere, though even his senior adviser Alan Goodison doubted the benefits of delay, for while this might give Kissinger time to coral both sides into agreement it might also permit the 'massacres, mass expulsions, mass movements of panic-stricken refugees, and preparations for war in Greece and regrouping for war in Turkey ... we need an agreement, not a diplomatic trick, now. I do not believe we can secure this.'[305]

No one harboured any illusions that Turkey meant business when the conference resumed on the final day of Wednesday, 14 August 1974. Defence chiefs in London made ready to order another evacuation from the dormitory towns but only when a Turkish attack was certain for despite all the information pointing to a dawn attack they could find no local intelligence reports to substantiate that assessment. Neither London nor Washington could once again be sure whether this was Turkish bluff.

When all the leaders met at 10.00 am in Geneva, Clerides gave Denktaş a counter proposal accepting autonomy and a grouping of villages but rejecting regional separation or population movements. Can you at least concede the principle of geographic separation pleaded Callaghan rather wearily while 'coming to the personal view that the least dangerous solution was letting the Turks to concentrate in a single zone within a federated state'.[306] Clerides refused. Opinion was not ready in Cyprus nor was Makarios, so all the Cypriot acting president offered was for Mavros and him to consult their respective governments and return with a clearer answer tomorrow night. This emitted a single ray of hope as a senior Greek diplomat Angelos Vlachos in Athens suggested privately that if Britain and the United States made the proposals, Athens and Nicosia might at least agree percentages, though excluding Famagusta and Kokkina, which were chief Turkish objectives.

Güneş inevitably refused any extension when Callaghan passed on the news an hour later and insisted the deadline remain 10.00 pm, saying that he must leave tonight with or without agreement. Callaghan exhorted Kissinger just after midday to get Ecevit's agreement for another extension, and also let off some steam about Güneş treating him in an unforgiveable manner by refusing an extension while giving no time to consider the ultimatum. Bill Macomber in Ankara duly urged another thirty-six hour adjournment on Ecevit who, having agreed one already and with his military ready to move, resisted.

Kissinger then told the Turkish prime minister that if he could not give thirty-six hours the United States would oppose Turkey without being clear on what this meant.

To apply pressure, the Department of State issued another statement against 'unjustified military action' with a supporting carrot to show understanding by saying 'we recognize the position of Turkish Cyprus requires considerable improvement and protection. We have supported a greater degree of autonomy for them.' Greek nationalists again misinterpreted this as a coded green light not the true purpose in trying to influence a country over which Washington had minimal control, and which now considered itself isolated from most of the Western world.

Kissinger briefed new President Gerald Ford in the early afternoon on the consequences of a conference breakup. The United States would condemn Turkey in the UN and make every effort to stop war between the two countries, 'but if it came to that, Turkey is more important to us and they have a political structure which could produce a Qadhafi [sic]'. Kissinger explained he was resisting internal pressure for an embargo because this was not in the United States' interests as 'There is no American reason why the Turks should not have one-third of Cyprus'.[307] Besides this, opium was a more important issue affecting middle America and continuing to haunt relations with Ankara, Nixon having prepared another letter of complaint to send out before resigning. They decided to delay issuing the letter and see how events unfolded in Cyprus.

The United States did not have many options as Sisco's analysis paper later that day revealed. This submission cleared by expert John Day bleakly anticipated one of three outcomes: a breakdown of talks without Turkish action, one with military action and one that saw Greek-Turkish fighting outside Cyprus. American experts concluded,

> Our goal, as in July [1974], should be to prevent Greek-Turkish hostilities and to get talks started. But the situation will be worse than in July – both governments will be passionately united, talking will appear to have been unproductive, and the Greeks will have no military option whatsoever on Cyprus, so that Thracian hostilities are more likely.[308]

At 6.40 pm in Geneva, Jim Callaghan opened the most extraordinary meeting of his political career. In a tense atmosphere and working to Ecevit's deadline, the four delegations spent seven hours disagreeing, reciting history, making claims and counter claims in acts of sober theatre, anger and sorrow. Güneş summarised his latest proposals before opening a debate about the continued failure of the Greek National Guard to evacuate Turkish-Cypriot enclaves and refused an extension for Mavros and Clerides to consult in Athens and Nicosia. Callaghan's appeals for 36 hours to solve a 200-year-old problem had no effect. Round and round went the arguments until they adjourned at 9.00 pm.

When resuming at 10.15 pm, Güneş presented two proposal: one, the cantonal plan of the previous evening for a large northern region and five smaller cantons in the south, and the second for a straightforward division incorporating the Turkish part of Famagusta and Turkish controlled Nicosia, continuing westwards amounting to 34 per cent of Cyprus. Size and detail were negotiable he said whereas geographical separation and federation in a single state were not.

Clerides requested forty-eight hours to consult their respective governments about what appeared modified ideas. Güneş refused, saying these proposals had been known about before the conference and they had all been beating about the bush since 8 August 1974. Mavros and Clerides insisted on consultation against an ultimatum by gun as did Callaghan, which the Turkish delegation dismissed as more prevarication. They adjourned again around 1.20 am.

In Ankara, Prime Minister Bülent Ecevit had to make a final decision. From the Turkish perspective, nothing had been achieved over five days apart from Greek prevarication on positions aired before the conference, with time favouring Karamanlis's government gaining in international prestige and Greek troops reinforcing themselves against Turkish positions, which though steady and well-armed were squeezed into small areas vulnerable in the long term. The balance of risk lay in sticking to the plan.

By contrast, Cypriot Acting President Clerides had a gun to his head from many sides, including Makarios and needed time to bring opinion along, if this were even possible, for either of the proposals meant displacing tens of thousands of Greek Cypriots. In Athens, Prime Minister Konstantinos Karamanlis, however pragmatic, led a weak government of a sore and humiliated country, which could not impose a solution without Cypriot consent.

Turkish Foreign Minister Turan Güneş was enjoying some refreshments during the break when a member of his delegation, Haluk Ulman, gave him a personal message from the prime minister. Apparently, Güneş's daughter had finished her holiday preparations and Ecevit had said she can go. A bemused Ulman did not understand why on earth the prime minister would be concerned with such a trivial matter given the affairs at stake. Güneş understood perfectly.

At 1.40 am, he went back to the talks for another twenty minutes of repeated arguments before boiling down the issues to one question, whether they all agreed the principal of regionalism in the form of two zones and cantons over 34 per cent outlined in his map. Clerides, supported by Callaghan, stated that they needed forty-eight hours to consider them with an open mind. Güneş said that, in that case, the conference was finished. Callaghan tried to forestall him by reading out a note supporting an extension from French ambassadors in Ankara and Athens on behalf of the European Community, which the foreign secretary had requested a few hours earlier. These did not move Güneş who said his words were final.

That was it. Callaghan, Mavros and Clerides confirmed their willingness to return on Thursday, Denktaş agreed if that was the wish of Turkey, but Güneş said nothing, rose from the table and parted with his aides, in Callaghan's view ungraciously, ending the meeting at 2.25 am. The others shook hands and wandered out.

Turkey began Operation Drop Star 4 thirty-five minutes later.

Chapter 20

RECRIMINATION, REAPPRAISALS AND ASSASSINATION

Henry Kissinger became the focus of everyone's attention. Prime Minister Konstantinos Karamanlis stayed defiant in refusing to meet President Gerald Ford until the United States forced Turkey to withdraw, supported by many in Congress and Britain, who similarly maintained that Kissinger should apply pressure on Turkey. Kissinger held out fearing damage to the United States' long-term interest and conscious not to repeat the mistakes of 1964 and 1967, though with one ambassador slain he began feeling the personal load of his responsibility.

With the Turkish operation more or less over, Callaghan, conscious of Britain's own continuing 1960 responsibilities, pushed Turkey and Greece with American backing to restart the Geneva process. He wrote to Ecevit on Tuesday, 20 August 1974 for five-way talks on the basis of two regions provided Turkey made gestures, including troop withdrawals; and repeated these terms to Karamanlis arguing that delay would inevitably reduce the prospects of securing concessions from the Turks.

Injected into his thinking were Whitehall defence recommendations for British forces to leave Cyprus. Troop numbers had already been reduced in the first defence review but now officials, spooked by vulnerability to ethnic conflict and forced to find more cuts, wanted out as much as possible. By no means a universal view it was the deciding one when Sir Geoffrey Arthur, a seasoned ambassador and influential chair of the Joint Intelligence Committee, submitted a brutal assessment on 20 August 1974 that the bases 'are more liability than an asset'. Turkey, he pointed out, had expected Britain to intervene after the coup as had Greece afterwards to stop a Turkish assault, 'We did neither, though to all appearances we were best placed, since we alone commanded bases in Cyprus, to do both'. And, he added, while the bases had saved countless lives protecting refugees and UNFICYP 'we shall get little thanks'.[309]

Arthur realised practical issues stopped complete abandonment. The Soviet Union must be denied the island, the United States clearly would not countenance it and there were thorny problems about which Cypriot community should get the land and who would support UNFICYP. Nonetheless, he made clear the significance of the bases 'has declined, is still declining, and may soon vanish',[310] which still set in train a process for further force reductions and an almighty row with Washington.

Henry Kissinger faced his own problems in calming congressional passion for injunctions on Turkish aid, which become the new threat. President Gerald Ford and he briefed a bipartisan congressional lobby that same day to keep them sweet, arguing that an aid injunction would not have changed the outcome and risked making Turkey a rogue state. He pointed out that American policy was to encourage Britain to present a federal solution with the United States playing a more active role. Ford admitted the Greek community did not think much of him but would likely come around – a comment that fell flat for congressional action was tempered but not eliminated.

Rodger Davies's body was returned to Washington on Wednesday, 21 August 1974. Dana, 20, and John, 15, disembarked from the plane at Andrews Air Force Base greeted by President Gerald Ford and Henry Kissinger to a nineteen-gun salute. Ford praised Davies as 'a great patriot, one of our most respected and admired diplomats'[311] and presented Dana with the folded Stars and Stripes. Kissinger awarded Davies the highest possible award for an American diplomat, the Secretary of State Award; the citation reading 'Ambassador Rodger P. Davies: For inspiring leadership, outstanding courage and dedication to duty for which he gave his life, Nicosia, Aug. 19, 1974.' The United States Air Force 707 flew on to Hamilton Air Force Base, California, where Davies was laid to rest in Berkeley.

Lindsey Grant, back in Nicosia as deputy ambassador, came face to face with local feeling when Cypriot Foreign Minister Ioannis Christophides signed Davies's book of condolence. Christophides told Grant how Davies had been 'murdered by the CIA because he was too soft on the Greeks, that it was all our fault that the war started, we had put the junta up to it. It was just an incredible reversal in a week. A week before he had had nothing to say about a US role.'[312]

William Crawford, the current ambassador to Yemen and an expert on Middle Eastern affairs, was named as Davies's permanent replacement. He was hiking on holiday in the Norwegian Fjords when he found the local police waiting for him atop one of the highest peaks and was later flown to the American Embassy to learn Henry Kissinger had ordered his return to Washington.

On the diplomatic front, a wide gulf between Turkish and Greek demands hampered Kissinger's statecraft. While Bülent Ecevit said he was ready to discuss the size of the Turkish zones and phased troop reductions, the Department of State doubted the extent as the Turkish army was digging in for winter, planned mopping up operations and was sitting pretty with no moral or diplomatic-political pressure to concede land. Ecevit also said Greek Cypriots would not be expelled from Turkish zones, while admitting to British Ambassador Horace Phillips those who left 'would not be invited to return'.[313]

And neither Prime Minister Konstantinos Karamanlis nor Acting President Glafcos Clerides had reason to start any negotiation in the face of Turkey's *fait accompli*. Both were hostages to embarrassment, each privately recognising the importance of concessions yet each unable to yield anything given their enemies on the right and the left. Karamanlis still refused the American invitation and insisted Turkey withdraw to a ceasefire line of Friday, 9 August 1974. Callaghan again appealed to Kissinger on Thursday, 22 August 1974, to push the Turks on troop reductions as the only way to save Greek honour and get them to Geneva. This Kissinger would not do for fear of losing Ankara, though every day that passed strengthened the national and international mood in the other direction.

Stung by the whole affair, not the least American criticism, Callaghan grasped Arthur's withdrawal recommendations about withdrawing with both hands. In his view,

> We should now prepare plans for closing them [the RAF bases] down. I see no future in Cyprus for us. Politically whatever we patch up in Geneva III ... will be unlikely to last if the Greeks sometime later insist on revenge. Then we should be embarrassed once more. So let's not be too long about getting out.[314]

He wanted to know when to talk to the Americans 'because our major interest is not a UK interest any more [*sic*], but a general interest in preventing the Island from being used for anti-Western purposes'.[315]

The Soviet Union exploited the lack of progress with proposals for a UN international conference and a joint guarantee with the United States, which Britain thought were intended to sabotage efforts to restart Geneva. Konstantinos Karamanlis flirted with the idea to win attention from the West. This worried Kissinger who foresaw the growth of the left wing in Greece, ever nationalistic armed forces and a weakening Greek prime minister who could not afford to make any deals so instead stoked anti-American sentiment. And he was becoming the personal brunt of it all with minimal influence, which now risked the American military being kicked out of Greece, while West Germany and France jockeyed to replace the United States creating the image of Europe for the Greeks and the United States for the Turks. Accusations of responsibility for Davies's death did not help his mood.

He wrote to Callaghan about these concerns on Saturday, 24 August 1974, stressing that Greece must be brought round to negotiations and support Clerides to reach agreement with Turkish Cypriots, adding that pressure on Turkey should only be done within the context of a negotiated solution. The letter disrupted Callaghan's holiday in the hot August sunshine. The foreign secretary was in no mind to leave this comfort and look ridiculous waiting for participants in Geneva who might never show up and anyway expected Prime Minister Harold Wilson imminently to call a general election, which for this senior Labour politician harbouring his own leadership ambitions was more important. Not wanting to be caught out by further press briefings and worried by Kissinger's complaints about Europe, he sent over senior diplomats John Killick and Michael Alexander to Washington as Kissinger did not appear 'in his present attitude ... taking sufficient account of the longer-term consequences of failure.'[316]

In the meantime, Washington and London started what groundwork they could to resume negotiations before the island became permanently divided, though the Foreign and Commonwealth Office was convinced not much could happen without American pressure. Ambassador Robin Hooper wrote from Athens,

If Dr [Henry] Kissinger is prepared to pay this sort of price, well and good. But unless he is, and unless the pressure succeeds in producing the sort of package that the Greeks could be pushed into accepting as a basis for discussion, I fear we shall get nowhere [and in which case the initiative should not be attempted].[317]

The United States had few levers to apply in the face of Turkish intransigence riding on the back of whipped up nationalism. Ecevit was prepared to discuss troop withdrawal only when a main agreement was reached and to reduce Turkish controlled land only once Turkish Cypriots went northwards – refusing to consider Greek refugees until a permanent settlement was reached. Ankara's tight reins on Rauf Denktaş also limited any local progress.

On Tuesday, 27 August 1974, William Crawford's confirmation hearing as ambassador to Cyprus was rushed through by the Senate in two hours. New York Senator Jacob Javits warned Kissinger:

> Greek Americans have never exercised national political influence ... They've never before exercised this essentially tremendous weight on a national level. But the Cyprus issue has galvanized them as they have never been galvanized before, and they have a structure through which to bring political influence to bear on the national level. If from time to time, Dr [Henry] Kissinger, you have had reason in your mind to take issue with the Jewish lobby, just wait till the Greek lobby hits you.[318]

Laughter followed his comments, but their force proved true within weeks.

During his ceremony, Crawford spoke about an island whose very independence and unity were threatened without fast action to prevent permanent division. 'Word came down through Arthur Hartman, the Assistant Secretary for European Affairs, that the Secretary had rather blown up about his new ambassador in Cyprus making policy before he even arrived on the island'. Crawford defended himself saying that he was stating the obvious. 'Well, the Secretary is angry', replied Hartman. And became more so when Crawford confessed, he was calling on Makarios on the way over to Cyprus. 'Arthur looked troubled. I guess he realized more than I did at that point the extent to which the ... Secretary of State did not like Archbishop Makarios, and vice versa.'[319] Hartman shrugged his shoulders and said he would tell Kissinger that Crawford could not turn down an official invitation without causing insult.

John Killick, a much-respected British diplomat sporting a fine moustache conveying the aura of an Indian general, and Michael Alexander, Callaghan's private secretary and a former Olympic fencer, did not move Kissinger when meeting later in the day. Little time passed before the secretary of state wondered why 'I seem to be the villain of your negotiations and I wonder how I got there',[320] pointing out that American policy would have been the same without Watergate. Killick described Britain's predicament of being criticised by all sides for not using military force, to which Kissinger wryly noted the Turks were not unhappy.

Both sides agreed they must stop the Cyprus position crystallising but differed starkly on the approach. Britain wanted fast movement fearing Greek action and worrying about refugee conditions. Killick warned that 'Callaghan is not prepared to put the UK in an exposed position in this sense without the US making a major effort to persuade the Turks to make concessions. It will depend on your leverage and how you would go about it'. An unmoved Kissinger did not intend submitting American ideas without knowing everyone's position saying, 'Last time round, the US had been sufficiently involved to carry some responsibility but not sufficiently to have control'. This was not going to happen again, he continued; 'You want a US "heave". I am not at all eager for us to be in a position where it can be alleged that the UK failed because we did not do enough. Failure would, therefore, be the US fault.'[321]

He also thought Callaghan's initiative premature saying, 'I am very worried that if the Turks do not play, then the UK will announce that the beastly Turks had thwarted their efforts.'[322] Besides he wanted Greece to stop bashing the United States. Killick said they were not here lay the blame but wanted to avoid repeat charges of impotence when 'we had responsibility without power'.[323] 'Until the Greeks stop picking on us, we will do nothing to help them',[324] replied Kissinger, conceding that he would apply pressure but only in the right way and time and not publicly and not by using aid for the complexities of getting it restarted by Congress. 'My concern now is that the outcome be such that it [does] not cause the Greeks to dance in the streets. The Turks have gained and the Greeks have lost, but in the negotiations the Greeks will have to gain something and the Turks will have to lose something'.[325]

Kissinger briefed Gerald Ford who agreed Britain should stay in front and Killick briefed Callaghan by telephone who consequently decided to abandon his negotiations initiative.

A day later, Prime Minister Konstantinos Karamanlis, with few levers apart from pressure on the international community, formally announced a military withdrawal from NATO, accusing the alliance of reacting with surprising apathy and acting as a mere bystander. His actions were intended to soothe his own people for Greece had more to lose in funding, training, courses and access to facilities, for which reason the mechanism for leaving was deliberately vague as was a threat to close American bases. NATO politicians ignored the announcement unless Greece pushed the matter.

On his way to take up appointment in Nicosia, American Ambassador William Crawford met Makarios in London on Friday, 30 August 1974 to try and win over the deposed Cypriot president. This mattered, for Crawford felt

> it helped pull back on the suspicion, which Makarios really had, that the United States had not only supported the junta, but also its effort to remove him. So it helped to get me off on a better foot. At least I didn't have Makarios and his supporters against me.[326]

Crawford then arrived in Cyprus to rigid security, assigned two American bodyguards who stayed with him even in the residence.

> The windows were blocked off with sheets of steel, so it was very hard to tell when it was daytime or nighttime. I got out very little. When I did, it was always accompanied by two extra cars of Cypriot police, all armed fore and aft. In the car there was so much bullet-proofing, I couldn't see out of my own window. And a great deal of hostility. The Greek Cypriots, by and large, people I had known socially in the earlier period, few of them came forward to offer anything. Those who did knew they were risking their lives or, at minimum, violent criticism. I was enormously grateful to the brave few who did.[327]

Chapter 21

CREATION OF A VILLAIN

A race began to achieve another ceasefire in more difficult circumstances, but this time with a strange calm among Western politicians, who, having no levers to influence the Turkish consolidation, resigned themselves to hopes of a swift operation.

Tired and angry, Callaghan held an immediate press conference squarely blaming Turkey's refusal to give Greece thirty-six hours to consider proposals, saying 'I cannot believe that in view of the assurances that have been given to me day after day by the Turkish Foreign Minister. There can be no military solution to the problems of Cyprus.'[328]

As if to cause affront, Turkey started Operation Drop Star 4 even while he was speaking with fighter bombers in action east of Nicosia and firing across the demarcation line. One Turkish plane flew over the Hilton hotel of BBC journalist John Sergeant strafing the swimming pool and the roof in a terrifying few moments. The telephone lines were cut again so Sergeant filed his report through a fellow Fleet Street journalist. Aircraft firing at Famagusta began their attacking runs over RAF Dhekelia land with return fire by National Guard anti-aircraft positions, causing warnings to all service families to stay in their quarters. Turkey provided assurances about the safety of the bases.

John Aiken, swiftly recalled from holiday in Rome, ordered another early morning evacuation of service families back to the bases, which this time was 'very much simpler, faster and altogether less dramatic than the first evacuation'.[329] To avoid any repeat of overcrowding, Aiken had families fly straight back to the United Kingdom from RAF Akrotiri with flights every thirty minutes between 14 and 16 August 1974. He ignored Turkey's imposition of a no-fly zone, signalling the

Turkish general staff that 'I do not recognise this "newly imposed danger area ... Any attack on my aircraft or ships carrying out their lawful business will be construed as that of one against the aircraft or ships of a NATO ally."'[330]

Henry Kissinger who learnt of the new fighting while at an Egyptian Embassy dinner in honour of visiting Foreign Minister Ismail Fahmi sent out cables urging calm to Athens, Ankara and Nicosia; and, to work hard on the aggrieved Greeks, invited Prime Minister Konstantinos Karamanlis to meet with President Gerald Ford in Washington.

Karamanlis, for his part, assembled his new Cabinet at 5.00 am in the Greek Pentagon to make the most important decision any politician could. Should they go to war against a dominant military force with only one outcome likely? Could Greece start a contained fight in Thrace where it enjoyed a better balance of forces? In a remarkable act of statesmanship, he resisted calls for war and instead requested immediate NATO support under the collective defence arrangements, avoiding a conflict that may have caused ethnic savagery against Turks in Thessaloniki and smaller Greek communities in Turkey and split the Western alliance.

In reality, the Greek prime minister had no option for the defence position had not improved since the military told Ioannidis two weeks earlier that demoralised forces were not ready to fight Turkey. How could Greece now defend its northern border, the Aegean Islands and Cyprus with a military disrupted by seven years of convulsion and an air force incapable of reaching the island in one leg? Even his resort to diplomatic levers had limitations for NATO had no intention of supporting one member state against another. Athens, therefore, informed NATO boss Dr Joseph Luns that Greece was withdrawing its military membership from the Alliance.

His government still explored limited ways to send some supplies and reinforcements, first testing whether this could be done in concert with Britain or with the United States. Foreign Minister George Mavros asked British Ambassador Robin Hooper about joint action under the Treaty of Guarantee of 1960, sending out a Greek division from Crete. What was Britain's reaction? Would it provide air cover once Greek jets went beyond their range? This was no more likely than Britain helping Turkey after the coup against Makarios, and the last thing the West wanted was wider conflict. Kissinger got wind of the request and quickly made his opposition known.

As Callaghan and his downbeat delegation flew back to London, diplomat Peter Goulden saw how the beleaguered foreign secretary still found time for his staff:

> Everybody was exhausted, [Jim] Callaghan more than anybody probably, but he went right round the plane thanking every clerk and every secretary. He sat by them one by one, patted them on the knee saying, 'I saw what you did, I appreciated what you did on that day, it made a difference for me.' And I thought that was a great politician using his political instincts to very good effect. But it was overall a failure, and it was probably the best opportunity that we had to solve the crisis.[331]

Art Hartman and Bob Oakley hitched a lift back giving them chance to chew the cud with the foreign secretary. Callaghan made a prescient comment presaging future changes in foreign policy telling Hartman that 'Henry [Kissinger] is a good friend of mine. When you go back tell him I don't mind ... but he has got to show there is a humanitarian concern in most of the initiatives.' Hartman defended his boss saying that he thought Kissinger had shown concern for the Turks because the Greeks did not appreciate the harm they had caused. The foreign secretary replied that 'there were things on both sides and the Greeks remember what the Turks did'.[332]

Callaghan got back to London, refreshed himself and spoke to Kissinger in a now calmer atmosphere at 1.45 pm with both concluding there was nothing more to do until Turkey quickly grabbed its proposed line, after which diplomacy could restart. From Callaghan's perspective 'the Turks have got a good case, which can only be resolved by the creation of a zone ... [and] let diplomacy take over when we see the opportunity once more.' In the meantime, 'Greece will need massaging because the Turks are too jingoistic, indeed too close to [Adolf] Hitler for my liking'. He also warned Kissinger to beware Greece turning on the United States as it started to on Britain, 'You're not going to act, we're not going to act unilaterally and the UN is going to get out of the way'.[333] To mend badly damaged fences between them, newly installed President Gerald Ford sitting next to Kissinger thanked Callaghan for his efforts.

A few minutes later, Callaghan, Harold Wilson, Secretary of Defence Roy Mason and senior officials killed off any idea of military support for Greece. Callaghan saying conclusively that 'the US would do nothing militarily. The UK could not act unilaterally. The UN would ... keep their heads down ... [and] ... the Turks were very concerned not to embarrass us and would leave the SBAs [sovereign base areas] alone.'[334] Wilson, therefore, decided there was no question of British intervention, which meant war with Turkey, but, in fact, there probably never was.

A meeting with Kurt Waldheim in London at 3.30 pm elicited actions only for UN diplomacy. Callaghan blamed Turkish intransigence and lost no time denouncing Güneş's 'delaying and deadline tactics'. He also blamed the Americans, saying they themselves now realised had acted too late, mentioning an American official – probably Art Hartman on the plane back – telling him that 'we did not give the backing you needed'.[335] Callaghan, therefore, gave Waldheim only moral support for Britain was not lending UNFICYP any more troops.

Kissinger set out the United States' response that afternoon to the Special Actions Group while Turkey was advancing but Greek forces had not yet reacted. Director of Central Intelligence William Colby was not entirely sure of Turkey's plans but thought a Greek-Turkish war unlikely. 'Our major strategy now', said Kissinger, 'is not to get ourselves in a position that would give vent to righteous indignation on the part of either the Greeks or the Turks' and to keep in with both government. 'We don't want to contribute to the Greek humiliation, and we don't want the Turks to feel that we have turned against them ... What we want now is to get a disengagement of forces'. In doing so, he all too quickly dismissed Sisco's prophetic concern about growing anti-American sentiment, arguing that 'We don't really care at this point about rising anti-Americanism in Greece. We're not playing 48-hour politics here. Our interest is in what happens three weeks from now'.[336]

No more could be done until all three affected American ambassadors reported back, and an assessment made of the Greek and Turkish positions. As they waited, Thursday, 15 August 1974 saw Sisco's comments about Greek anger come to life, incensed at the sight of 200,000 refugees fleeing south particularly from Famagusta. Many along with Turkish refugees coming the other way sought refuge in the British bases arriving 'on foot, in small cars, on tractors and on mule drawn carts. Some managed to travel on buses and it was a daunting experience to see so many people with dazed and fearful expressions peering through the windows.'[337]

These refugees provided fuel to turn on the United States. Diplomat James Williams stationed in Cyprus saw this mood swing when accompanying Ambassador Rodger Davies to see Clerides. As their flag-bearing Cadillac arrived, huge numbers of refugees milling around turned angry and started bashing the car.

We had a police escort so we didn't think we were in any danger. It was becoming a mob, and it was clearly not friendly ... We got out of there as quickly as we could because the mob was getting bigger and as I said was just not friendly. Again, nobody was hurt, there were no rocks thrown or any other objects, but it was an ugly mood.[338]

Ambassador Rodger Davies submitting his report to the Department of State later that day lamented how a typical Greek-Cypriot man willingly believes reports of US support for Turkey. A returned Art Hartman found the mood in Congress turning as well:

I came home and faced a barrage from some of my old friends in Congress. Paul Sarbanes and his friend, John Brademas ... I was attacked because they couldn't get their hands on Henry [Kissinger]. He was doing his important work of shuttle diplomacy in the Middle East, of all these guys who had both Greek and Jewish constituents were a little rough, but with me the gloves were off and they really let me have it. I went up and defended a more even-handed policy, which they thought was indefensible and they began attaching all kinds of restrictions to legislation. It was not good ... The scars from that remain with me.[339]

In front of television cameras, Prime Minister Konstantinos Karamanlis solemnly told his people why Greece was not going to war. Wearing a black suit, white shirt and black tie, he condemned the deplorable and senseless action of the junta and Turkey's exploitation of events, and explained how opposing the Turks in Cyprus was made impossible by the distance from the mainland and the risk of weaking the defences of Greece. In Ankara, Bülent Ecevit certainly did not want war assuring Ambassador Bill Macomber that Turkey wanted only a third of the island.

An afternoon Turkish trespass onto a British base startled local commanders when an observation post spotted thirty-five Turkish tanks advancing on Famagusta 3 miles north of RAF Dhekelia. The column suddenly changed direction and headed right for the northern tip of the base, with seven tanks splitting off and travelling to within a few hundred yards of the north-west boundary where they fired three shells into the base narrowly missing a Ferret Scout car and a white Thames Television van. The Ferret driver snappily drove off taking the television crew with him. The Turkish column then regrouped in seeming preparation to attack the nearby National Guard camp, which returned fire, one shell passing through the NAAFI roof and another starting a fire on scrubland east of the base, which a fortuitous wind directed away. John Aiken quickly told the Turkish commander in chief through the UN and the High Commission that 'Your troops have entered British Sovereign Territory and fired on British Troops. This is to cease forthwith.'[340]

An assurance swiftly followed but the tanks stayed put so two curious colonels, Ian Cartright, commanding the Royal Fusiliers, and H.A. Johnstone, commanding 9th Signals Regiment, brazenly walked out 2 miles by themselves unarmed to have a look. They eventually came across the crews of three squadrons of Turkish tanks and one company of mounted infantry having a brew up. Cartright and Johnstone 'were relieved to learn that the Turks had strict orders not to fire on the SBAs [sovereign base areas] and they were able to explain to them the position of the boundary'.[341] No explanation was given for the tank fire however, with one report even ending up on Henry Kissinger's desk suggesting Turkey was attacking the RAF base.

A Turkish staff officer flew into RAF Akrotiri to give further assurances. This did not stop another shock an hour later when a lone Turkish tank drove up to the base boundary scaring Greek-Cypriot refugees pouring in and British soldiers alike. Contact was tentatively made with the isolated tank crew, which were found to be hopelessly lost, out of ammunition and fuel and suffering from a broken radio and a jammed machine gun. Fuel was quickly found to escort the tank to the northern edge of the base and then sent on its way to the known Turkish position.

From London, Callaghan told Kissinger he had formally turned down the Greek reinforcement request. He then annoyed the secretary of state by saying he was taking a holiday with no intention of rushing back to Geneva if talks resumed, leaving Foreign Minister Roy Hattersley on hand if needed. This confirmed for Kissinger his growing personal view about Callaghan's reliability in high-level diplomacy. Other points of difference resurfaced when Callaghan said he feared a buoyant Turkey might act outside of Cyprus, which Kissinger doubted though said he would crack down on military supplies in that case.

Kissinger dismissed similar worries from his own staff later that morning at the Special Actions Group when even Director of Central Intelligence William Colby suggested Turkey might move into the south-west causing Konstantinos Karamanlis to fall in Athens. He disagreed, 'Well, I think that once this Turkish operation runs its course, they won't go any further. We won't stand for it. We just can't stand for any more Turk operations. They have already stretched us to the limit'.[342] For good measure, President Gerald Ford issued a press statement disapproving of Turkish military action on Cyprus and strongly urging immediate compliance with relevant United Nations ceasefire resolution.

Towards the end of the afternoon, Kissinger decided on an initiative to restart the Geneva process telling his senior staff that 'I am persuaded that Callaghan does not know how to do these things himself. He should have taken a more neutral position and put concrete proposals on the table.'[343] However, he now realised the extent of Greek grievance as Karamanlis had still not replied to the invitation to visit Washington, so had senior aide Wells Stabler set down everything American had done to avert Turkish action and show Athens his even handedness. In considering positions, he thought it best 'to have the Turks give up 10 per cent of the 30 per cent of the territory they have'.[344]

He spoke first with Bülent Ecevit who said that Operation Drop Star 4 would finish at noon the next day. In turn, Kissinger agreed to try and influence a vote on an impending French drafted Security Council resolution calling on Turkey to withdraw from Cyprus. (France, already a significant provider of military equipment to Greece, sensed a chance to displace the United States in sore Greek political hearts by sponsoring another resolution criticising Turkey.)

An hour later, he had a difficult conversation with the Greek prime minister who rebuffed his invitation, saying, 'I don't think because you know it is difficult for me to leave the country. We have many problems. The people are very bitter, angry, the armies are upset. It is difficult to leave the country. Maybe a little later, but just now it is impossible.'[345] You must get the Turks out not just advise them insisted Karamanlis. Kissinger diplomatically offered to call him again the next day.

At midday on Friday, 16 August 1974, Prime Minister Bülent Ecevit agreed with his generals and his Cabinet that Turkey had achieved its prime object enough to consider a ceasefire, which he later told Kissinger could come by 3.00 pm. This ceasefire, while welcome, did not calm fury across the Greek-speaking community, whose American constituents marched in Washington on what became the first of eighteen significant demonstrations.

Prime Minister Harold Wilson sent Karamanlis a personal message explaining why sending in a Greek division was unwise and encouraged him to work for a negotiated settlement. The best way of bringing Turkey to the table, he added, was to avoid prolonging the fighting, gain international support and, realistically, push the federal solution.

Later in the afternoon, Ecevit told the United States and Britain he was ready to resume Geneva at any time, adding that if the Greeks did not want to negotiate there would inevitably be two separate areas without any uniting bond of a central government. He confirmed there would be no major violation of the current demarcation line.

Meanwhile, British diplomats tried working out their own position. Senior official Alan Goodison thought 'we should not go to the conference table until we are sure of the basic ingredients of a settlement in terms of the broad policies and attitudes of the parties'.[346] He considered a bi-regional federation – a term the Foreign and Commonwealth Office now used to avoid saying partition – was the realistic solution with Turkey having under 34 per cent of the land. Callaghan was clear what he wanted before returning to this negotiating nightmare: Greece should accept diplomatic defeat and everyone offer concessions with Turkey reducing the land held and Clerides agreeing two zones – and, growing ever more important in his mind, Britain must escape its 1960 and UNFICYP entanglements.

Rubbing against Callaghan's wounds was louder American criticism, which prominent *The New York Times* journalist Bernard Gwertzman laid bare in a piece reporting the Department of State's disappointment in the foreign secretary. One sentence read that 'officials here have made no secret in recent days of their view that Mr Callaghan has not proven the most effective mediator'.[347] Callaghan's steam from London could be seen from the seventh floor of the Department of State with Kissinger again having to soothe hurt feelings in a call to British Ambassador Peter Ramsbottom later that evening.

Turkey's advance stopped at 5.00 pm leaving the Turks on the edge of RAF Dhekelia. Firing did not stop completely as Turkish troops spent several days winning small tactical advantages to fortify their positions against a future counterattack.

Henry Kissinger on the back of the previous day's rough call with the Greek prime minister examined with his senior diplomats how to prove American support without showing 'excessive eagerness and not now tilt toward Greece and lose the Turks'. His challenge was getting an obstinate Karamanlis to negotiate while stopping personal attacks whipping up anti-American opinion on the streets. This meant Turkish concessions, which the secretary wondered whether 'Ecevit is subtle enough to do it, but can he get the military on board?'[348] A question no one could answer.

By the end of the day, the UN passed French-sponsored Resolution 360 disapproving of unilateral action, which implied

Turkey, affirming the ceasefire and urging a return to talks. Turkey was furious as Kissinger had finally decided the motion was tame enough not to invite Soviet meddling and had the United States' vote in support.

Continuing minor Turkish action to seize high land beyond Famagusta on Saturday, 17 August 1974, incensed Athens and increased anti-American demonstrations. James Williams and his colleague Mike Austrian at the American Embassy in Cyprus decided to tour Nicosia to inspect the situation. When they returned and Austrian started filing his report, the embassy's general services officer called them back over to the car and showed them a hole on the passenger side. A bullet had passed close to where Williams had been sitting.

Nationalist fervour rode equally high in Turkey proving a mixed blessing for Prime Minister Bülent Ecevit as his close-run military victory had bolstered his generals and hard-line nationalist groupings limiting any room for concessions in negotiations. Opinion among ordinary Turks in the ancient coffee houses of the capital vented annoyance at Britain, which the British Embassy's defence attaché, Brigadier H.H. Marston, described as vituperative, 'We are held to be anti-Turkish and by our own attitudes and statements we are responsible for much of the present world criticism of Turkey'.[349]

World opinion had certainly turned against Turkey, sometimes accusing its soldiers of barbarity, causing consternation in Ankara when its own people read about alleged atrocities against fellow Turks in Cypriot enclaves. One incident in particular caused outrage when a Turkish journalist was allegedly blindfolded and shot in cold blood by the Cypriot National Guard: he was given a state funeral in all but name in Ankara attended by Ecevit and his Cabinet.

With little progress and the United States becoming a target, Kissinger decided to get tough on Karamanlis for, 'We have no interest in supporting a country which follows a professional anti-US position ... The word has gone forth that the US will not be pushed around. This campaign must stop.'[350] He sent out a cable telling the Greek prime minister,

[it] is totally unjustified for the blame to be laid on the US; nor do we believe it is in the interest of Greece to do so ... Both Greece and the US were put in the situation in which we now find ourselves by the irresponsible and unwise actions of the Greek junta in upsetting the balance of forces on Cyprus.[351]

Karamanlis was assured that the United States understood his position and would help find a reasonable solution but should not press for what was no longer realistic.

Bill Macomber in Ankara pushed Ecevit to stop the minor advances and make a 'generous prior gesture' implying this should be land. This was done gently for Kissinger wanted Ecevit 'to know that the United States has not changed its position with regard to Cyprus nor its sympathy for an acceptable and lasting resolution of the problems the Turkish Cypriots have so long faced'.[352]

By Sunday, 18 August 1974, the Greek lobby began pushing President Gerald Ford for action and accusing Kissinger of being pro-Turk for resisting an aid embargo. Indiana's Representative John Will, a senior Democrat and son of a Greek restauranteur, argued that a strong show of anger could have stopped the Turks. New York representative Bella Abzug, a prominent rights activist hailing from Russian Jewish immigrants, marched with 50,000 others in Washington carrying placards that denounced 'Killer Kissinger', 'Kissinger Murderer' and 'CIA out of Greece'. Congressman Peter Kyros, another second-generation Greek, urged protesters to lobby Congress to get Turkey out.

American journalists increased their criticism. *The New York Times* foreign correspondent Alvin Shuster wrote the 'month old Cyprus crisis has left the Turks satisfied, the Greeks dismayed and angry and European experts in bewilderment over whether Secretary of State [Henry] Kissinger has lost his diplomatic touch'. Shuster finished by quoting an unnamed NATO diplomat saying, rather accurately, that 'Kissinger is a man who understands power ... And in this case Turkey had all the power.'[353]

All of which created the conditions for something bad to happen as it duly did on Monday, 19 August 1974, though no one at the American Embassy in Nicosia early in the morning had any reason to suspect an unfolding tragedy. James Williams joined the staff meeting as normal on this cloudless summer day to learn as he had many times before about a demonstration, this one by the Cypriot civil service. Fourteen American marines protecting the embassy were given a routine briefing.

It started with a 400-strong crowd gathering outside a trade union office a few streets away increasing in vigour and number when marching to the embassy compound with banners reading 'Kissinger – Hitler and NATO – murderers of Cyprus'. Williams heard them approaching around 10.00 am. Roused to anger the protesters threw stones on one side of the embassy and set eight cars alight, so marines closed the compound gates, readied their tear gas cannisters and staff pulled down all the wooden shutters to protect the windows. Some protesters still climbed the 8-foot iron railings making it to the flagpole, burning the American flag with others burning an effigy of Kissinger.

Williams, though anxious like his colleagues, thought the demonstration would ease off once the crowd let off steam. Embassy staff nonetheless appealed to the police and the National Guard for protection and repeated the call at 11.00 am, which eventually produced around forty unarmed police officers, an outnumbered few who could do little to quell the mob. An unwitting small convoy of British soldiers coincidently passed by but turned back when set on by the stone-throwing crowd.

Rocks continued hitting the building, windows broke and shouting grew fiercer. Ambassador Rodger Davies, fearing that an exploding car might spray debris through the large windows, moved his thirty-eight-civilian staff to the supposedly safer area of a second-floor hallway. Here Williams and his colleagues braved out the violence in humid conditions as the air conditioning system struggled to keep the over-crowded area cool while awaiting the intervention of Greek-Cypriot authorities.

After a short while, Williams and his colleague Mike Austrian decided to get a better look and made their way to the roof and the ambassador's residence. Looking over the balcony Williams saw his own car in flames and watched a gas tanker explode raising its rear end. Then he heard several pops, which he did not immediately recognise as guns shots, though a pierced water tower on top of the building made the cause obvious. He then ran over to the back of the balcony and leaned over to see marines throw tear gas on the empty small car park to deter the crowd moving there. Unfortunately, he was not far enough away to stop his eyes from stinging and fell to the floor rubbing his eyes.

Some soldiers of the Cypriot National Guard arrived and fired shots into the air, why was not clear, adding to the confusion with rounds of gunfire coming from different directions. Then terrifying rips of a semi-automatic gun fire zipped over Williams's head through the bamboo shoots in the patio garden, probably deliberately aimed as this is where Rodger Davies would retreat when the embassy came under attack.

Williams's life might very well have been saved by the C2 gas for he was crawling when he heard the fire and curled up like a baby at the top of the inside stairs. He picked himself up, got downstairs to clean his eyes and then rushed back to the balcony where Austrian was helping the marines throw new gas canisters into the car park. But Austrian, a civilian new to military action, could not open his cannister so placed it between his legs to gain leverage, which worked sending a white spray into his crotch and over his face, causing the marines to fall about laughing, while he writhed in agony from the burning. Williams dragged his wailing colleague with hands gripping his crotch, downstairs for more water.

Another gunman opened fire from the third floor of an adjacent building at the ambassador's empty office close to his desk. These high-velocity rounds penetrated the closed window, carried on through the office and by a dreadful coincidence hit Ambassador Rodger Davies as he stood in the hallway, killing him instantaneously through the heart. Another bullet tore through the head of Antoinette Varnava, a local Cypriot employee, who tried to catch Davies as he fell. They died together. The casing of a third bullet struck the thigh of economic officer, Jay Graham.

Williams and Austrian made their way down to the second floor when the message came through on the marines' radio of injuries. Amid the screaming, yelling and tear gas lay the still bodies of Davies and Antionette Varnava. Graham stood with blood trickling down his thigh. They had to wait another thirty minutes as the crowd shouted and fired more shots in the air until slowly the Greek-Cypriot police arrived in numbers, not knowing of the fallen ambassador inside.

Assistant public affairs officer David Grimland raced out in his car 1.5 miles to the general hospital securing two ambulances, which both turned back when they could not pierce the throng of protesters. Acting President Glafcos Clerides heard the news in the middle of a press conference and dashed over to the embassy with his public information minister. They wore facemasks to walk through the prevailing gas outside and climbed the stairs when Clerides horrified by the scene threw off his mask and knelt over the ambassador's body.

A Canadian UNFICYP contingent arrived to help disperse the still agitating crowd, some throwing stones at their vehicles. Eventually, a fire department ambulance took Davies to a private clinic, Clerides following behind, where the ambassador was pronounced dead. Davies, a popular man in the department and a fine eastern affairs expert, had arrived only a month before with his two children, Dana and John, to start a new life after the loss of his wife, Sally.

Not far away, Williams's pregnant wife, Ann, whom only the day before Davies had let return from the embassy to their home with her 4-year-old son, Ben, knew someone had been shot from chatter over a walkie talkie. Williams managed to assure her a few hours later he was fine and then himself worried that the mob might search homes for embassy staff such was the anger against anything American. To keep Ben's mind occupied, mother and young son made makeshift defences, including boiling water to throw on intruders and barricaded the top of the staircase to the house.

A loud knock came through their front door blocked by chairs. An English-speaking man asked to come in, which Ann declined demanding to know who he was and what he wanted, while reassuring her son and having him turn up the flames to boil the water. 'We're Canadians',[354] came the reply. Thinking how to make sure, she asked them to name the capital city and then realised she could not remember herself. To her relief, she heard a Canadian soldier turn to his colleague and ask who this nutcase was. Ann pushed the buzzer, and UNFICYP troops swarmed in with their rifles ready saying that a crazy Greek lady told them Ann was under attack. Ann then realised she had told her maid, Maria, to leave if the compound was attacked; and Maria had the wit to flag down a patrol helping at the burning embassy. The Canadians later took Ann and Ben to a UNFICYP officer's club on the airport road. This time there was no question of not being evacuated, pregnant or not.

Other demonstrations were held in Athens where some 4,000 protesters clashed with police and another large protest took place in Washington.

Clerides expressed his sorrow to Kissinger in the middle of the afternoon giving the secretary of state chance to insist that anti-American agitation in Cyprus and Athens must stop or 'we will wash our hands of everything and let Turkey and Greece handle it themselves'.[355]

Prime Minister Bülent Ecevit also offered his condolences giving Kissinger opportunity to explain he wanted a press statement saying the United States would not tolerate pressure and asking Turkey to agree troop reductions. Do you consent? Ecevit did not, because Turkish military positions had to be fully secured, Turkish Cypriots protected from alleged atrocities and a final settlement agreed first. Instead, Ecevit called back two hours later with suggested words about security, terrorism and reductions when conditions allow. Kissinger pushed him for a simpler statement but all he agreed was a line that 'the Turkish Government has assured me that they consider the demarcation line negotiable'.[356]

Henry Kissinger, therefore, went as far as possible in a press statement to quieten alarm after Davies's death. The ceasefire must be maintained, negotiations started with American support, Turkey must show flexibility to Greek sensitivities in land held and troop numbers, and Prime Minister Bülent Ecevit had assured him about keeping to the demarcation line and carrying out the Geneva Declaration for troop reductions at the right time. He added that while Greek friendship was valued, the United States would not be 'pressured by threat of withdrawal from the [Treaty of] Alliance, which Greece joined in its own interest, or by anti-American demonstrations'.[357]

This press statement, especially words about Greek threats, maddened Athens. 'We were very sorry to see Dr [Henry] Kissinger's statement', said a Greek government official, 'We did not threaten anybody. We can't – we don't have the fleet'.[358] Its Ministry of Press accused the secretary of state of 'dangerously underestimating'[359] the sadness felt by Greeks toward the United States over Cyprus.

Lewis Dean Brown, a deputy undersecretary for management, Normandy landings veteran and former ambassador to Jordan where he kept a pistol handy during the brief civil war to avoid becoming an embarrassing hostage for the United States, was parachuted in to take temporary control of the embassy in Nicosia. His arrival settled understandable tension between the traumatised staff arguing over who should take charge, for they did not have a deputy chief of mission. Lindsey Grant, who had filled this role, left a few days earlier when the situation appeared stable and was holidaying in Scotland when he got the call to return. James Williams, Mike Austrian, defence attaché Colonel Jessup and the CIA station chief remained as a core group supporting Brown. Many other staff suffering with broken nerves were allowed back to the United States.

Gerald Ford arranged for the repatriation of Ambassador Rodger Davies. Davies's children, Dana and John, and the cat to were flown back to Akrotiri from Beirut (where embassy staff had been evacuated) to collect their father's body. Art Hartman in Washington agreed with James Williams that his wife, Ann, and son, Ben, take that same flight home to the United States. Nicosia General Hospital staff prepared Davies's body with his death certificate stating a stray bullet as the cause of death.

Chapter 22

THE BATTLE FOR AID BEGINS

A race was on to stop the situation freezing into a permanent division and risking guerilla warfare, which Britain knew only too well from its bitter experience in the 1950s. But Henry Kissinger and Jim Callaghan had reasons to move at different speeds, the American secretary of state wanting everyone first to be ready with clear positions and the foreign secretary needing to forestall further Turkish action before a British election. Kissinger was, however, forced to into quicker than he wanted so he could control Congress, which meant trying to get some results in a near impossible situation before Turkey, Athens or the Cypriot communities were prepared.

Nerves on the island remained frayed as minor violations fuelled rumours of a Turkish third phase. On Tuesday, 3 September 1974, the Greek Embassy in London even warned that Turkey intended taking over Larnaca, unnerving refugee communities especially when an unexplained exchange of fire across the Green Line two days later caused panic. Only when Prime Minister Bülent Ecevit provided public assurances did fears recede though Greek Cypriots stayed on their guard.

Refugee problems gathered apace raising the prospect of more violence, a humanitarian crisis and new responsibilities for the British exchequer costing some £10,000/£15,000 a week particularly for 8,000 displaced Turkish Cypriots at Akrotiri. Here two camps, Happy Valley and Paramali Forest, provided supplies and medicines alongside two RAF nursing officers who managed baby clinics overseeing sixty-three births with not one child lost.

Community talks, which began at the formerly exquisite Ledra Palace Hotel in Nicosia now used by the UN as their new headquarters, were slow with Clerides moving carefully because of the influence of George Mavros in Athens and the archbishop in London. On Monday,

9 September 1974, Makarios reasserted his authority by announcing a return in the very near future and insisting that Turkey allow 200,000 Greek-Cypriot refugees home, undermining the very regional solution Clerides was gently pursuing with Rauf Denktaş and his position as acting president to his utter dismay.

Kissinger, who was still convinced the time not yet right to start negotiations but having to ward off congressional action, despatched senior diplomat Wells Stabler to Ankara and retired Ambassador William Tyler to Athens to test thinking around a two-region solution incorporating Turkish land and troop reductions. These were consultations only for he fended off persistent London requests to act on Turkey, telling Ambassador Peter Ramsbottom on Monday that Britain bore blame for not pushing Greece harder at Geneva. British press criticism also annoyed him for being singled out as 'the most criticised in the world press for the failure of the Geneva talks, when he had fallen over backwards both to support us when we had asked for American action, and to avoid diminishing your [Callaghan's] central role'.[360]

London, however, was less concerned about criticising Kissinger than getting out of Cyprus. The Cabinet Defence Committee endorsed Geoffrey Arthur's recommendations that same day for 'the total withdrawal of forces from Cyprus, which should, if possible, be presented in the context of satisfactory settlement to the Cyprus problem'.[361] Callaghan, recognising the United States would make overriding objections, had officials draw up a back-up plan, running down as much presence as possible without leaving.

Callaghan also assembled his chief diplomats in London to thrash out what next for Britain and Cyprus. Hooper, Phillips, Olver, Brimelow and Killick besides Alan Goodison and Anthony Ackland, and many others bruised and battered from their personal experiences, together with ministers Roy Hattersley and David Ennals scratched their heads over the same conundrum that had confounded their predecessors a decade earlier. Different views provided more questions than answers and little consensus. Did British interests lie with Greece or Turkey? What could be done given Greek refusal to negotiate? There was also the issue of what to do about Makarios, which Robin Hooper pointed out no Greek politician had ever resolved. Their conclusion was to push discussions between Clerides and Denktaş with Greek and Turkish support rather than resume the Geneva process, and somehow facilitate an eventual political settlement, which did not entangle Britain.

In Athens, Prime Minister Konstantinos Karamanlis and Minister Dimitrios Bitsios (soon to become foreign minister) gave visiting Ambassador William Tyler and resident Deputy Ambassador Monty Stearns a rough time, denouncing the United States and arguing that London and Washington could have prevented the coup and Turkey's landings. Anti-American sentiment was natural in Greece, said Karamanlis, and would only reduce if Washington admitted errors and found an agreeable solution, otherwise 'I would have to go to war or leave the country. I was welcomed back to Greece as a saviour. I could not let my own people down.'[362] Tyler did not let him get away with it, replying that the United States had no guilt, no mistakes to admit and was not responsible for the stupidity of the junta.

Bitsios then read out Greek conditions for indirect talks. Turkish land must mirror the size of its population in Cyprus, no population exchanges, refugees to return and a federal government with significant central powers. Tyler countered with Kissinger's more realistic ideas for two regions, which Karamanlis dismissed saying 'we accept this idea although the Greek Cypriots do not'[363] and if this, and a sizeable population exchange represented American thinking, there was little hope for success.

While Ambassador William Tyler refuted mistakes in Ankara, American intelligence admitted to some in Washington when on Tuesday, 10 September 1974, William G. Hyland, head of the Department of State's Intelligence and Research Bureau, sent Kissinger a punchy postmortem report on events leading up to Ioannidis's coup. Tasca's embassy drew much criticism alongside indecisive messages given by the United States to Ioannidis:

> One cannot conclude from the attached survey that we had what could be called 'warning' of an impending coup. What we did have were sufficient storm signals to warrant some diplomatic action – which, in retrospect, seems to have been weak and indecisive. Thus, it is possible that in Athens our policy was interpreted as seeming acquiescence in Ioannidis'[s] plans, especially since the Greek junta could not know of the various pulling and hauling between the Department and the Embassy.[364]

Crucially, Hyland conceded that although cloudy and even misleading, 'the weight of evidence pointed to an impending direct move against Makarios by Ioannidis'. The brigadier general may also have interpreted the United States' conflicting and weak signals as a green light and 'could have concluded that he had a free hand, insofar as the United States was concerned, as long as his gambit was intra-Greek'.[365] To sweeten this tough medicine, Hyland suggested the Aegean Islands dispute in early spring and early summer had distracted government attention as the likely flash point between Greece and Turkey.

Makarios continued intervening with ever stronger positions, telling Callaghan on Wednesday, 11 September 1974, that he wanted cantons and that population transfers were out of the question. He was shortly visiting Yugoslavia and Albania and hoped to address the UN General Assembly to internationalise the issue. An unimpressed foreign secretary noted privately to his officials that here was a very wicked man and his only rule in dealing with such people was to always speak the truth.

More pressure piled up over Turkish refugees on British bases with Ecevit's government formally requesting their evacuation by sea. While this tempting offer relieved Britain of watching the horrors of winter unfold on the beleaguered Turkish-Cypriot community, any transfer undermined Clerides's negotiations over population movements and laid London open to accusations of favouring the Turks. The request was therefore declined because no reciprocal arrangements existed for Greek Cypriots, which angered the Turks even more and causing them to accuse Britain of human rights violations and making their refugees hostages.

Anti-American sentiment was one reason why Ambassador Henry Tasca had a smaller farewell party than usual for an outgoing ambassador on Saturday, 14 September 1974 (he actually left his post the following Monday, 16 September 1974). Many Greek employees boycotted the party in protest against Washington with one saying, 'They are killing our brothers in Cyprus and giving us drinks to drink here'.[366] Tasca's personal style, which left him distant from many staff members, accounted for other absences. Organisers bunched guests together in the patio to give the appearance more people attended than were present.

Other manifestations of anti-Americanism appeared across Greece. That Saturday Greek pilots of Olympic Airways refused to fly with American employees and demanded the sacking of seven American pilots and four flight engineers working on transatlantic flights. Protests in Athens were so large that newly arrived Ambassador Jack Kubisch thought his previous experience of lively anti-Vietnam demonstrations small beer in comparison:

I had never seen demonstrations of the kind that took place in Athens. There were demonstrations of 200,000, 300,000 or 400,000 people that gathered in the centre of town all day long and then marched on the American Embassy, 200 to 300 abreast, marching by, using the worst, most obscene epithets in language, and trying to break into the embassy.[367]

Even after the tragedy in Nicosia, demonstrators still attacked the American Embassy, in Athens on one occasion breaking in and setting fire to parts of the compound. Kubisch anxious to avoid any situation creating a Greek martyr instructed his marines:

> [If] you were in the last extremity where they had you down, they were about to do you terrible damage, then you could draw your pistol and shoot. And those Marines, we had twelve at the time in the Marine security guard, did a wonderful job. They fought off the people breaking into the embassy with brooms and fire extinguishers and chairs and so on. A lot of people were hurt. There were a lot of broken bones, broken arms, broken clavicles and so on. A lot of police were badly injured, but no one was killed.[368]

Defence Minister Evangelos Averoff visited the damaged embassy late at night to apologise and the foreign ministry agreed to pay for all damage.

Kissinger's need for results were struck a hard blow when Ecevit's government started to crumble, just as Wells Stabler arrived on Friday, 13 September 1974 to warn Ankara it risked losing American military aid for misusing NATO equipment and not controlling poppy production. By Tuesday, 17 September 1974, Ecevit's coalition partner, the National Salvation Party, which demanded either partition or annexation in Cyprus, withdrew support for Ecevit's measured policy of an independent sovereign island under a federal government. Ecevit hoping his hero status on the street sufficient to win the day called its bluff by resigning, expectations that were not fulfilled as political wrangling over the next two weeks found no alternative coalition partners. His principal opponent, Süleyman Demirel and the Justice Party, similarly lacked enough backers to form a government so Ecevit struggled on in a caretaker role until Sunday, 17 November 1974.

By contrast, Harold Wilson went on British television to announce the much-anticipated United Kingdom general election for Thursday, 10 October 1974.

In Washington, impatient congressmen laid bills in both houses to stop Turkish aid, pulling the rug from underneath Kissinger, who consequently cancelled any thoughts of visiting Ankara under what might appear as pressure from the American legislature. Senior diplomat Art Hartman thought that Congressional positions exceeded anything sought by Prime Minister Konstantinos Karamanlis, who asked him why Washington could not control American politicians. Congress was not for turning though in a hostile atmosphere with some politicians thinking Kissinger had hoodwinked them over not yet imposing an arms embargo.

On Tuesday, 24 September 1974, the House of Representatives suspended aid to Turkey. President Gerald Ford used a presidential veto to ignore them in favour of shielding the United States' relationship with Ankara, but there was a limit on how many times this was possible. A huge battle of political wills followed, forcing Kissinger to find a solution before Congress removed his levers of power to bring one about. A congressional threat to implement an aid embargo made his task harder as an offended and now politically sterile Ankara had no reason to act, and Athens, thinking that American politicians would do its work for it, no reason to compromise.

He used the new UN session in New York to prepare positions. He told George Mavros that Turkey should realistically get more than the proportion of its population but not what was sought; and Turkish Foreign Minister Turan Güneş that 'we are now in a disintegrating state of US domestic politics. We have to face realities' and that as 'the situation in Greece is unstable. It is our intention to support the Karamanlis government'.[369]

Makarios did not help by announcing on Thursday, 26 September 1974 his return to Cyprus after the UN General Assembly debate. A depressed Clerides made noises about resigning and appealed for Athens' help to keep the archbishop away, but the Greek prime minister had to move carefully for Makarios had weight in the planned elections to restore elected civilian government in Greece.

President Gerald Ford and Secretary of State Henry Kissinger tried swaying congressional leaders, including Senator Mike Mansfield, former Vice President Hubert Humphrey and Senator William Fulbright over a White House breakfast. Kissinger appealed to reason, saying that an aid cutoff would cause Greece to expect unachievable concessions and at same time lose Turkey and destroy any hope of a settlement. This did not persuade hardened senators who needed to show progress for mid-term elections. Fulbright admitted that before the coup the Congressmen were out of touch with their US-Greek communities who supported the junta but now wanted to get back in touch with these constituents by being tough on Turkey. Reaching no consensus, the president agreed to insert tough language into the current congressional proposals, vainly hoping that eventual progress by Turkey would make them redundant.

To get that progress, Kissinger continued his diplomacy at the end of September 1974 assuring Clerides of American support for community negotiations and his intention to press Athens and stop Makarios from causing disruption. But he made little headway with Greek Foreign Minister George Mavros who, very much reflecting the archbishop's views, wanted cantons not a simple division of the island and 50,000 Greeks returned to Famagusta – and who still blamed Washington for the prevailing anti-American sentiment on the street, which could be resolved, he argued, through an embargo.

'Impossible', said Kissinger, who would not push Ankara for concessions in these circumstances because he was not about to become the 'whipping boy'.

> Why should we have to repair a situation that was started by the Greek Government? ... I don't accept the proposition we have done anything against Greece. I understand domestic reasons for your anti-Americanism. We too want you to succeed in the elections.[370]

Kissinger agreed to work on the Turks and get enough to support Clerides and Denktaş talks providing Greece dropped anti-American rhetoric.

American politics undermined him the next day and gave Greece a fillip when on Monday, 30 September 1974, the Senate voted to cut off aid by fifty-seven to twenty votes arguing that Turkey had used American arms in Cyprus. The House of Representatives adopted a similar resolution calling for a cessation of aid unless the president certified that Turkey was making substantial progress. Legislation would pass once both houses resolved differences in their respective resolutions.

Makarios exacerbated the situation in his grand UN speech on Tuesday, 1 October 1974, delighting communist and non-aligned African delegates while Arab spokesmen looked on coolly and the seats of the Turkish delegation stayed vacant. He rejected any geographical division while possibly accepting cantons and denounced Turkey as an 'aggressor', declaring that 'the victims of this aggression were in proportionate terms greater than the victims of many years in Vietnam'.[371] This speech formed part of his strategy to force Washington to change Ankara's approach, a position he thought possible having earlier told a journalist in London that Turkey should be made to behave. (Two days before that he gave an interview to Eric Rouleau, the prominent Egyptian born journalist of the French daily Le Monde, mischievously accusing the CIA of participating in the coup against him.)

Clerides threatened to resign, the only response possible to this challenge by the archbishop who also continued to inspire demonstrations on the island. He demanded a mandate from the Greek Cypriots, Athens and Makarios or else, which was a message as much to tease out support and have Konstantinos Karamanlis keep the archbishop away as any intention to resign.

Kissinger fared no better with the archbishop when they met at the Waldorf Towers on Wednesday, 2 October 1974. Makarios, lighting up cigarettes produced from a case hidden in his tunic, listened as the secretary of state explained that neither the United States nor Turkey responded to pressure and the Turks were unlikely to agree many cantons. 'My skill is to get the other party to do what needs to be done. It can't be done with threats ... I've no objection to asking the Turks to go back to five cantons ... But if the Greeks are going out on the streets of America calling me a killer, I have no interest.'[372] He also dismissed the archbishop's suggestions of CIA involvement as ridiculous.

Yet budge Makarios would not, insisting that Kissinger had personal influence on Ankara and rejected two regions even if Clerides and Karamanlis supported it. He mentioned Egyptian President Muhammad Sadat who recently told him the key is 'in the hands of Dr [Henry] Kissinger', to which the secretary of state replied that the 'Egyptians dealt with us on the basis of cooperation. The Greeks are dealing with us on the basis of blackmail.'[373]

Greek announcements for an election on Sunday, 17 November 1974 further reduced the likelihood of deals as any concessions by Athens were electoral suicide, ran the risk of invoking action by disgruntled armed forces and strengthened the left in Greece under Andreas Papandreou. Karamanlis had to stay tough and play the aggrieved party to keep his army on board.

Arab-Israeli shuttle diplomacy took Kissinger away until Tuesday, 15 October 1974 leaving Art Hartman to take more of the brunt of congressional assaults. To Kissinger's amusement Syrian President Hafez al-Assad accused him of arranging the Cyprus coup to win a NATO base from which to attack his country – and then asked why he was now helping Makarios since the United States would not get a base that way.

On Friday, 11 October 1974, Prime Minister Harold Wilson in Britain received the very result he hoped to avoid of being returned with a majority of only three, moving Labour from an exposed governing party to a very fragile one.

In the United States, both houses of Congress had by now reconciled their different resolutions to halt Turkish aid causing President Gerald Ford to wield another veto on Monday, 14 October 1974, warning that an embargo imperilled 'our relationship with our Turkish ally and

weaken us in the crucial Eastern Mediterranean'.[374] Massachusetts
Senator Edward Kennedy, brother to a slain president, accused the
administration of 'cynical use of tax dollars in support of policies
which prolong the Greek refugee problem and the Turkish occupation
of Cyprus'.[375]

A second congressional resolution three days later forced another
veto until Congress overcame the deadlock with a new resolution
allowing Ford to defer aid until Tuesday, 10 December 1974 on
condition Turkey stopped using American weapons in Cyprus, made
substantial progress towards an agreement and reduced its soldiers
on the island. Turks on the street saw this as Americans turning on
them. Their Greek equivalents already thought the United States was
behind their own woes – Cypriot students having days earlier staged
an anti-American protest in the form of a mock funeral for Henry
Kissinger.

Chapter 23

RETURN OF THE KING

Pressure was on to give congress evidence of Turkish progress before it took control of American foreign policy. Henry Kissinger had to pull this off against competing claims: a Turkey struggling internally with political arithmetic and insisting on one large zone in the north and five smaller ones in the south; Makarios wanting between ten and twenty cantons; and Athens insisting on areas representative of population size. And the archbishop due to return to his fiefdom.

Keeping influence over Ankara after congressional resolutions offended Turkish sentiment and damaged Ecevit's political standing was his initial hurdle. An aggrieved Ecevit told Ambassador Bill Macomber, 'Usually it is said that people get along and governments do not; this is a case where governments get along and the people are determined to do this to us, first on poppies and now on this'.[376] Ecevit, still prime minister but only just while struggling to find new coalition partners, wanted another planned UN General Assembly debate pushed back to Monday, 11 November 1974 so that Kissinger could visit without appearing subservient to Congress.

Kissinger examined how to do this with his senior diplomats on the morning of Thursday, 22 October 1974. In not especially good humour, he moaned this was the Suez Crisis all over again with the United States applauding itself over treatment of Britain and France so that '70 per cent of the troubles we have had with them since have been caused by our brutality in '56'. He wanted Turkey shown that the United States had tried to delay the debate: 'Has anyone in this building considered what will happen if there is an Israeli-Syrian war next summer and the Russians try to intervene, how we can operate in the Eastern Mediterranean, without the Turks?' All he could see was Turkish humiliation and Ford's government appearing impotent on foreign policy with plaudits going to the UN and Congress. As voting against any UN resolution risked the wrath of Congress and voting for risked Turkish indignation, he decided that what 'we have to do is to show the Greeks that only by working with the United States can they get something'.[377]

On this there was fat chance for Karamanlis's government saw matters sailing in its favour and the UN machine having once revised the date of the debate was not minded for another delay. On Monday, 28 October 1974, the UN General Assembly, therefore, adopted Resolution 3212 to respect Cypriot sovereignty, remove foreign troops, return refugees and engage the secretary general in a solution.

London meanwhile worried about senior Greek and Cypriot bureaucrats and politicians believing stories of Britain's failure to 'do something' as a guarantor power given the RAF bases on the island. Alan Goodison, the principle Foreign and Commonwealth Office expert, was harangued over a dinner party at the Dutch Embassy by the Cypriot high commissioner for failing to remove Sampson. The seasoned officer wearily concluded that we 'had better get used to hearing'[378] such accusations for a long time to come. It did not help that shortly afterwards he was lectured by a senior Turkish diplomat over refugees, who said that the Turks did not understand why Britain valued a solution in Cyprus over friendship with the Turkish people.

Kissinger used the opportunity of a UN food conference in Rome to get diplomacy moving. He whittled down Turkey's negotiating positions to geography as the basis for talks, a Greek statement on two regions and some Turkish refugees to go north in return for concessions including troop reductions. These he presented to Dimitrios Bitsios, now the Greek foreign minister, over an 8.00 am breakfast at the Hotel Excelsior. Bitsios wanted cantons and concessions, including the immediate return of Greek Cypriots to their homes. Kissinger thought cantons now implausible, so they agreed to explore talks without preconditions: 'we should not expect too much. I will try to help move along the cantonal solution and to get political talks started and we may discuss some gestures'.[379] At last, a basis for discussion was reached.

In discussing the detail, Kissinger could not avoid venting his constant frustrations about Callaghan:

> I consider the second Geneva meeting to be the most incompetently handled negotiation I have ever witnessed. The British thought that they could achieve a settlement there. In fact, we had encouraged the Turks to make a proposal so that there would be something on which to negotiate but Callaghan was so mad at the Turks that he could not get the process moving.[380]

Another sore was being opened when London resumed discussion on Friday, 8 November 1974 about retreating from Cyprus. Cabinet Secretary Sir John Hunt, the country's top civil servant, reviewed with defence mandarins and diplomats how to explain Britain's defence contraction and its opening gambit to leave Cyprus. They agreed on the tactics to consult with the United States: namely that Britain cannot afford the bases, the recent conflict had made them a liability, the RAF element was being reduced, the preference was to get out, which should help a political settlement if played carefully – what did the Americans think? If the United States objected, Hunt decided, the government must think again.

On Wednesday, 13 November 1974, Ecevit announced the return of 5,000 soldiers, a gesture largely lost on Congress, and which did little to help him at home, as the search continued for a replacement prime minister who commanded support in the Turkish Parliament.

Kissinger tried stopping any mischief-making by Makarios, shortly returning to Cyprus, when they meet a fourth time in Washington that Wednesday. Makarios supporters chanted outside the Department of State in favour of their archbishop, causing Kissinger to wonder whether these were his own students. He warned the archbishop against unsettling local talks and again suggested that only a bizonal arrangement was realistic. But because he was trying to tease out a solution and not impose one, Kissinger did not exclude the idea of cantons, giving Makarios the very basis for fomenting trouble the secretary of state hoped to avoid. The archbishop quickly let it be known publicly that Kissinger supported his canton ideas, causing jitters in Callaghan's Foreign and Commonwealth Office, which had been telling the Greeks quite firmly that two zones was the answer.

American officials did not object but went spare when listening to Hunt's presentation in Washington on Thursday, 14 November 1974 informing them of British plans to leave Malta, reduce armed forces including in West Germany, completely end residual commitments in the Far East and the Gulf, and prospectively get out of Cyprus. Secretary of Defense Jim Schlesinger, the youngest person to ever hold that position and as tough speaking as Kissinger, was positively spitting. Of all the areas of protest Cyprus was the line in the sand, home to intelligence assets and a vital component in Middle East calculations. Kissinger opposed any withdrawal increasing the relative decline of Western influence and rejected the weak notion that it helped a political settlement as Turkey, Cyprus and Greece had made no statements about the bases. At best, he was prepared for a reduction of forces in Cyprus.

In the meantime, Makarios's trouble making caused such alarm that British Ambassador Peter Ramsbottom had to clear the air with Kissinger on Saturday, 16 November 1974, when the secretary of state provided reassurance that he did not support the cantons proposal, which

> will never be. His [Makarios] efforts to get me to support his five cantonal plan have no chance, but I did not come out flatly and say this. In this way he could not say that I had insisted on a bi-zonal arrangement. Makarios is trying to turn us around by saying what he has. It is better for me to give my opinion after I have talked to the Turks – if I ever talk to them. But, in any case, you can assure Callaghan we are in total agreement on this matter.[381]

Kissinger also wrote to the electioneering Greek prime minister politely warning him off anti-American declarations while pushing for two zones – with a reduced size of the Turkish zone, and offering support for a Greek-Turkish settlement of regional issues in the Aegean Islands.

Democracy firmly re-established itself in Greece on Sunday, 17 November 1974, when Konstantinos Karamanlis and his New Democracy Party won convincingly in the general election with 220 of 300 parliamentary seats, which the British embassy thought the least corrupt in modern Greek history. Andreas Papandreou's Panhellic Socialist Movement (PASOK) won twelve seats and 13.58 per cent of the popular vote. A strong result did not free Karamanlis entirely of problems as the army was capable of interfering if alienated and Andreas Papandreou now had a platform to exploit Cyprus and American bases as political issue. Nonetheless, a strong performance made this elder statesman his own man and no longer the heir of the junta.

Prime Minister Harold Wilson congratulated him while politely drawing attention to a two-zone solution as the key to unlock the door to progress. Diplomats racked their brains on how to improve British-Greek relations against a prevailing Greek belief that Britain stood by in the whole saga and now espoused an 'extreme'[382] view in supporting two regions. They decided on restoring links between armed services, which might 'help extinguish the lingering suspicions of our connivance with the Turkish Armed Forces in Cyprus'.[383]

A glimmer of hope shone out of Ankara when that same day medical Professor Sadi Irmak, a 70-year-old independent senator, became the new prime minister in Turkey by appointment, not election, and formed a government of mostly academics and civil servants. His installation ended two months of political stalemate and provided a degree of stability, which raised hopes of negotiations. These were tempered by the realisation that Irmak's unelected government was not a long-term prospect and Cyprus was the only unifying factor among political parties, which all wanted two zones apart from the radical National Salvation Party.

Clerides, faced with the imminent return of his rival Makarios, prepared to brief the archbishop in London on Wednesday, 20 November 1974, their first meeting since the coup. He still forlornly hoped that Greece, London and Washington could prevent him returning but there was little prospect, for even a strengthened Karamanlis had limited control over the archbishop. Nonetheless, Clerides repeated his ultimatum to resign without a mandate to negotiate on two regions, a message he made public when boarding his flight by threatening to stop the talks unless a document were drawn up defining the framework for negotiations with the Turkish Cypriots and signed by the Greek government, Makarios and himself.

In London that day, Harold Wilson's Cabinet, faced with vehement American views on British defence cuts, decided on the fall-back plan to reduce forces in Cyprus as much as possible and reduce RAF Akrotiri from major military camp to staging post. This retention provided a sweetener when telling President Gerald Ford that Britain was still winding down its other international commitments, for it could not afford to 'keep forces stationed round the world' and would instead concentrate only on NATO defences in Europe.

Callaghan couched this decision as a deliberate change in British policy to placate Washington when writing to Kissinger. The 'fact that the US Administration and you personally attach such importance to our presence in Cyprus, together with your argument about the generally adverse effect of our withdrawal on the region as a whole, was the determining consideration.' It was not done without a swipe at still having 'responsibility without power', Callaghan said,

[He was] not entirely happy about the prospect which our decision in Cyprus entails ... the mere fact of our continued presence on the island ... is bound, whatever we may say, to imply some kind of continuing special role and responsibility for the British Government.[384]

Kissinger sent his return thanks, which did not fully reflect views in Washington where the defence community seethed about British cuts.

The next day, on Thursday, 21 November 1974, a smoke-piping Clerides thought he reached an understanding with Makarios in a seven-hour meeting about his powers as official Greek-Cypriot negotiator. At a following press conference, he announced the return of his master carefully denying any disagreement between them while pointedly emphasising that a settlement in Cyprus needed a federal system of 'distinct geographic areas'. Makarios, by contrast, bade his time and refrained from any comment, immune to influence as many leaders came to realise.

Matters were similarly not straightforward in Ankara when Professor Sadi Irmak's government hit the rocks on Friday, 29 November 1974 after only days in office. The Turkish Parliament threw out his legislative agenda causing his government without any main-stream political support to collapse; he resigned but was reappointed caretaker prime minister until spring elections. Irmak still had strong words over Cyprus that attracted widespread support across the Turkish Parliament, expressing discontent about the return of Makarios and threatening to proclaim an independent Turkish-Cypriot Republic and rescue stranded communities if the archbishop's presence caused more fighting. His position was partly conditioned by deep feelings on the street with Turks demanding to know why their government was allowing the return of their chief enemy. In Cyprus, Turkish-Cypriot leader Rauf Denktaş told a newspaper that without knowing Makarios's intentions, he foresaw a future of his eldest son fighting on the 'Green Line' and his younger one growing up defending it.

On Thursday, 28 November 1974, Prime Minister Konstantinos Karamanlis met Makarios and Clerides in Athens to discuss the terms for Clerides to remain as negotiator. Karamanlis may have thought he had won a commitment from the archbishop – who received a hero's welcome by thronged masse – that laid the ground for talks with Turkey but dealings with the byzantine Makarios were never so easy. While appearing to acknowledge a geographical solution with one major Turkish zone accompanied by others mirroring population sizes, the archbishop gave himself space to decide a position later and astutely refused to sign any document until after his return to Cyprus. The reality was no agreement was valid without his blessing for even after all this time only he could carry most Greek Cypriots.

On this basis, Makarios was allowed to return to his island. Word went out to the Greek officers commanding the reforming National Guard and the Cypriot police to protect the archbishop when he arrived. EOKA-B, down but not out, was not expected to cause immediate trouble, the chastened advocates of *enosis* waiting to see what happened. Just in case, Greek armed forces were placed on alert to both counter any EOKA-B threat and respond to Turkish ones. Likewise, Turkish troops and Turkish-Cypriot irregulars and stood ready for trouble.

Makarios was returning to a land of two countries from the single nation he fled in August. One third now ruled by Turkish Cypriots in an 'Autonomous Turkish Administration' applying Turkish import, export and customs rules, and using Turkish-Cypriot license plates and currency. Parts of Famagusta and Kyrenia were ghost towns where Turkish soldiers had painted over Greek street and shop lettering and written *'Turk Evi'* ('Turkish house') on houses taken over by Turkish Cypriots. In the other two thirds the weight of Greek-Cypriot expectation wanted him to restore burnt homes, rehouse over 150,000 refugees, mend damaged businesses and rebuild a diminished economy where 30 per cent of workers were now unemployed and much rich agricultural land, Kyrenia tourism trade and the income from the deep-water port of Famagusta lost to Turkey.

Such concerns were lost in the immediate moment when the thrice elected president Archbishop Makarios III arrived home on Saturday, 7 December 1974. Twice had he been exiled and twice returned as saviour to his people, this time arriving from Athens in a Greek plane landing at RAF Akrotiri and then by UN helicopter to Nicosia, the very way he left.

Thousands lined the streets to the shell-strewn archbishopric with hundreds pushing their way onto dangerously overcrowded rooftops waving banners, large colourful wreaths and pictures of their adored leader. There were reckless onlookers, including a television crew seeking the best shots balanced atop a bell tower with barely an inch to spare. Spectators sang patriotic songs and chants some with anti-American and anti-NATO flavours. Then their leader appeared on the long, busy balcony causing a frenzy of arm waving and deafening calls of adulation awaiting his words.

Yet just as Makarios had spurned the independence arrangements he had helped shape and sign in 1960, so he brushed aside the tentative deal worked out in Athens and the opportunity for true statesmanship. Instead of offering a solution he used a forty-five-minute speech to declare,

This is not the time to set out my views as to how the problem should be solved … I only say that we shall not accept any solution involving transfer of populations and amounting to partition of Cyprus …We Greek Cypriots, however, are on no account prepared to recognize and accept accomplished facts brought about by military operations.[385]

Instead, he offered an amnesty to Greek Cypriots who tried to kill him in July 1974, saying 'I do not wish to rake up old wounds that I want to see heal ... I forgive them all for their sins and grant them amnesty in the hope that the desired concord and unity among our people will come about.'[386]

Not a single mention did he make of Clerides who had steered Cyprus through a near civil war and begun the process of negotiation and humanitarian discussions with his opposite number Denktaş. Clerides, present and listening to the speech, left the palace immediately after the archbishop finished to lunch with his wife and daughter at the Hilton hotel's coffee shop rather than with Makarios.

In the space of two months, one leader had fallen in Nicosia, a statesman had restored Greek democracy, the Turkish poet prime minister most likely to deliver a deal was replaced by an academic and Makarios returned as president of Cyprus. One other hopeful leader did not make it in this shuffling of the deck, for amid all the jubilation the man who had long anticipated a warm reception from his people was severely disappointed.

Prime Minister Konstantinos Karamanlis granted young King Constantine II a referendum on the return of the monarchy the day after Makarios returned to Cyprus. But once again the Greek monarch was rejected, this time decisively by 30.8 per cent to 69.2 per cent in a result which severed the 114-year-old ties between a king and his people, who now favoured a republic. King Constantine II never stood a chance, for the Greeks remembered his troubles with prime ministers that caused the junta's rise in 1967 and his naïve endorsement of its regime. Besides, there was little love for the royal family's German ancestry stretching back to the German-Danish dynasty in 1863, especially King Constantine II's grandfather, a Germanophile who prevaricated over supporting the Allies and married Kaiser Wilhelm I's sister, who was King Constantine II's grandmother. Nearly as many people turned out to celebrate the result in Athens' central square as had welcomed Makarios on his way to Cyprus, with some chanting 'The German will die tonight'.

King Constantine II lived out his contented exile mostly in Britain always insisting on being called 'King'.

Chapter 24

OUT OF TIME

Henry Kissinger acutely conscious of the looming December deadline set by Congress pushed even harder to get a deal before he lost control of foreign policy.

On Wednesday, 4 December 1974, the Senate renewed an extension until Friday, 14 February 1975 while seven days later the House of Representatives refused any more time and brought the ban into effect. This legislative muddle gave him time to bring about a settlement. By good fortune foreign leaders assembled for a NATO meeting in Brussel between Wednesday, 11 and Thursday, 13 December 1974 affording chance to work on Greece and Turkey.

He tested Turkish thinking over breakfast in Brussels on 11 December with new Turkish Foreign Minister Melih Esenbel, a career diplomat and former ambassador to Washington, who, angered by the latest congressional moves, refused any Turkish gestures and insisted on two zones.

Greek Foreign Minister Dimitrios Bitsios proved more flexible later that morning when they met in a palatial suite of the Hilton in Brussels. Bitsios explained that Prime Minister Konstantinos Karamanlis, fresh from political victory and wanting a swift solution to Cyprus and improved relations with Turkey, might agree a federal solution with one large Turkish area around Kyrenia and smaller cantons in the north reflecting an eighty to twenty population split. However, two zones remained out of bounds. Perhaps thinking of the loose arrangement discussed in Athens, Bitsios remarkably claimed that even Makarios supported this idea.

Although far from Turkey's position, this new Greek line offered prospects for a breakthrough. The game was on to stop the executive of the United States ceding control of foreign policy to Congress.

Kissinger agreed to tell Turkish Foreign Minister Melih Esenbel that Greece supported local community negotiations and both Athens and the United States would back Clerides if Makarios caused problems. If Esenbel refused, he would try Ankara. Two things must stand, Kissinger told Bitsios: the United States was not going to get directly involved and risk becoming a whipping boy if the ideas failed though he would support them; and threats to withdraw from NATO or to undermine Greek-American relations must stop. Bitsios side-steeped this last point saying that Karamanlis was only responding to public pressure.

A hesitant Esenbel did not like the sound of any of this when told, for he distrusted Makarios and doubted anyone could control him. Kissinger pushed harder, explaining this opportunity was not to be missed and offered a public letter of support for Esenbel to sleep on overnight.

Kissinger updated Bitsios at 11.00 pm, drafted the letter and told President Gerald Ford of hopes to influence Congress:

This makes the outcome of the Congressional vote very decisive. If aid remains cut off either the negotiations will fail or they will quickly stalemate. On the other hand, we have a chance now to get things moving and I have the impression that [Prime Minister Konstantinos] Karamanlis is eager for a rapid settlement.[387]

His hope was not misplaced for next day Esenbel persuaded Ankara that negotiations underpinned by American assurance were worth a punt, provided it was Clerides who made the formal request to Denktaş for community discussions. Talks must also move slowly, Esenbel told Kissinger, when passing on Turkey's tentative agreement late at night, and must address practical issues such as reopening the airport to test whether Clerides had power. Kissinger preferred quicker progress on a political settlement, but his letter still met Esenbel's approval with the American government undertaking 'to use its full influence to the end that agreements reached in these negotiations are fairly and fully implemented'.[388]

Those agreements appeared tantalisingly close. Greece now wanted a settlement, Greece and Turkey agreed to talk for the first time about a political solution besides practical matters and the time looked auspicious to move before Makarios caused delay. And from Kissinger's perspective, he was not inveigled in talks should they fail and, crucially, he had evidence to influence political discussions in Washington.

An optimistic Kissinger asked Bitsios to meet him straightaway regardless of the hour, which a tired Greek foreign minister feigned illness to put off until the next morning, Thursday, 13 December 1974, when he duly agreed. His price was also an assurance that talks would not start on the presumption of two zones. Kissinger could not get either side to budge on this issue but manoeuvred them to not make it a barrier to negotiations. A deal was therefore struck under the hanging sword of Congress with Henry Kissinger briefing President Gerald Ford that 'I believe we have made good progress here to unblock the negotiating situation on Cyprus. I am convinced that if we lose this opportunity due to congressional action, we may not have another chance.'[389]

He flew to Martinique for planned discussions with the French president and then, still tired from all the travelling, rushed back to Washington armed with the Brussels letter to appeal for another extension from Congress. He briefed leading pro-Greek senators, including Paul Sarbanes and John Brademas, late at night in the speaker's office to persuade them that Turkey was on the verge of withdrawing troops and allowing some Greek Cypriots home.

Circumstances favoured him as most American politicians did not want to delay the overall aid bill for fear of holding up supplies to Israel – and, showing progress, Clerides had initiated community talks with Rauf Denktaş on the basis of the Brussels letter. Consequently, on Wednesday, 18 December 1974, Congress passed the fiscal year 1975 Foreign Assistance Act resuming aid to both Turkey and Greece until Wednesday, 5 February 1975, but on condition that President Gerald Ford in February formally advise them that substantial progress had been made. This time Ford signed the bill making the new deadline a tough target to move again. Kissinger had at least won a short extension.

Any relief soon gave way to the next, much tougher race for results by 5 February, as events quickly unravelled the Brussels deal. On 19 December 1974, Clerides opened talks with Denktaş, who accepted him as the fully empowered representative of the Greek-Cypriot community to make the point that agreements reached must stand. They agreed to discuss the powers of a federal government, the nature of the federation (bizonal or multiregional) and economic and humanitarian issues. Then Denktaş threw a spanner in the works next day when unexpectedly raising the question of guarantees from Turkey, Greece and Britain. Makarios interfered by extending this list to include UN Security Council countries – Clerides checked with Athens, which, in no mood to rush, wanted to see how the threat of an American aid embargo affected Ankara.

This was all no help to Kissinger as the year turned to 1975. Swift results were needed if both community leaders were to resume talks on 6 January 1975, leaving only four weeks before the congressional axe fell. Kissinger changed tack, deciding the local talks should address less contentious issues to show progress and create an atmosphere of trust for the tougher political problems. He pushed Turkish Foreign Minister Melih Esenbel on Tuesday, 7 January 1975, to support Denktaş and address practical solutions, such as reopening Nicosia airport, some troop withdrawals and over refugees any of which might satisfy Congress. Esenbel annoyingly wanted the guarantor countries to validate any decision reached.

This made results even more unlikely causing Kissinger to tell President Gerald Ford that 'we have to get a longer extension this time', which was improbable so he fretted that 'We will pay for this for years to come'.[390]

In the meantime, Director of Central Intelligence William Colby reported on his own agency's performance, affirming the earlier findings by the Department of State's intelligence chief, Hyland. Colby admitted failures to predict the Cypriot coup, writing that intelligence analysts had 'in early July [1974], notwithstanding their earlier concern, conveyed the impression to the policy makers that the world had been granted a reprieve: Ioannidis, they suggested, had now decided not to move against Makarios, at least for the time being'. His agency also provided 'confused and unconvincing'[391] advice of Turkey's second intervention catching the Department of State off guard again. These errors he attributed to an over reliance on limited human intelligence contacts – as information had almost exclusively come from CIA station chief Stacy Hulse, his deputy Ron Estes and head of operations Gust Avrakotos.

But Colby was not shouldering all the blame. Ambassador Henry Tasca's embassy did not escape criticism as 'reporting from the embassy in Athens, especially in the pre-coup period, was weak; it fairly consistently downplayed the likelihood of serious trouble over Cyprus, even in the face of repeated expressions of great concern from Nicosia and Washington'. And there was a dig at Kissinger and his top diplomats claiming that analysis suffered from 'the nonavailability of certain key categories of information, specifically those associated with private conversations between US policy makers and their representatives on the scene and between these policy makers and certain principals in the dispute'. Alongside 'exemplary successes', including accurate reporting on Soviet intentions and forewarning of the first Turkish intervention – which rather got muddled by the

Department of State, errors were ultimately ascribed to that 'old and familiar' willingness to believe that irrational moves 'will not be made by essentially rational men'.[392]

Rational men were trying hard in Cyprus with Clerides and Denktaş eventually resuming discussions on 14 January 1975 though only to talk about preliminaries giving Kissinger now three weeks.

Elsewhere, refugee issues renewed anti-Western sentiment in Greece and Cyprus when on Tuesday, 15 January 1975, Jim Callaghan finally decided to transfer 9,400 Turkish Cypriots northwards on compassionate grounds. Without reciprocating measures, outrage gripped Greeks and Greek Cypriots endorsing their suspicions of British collusion with Turkey. Protesters made their way from Limassol, broke through the perimeter of RAF Akrotiri blocking the transfer route and attacked a small UN convoy setting one vehicle alight. British soldiers replied with water cannons and tear gas. Tragically a UN vehicle going to help the burning vehicle struck a protester, an 18-year-old Greek Cypriot, Panikos Dimitriou, a refugee from a village near Famagusta, who died on the way to hospital at RAF Akrotiri. This created a minor cause celebre and further heightened community tension.

The next day, 18 January 1975, three Turkish Airlines' Boeings packed with Turkish Cypriots flew out starting the two-week transfer process and landed in Ankara, where disembarked refugees received a hero's welcome to band music. Some had mixed feelings about leaving their homes and businesses, but realising relations with their neighbours were irreparable broken kissed the ground in thanks.

Greek Cypriots again reacted furiously accusing Britain of condoning partition. Five thousand youths burnt the consulate and turned on the British Council ransacking and burning the library. British service stores in Limassol were set alight, as were effigies of Queen Elizabeth II, the Turkish flag and cars at different locations, including a British facility on Mount Troodos. In Athens 2,000 students broke through a police line into the courtyard of the British Embassy where they smashed windows, painted slogans on walls and burnt a car, eventually leaving in frustration when unable to break in.

Protesters again set on the American Embassy in Nicosia, breaking into the compound, setting cars alight, and burning the ground floor pharmacy before trashing the economic section on the next floor.

Frederick 'Fred' Z. Brown, the newly arrived deputy chief of station, brought in for his military and refugee experience by new Ambassador William Crawford, witnessed the scenes with marines firing tear gas into the crowds and embassy staff sent upstairs to a vault in the roof for 'either the last stand. Or for protection. Or evacuation by the UN peacekeeping contingent, when the Greek-Cypriot mob broke into the building and almost killed us'. Brown himself went up the stairs with his two 'Greek Cypriot guards, my chief marine gunny who had a couple of shotguns, and our security officers. We had decided that if the mob came around the corner and up the stairways, we would fire. We had used all of our teargas.'[393] Fortunately, this was not needed as once again a Canadian UNFICYP contingent arrived to beat back demonstrators.

Kissinger learning of the attack warned Makarios that he would close the whole American mission and turn his back on Cyprus if a single American was killed. Brown delivered that very message,

'I have instructed Mr [Frederick] Brown to tell you that if there is any further attack on the American embassy, if an American citizen or any Greek Cypriot employee of the American embassy, is harmed in any way, the United States will cease all activities having to do with Cyprus, will cut off negotiations and will have nothing further to do with the attempt to find a solution on Cyprus. Yours truly, Henry Kissinger.' So I went over in the clothing I was wearing. Full of stink and tear gas and a little bit of blood. I went over and called on the Foreign Minister and delivered this note. Just put it on the table and said, 'This is what we have to say to you.' That took care of it.[394]

By good fortune, political officer James Williams who had lived through the first ordeal had just arrived back in Arlington, Virginia for the birth of his second child, Laura.

Coincidentally, the day Laura was born the headline story in the Post with pictures was of the next Greek Cypriot demonstration that attacked the embassy, and this time they torched the place ... Certainly nobody was shot, thank God, but it was an ugly reminder of how volatile the situation still was.[395]

His wife, Ann, understandably wanted him out of what she thought was a hell hole, so Williams did just that, having been one of the few to stay on and settle the embassy after Davies's death, telling William Crawford he wanted out. Crawford, who had carefully selected the people to rebuild the embassy's morale, gave him a rough time and even considered disciplinary action before relenting. John left six months later.

Local talks deteriorated on 31 January 1975 when Denktaş rejected proposals to reopen Nicosia International Airport with both sides wanting management unacceptable to the other and over Greek-Cypriot use of the Famagusta seaport. The United States hurriedly tried brokering a joint Greek-Turkish board with a neutral country running the airport.

With talks adrift and only four days to go before the cut off, Kissinger's armoury was empty. On 1 February 1975, he made a last-ditch appeal to select congressmen Brademas, Sarbanes, Representative Benjamin Rosenthal of the Queens district of New York and Missouri Senator Thomas Eagleton. He gave them an honest appraisal admitting there 'has not been much progress. We have tried to move the negotiations along as quickly as possible but up to now the progress that has been made has really been of minor nature. I could, therefore, not recommend that the President find that substantial progress has been achieved.'[396]

Then he recited all the reasons against an embargo, impressing on them the likely damage:

> I must say to you in all seriousness that I consider it to be a foreign policy disaster. It hurts the chances of a Cyprus negotiation. It will not in any way help us with the Greeks. It will be looked upon by others in the area as calling into question the good sense of the United States in taking care of our long term interests.[397]

Such powerful words did not move the senators. Turkey had not made serious progress, said Brademas, and there was no progress over Greek-Cypriot refugees. From the congressman's perspective,

> it looks to us as though the Turks are taking even more of a hard line. But we cannot share your view that this has been a disaster. You must see this in the context that American arms have been used in violation of the law and, therefore, from our point of view, it would be a disaster not to react. We believe that the law must be enforced and that, therefore, aid must be cut off.[398]

Sarbanes was equally strong, insisting that no rationale argument existed for an extension. Brademas also warned Kissinger of a clobbering if President Gerlad Ford used another veto.

Thus, after several months of trying to protect the right of the American government to make its own foreign policy, Kissinger and Ford lost their battle with the legislature. Section 620(X) of the

Foreign Assistance Act of 5 February 1975 banned military aid to Turkey. The president tried soothing the effect with a public statement that suspension 'cannot be in the interest of the United States to take action that will jeopardize the system on which our relations in the Eastern Mediterranean have been based for 28 years'. He added that the 'Administration judges these adverse effects of a suspension of aid to Turkey to be so serious that it urges the Congress to reconsider its action and authorize the resumption of our assistance relationship with Turkey'.[399]

Turkey appreciated the gesture but not the result and did not buckle as the Greek lobby very much hoped and Kissinger had predicted all along. Community talks stayed deadlock causing the alarmed Cyprus ambassador in Washington, Dimis Dimitriou, to threaten taking the matter to the UN for results. A dispirited Kissinger did not care, for this grand exponent of strategy had his efforts undermined by the manoeuvrings of the Greek lobby in concert with Athens and Makarios, damaging relations with Turkey and revealing the limits of American policy to the world. His aides beseeched him to send messages backing community talks, but he was in sterner mood when discussing the subject on Saturday, 8 February 1975. As far as he was concerned, 'We are prepared to assist, and that's it. And we're not going to beg these guys, and I want to have a tough and aloof line.' He then summed up future American policy,

> You tell him [Makarios] if he internationalizes it, we will be in exact step with the international community … If he does, we are willing to help, but it's entirely up to them. And we're sick and tired of them playing around in our domestic politics. That's the posture we're going to take with the Greeks, and Turks as well.[400]

None of this mattered for on Thursday, 13 February 1975, Rauf Denktaş declared the creation of a Turkish Federated State of Cyprus. Seven months after the coup unseating Makarios, Cyprus was now divided in the very partition neither Greece nor Turkey had originally wanted but reflected the reality of life on the ground.

Greek Cypriots pulled out of negotiations, Western countries condemned the action and refused to recognise the new entity, while pragmatists saw the declaration as inevitable. Even the left-leaning British *The Guardian* newspaper wrote,

> No amount of global denunciation has budged Ankara one jot. The cut-off in American military aid has been immediately counter-productive.

Mr Denktash [Rauf Denktaş] has 35,000 regular troops on his patch and, thus, all the solid arguments ... the Greeks must sooner or later begin talking within Mr Denktash's unrelenting frame of reference. They must also accept that a lot of northerners who lost their homes and lands will not get them back again.[401]

Fearing that angry Greek Cypriots might turn on the vulnerable bases, Jim Callaghan stayed on his hobby horse:

If the Greeks push us too hard, then I shall raise again the question of evacuating Cyprus. We are staying there in general Western interests – not our own: and the Greek Cypriots may have to face the alternatives of us pulling out or of replacement by a NATO force – neither of them desirable alternatives for the Greek Cypriots.[402]

Henry Kissinger, his efforts exhausted, updated the president in a short note on Thursday, 14 February 1975, writing that a new Turkish-Cypriot state 'will have little practical effect on the ground since there is already almost complete separation of populations and administrations ... However, the impact on the negotiations and the prospects for progress on a Cyprus settlement will be far-reaching and serious.'[403]

And so it has proved to be with an island still divided decades later.

Chapter 25

A LONG SHADOW

Henry Tasca, recalled from Cyprus in September 1974, resigned from the diplomatic service at the age of 62 and moved with his Italian wife to Rome, a post he had favoured above reappointment to Athens, where he began a business career. He died in a Swiss car accident five years later in 1979, which his 15-year-old son, John, survived, also leaving behind a wife and three daughters.

The United States' top CIA staff in Athens, reviewed by the CIA's inspector general who found nothing wanting, continued in their posts until each moved on for routine career reasons. Stacy Hulse finished his tour as station chief in 1975 earning promotion as head of Soviet affairs in Langley until his retirement three years later. His deputy Ron Estes stayed on for two more years, temporarily becoming head of station, followed by appointments in Langley then Spain before heading one of the agency's clandestine divisions, retiring in the 1980s. Along the way Estes married a Russian actress, Luba, whom he had first recruited in Beirut in the early 1970s to spy on officers of the Комитет государственной безопасности (Komitet Gosudarstvennoy Bezopasnosti or abbreviated to KGB), Russia's domestic secret service.

Head of operations Gust Avrakotos went on to win notoriety and unwanted Hollywood stardom as head of the CIA's activity to arm the Afghan *mujahedeen* (guerilla fighters) in their war against invading Soviet forces in 1979. He worked closely with Texas congressman Charlie Wilson in highly unconventional procurement methods, which formed the subject of a book (2003) and film (2007), *Charlie Wilson's War*, but his uncomfortable down-to-earth manner and criticism of the Iran-Contra affair led to subsequent downgraded appointments in Africa before his retirement. He died in 2005.

The United States' CIA mission in Athens witnessed another tragedy affecting agency morale. On 23 December 1975, new CIA Athens station chief Richard 'Dick' Welch and his wife, Kika, were driven home from an afternoon Christmas party organised by new Ambassador Jack Kubisch where they chatted to embassy staff and journalists and watched some Greek dancing. They arrived back at 10.00 pm, got out of the car and walked to their house when another car, trailing them home, pulled up. Three armed men got out and ran over with one telling Dick Welch to put his hands up. Welch questioned 'what?' at which the man opened fire hitting the CIA boss three times, the first bullet killing him instantly. All three men then sped off in the waiting vehicle.

Ron Estes was first on the scene when the protection officer who had driven Welch home rushed over to fetch him. He got there to find Kika embracing her lifeless husband. The driver called for an ambulance, which did not arrive quickly, so Estes and the officer put Welch into the car and followed a police escort to the hospital where waiting doctors confirmed the obvious.

Monty Stearns, the embassy's deputy, parachuted in to support Henry Tasca, soon heard the news about the friend he been delighted to welcome to Athens:

> My wife, Toni, rushed over to the Welch house which was not far from ours and I went down to the chancery... It turned out, of course, it was part of the plot which resulted in a group of terrorists gunning him down in his own driveway in front of his wife. My wife went over to the house and slept there that night. His father was visiting. His birthday party had occurred just a week before. We had gone to it. Toni's best or worst recollection of it is lying half asleep on the sofa in the Welch living room and seeing Dick's father coming down the stairs for an early cup of coffee, not yet knowing what had happened.[404]

This second assassination hit Washington terribly. Welch, like Rodger Davies, popular and respected by fellow officers and diplomats, was a most unlikely looking spy in appearance and demeanour. With round rimmed glasses he bore the looks of a kindly academic underscored by his Harvard University education in classical Greek language and history, which he later converted to modern Greek, confounding many native speakers with his sophisticated fluency. After appointments in South America, Welch quickly rose through the ranks replacing Stacy Hulse in a dream appointment with his love of Greek history. He was Estes's friend, the two having worked closely on a previous tour of duty in Nicosia, and found time to sail together when reunited in Athens. Welch, aged 46, left behind a wife and three children.

Welch's murder augured an age of terrorism from an organisation called 17 November, bearing the date of the student action against the junta in 1973, which held the West, primarily the United States and Britain, responsible for Greek woes.

Cyprus also affected the 1976 American presidential election with the Greek lobby supporting democratic hopeful James 'Jimmy' Earl Carter Jr, the former governor of Georgia, who ousted incumbent Gerald Ford in a tight result. Carter's apparent support for the Greek cause pushed Turkish Cypriots to denounce him as an organ of Greek propaganda.

American Ambassador William Crawford, the permanent replacement for the assassinated Rodger Davies, heard about the word spreading from the Greek lobby that 'When our man Carter gets in, we will make sure that anybody who has had anything to do with Cyprus during this disastrous period is eliminated.'[405] Sure enough, out went the head of the Department of State's European Affairs, Art Hartman, though in his case to become ambassador to France, a position he was born for, and afterwards as ambassador to the Soviet Union. (Hartman's deputy Wells Stabler became ambassador to Spain in 1975.) Bill Macomber left Ankara in June 1977 and, with his fine cultural tastes, became president of The Metropolitan Museum of Art in New York. Jack Kubisch left his Greek ambassadorial post in July 1974 to serve as vice president of the United States' National Defense University.

William Crawford learnt the lobby was similarly gunning for him and prepared for the worse. He had though won supporters along the way most notably Makarios himself who made the difference when they met shortly before the American elections:

He had this benign, lovely look, with his big, tall hat. He said, 'Mr Ambassador, isn't it true that under your system, ambassadors submit their resignations when a new President comes in?' I said, 'Yes, your Beatitude, it is.' He said, 'Wouldn't that be in your case, also, as a career officer, that you would submit your resignation?' I said, 'Yes, your Beatitude.' He said, 'What are your wishes?' ... I said, 'Your Beatitude, if the time has come when I can no longer serve the cause of peace in Cyprus, I'll be happy to go. If there's still something to be of use based on my knowledge of the island and experience here, I would prefer to stay.' He just smiled very faintly, having made the point that he could remove Kissinger's envoy at will. And I stayed for another three years.[406]

Splits in the Department of State over Cyprus in 1974 affected the careers of the fourth-floor experts. Tom Boyatt, the expert on Cyprus, who thought he had effectively been sacked for writing an August 1974 dissent memorandum was placed on a year-long seminar course, after which his career was salvaged with an appointment to Chile before serving as ambassador to Upper Volta and Columbia. His colleague Bob Dillon, also fearing repercussions, served in Malaysia, Turkey and Egypt and then became ambassador to Lebanon. John Day on the Greek desk suffered most and never progressed much further in the foreign service, whereas Harmon Kirby, the expert on Turkey, eventually wound up as ambassador to Togo.

Joe Sisco, the tough talking Italian-Chicago undersecretary, left the Department of State in 1976 to become president of Washington College for four years. However, after government service he found fundraising rather distasteful, so to stay involved in world affairs founded his own consultancy advising on political and economic analysis and punditry, dying in 2004.

Henry Kissinger the last surviving principal of the whole affair died in December 2023 shortly before the fiftieth anniversary of events in Cyprus. He never again held office when President Gerald Ford lost power despite being only 54. His realpolitik ideas were out of fashion as much with the human rights-based approaches of Jimmy Carter as with newer Republicans, who eventually congregated around President Ronald W. Reagan and eschewed compromise with the Soviet Union. His legacy, while controversial, is judged by Cold War achievements, including *détente*, the reopening of China, withdrawal from Vietnam and facilitating peace between Israel and Arab countries. These global events dwarfed what happened on the Mediterranean island of Cyprus with some obituary writers not even mentioning the subject. Kissinger, though, always regarded Cyprus as one of his greatest regrets.

American relations with Turkey suffered pretty much as Kissinger had feared after the congressional embargo. Ankara reacted with its own surprisingly tough measures, temporarily closing American military bases harming intelligence gathering. The Turkish ambassador in Cyprus told American Ambassador William Crawford that

Turkey is an imperial power and a continental power. That we are unnaturally prevented from breathing to the north and the east by the presence of the Soviet Union makes it all the more important that we be able to breathe to the south and to the west. 1974 solved the southern dimension. It remains to solve the Western dimension.[407]

President Jimmy Carter eventually fought his legislature to lift sanctions in 1978, an act he described as the most important foreign policy issue facing Congress. This and a defence deal with Ankara partly repaired relations but not completely, for Turkey rejected use of the bases to help Carter's ill-fated rescue of American hostages in Iran in 1980 and to monitor Soviet compliance with arms reduction talks.

Poet and left-wing nationalist Bülent Ecevit became Turkish prime minister three more times. His second term ended in November 1979 shortly before another coup, when the army ruled the country for a further three years, jailing him twice for speaking to foreign journalists. His final term, in his 70s between 1999 and 2002, saw him lead the campaign for the European Union to accept Turkey as a candidate member. Poor responses to earthquake disasters and a failing economy caused his decisive final defeat at the polls by Recep Tayyip Erdoğan and the Justice and Development Party. This most curious Turkish politician, who as the country's only left-wing prime minister possessing mannerisms of a bookish professor, which disguised forceful nationalist urges and who lived frugally and honestly, died in 2006.

In spring 1976, Foreign Secretary Jim Callaghan won anointment from Prime Minister Harold Wilson as his chosen successor, which together with his general popularity across Labour saw him elected by the party but not by the country to become the new premier. This was a tough mantle for anyone aged 64 amid a bleak picture of 1970s Britain afflicted by strikes and economic gloom. Despite holding four offices of state, including as foreign secretary managing an international crisis nearly seeing British troops in foreign battles, he is unfairly remembered for comments he never actually made as prime minister.

On returning from a sun-soaked international conference with foreign leaders, including President Jimmy Carter, he was greeted by journalists at Heathrow Airport in the low February clouds of 1976 demanding to know about his cures for the country's problems. His ill-informed response, 'I don't think that other people in the world would share the view that there is mounting chaos', was converted the next day by creative journalists of The Sun newspaper to damming headlines of 'Crisis, what crisis?' This saying hung round his neck when facing his only election as prime minister three years later against Britain's first female political leader, Margaret 'Maggie' Thatcher, who squarely beat him.

Few obituary writers even mention Cyprus when reflecting on Callaghan's record of successes and failures. Of his own management of Cyprus, he wrote in his autobiography that 'Britain behaved honourably and fulfilled her obligations to the limit of the possibilities open to us … Others may attribute blame but I do not feel ashamed of what we tried to do.'[408]

Similarly, barely a mention is made of Cyprus in commemorations of Callaghan's principal adviser, Alan Goodison, who later became ambassador to Ireland making a significant contribution to the Good Friday Agreement besides becoming a colourful lay preacher at Hampstead parish church.

Air Marshal John Aiken stayed on for two more years, then became the RAF's personnel officer before retiring in 1978 into the post of director general of intelligence at the Ministry of Defence.

On the diplomatic side, British Ambassador Robin Hooper left his final posting in Greece 1974 and returned home where he was sought after by historians anxious for more details of his war experiences. Hooper had crash landed in occupied France with a Lysander aircraft on a Special Operations Executive (SOE) mission and hid with the French Resistance until flown out a month later. He died aged 74 in 1989. High Commissioner Stephen Olver retired with a knighthood. British Ambassador Horace Phillips stayed on in Ankara until 1977, when he retired to start his second career working for the engineering and construction company Taylor Woodrow.

A rundown of forces on Britain's sovereign bases in Cyprus left only the permanent stationing of helicopter units as all other flight squadrons, including the mighty Vulcan bombers, departed. In January 1975, with only three weeks' notice, RAF pilot Ken Watson returned with 35 Squadron from warm Mediterranean delights to the bleak drizzle of RAF Scampton in Lincolnshire. RAF bases on Cyprus, which diplomats so eagerly wanted to relinquish, have subsequently provided crucial services in nearly every British foreign engagement from the Falklands islands to the intervention in Libya and, at the time of writing, are used in Middle East peace operations.

Greek-American relations waned for several years after 1974. Athens resisted rejoining NATO and lobbied to retain the embargo on Turkey, eventually rejoining the Alliance in October 1980 when, ironically, supported by a Turkish government now ruled by generals. Andreas Papandreou, the much maligned left-wing politician, who eventually became prime minister in the 1980s, never implemented his threats to kick out the United States.

In August 1975, Dimitrios Ioannidis received a life sentence for his role in suppressing the student protests at Athens Polytechnic in trials that have been described as the Greek Nuremburg, when the government of Prime Minister Konstantinos Karamanlis prosecuted former junta leaders. Fellow conspirators, whom Ioannidis had worked with to overthrow democratic Greek rule in 1967, namely former Georgios Papadopoulos, Stylianos Pattakos and Nikolaos Makarezos received death sentences commuted to life imprisonment. Sixteen others were tried.

They enjoyed comfortable conditions in the Athens high-security Korydallos Prison, with Ioannidis even arranging parties by former colleagues in the secret military police. Ioannidis kept himself apart from the colonels as some regarded him a traitor for turning on them in 1973. He stayed defiant to the day of his death in 2010, aged 87, insisting victory over Turkey was his had chiefs of the armed forces not disobeyed orders to attack. Papadopoulos gave no plea during his trial and did not recant when dying in a prison hospital in June 1999.

None of the generals who removed Ioannidis from power in August 1974 were prosecuted. Grigorios Bonanos, who commissioned the coup against Makarios on instruction from Ioannidis, and head of the army Andrea Galatsanos were simply replaced in August 1974. Head of the air force Alexandros Papanikolaou left service as honorary air marshal in January 1975 when Admiral Petros Arapakis left with his own honorary title.

Greek Prime Minister Konstantinos Karamanlis continued to shepherd his country to full democracy paving the way for European Union admission in 1981. After leaving office in 1980, he served for two terms as president and died in 1998, aged 91, possibly as Greece's most successful politician or at least its post-war saviour.

Deposed Greek King Constantine II lived out his isolation mostly in his Hampstead Heath realm in London until his death in 2023, his visits to Greece were limited until 2013 when he was allowed to return as a private citizen, all thoughts of a restoration extinguished.

In Cyprus, usurper and eight-day president, Nikos Sampson, received a twenty-year prison sentence in 1976 for his role in the coup with leniency three years later allowing him a decade in France for medical treatment. His subsequent return to prison was soon suspended on health grounds, so he spent the next ten years in journalism before dying in 2001 unrepentant of his role, which he maintained was thrust upon him.

Six people were tried in 1977 over events surrounding the death of American Ambassador Rodger Davies. Two were acquitted, two received small jail sentences when pleading guilty and two others, linked to EOKA-B who were tried for alleged murder, had charges reduced to gun possession when evidence was lost in the prosecuting process.

Political priest Archbishop Makarios III, president of Cyprus and *ethnarch* to Greek Cypriots, having escape countless assassination attempts died from the simpler cause of heart failure, aged 62, most likely exacerbated by his chain-smoking habit, leaving his ideas and ambitions for himself and Cyprus never really understood. His immediate legacy was the election of a protégé, Spyros Kyprianou, yet another British educated barrister, who refused to compromise with the northern Turkish community in the following two terms as president. Kissinger later wrote that when Makarios died so did the best hope for a settlement:

> When all was said and done, Makarios more than any other Cypriot leader had the imagination to accept reality and prestige to lead his compatriots in the direction of their necessities. Makarios was, after all, a big man in a world not blessed with them.[409]

His political rival, Glafcos Clerides, enjoyed longer years dying aged 91 in 2013, though time had to pass before Greek Cypriots accepted his realistic views. He first continued as negotiator eventually resigning in 1976 unable to win support from Makarios. Ten years then passed with lost election campaigns before Clerides won the Cypriot presidency himself between 1993 to 2003, by which time his own views towards Turkish Cypriots hardened. His period in office increased tension with them and Ankara, particularly after he purchased long-range missiles capable of reaching Turkey.

Clerides's respect for his opposite number, Rauf Denktaş, who died the year before him, did not dull. Denktaş led the northern half of Cyprus as it changed status unilaterally declaring itself the Turkish Republic of Northern Cyprus in 1983, still unrecognised by the UN. Denktaş served as president of this isolated republic four times with as unbending mentality as Makarios by not budging from his insistence on a two-zone solution. He eventually left office in 2005.

Anyone trying to resolve the problems of Cyprus requires bravery, ingenuity and an intelligent understanding of the island's complex and colourful history. This includes an accurate knowledge based on evidence of the immediate causes that led to the temporary toppling of a democratically elected president and two subsequent military interventions by Turkey in summer 1974.

People of any nation when hit by calamity search for reason to explain what has befallen them. All too easily narratives develop of malign interference or manipulation by foreign powers, which in this case many in the Greek speaking world – and for obverse reasons some in Turkey – put at the door of Washington and sometimes London. Events that left Cyprus divided today are complex but in a nutshell are a story about a Greek military officer who seized power in Greece and made a terrible miscalculation. His attempted coup against Makarios gave Ankara a once in a generation opportunity to protect its people and solve a longstanding defence concern.

No one was blaming Americans in the Greek-speaking world on a significant scale until the second Turkish incursion in August 1974. Thereafter, a humiliated Greek people hunted for scapegoats and settled on Washington partly from the memories that President Lyndon Johnson had restrained Turkey in the 1960s and partly from a mistaken view that the United States had engineered the rise of the junta. Anti-Americanism in Greece became so entrenched that even *The Economist* newspaper wrote a piece on Saturday, 7 September 1974 trying to disprove conspiracy fantasies.

The United States and Britain had tried to solve the problem with their own perspectives and interests when imprisoned by their own affairs, Watergate for the former and the economy for the second. Their work was influenced by what was possible without power to control the activities of foreign nation states.

Cyprus remains divided very much as Tom Boyatt and his colleagues foresaw decades ago. For Boyatt, the 1967 Cyrus Vance mission 'managed to avert a war, and indeed he managed to get a mechanism for negotiations established, which exists to this day. It must be the longest on-going negotiation in the history of the world, still unsuccessful.'[410]

Can that change? Henry Kissinger notably told Makarios during a fleeting visit that he never wanted to touch the seemingly intractable problems of either Northern Ireland or Cyprus. One is now enjoying a slow but steady twenty-year course of peace and progress. Has the time for Cyprus arrived?

ACKNOWLEDGEMENTS

I should like to thank all the many service personnel who kindly shared their fascinating stories with me especially John 'Taff' Lee, Wing Commander Ken Watson, Helen Watson and Air Marshal Clifford Spink; Heather Ashe at the Association for Diplomatic Studies and Training of the Department of State and the entire unit for its priceless interviews with former American diplomatic personnel; staff at the Gerald R. Ford Presidential Library; Ralph Mariani; Ambassador Tom Boyatt; Burak Gursel; and the Association of Former Intelligence Officers (AFIO).

BIBLIOGRAPHY

Articles

Dimitrakis, P., 'The Value to CENTO of UK Bases on Cyprus', Middle Eastern Studies, Volume 45, Issue No. 4, 2009

Stern, Laurence M., 'Bitter Lessons: How We Failed in Cyprus', Foreign Policy, Volume 19 (summer 1975), Slate Group, LLC, United States,

Yellice, Gurhan, 'The American Intervention in the 1964 Cyprus Crisis and the Greek Political Reaction (February–August 1964)', Journal of Modern Turkish History Studies, XVII/35, autumn 1964

Books

Anderton, Michael, *RAF 'Plumber', My 30 Years in the Armaments Trade 1953–83*, Woodfield Publishing, Bognor Regis, 2006

Asmussen, Jan, *Cyprus at War: Diplomacy and Conflict During the 1974 Conflict*, I.B Tauris, London, 2008

Ball, George W. *The Past Has Another Pattern: Memoirs*, W.W. Norton & Co., New York, United States, 1982

Callaghan, James, *Time and Chance*, Politicos Publishing, Tunbridge Wells, 2006

Constandinos, Andreas, *America, Britain and the Cyprus Conspiracy of 1974: Calculated Conspiracy or Foreign Policy Failure?*, AuthorHouse, Milton Keynes, 2009

Drousioitis, Makarios, *Cyprus 1974: Greek Coup and Turkish Invasion*, Bibliopolis, Mannheim and Möhnesee, Cyprus, 2006

Erickson, Edward J. and Uyar, Mesut, *Phase Line Atilla: The Amphibious Campaign for Cyprus, 1974*, Marine Corps University Press, Virginia, United States, 2020

Hamilton, Keith and Salmon, Patrick (eds.), *The Southern Flank in Crisis 1973–1976*, Routledge, London, 2006

Heckman, Timothy and Friedman (eds.), B.A., *On Contested Shores: The Evolving Role of Amphibious Operations in the History of Warfare*, Marine Corps University Press, Virginia, United States, 2020 (Guvenc, Serhat and Uyar, Mesut, 'Chapter 13: Against All Odds – Turkish Amphibious Operation in Cyprus, 20–23 July 1974')

Henn, Francis, *A Business of Some Heat: The United Nations Force in Cyprus Before and During the 1974 Turkish Invasion*, Pen & Sword Books, Barnsley, 2004

Holland, Robert, *Blue-Water Empire: The British in the Mediterranean Since 1800*, Allen Lane/Penguin, London, 2012

Holland, Robert, *Britain and the Revolt in Cyprus, 1954–1959*, Clarendon Press, Oxford, 1998

Horace, Phillips, *Envoy Extraordinary: A Most Unlikely Ambassador*, Radcliffe Press, Chippenham, 1995

Horne, Alistair, *Kissinger: 1973, The Crucial Year*, Simon & Shuster, United States, 2009

Hynes, Catherine, *The Year That Never Was: Heath, the Nixon Administration and the Year of Europe*, University College Dublin, Dublin, Republic of Ireland, 2009

Kissinger, Henry, *Years of Upheaval*, Weidenfeld & Nicolson, London, 1982

Kissinger, Henry, *Years of Renewal*, Weidenfeld & Nicolson, London, 1999

Mayes, Stanley, *Cyprus and Makarios*, Putnam, London, 1960

O'Malley, Brendan and Craig, Ian, *The Cyprus Conspiracy: America, Espionage and the Turkish Invasion*, I.B Tauris, London, 2001

Seargent, John, *Give Me Ten Seconds*, Macmillan, London, 2001

Stearns, Monteagle, *Entangled Allies: US Policy Toward Greece, Turkey, and Cyprus*, Council on Foreign Relations Press, New York, United States, 1992

Van Atta, Dale, *With Honor, Melvin Laird in War, Peace, and Politics*, University of Wisconsin Press, Wisconsin, United States, 2008

van der Bijl, Nick, *The Cyprus Emergency: The Divided Island, 1955–1974*, Pen & Sword Books, Barnsley, 2014

Wilson, Harold, *Final Term, The Labour Government 1974–1976*, Weidenfeld & Nicolson, London, 1979

Magazines Referenced
Playboy

Newspapers Referenced
Le Monde
Mahi
Pravda
The Economist
The Observer
The Sun
The Washington Post

Books Referenced

Crile, George, *Charlie Wilson's War*, Atlantic Monthly Press, New York, United States, 2003

Shakespeare, William, *Othello*, 1603

Woodward, Bob and Bernstein, Carl, *All the President's Men*, 1974 (republished *All the President's Men: The Most Devastating Political Detective Story of the 20th Century*, Simon & Shuster, United States, 2006)

Films Referenced

Charlie Wilson's War, 2007

How the West Was Won, 1962

The High Bright Sun, 1964

The French Connection, 1971

Radio Programmes Referenced

British Forces Broadcasting Service (British forces' radio)

Round the Horne (BBC)

Radio Stations Referenced

Paphos Free Radio, Cyprus

Radio Moscow, Russia

Television Programmes Referenced

BBC News (BBC)

BBC World Service (BBC)

Kojak (CBS)

Websites

https://ekathimerini.com

https://greekreporter.com

Images

All images contained in this book supplied courtesy of Alamy.
© Alamy.

Use of Quotations

The author has endeavoured to contact all copyright holders, providing full and proper credits for any text quoted throughout this book. If there are any omissions, this is a genuine oversight, so please make yourself known to the publisher so that this may be corrected in any reprint or future edition.

Sources

Association for Diplomatic Studies and Training Oral History Collection of American Diplomatic Staff: Frank Athanason, Thomas 'Tom' David Boyatt, Elizabeth 'Ann' Brown, William R. Crawford, Robert 'Bob' S. Dillon, Samuel Gammon, Douglas G. Hartley, Arthur 'Art' Adair Hartman, Richard L. Jackson, Charles Stuart Kennedy, Barrington King, Harmon Elwood Kirby, Lindsey Grant, William Butts Macomber, Robert 'Bob' McCloskey, E. Wayne Merry, Michael Metrinko, James H. Morton, Robert 'Bob' Bigger Oakley, Walter J. Silva, James W.S. Spain, James Alan Williams, John Wolf and Dan Zachary

The British Diplomatic Oral History Programme maintained by Churchill College Cambridge: Donald Cape, Derek Malcolm Day, Peter John Goulden, John Killick, Richard Parsons, Horace Phillips and John Wilson

Office of the Historian, online
Documents on British Policy Overseas, Series II, Volume 5
Eastern Europe, Eastern Mediterranean, 1969–1972
Foreign Relations of the United States, 1969-1976, Volume XXX
Foreign Relations of the United States, 1969–1976, Volume XXIX
Greece, Cyprus, Turkey; Eastern Mediterranean, 1973-1976

The Southern Flank in Crisis 1973–1976 – Hamilton, Keith and Salmon, Patrick (eds.), Routledge, London, 2006

The Gerald R. Ford Presidential Library
The Cyprus Crisis papers online

Public Record Office Kew
DEFE, CAB, PREM AND FCO files

Hansard
RAF Akrotiri Station book 1974

Report to the Congress
United States Economic Assistance to Turkey by the Controller of the United States, Washington DC, September 1964

Newspapers
Milliyet
The Guardian
The Independent
The New York Times
The Times
The Washington Post
Time (magazine)
To Vima
ekathimerini.com
greekreporter.com

United Nations Digital Library
Security Council official records
AFIO interviews
Private interviews and information
British Pathé newsreel archive 1896–1978

Crisis on Cyprus: 1975 One Year After Invasion – A Staff Report Prepared for the Use of the Subcommittee to Investigate Problems Connected With Refugees and Escapees of July 1974, United States Congress, Senate Committee on the Judiciary

NOTES

Introduction

1   Page 36, ADST Oral History Project, interview with Charles Stuart Kennedy by Brandon Grove, 4 September 1996.

2   Page 35, ADST Oral History Project, interview with Colonel Frank Athanason by Charles Stuart Kennedy, 10 June 2005.

Chapter 1 – An Intractable Problem

3   Words spoken by Cassio in Act 11, Scene 1 in the tragedy *Othello* by William Shakespeare published in 1622.

4   Convention of Defensive Alliance between Great Britain and Turkey, with respect to the Asiatic Provinces of Turkey, signed at Constantinople on 4 June 1878.

5   Page 15, The Association for Diplomatic Studies and Training (ADST) Foreign Affairs Oral History Project, Interview with Ambassador Barrington King by Charles Stuart Kennedy, 18 April 1990.

6   Page 350, Ball, George W., *The Past Has Another Pattern: Memoirs*, W.W. Norton & Co., New York, United States, 1982

7   Page 32, ADST Oral History Project, interview with Herbert Daniel Brewster by Charles Stuart Kennedy, 11 December 1991.

8   Page 394, Yellice, Gurhan, 'The American Intervention in the 1964 Cyprus Crisis and the Greek Political Reaction (February–August 1964)', *Journal of Modern Turkish History Studies*, XVII/35, autumn 1964.

9   Page 12, ADST Oral History Project, interview with Ambassador Thomas David Boyatt by Charles Stuart Kennedy, 8 March 1990.

10 Page 70, ADST Oral History Project, interview with Ambassador Robert V. Keeley by Thomas Stern, 19 December 1991.

11 Page 71, ibid, ADST, Ambassador Robert V. Keeley interview, 1991.

12 Page 17, ADST Oral History Project, interview with Ambassador William Rex Crawford Jr by Charles Stuart Kennedy, 24 October 1988.

13   Page 74, British Diplomatic Oral History Programme (BDOHP), Churchill College, Cambridge, interview with Ambassador The Honourable Sir Peter Ramsbottom by Malcolm McBain, 9 January 2001.

14   Page 13, BDOHP, interview with Sir Derek Malcolm Day by Jane Barder, 11 March 1996.

15   Page 15, ADST Oral History Project, Thomas David Boyatt interview, op cit.

16   Page 18, BDOHP, interview with Richard Oliver Miles by Malcolm McBain, 27 August 2004.

17   Page 17, ADST Oral History Project, interview with Ambassador Robert McCloskey by Charles Stuart Kennedy, 8 May 1989.

18   *The New York Times*, 'Thousands at Rites as Grivas is Buried at Cyprus Hideout', 31 January 1974.

19   Page 29, ADST Oral History Project, William Rex Crawford Jr interview, op cit.

20   Page 28, ADST Oral History Project, interview with James Alan Williams by Ray Williams, 31 October 2003.

21   Page 35, Stern, Laurence M., 'Bitter Lessons: How We Failed in Cyprus', Foreign Policy, Volume 19 (summer 1975), Slate Group, LLC, United States.

Chapter 2 – British Exposure

22   Page 28, BDOHP, interview with Sir John Weston by Liz Cox, 13 June 2001.

23   Page 19, BDOHP, Richard Oliver Miles interview, op cit.

24   Private information.

25   Page 103, Anderton, Michael, *RAF 'Plumber': My 30 Years in the Armaments Trade, 1953–83*, Woodfield Publishing, Bognor Regis, 2006.

26   Sir Alan Goodison, *The Times* obituary, 13 July 2006.

Chapter 3 – Turkish Independence

27   Page 34 ADST Oral History, Lindsey Grant interview, op cit.

28   Page 25, ADST Oral History Project, interview with Ambassador James W.S. Spain by Charles Stuart Kennedy, 31 October 1995.

Chapter 4 – American Distraction

29   Page 21, ADST Oral History Project, interview with Peter W. Rodman by Charles Stuart Kennedy, 22 May 1994.

30   Page 81, ADST Oral History Project, interview with Ambassador Arthur Adair Hartman by Charles Stuart Kennedy, 20 October 1999.

31   Ibid.

32   Page 21, ADST Oral History Project, interview with Ambassador Barrington King by Charles Stuart Kennedy, 18 April 1999.

33   Page 62, ADST Oral History Project, interview with Ambassador Harmon Elwood Kirby by Charles Stuart Kennedy, 31 August 1995.

34   Page 48, ADST Oral History Project, interview with Walter J. Silva by Charles Stuart Kennedy, 23 January 1995.

35   Page 27, ADST Oral History Project, interview with Richard L. Jackson by Charles Stuart Kennedy, 17 August 1998.

36   Page 26, ADST Oral History Project, interview with Elizabeth 'Ann' Brown by Thomas J. Dunnigan, 30 May 1995.

37   Page 34, ADST Oral History Project, interview with Charles Stuart Kennedy by Brandon Grove, 4 September 1996.

38   Kennedy, ibid.

39   Page 30, ADST Oral History Project, James Alan Williams interview, op cit.

40   Ibid.

Chapter 6 – An Incomplete Picture: January to June 1974

41   Page 7, ADST, Thomas David Boyatt interview, op cit.

42   Minutes of Secretary of State Dr Henry Kissinger's regional staff meeting, Washington, 20 March 1974, Foreign Relations of the United States (FRUS), 1969–1976, Volume XXX, Greece; Cyprus; Turkey, 1973–1976.

43   Ibid.

44   Document 8, letter from High Commissioner Stephen Olver (Nicosia) to Sir Alan Goodison, Nicosia, 25 March 1974, DBPO, Series III, Volume V.

45   Page 56, ADST, Ambassador Harmon Elwood Kirby interview, op cit.

46   Ibid.

47   Greece Under Ioannidis: Implications for US-Greek Relations, interagency intelligence memorandum, Washington, 18 April 1974, FRUS, Volume XXX.

48   Page 7, ADST, Thomas David Boyatt interview, op cit.

49   Footnote 6, Document 15, letter from Mr J.R. Leeland (Ankara) to Mrs G.S. Wright, Ankara, 7 June 1974, and Footnote 5, Document 16, letter from High Commissioner Stephen Olver (Nicosia) to Sir Alan Goodison, Nicosia, 19 June 1974, DBPO, Series III, Volume 5.

50   Document 16, letter from High Commissioner Stephen Olver (Nicosia) to Sir Alan Goodison, Nicosia, 19 June 1974, DBPO, Series III, Volume V.

51   Foreign policy views of Brigadier General Dimitrios Ioannidis, telegram from the embassy in Greece to the Department of State, Athens, 14 June 1974, FRUS, Volume XXX.

52   Footnote 3, Document 77, telegram comments from Nicosia embassy to telegram from the Department of State to the embassies in Greece and Cyprus, Greece-Cyprus relations, Washington, 29 June 1974, FRUS, Volume XXX.

53   Page 44, ADST Oral History Project, interview with Ambassador Robert S. Dillon by Charles Stuart Kennedy, 17 May 1990.

54   Ibid.

55   Page 7, ADST, Thomas David Boyatt interview, op cit.

56   'Athens Junta Was Open in Dislike of Archbishop', *The New York Times*, 16 July 1974.

57   Page 35, ADST Lindsey Grant interview, op cit.

58   Ibid.

59   Page 44, ADST, Ambassador Robert S. Dillon interview, op cit.

60   Page 8, ADST, Ambassador Thomas David Boyatt interview, op cit.

61   Page 44, ADST, Ambassador Robert S. Dillon interview, op cit.

62   Page 31, ADST, James Alan Williams interview, op cit.

63   Page 32, ADST, Lindsey Grant interview, op cit.

64   Ibid.

65   Page 19, ADST, Ambassador William Rex Crawford Jr interview, op cit.

66   Ibid.

67   Page 8, ADST, Ambassador Thomas David Boyatt interview, op cit.

68   Page 335, Callaghan, James, *Time and Chance*, Politicos Publishing, Tunbridge Wells, 2006.

69   Page 8 ADST, Ambassador Thomas David Boyatt interview, op cit.

70   Page 8, ADST, Ambassador Thomas David Boyatt interview, op cit.

71   Ibid.

Chapter 7 – An Unexpected Coup: Monday, 15 July 1974

72   Private information.

73   Document 19, Foreign Secretary James Callaghan to Ambassador Sir Robin William John Hooper (Athens), FCO, 15 July 1974, DBPO, Series III, Volume V.

74   Footnote 1, Document 20, Foreign Secretary James Callaghan to Ambassador Sir Robin William John Hooper (Athens), FCO, 16 July 1974, DBPO, Series III, Volume V.

75   Page 32, ADST Oral History Project, interview with Colonel Frank Athanason by Charles Stuart Kennedy, 10 June 2005.

76   Page 32, ibid.

77   Document 80, Cyprus, minutes of meeting of the Washington Special
     Actions Group. Washington, 15 July 1974, FRUS, Volume XXX.

78   Ibid.

79   Document 81, Cyprus: Further reflections from Athens, telegram from
     the embassy in Greece to the Department of State, Athens, 15 July 1974,
     FRUS, Volume XXX.

80   Ibid.

81   Document 82, Cyprus Coup: For Ambassador from the Secretary,
     telegram from the Department of State to the embassy in Greece,
     Washington, 15 July 1974, FRUS, Volume XXX.

82   Report by commander of British forces Near East on the Cyprus
     Emergency, 15 July–16 August 1974, 15 May 1975, DEFE 25/385.

83   Ibid.

84   Document 83, transcript of telephone conversation between Secretary of
     State Dr Henry Kissinger and the Soviet Ambassador Anatoly Dobrynin,
     Washington, 15 July 1974, FRUS, Volume XXX.

85   Document 84, transcript of telephone conversation between Secretary of
     State Dr Henry Kissinger and the Soviet Ambassador Anatoly Dobrynin,
     Washington, 15 July 1974, FRUS, Volume XXX.

86   Ibid.

Chapter 8 – Turkey Goes Through the Motions: Tuesday, 16 July 1974

87   Footnote 5, Document 20, Foreign Secretary James Callaghan to
     Ambassador Sir Robin William John Hooper (Athens), FCO, 16 July 1974,
     DBPO, Series III, Volume V.

88   Hansard, column 247, Volume 877, *Cyprus*, debated on Tuesday, 16 July
     1974.

89   Page 8, British Forces Near East report, DEFE 25/385, op cit.

90   Document 88, Cyprus Coup, meeting with Brigadier General Dimitrios
     Ioannidis, telegram from the embassy in Greece to the Department of
     State, Athens, 16 July 1974, FRUS, Volume XXX.

91   Ibid.

92   Ibid.

93   Ibid.

94   Document 86, Cyprus, minutes of meeting of the Washington Special
     Actions Group, Washington, 16 July 1974, FRUS, Volume XXX.

95   Page 44, ADST, Ambassador Robert S. Dillon interview, op cit.

Chapter 9 – Tones of Difference Emerge: Wednesday, 17 July 1974

96   Footnote 3, Document 23, High Commissioner Stephen Olver (Nicosia) to Foreign Secretary James Callaghan, Nicosia, 17 July 1974, DBPO, Series III, Volume V.

97   'Makarios, in London, Gets Britain's Strong Backing', *The New York Times*, 18 July 1974.

98   Ibid.

99   Document 90, Cyprus Coup: Am-PriMin Meeting, telegram from the embassy in Turkey to the Department of State, Ankara, 17 July 1974.

100   Columns 447 and 448, Volume 887, Cyprus, debated on Wednesday, 17 July 1974, Hansard.

101   'US Begins Talks with Chiefs of New Cyprus Regime', *The New York Times*, 18 July 1974.

102   Ibid.

103   Document 91, Cyprus, minutes of meeting of the Washington Special Actions Group, Washington, 17 July 1974, FRUS, Volume XXX.

104   Ibid.

105   Document 23, High Commissioner Stephen Olver (Nicosia) to Foreign Secretary James Callaghan, Nicosia, 17 July 1974, DBPO, Series III, Volume V.

106   Footnote 5, ibid.

107   Annex G Flash, 17 July, 2245, report by commander of British Forces Near East on the Cyprus Emergency 15 July–16 August 1974, 15 May 1975, DEFE 25/385.

108   Document 92, transcript of telephone conversation between Secretary of State Dr Henry Kissinger and British Foreign Secretary James Callaghan, 17 July 1974, FRUS, Volume XXX.

109   Ibid.

110   Footnote 10, Document 25, record of conversation between Prime Minister Harold Wilson, Foreign Secretary James Callaghan, Secretary of Defence Roy Mason, Turkish Prime Minister Bülent Ecevit, Acting Foreign Minister Hasan Işik and Mr Asilturk after dinner at No. 10 Downing Street, on Wednesday, 17 July 1974, DBPO, Series III, Volume V.

111   Document 25, ibid.

112   Document 93, transcript of telephone conversation between President Richard Nixon and Secretary of State Dr Henry Kissinger, 17 July 1974.

113   Footnote 8, Document 26, Ambassador The Honourable Sir Peter Ramsbottom (Washington) to Foreign Secretary James Callaghan, Washington 17 July 1974, DBPO, Series III, Volume V.

114   Footnote 5, Document 26, ibid.

115   Page 231, Constandinos, Andreas, *America, Britain and the Cyprus Conspiracy of 1974: Calculated Conspiracy or Foreign Policy Failure?*, AuthorHouse, Milton Keynes, 2009.

116   Page 46, ADST, Ambassador Robert S. Dillon interview, op cit.

117   Ibid.

118   Ibid.

119   Page 9, ADST, Ambassador Thomas David Boyatt interview, op cit.

Chapter 10 – Don't Legitimise Makarios: Thursday, 18 July 1974

120   Document 27, minutes from Sir John Edward Killick to Sir Alan Goodison, FCO, 18 July 1974, DBPO, Series III, Volume V.

121   Footnote 9 to Document 27, Minute from Sir John Edward Killick to Sir Alan Goodison, FCO, 18 July 1974, DBPO, Series III, Volume V.

122   Footnote 12, Document 25, record of dinner conversation, op cit.

123   'Sampson Defends the Cyprus Coup', *The New York Times*, 19 July 1974.

124   Ibid.

125   Footnote 3, Document 28, Foreign Secretary James Callaghan to High Commissioner Stephen Olver (Nicosia), FCO, 18 July 1974, DBPO, Series III, Volume V.

126   Document 96, editorial note, FRUS, Volume XXX

127   Document 94, Cyprus, minutes of meeting of the Washington Special Actions Group, Washington, 18 July 1974, FRUS, Volume XXX.

128   Ibid.

129   Document 95, Cyprus Crisis, memorandum of conversation, Washington, 18 July 1974, FRUS, Volume XXX.

130   Ibid.

131   Document 97, Subject: Policy Considerations in Cyprus Situation, telegram from the Department of State to certain posts, Washington, 18 July 1974, FRUS, Volume XXX.

132   Ibid.

133   Document 95, memorandum, op cit.

134   Document 28, Foreign Secretary James Callaghan to High Commissioner Stephen Olver (Nicosia), FCO, 18 July 1974, DPBO, Series III, Volume V.

Chapter 11 – The Sisco Mission: Friday, 19 July 1974

135   Page 53, ADST Oral History Project, interview with Ambassador Robert Bigger Oakley by Charles Stuart Kennedy and Thomas Sten, 7 July 1992.

136   Page 9, ADST, Ambassador Thomas David Boyatt interview, op cit.

137 Page 53, ADST, Ambassador Robert Bigger Oakley interview, op cit.

138 Page 53, ADST, Ambassador Robert Bigger Oakley interview, op cit.

139 Page 9, ADST, Ambassador Thomas David Boyatt interview, op cit.

140 Ibid.

141 Document 99, For Secretary from Joseph John Sisco, telegram from the embassy in Greece to the Department of State, Athens, 19 July 1974, FRUS, Volume XXX.

142 Page 24, ADST Oral History Project, interview with Ambassador John Wolf by Kenneth Brown, 14 October 2014.

143 Ibid.

144 Footnote 5, Document 29, Sir Edward Emile Tomkins (Paris) to Ambassador The Honourable Sir Peter Ramsbottom (Washington), Paris, 19 July 1974, DPBO, Series III, Volume V.

145 Document 29, Ibid.

146 Footnote 3, Document 29, ibid.

147 Ibid.

148 Excerpts from Archbishop Makarios III's statement to the UN Security Council, *The New York Times*, 20 July 1974.

149 Footnote 6, Document 29, DPBO, op cit.

150 Page 342, Callaghan, James, *Time and Chance*, op cit.

151 Page 54, ADST Oral History, Ambassador Robert Bigger Oakley interview, op cit.

152 Ibid.

153 Page 9, ADST Oral History, Ambassador Thomas David Boyatt interview, op cit.

154 Ibid.

155 Page 45, ADST Oral History, Ambassador Robert S. Dillon interview, op cit.

156 Page 26, ADST Oral History Project, interview with Ambassador William Butts Macomber Jr by Warren Uma, 19 September 1993.

Chapter 12 – The First Assault: Saturday, 20 July 1974

157 Page 40, ADST, James Alan Williams interview, op cit.

158 Annex U, BFBS Special Announcement, 20 July 1974, DEF 25/385, op cit.

159 Document 100, transcript of telephone conversation between Secretary of State Dr Henry Kissinger and Secretary of Defense Dr James Schlesinger, 19 July 1974, FRUS, Volume XXX.

160 Page 343, Callaghan, James, *Time and Chance*, op cit.

161 Footnote 4, Document 30, Ambassador Sir Horace Hyman Phillips (Ankara) to Foreign Secretary James Callaghan, Ankara, 20 July 1974, DBPO, Series III, Volume V.

162 Document 101, transcript of telephone conversation between Secretary of State Dr Henry Kissinger and Ambassador at Large Robert McCloskey, 19 July 1974, FRUS, Volume V.

163 Annex W, BFBS Special Announcement 20 July, British forces report, DEF 25/385, op cit.

164 Ibid.

165 ITN news reel archive, 20 July 1974, broadcasting Michael Nicholson's report from Cyprus.

166 Document 102, transcript of telephone conversation between Secretary of State Dr Henry Kissinger and Director of Central Intelligence William Colby, 19 July 1974, FRUS, Volume V.

167 Document 103, transcript of telephone conversation between President Richard Nixon and Secretary of State Dr Henry Kissinger, San Clemente, 19 July 1974, FRUS, Volume V.

168 Footnote 6, Document 31, Foreign Secretary Callaghan to Ambassador Sir Robin William John Hooper (Athens), FCO, 20 July 1974, DBPO, Series III, Volume V.

169 Quoted in *The Truth in a 'Dark Room*, excerpts from Alexis Papachelas's forthcoming book, ekathimerini online newspaper (ekathimerini.com), 14 October 2021, using material from Papahelas, Alexis, *Greece and Cyprus in a Dark Room, 1967–74*, Metaixmio, November 2021.

170 Footnote 7, Document 32, Ambassador Sir Robin William John Hooper (Athens) to Foreign Secretary James Callaghan, Athens, 20 July 1974, DBPO, Series III, Volume V.

171 Quoted in *The Dramatic 38 Minutes of a National Tragedy*, 20 July 2022, ekathimerini, op cit, using material from *Greece and Cyprus in a Dark Room, 1967–74*, op cit.

172 Page 32, ADST Oral History Project, interview with Colonel Frank Athanason by Charles Stuart Kennedy, 10 June 2005.

173 Ibid.

174 Ibid.

175 Ibid.

176 Document 104, editorial note, FRUS, Volume XXX.

177 Page 35, ADST, Ambassador Wolf interview, op cit.

178 Ibid.

179 British forces report, DEF 25/385, op cit.

180 Document 32, Ambassador Sir Robin William John Hooper (Athens) to Foreign Secretary James Callaghan, Athens, 20 July 1974, DBPO, Series III. Volume V.

181 Ibid.

182 Annex V, British forces report, DEF 25/385, op cit.

183 British forces report, DEF 25/385, op cit.

184 Private information.

185 Footnote 8, Document 32, DBPO, op cit.

186 Page 52, ADST, James Alan Williams interview, op cit.

187 Document 105, Cyprus, minutes of meeting of the Special Washington Actions Group, Washington, 20 July 1974, FRUS, Volume XXX.

188 Page 280, Constandinos, Andreas, *America, Britain and the Cyprus Crisis of 1974*, op cit.

189 Document 106, transcript of telephone conversation between Secretary of State Dr Henry Kissinger and the Deputy Secretary of State Robert Ingersoll, 20 July 1974, FRUS, Volume V.

190 Ibid.

191 Footnote 6, Document 106, ibid.

192 Document 109, transcript of telephone conversation among Secretary of State Dr Henry Kissinger, the Deputy Secretary of State Robert Ingersoll, and the Assistant Secretary for International Organization Affairs William Buffum, 20 July 1974, FRUS, Volume XXX.

193 Document 108, transcript of telephone call between President Richard Nixon and Secretary of State Dr Henry Kissinger, San Clemente, 20 July 1974, FRUS, Volume XXX.

194 Ibid.

Chapter 13 – Turkish Prevarication: Sunday, 21 July 1974

195 Page 137, *Crisis on Cyprus, 1975: One Year After the Invasion*, a staff report prepared for the use of the Subcommittee to Investigate Problems Connected with Refugees and Escapees of the Committee on the Judiciary, United States Senate, Ninety-Fourth Congress, first session, 20 July 1974.

196 Document 110, Cyprus, minutes of meeting of the Washington Special Actions Group, Washington, 21 July 1974, FRUS, Volume XXX.

197 Page 138, Crisis on Cyprus, Congressional staff report, op cit.

198 British forces report, DEF 25/385, op cit.

199 152, Sergeant, *Give Me Ten Seconds,* op cit.

200 Private information.

201 Page 22, ADST Oral History Project, interview with Ambassador James W.S. Spain by Charles Stuart Kennedy, 31 October 1995.

202 Document 110, Minutes, FRUS, op cit.

203 Ibid.

204 Ibid.

205 Page 288, Constandinos, Andreas, op cit.

206 Footnote 6, Document 34, Foreign Secretary James Callaghan to Mr Dobbs (Moscow), FCO, 21 July 1973, DBPO, Series III, Volume V.

207 Document 111, transcript of a telephone conversation between Secretary of State Dr Henry Kissinger and Turkish Prime Minister Bülent Ecevit, 21 July 1974, FRUS, Volume XXX.

208 Footnote 1, Document 35, Ambassador Sir Robin William John Hooper (Athens) to Foreign Secretary James Callaghan, Athens, 21 July 1974, DBPO, Series III, Volume V.

209 Document 36, Foreign Secretary James Callaghan to Sir Edward Emile Tomkins (Paris), FCO, 21 July 1974, DBPO, Series III, Volume V.

210 Footnote 5, Document 36, ibid.

211 XXX

212 'A Greek-Turkish Truce Accord on Cyprus is Announced by US; Ceasefire is Scheduled Today', *The New York Times*, 22 July 1974.

Chapter 14 – Relief: Monday, 22 July 1974

213 British forces report, DEF 25/385, op cit.

214 Page 296, Constandinos, Andreas, op cit.

215 'Ankara Claiming Permanent Base', *The New York Times*, 23 July 1974.

216 Private information.

217 Page 55, ADST, Ambassador Robert Bigger Oakley interview, op cit.

218 Page 56, ibid.

219 Page 9, ADST, Ambassador Thomas David Boyatt interview, op cit.

220 Page 10, ibid.

221 Page 68, Stern, Laurence M., op cit.

222 Ibid.

223 Document 37, Extract from Conclusions of a Meeting of the Cabinet held at 10 Downing Street on 22 July 1974 at 12 noon, DPBO, Series III, Volume V.

224 Document 117, telegram from the Department of State to the embassies in Turkey and Yugoslavia, Washington, 23 July 1974, FRUS, Volume XXX.

225 Document 113, Cyprus, minutes of meeting of the Washington Special Actions Group, Washington, 22 July 1974, FRUS, Volume XXX.

226   Document 114, transcript of telephone conversation between Secretary of State Dr Henry Kissinger and Foreign Secretary James Callaghan, 22 July 1974, FRUS, Volume XXX.

227   Footnote 4, Document 38, Note by Mr. Acland, FCO, 22 July 1974, DBPO, Series III, Volume V.

228   British forces report, DEF 25/385, op cit.

229   Document 115, memorandum of conversation, Washington, 22 July 1974, FRUS, Volume XXX.

230   Ibid.

Chapter 15 – Greek Fall: Tuesday, 23 July 1974

231   Page 129, Phillips, Horace, *Envoy Extraordinary: A Most Unlikely Ambassador*, Radcliffe Press, Chippenham, 1995

232   Ibid.

233   Annex BB, British forces report, DEF 25/385, op cit.

234   British forces report, DEF 25/385, op cit.

235   Ibid.

236   Annex CC, British forces report, DEF 25/385, op cit.

237   British forces report, DEF 25/385, op cit.

238   Ibid.

239   Ibid.

240   Footnote 2, Document 119, Cyprus Crisis, memorandum of conversation, Washington, 23 July 1974, FRUS, Volume XXX.

241   Footnote 9, Document 40, Foreign Secretary James Callaghan to British Representatives Overseas, FCO, 25 July 1970, DBPO, Series III, Volume V.

242   Page 78, ADST Oral History Project, interview with Ambassador Monteagle Stearns by Charles Stuart Kennedy, 30 April 2013.

243   Ibid.

244   'Junta's Rule Ends', *The New York Times*, 24 July 1974.

245   Document 118, briefing memorandum from the Assistant Secretary of State for European Affairs (Hartman) to Secretary of State Dr Henry Kissinger, Washington, 23 July 1974, FRUS, Volume XXX.

246   Page 348, Callaghan, James, *Time and Chance*, op cit.

247   Document 119, Cyprus Crisis, memorandum of conversation, Washington, 23 July 1974, FRUS, Volume XXX.

248   Ibid.

249   Ibid.

250   Ibid.

251 Ibid.

252 Ibid.

253 British forces report, DEF 25/385, op cit.

Chapter 16 – Karamanlis Returns: Wednesday, 24 July 1974

254 Annex DD, British forces report, DEF 25/385, op cit.

255 British forces report, DEF 25/385, op cit.

Chapter 17 – The First Conference

256 Annex FF, British forces report, DEF 25/385, op cit.

257 British forces report, DEF 25/385, op cit.

258 Ibid.

259 Footnote 7, Document 41, Mr D.H.T. Hildyard (UKMIS Geneva) to FCO, Geneva, 26 July 1974, DBPO, Series XXX, Volume V.

260 Document 41, ibid.

261 Footnote 3, Document 42, note by Sir Alan Goodison, Geneva, 27 July 1974, DBPO, Series III, Volume V.

262 Page 80, ADST, Ambassador Monteagle Stearns interview, op cit.

263 Footnote 2, document 45, Mr D.H.T. Hildyard (UKMIS Geneva) to FCO, Geneva, 29 July, DBPO, Series III, Volume V.

264 Footnote 3, Document 45, ibid.

265 Document 45, ibid.

266 Page 326, Constandinos, *America, Britain and the Cyprus Crisis*, op cit.

267 Document 44, note by the Defence Policy Staff of the Chiefs of Staff Committee, Cabinet Office, 29 July 1974, DBPO, Series III, Volume V.

268 Document 124, *Memorandum of Conversation*, Washington, 29 July 1974, FRUS, Volume XXX.

269 Ibid.

270 Document 48, Mr D.H.T. Hildyard (UKMIS Geneva) to FCO, Geneva, 30 July 1974, DBPO, Series III, Volume V.

271 Document 49, chronology of events of 30 July 1974, at the Palais des Nations, Geneva, DBPO, Series III, Volume V.

Chapter 18 – Fall of a President

272 Footnote 3, Document 52, High Commissioner Stephen Olver (Nicosia) to Foreign Secretary James Callaghan, Nicosia, 5 August 1974, DBPO, Series III, Volume V.

273 Page 25, ADST, Elizabeth 'Ann' Brown interview, op cit.

274 Page 56, ADST, Ambassador Robert Bigger Oakley interview, op cit.

275   Page 85, ADST, Ambassador Arthur Adair Hartman interview, op cit.

276   Ibid.

277   Footnote 4, Document 53, Steering Brief for the United Kingdom to Stage II of the Geneva Talks on Cyprus, FCO, 7 August 1974, DBPO, Series III, Volume V.

278   Footnote 8, Document 53, ibid.

279   Document 52, High Commissioner Stephen Olver (Nicosia) to Foreign Secretary James Callaghan, Nicosia, 5 August 1974, DBPO, Series III, Volume V.

280   Footnote 3, Document 53, steering brief, DBPO, op cit.

281   Document 54, record of a conversation between James Callaghan and Arthur Adair Hartman at the FCO on 8 August 1974 at 10.30 am, DBPO, Series III, Volume V.

282   Footnote 5, Document 52, High Commissioner Stephen Olver to Foreign Secretary James Callaghan, DBPO, op cit.

283   Page 191, Asmussen, Jan, *Cyprus at War: Diplomacy and Conflict During the 1974 Conflict*, I.B. Tauris, London 2008.

Chapter 19 – Second Assault

284   Footnote 5, Document 82, Draft Paper by Sir Geoffrey Arthur, DBPO, Series III, Volume V.

285   Document 55, Miss A.M. Warburton (UMKIS Geneva) to FCO, Geneva 8 August 1974, DBPO, Series III, Volume V.

286   Page 83, ADST Oral History Project, interview with Ambassador James G. Lowenstein, interviewed by Denis Kux, 8 February 1994.

287   Document 126, telegram from the mission in Geneva to the Department of State, Geneva, 9 August 1974, FRUS, Volume XXX.

288   Footnote 5, Document 57, record of a conversation between Foreign Secretary James Callaghan and Foreign Minister Turan Güneş, on 9 August 1974, DBPO, Series III, Volume V.

289   Document 125, telegram from the mission in Geneva to the Department of State, FRUS, Volume XXX.

290   Ibid.

291   Page 52, ADST, Ambassador Robert Bigger Oakley interview, op cit.

292   Page 57, ADST Oral History Project, interview with David M. Evans by Charles Stuart Kennedy, 22 November 1986.

293   Page 37, ADST Oral History Project, interview with Ambassador Jack B. Kubisch by Henry E. Mattox, 6 January 1989.

294   Document 60, Miss A.M. Warburton (UMMIS Geneva) to FCO, Geneva, 10 August 1974, DBPO, Series III, Volume V.

295 Document 127, transcript of telephone conversation between President Gerald R. Ford Jr Ford and Secretary of State Dr Henry Kissinger, Washington, 10 August 1974, FRUS, Volume XXX.

296 Document 61, Mr Richard (UKMIS New York) to Foreign Secretary James Callaghan, New York, 11 August 1974, DBPO, Series III, Volume V.

297 Document 62, record of a meeting between James Callaghan and Arthur Adair Hartman at UKMIS Geneva on 11 August 1974, DBPO, Series III, Volume V.

298 Document 63, record of a telephone conversation between Foreign Secretary James Callaghan and Joseph John Sisco on 11 August 1974, DBPO, Volume V.

299 Footnote 2, Document 64, Record of a conversation between Foreign Secretary James Callaghan and Foreign Minister Turan Güneş in the Palais des Nations, Geneva, on 11 August 1974, DBPO, Series III, Volume V.

300 Document 68, Miss A.M. Warburton (UKMIS Geneva) to Ambassador The Honourable Sir Peter Ramsbottom, Geneva, 12 August 1974, DBPO, Series III, Volume V.

301 Page 21, British Diplomatic Oral History Programme, Recollections of Sir Peter John Goulden GCMG, recorded and transcribed by Abbey Wright, 26 March 2019, Churchill College Archives Centre.

302 Page 22, ibid.

303 Document 128, Cyprus, memorandum of conversation, Washington, 12 August, FRUS, Volume XXX.

304 Footnote 6, Document 68, DBPO, op cit.

305 Footnote 7, Document 72, record of a conversation between Foreign Secretary James Callaghan and Foreign Minister Turan Güneş at the Palais des Nations, Geneva on 12 August 1974, DBPO, Series III, Volume V.

306 Footnote 1, Document 73, Miss A.M. Warburton (UKMIS Geneva) to FCO, Geneva, 13 August 1974, DBPO, Series III, Volume V.

307 Document 129, *Memorandum of Conversation*, Washington, 13 August 1974, FRUS, Volume XXX.

308 Document 130, Cyprus Contingencies, paper prepared in the State Department, Washington undated, FRUS, Volume XXX.

Chapter 20 – Recrimination, Reappraisals and Assassination

309 Document 82, Draft Paper by Sir Geoffrey Arthur, FCO, 20 August 1974, DBPO, Series III, Volume V.

310 Ibid.

311 President Gerald R. Ford Jr and Dr Henry Kissinger in Tribute to Slain Cyprus Envoy, *The New York Times*, 22 August 1974.

312   Page 34, ADST, Grant interview, op cit.

313   Footnote 6, Document 83, Ambassador Sir Robin William John Hooper (Athens) to Foreign Secretary James Callaghan, Athens, 26 August 1974. DBPO, Series III, Volume V.

314   Footnote 14, Document 82, DBPO, op cit.

315   Ibid.

316   Footnote 1, Document 83, DBPO, op cit.

317   Document 83, DBPO, op cit.

318   Page 38, ADST, Ambassador William Rex Crawford Jr interview, op cit.

319   Page 31, ibid.

320   Document 146, memorandum of conversation, Washington, August 27, 1974, FRUS, Volume XXX.

321   Ibid.

322   Ibid.

323   Document 84, record of a meeting between Secretary of Dr State Henry Kissinger and Sir John Edward Killick held in the Department of State, Washington, 27 August 1974, DBPO, Series III, Volume V.

324   Ibid.

325   Document 146, FRUS, op cit.

326   Page 31, ADST, Ambassador William Rex Crawford Jr interview, op cit.

327   Page 34, ibid.

Chapter 21 – Creation of a Villain

328   'Cyprus Fighting Resumes as Peace Talks Collapse: UN Called Into Session', *The New York Times*, 14 August 1974.

329   British forces report, DEF 25/385, op cit.

330   Ibid.

331   Page 22, BDOHP, Sir John Peter Goulden interview, op cit.

332   Page 83, ADST, Ambassador Arthur Adair Hartman interview, op cit.

333   Document 77, record of a telephone conversation between Foreign Secretary James Callaghan and Secretary of State Dr Henry Kissinger on 14 August 1974, DBPO, Series III, Volume V.

334   Footnote 6, Document 77, ibid.

335   Document 78, record of a meeting between Foreign Secretary James Callaghan and Dr Kurt Waldheim in the FCO ON 14 August 1974, DBPO, Series III, Volume V.

336   Document 131, Cyprus, minutes of the Special Actions Group, Washington, 14 August 1974, FRUS, Volume XXX.

337 British forces report, DEF 25/385, op cit.

338 Page 50, ADST, James Alan Williams interview, op cit.

339 Page 83, ADST, Ambassador Arthur Adair Hartman interview, op cit.

340 British forces report, DEF 25/385, op cit.

341 Ibid.

342 Document 132, Cyprus, minutes of the Special Actions Group, Washington, 15 August 1974, FRUS, Volume XXX.

343 Ibid.

344 Document 133, Cyprus, memorandum of conversation, Washington, 15 August 1974, FRUS, Volume XXX.

345 Document 135, Transcript of Conversation Between Secretary of State Dr Henry Kissinger and Greek Prime Minister Konstantinos G. Karamanlis, 15 August 1974, FRUS, Volume XXX.

346 Document 80, draft paper by Sir Alan Goodison, FCO, 16 August 1974, DBPO, Series III, Volume V.

347 'US Offering to Mediate in Negotiations on Cyprus', *The New York Times*, 16 August 1974.

348 Document 136, Cyprus, memorandum of conversation, Washington, 16 August 1974, FRUS, Volume XXX.

349 Footnote 7, Document 80, DBPO, op cit.

350 Document 137, Cyprus, memorandum of conversation, Washington, 17 August 1974, FRUS, Volume XXX.

351 Footnote 2, Document 137, ibid.

352 Document 138, telegram from the Department of State to the embassy in Turkey, FRUS, Volume XXX.

353 'Kissinger's Role in Cyprus Crisis Criticized', *The New York Times*, 19 August 1974.

354 Page 59, ADST, James Alan Williams interview, op cit.

355 Document 139, transcript of telephone conversation between Secretary of State Dr Henry Kissinger and Acting Cypriot President Clerides, 19 August 1974, FRUS, Volume XXX.

356 Document 140, transcript of telephone conversation between Secretary of State Dr Henry Kissinger and Turkish Prime Minister Bülent Ecevit, 19 August 1974, FRUS, Volume XXX.

357 'Kissinger Seeks to Assure Athens on Cyprus Issues', *The New York Times*, 19 August 1974

358 'Athens Said to Rebuff US in Accepting Soviet Plan', *The New York Times*, 20 August 1974.

359 Ibid.

Chapter 22 – The Battle for Aid Begins

360 Footnote 9, Document 90, Foreign Secretary James Callaghan to Ambassador The Honourable Sir Peter Ramsbottom (Washington), FCO, 11 September 1974, DPBO, Series III, Volume V.

361 Footnote 14, Document 82, DBPO, op cit.

362 Document 149, Cyprus, second Caramanlis-Tyler meeting, telegram from the embassy in Greece to the Department of State, Athens, 11 September 1974, FRUS, Volume XXX.

363 Ibid.

364 Document 150, Cyprus: Coup Post-Mortem, memorandum from the Director of the Bureau of Intelligence and Research (William G. Hyland) to Secretary of State Dr Henry Kissinger, Washington, 10 September 1974, FRUS, Volume V.

365 Ibid.

366 'Greeks Boycott Envoy's Sendof [sic]', *The New York Times*, 8 September 1974.

367 Page 39, ADST, Ambassador Jack B. Kubisch interview, op cit.

368 Page 40, ibid.

369 Document 210, secretary's meeting with Turkish Foreign Minister Turan Güneş, memorandum of conversation, New York, 24 September 1974, FRUS, Volume V.

370 Document 153, secretary's meeting with Foreign Minister George Mavros, memorandum of conversation, New York, 29 September 1974, FRUS, Volume XXX.

371 'Makarios at UN, Rejects a Federation for Cyprus', *The New York Times*, 2 October 1974.

372 Document 154, memorandum of conversation, New York, 2 October 1974, FRUS, Volume XXX.

373 Ibid.

374 'Ford Vetoes Spending Bill That Halts Aid to Turkey', *The New York Times*, 15 October 1974.

375 Ibid.

Chapter 23 – Return of the King

376 Document 156, minutes of Secretary of State Dr Henry Kissinger's staff meeting, Washington, 22 October 1974, FRUS, Volume XXX.

377 Ibid.

378 Document 56, letter from Sir Alan Goodison to John Day (Nicosia), FCO, 1 November 1974, DBPO, Series III, Volume V.

379 Document 157, memorandum of conversation, Rome, 5 November 1974, FRUS, Volume XXX.

380 Ibid.

381 Document 160, memorandum of conversation, Washington, 16 November 1974, FRUS, Volume XXX.

382 Footnote 5, Document 99, Foreign Secretary James Callaghan to Ivor Richards (Athens), FCO, 15 November 1974, DBPO, Series III, Volume V.

383 Document 102, extract from Ivor Richards (Athens) to James Callaghan, Athens, 27 November 1974, DBPO, Series III, Volume V.

384 Document 101, Foreign Secretary James Callaghan to Ambassador The Honourable Sir Peter Ramsbottom (Washington), FCO 26 November 1974, DBPO, Series III, Volume V.

385 Ibid.

386 Ibid.

Chapter 24 – Out of Time

387 Document 164, memorandum from the president's Deputy Assistant for National Security (Scowcroft) to President Gerald R. Ford, Washington, 12 December 1974, FRUS, Volume XXX.

388 Document 168, letter from Secretary of State Dr Henry Kissinger to Turkish Foreign Minister Melih Esenbel, Washington, 13 December 1974, FRUS, Volume XXX.

389 Document 167, memorandum from the president's Deputy Assistant for National Security (Scowcroft) to President Gerald R. Ford, Washington, 13 December 1974, FRUS, Volume XXX.

390 Document 170, memorandum of conversation, Washington, 7 January 1974, FRUS, Volume XXX.

391 Document 171, study prepared by the Intelligence Community Staff for Director of Central Intelligence William Colby, Washington, January 1975, FRUS, Volume XXX.

392 Ibid.

393 Page 41, ADST Oral History Project, interview with Frederick Z. Brown by Charles Stuart Kennedy, 2 February 1990, FRUS, Volume XXX.

394 Page 44, Ibid.

395 Page 64, ADST Oral History Project, James Alan Williams interview, op cit.

396 Document 172, memorandum of conversation, February 1, 1975, FRUS, Volume XXX.

397 Ibid.

398 Ibid.

399 Document 173, editorial note, FRUS, Volume XXX.

400 Document 174, minutes of Secretary of State Dr Henry Kissinger's staff meeting, Washington, 7 February 1975, FRUS, Volume V.

401 'Parting is Sour Sorrow', *The Guardian*, 14 February 1975.

402 Footnote 14, report by the Joint Intelligence Committee, Cabinet Office, 13 February 1975, DBPO, Series III, Volume V.

403 Document 176, memorandum from the president's Assistant for National Security Affairs (Kissinger) to President Gerald R. Ford, Washington, 14 February 1975, FRUS, Volume XXX.

Chapter 25 – A Long Shadow

404 Page 83, ADST Ambassador Monteagle Stearns interview, op cit.

405 Page 38, ADST, Ambassador William Rex Crawford Jr interview, op cit.

406 Page 39, ibid.

407 Page 36, ADST, Ambassador William Rex Crawford Jr interview, op cit.

408 Page 357, Callaghan, James, *Time and Chance,* op cit.

409 Page 238, Kissinger, Henry, *Years of Renewal*, Weidenfeld & Nicolson, London, 1999

410 Page 4, ADST, Ambassador Thomas David Boyatt interview, op cit.

INDEX

1st Airborne Division (Turkish), 127
2nd Airborne Division (Turkish), 127
3rd Airborne Division (Turkish), 127
4th Airborne Division (Turkish), 127
5th Avenue, United States, 108
6th Corps (Turkish), 113
9th Signals Regiment (British), 25, 227
11 Marine Craft Unit (British), 127
12 Light Air Defence Brigade (British), 97
19 Brigade (British), 97
35 Squadron (British), 137, 267
39th Infantry Division (Turkish), 81, 104, 131, 157
50th Infantry Regiment, 131, 142
56 (Lightnings) Squadron (British), 77, 135
70 Squadron (British), 147
84 Squadron (British), 26, 90, 158, 162
111th Squadron (Turkish), 149
280 Signals Unit (British), 122, 156
509th Airborne Infantry (American), 140

A4 Skyhawks (aircraft), 143
ABBA, 14
ABC News, 140
Abzug, Bella, 231
Acheson, Dean, 9, 23
Ackland, Anthony, 96, 103, 237
Adana, Turkey, 34, 90, 96, 167
Adatepe, see TCG *Adatepe*
Aden, 14

Aegean Islands, 32, 35–6, 54, 59–67, 76, 84, 113, 223, 238, 248
Afghanistan/Afghan, 262
AFIO (Association of Former Intelligence Officers), *see* Association of Former Intelligence Officers
Africa/African, 242, 262
Agent Orange, 41
Agirda mountain area, Cyprus, 142
Agnew, (American) Vice President Spiro, 40
Aiken, Air Chief Marshal Sir John Alexander Carlisle, 79, 88, 90, 92–3, 100, 105–106, 117, 119, 123, 126, 133–6, 146, 149, 156–8, 162, 164, 166–9, 179–80, 183, 185, 198, 222, 227, 267
Air Force One, 36
AKEL (Ανορθωτικό Κόμμα Εργαζόμενου Λαού/Progressive Party of Working People) (Cypriot), 12–3, 59, 81
Akinci, General Eşref, 90
Akrotiri, Cyprus, 7, 13, 23, 25–6, 82, 85, 88–90, 92, 122, 135–7, 147, 156, 158, 169, 202, 222, 227, 235–6, 249, 251, 257, 275
Akrotiri, RAF, *see* RAF Akrotiri
al-Assad, (Syrian) President Hafez, 243
Albania/Albanian, 239
Alexander, Michael, 175, 218–9
Aliquippa, United States, 46
All the President's Men (book), 69, 274

All the President's Men: The Most Devastating Political Detective Story of the 20th Century (book), 274

Alliance, Treaty of, 7, 33, 223, 235, 267

Allies, 4, 252, 273

America, see USS *America*

America/American, *see* United States/American

American Embassy, 11, 33–4, 41–2, 45–6, 51, 66, 71–3, 131, 217, 230–1, 239–40, 257

    Defense Attaché Office, 66

American government, *see* United States government

American presidents, *see* Dwight D. Eisenhower, President Gerald R. Ford Jr, President, Lyndon B. Johnson, President John F. Kennedy, President Abraham Lincoln, Richard M. Nixon, President Ronald W. Reagan and Harry S. Truman

    see also Vice President Spiro Agnew and Vice President Hubert Humphrey

Anderson, Robert, 93, 98

Anderton, Michael, 26, 272, 278

Anderton, Pauline, 26

Anderton, Susan, 26

Andrews Air Force Base, United States, 216

Andromeda, see HMS *Andromeda*

Androutsopoulos, (Greek) Prime Minister Adamantios, 19, 58, 61, 71, 73, 114, 129, 143–4, 146, 149, 154, 164

Ankara, Turkey, 5, 7–9, 11, 18, 25, 30–1, 33, 57–60, 63, 65, 67, 80, 82, 84, 86–7, 89, 92, 96, 99, 101, 104, 106–108, 110–1, 115, 117–9, 122, 124–6, 128, 130, 132–3, 136, 138–9, 142–3, 146, 149, 153, 155, 157–8, 161, 164, 166–7, 169–70, 172, 178–80, 183, 186–91, 194, 196, 200–202, 205–207, 209–14, 217, 219, 223, 226, 230–1, 237–8, 240–3, 245, 248, 250, 254–5, 257, 260, 264–7, 269–70, 279, 282, 285, 287

Anorthotikó Kómma Ergazómenou Laoú (AKEL) (Cypriot), *see* AKEL

Antalya, Turkey, 96

Aphrodite, 129

Arabia/Arabian, 54

Arab-Israeli War, 24

Arabs, 2, 4, 13, 24–5, 27, 38, 75, 161, 181, 242–3, 265

Arapakis, Admiral Petros, 53, 133, 145, 153–4, 170–1, 268

Argentina/Argentinian, 184

Argosy (aircraft), 92–4

Arlington, United States, 258

Armstrong, Chester, 26

Arthur, Sir Geoffrey, 215–7, 237, 290–1

Ashe, Heather, 271

Association for Diplomatic Studies and Training of the Department of State, 271

Association of Former Intelligence Officers (AFIO), 271

Atatürk, General Mustafa Kemal, 4, 29–30, 32

Athanason, Colonel Frank, 83, 131–2, 275, 277, 280, 285

Athens airport, Greece, 133

Athens Polytechnic, Greece, 19, 52, 267

Athens, Greece, 1, 6, 8–11, 15, 19, 31, 34, 41–3, 45–7, 51–7, 59, 61–4, 66, 68, 70–4, 76, 80–1, 83–4, 87, 94–5, 98, 100, 103, 106–109, 111, 113–6, 121, 123–6, 128–9, 131–4, 136, 144–5, 148, 152–3, 155–6, 158–60, 164, 169–73, 175–6, 182, 186–7, 193, 195–6, 203, 205, 209–11, 213–4, 218, 223, 227–8, 230, 234–41, 243, 245, 250–7, 260, 262–3, 267–8, 279–81, 284–5, 287, 292–5

Athens, University of, 1

Augusta, United States, 83
Austria/Austrian, 146, 151–2, 156,
    158–9, 200
Austrian, Mike, 230, 232–3, 235
Averoff, (Greek) Defence Minister/
    Foreign Minister Evangelos, 171,
    173, 240
Avrakotos, Gust Lascaris, 46, 63, 67,
    71, 73–4, 256, 262
Avro Vulcans (aircraft), 116
Ayios Nikolaos, Cyprus, 25

Ανορθωτικό Κόμμα Εργαζόμενου
    Λαού (AKEL/Progressive Party
    of Working People) (Cypriot), see
    AKEL

Baghdad Pact, see CENTO
Ball, (American) Undersecretary
    George W., 9, 23, 272, 277
Bangladesh/Bangladeshi, 24
Bayülken, Ümit Haluk, 144
BBC (British Broadcasting
    Corporation), 17, 58, 106, 124–5,
    127, 147, 157, 166, 198, 222, 274
BBC News (television programme),
    198, 274
BBC World Service, 125, 157, 166, 274
Beattie, Colonel C.E., 192
Beijing, China, 36
Beirut, Lebanon, 15, 137, 163,
    235, 262
Belfast, Northern Ireland, 79
Belgium/Belgian, 136, 144, 253, 255
Belgravia, England, 103
Beliaev (Soviet diplomat), 80
Berk (destroyer), 158
Berkeley, United States, 216
Berlin Airlift, 134
Berlin, Germany, 44, 134, 147
    West, 44
Bernstein, Carl, 69, 274
Bisley, England, 90
Bitsios, Minister Dimitrios, 190, 238,
    246, 253–5

Black Sea, 33
Boeings (aircraft), 257
Bogarde, Dirk, 6
Bogazköy, Turkey, 127
Bombs, see Weapons
Bonanos, Grigorios, 58, 69, 114,
    129–32, 144–5, 151, 153–4, 159–60,
    170, 173, 268
Bosporus Strait, 34
Boston, United States, 1, 42, 45
Boyatt, Thomas 'Tom' David, 10, 13,
    46, 55, 57, 61–5, 68–9, 71–3, 75–7,
    84, 93, 99, 103–104, 114–5, 119–20,
    159, 200, 265, 270–1, 275, 277–80,
    283–4, 287, 296
Brademas, John, 47, 226, 255, 259
Brandon, Mr, 115
Branson, Captain Cecil Robert Peter
    Charles, 167
Brewster, Herbert Daniel, 10, 277
Brezhnev, Leonid, 37–8
Brighton, see HMS Brighton
Brimelow, (British) Permanent
    Secretary Sir Thomas, 80, 237
Britain/British, passim
    see also United Kingdom
Britannia Airways, 76
British Airways, 108
British Army, 90, 167
    see also British Army Air Corps
        and Coldstream Guards
British Army Air Corps, 167
    see also British Army
British Broadcasting Corporation
    (BBC), see BBC
British Cabinet, see Cabinet
British Council, 257
British Defence Committee, 196, 237
    see also Cabinet
British Embassy, 230, 257
British Empire, 3, 58
British Forces Broadcasting Service,
    85, 274
British forces' radio, see British
    Forces Broadcasting Service

British government, 22–3, 27, 64, 76,
    102, 106–107, 160, 174, 179, 187, 196,
    199, 237, 247, 249, 287, 289, 296
        see also British Treasury,
            Cabinet, Downing Street,
            MOD and Whitehall
British High Commission, 81, 88
British International School,
    Cyprus, 80
British Joint Intelligence Committee,
    117, 201, 215, 296
British Ministry of Defence (MOD),
    25, 97, 99, 106, 185, 189, 204, 267
British MOD (Ministry of Defence),
    see British Ministry of Defence
        see also British government
British Near East Joint Intelligence
    (British), 79
British prime ministers, see Prime
    Minister Anthony Eden, Prime
    Minister Margaret 'Maggie'
    Thatcher and Prime Minister
    Harold Wilson
British royal family, 32, 257
        see also Greek royal family,
            Prince Philip of England
            and Queen Elizabeth II of
            England
British Treasury, 23, 187, 196
        see also British government,
            Cabinet and Downing Street
Brown, (American) Ambassador
    Lewis Dean, 235
Brown, Elizabeth 'Ann', 45, 71, 193,
    275, 279, 289
Brown, Frederick 'Fred' Z.,
    257–8, 295
Brown, Kenneth, 284
Brussels, Belgium, 144, 253, 255
Buchanan, Wiley T., 153
Buckinghamshire, England, 135
Buffum, William 'Bill', 111, 116, 162,
    184, 187–8, 194, 286
Bulgaria/Bulgarian, 3
Burger, Warren (chief justice), 202

Burton, Richard, 14
Byzantium Empire, 2

Cabinet, 15, 30, 42, 73, 76, 81, 102,
    106–107, 119, 130, 139, 150, 152,
    154, 160, 169, 196–7, 199, 206, 209,
    223, 228, 230, 237, 247, 249, 287,
    289, 296
        British, 102, 106–107, 152, 160,
            196, 199, 237, 247, 249, 287,
            289, 296
        see also British Defence
            Committee, British
            government and
            Downing Street
    Cypriot, 15, 81, 130, 169
    Greek, 42, 73, 76, 154, 197, 223
    Turkish, 30, 119, 139, 150, 206,
        209, 228, 230
California, United States, 41, 47, 102,
    113, 118, 121, 216
Callaghan, (British) Foreign
    Secretary Leonard James 'Jim',
    21, 24, 27–8, 30, 59, 75, 80, 82, 89,
    92, 96–7, 99–103, 106–10, 112–3,
    117–21, 125–6, 128, 130–1, 133–4,
    145–6, 148, 150–3, 156, 160–2,
    164, 166–7, 171–2, 174–5, 178–80,
    183–92, 195–6, 198–215, 217–8,
    220, 222, 224–5, 227–9, 236–7, 239,
    246–9, 257, 261, 266–7, 272, 280–5,
    287–92, 294–6
Callaghan, Audrey, 198
Camden, England, 22
Canada/Canadian, 147, 184,
    233–4, 258
Cape Apostolos Andreas, Cyprus,
    134
Caradon, Lord, see Sir Hugh Foot
    (Lord Caradon)
Cardiff South (constituency), 21
Carlos of Spain, King, 44
Carlyle (hotel), The, United
    States, 108
Cartright, Colonel Ian, 227

Carver, Sir Michael 'Mike', 92, 110, 168

Castro, Fidel, 7, 12, 93

Catholic, 3
   see also Roman Catholic Church

CENTO (Central Treaty Organization), 23, 272

Central Intelligence Agency (CIA) (American), see CIA

Central Treaty Organization (CENTO), see CENTO

Centre Union, see EDEK

Chand, Lieutenant General Dewan Prem, 175–6, 178–80, 184

Charlie Wilson's War (book), 262, 274

Charlie Wilson's War (film), 262, 274

Charybdis, see HMS Charybdis

Chatos, Cyprus, 161

Chicago, United States, 39, 265

Chile/Chilean, 265

China/Chinese, 24, 36–8, 55, 59, 80, 119, 140, 154, 265

Christian, 2

Christmas Massacre, 8

Christophides, (Cypriot) Foreign Minister Ioannis, 56, 216

CIA (Central Intelligence Agency) (American), 43–6, 54, 56–7, 63–4, 67–76, 84, 93, 103, 114, 117, 119, 141, 143, 151, 162, 216, 231, 235, 242–3, 256, 262–3

Civil Service, 21

Clarridges (hotel), England, 96, 100

Clements Jr, (American) Secretary of Defense William 'Bill' Perry, 98

Clerides, (Cypriot) Acting President Glafcos Ioannou, 17–8, 20, 30, 60, 81, 95, 99, 101, 103, 111, 120–1, 123–6, 128, 151, 160, 162, 169–70, 172, 174–7, 182, 184, 190, 192, 195, 197, 201, 203–204, 207, 209–11, 213–4, 217–8, 225, 229, 233–4, 236–7, 239, 241–3, 249–50, 252, 254–5, 257, 269, 293

Clerides, Lila Irene, 17

Colby, William, 93, 98–9, 110, 118, 128, 150–1, 225, 227, 256, 285, 295

Cold War, 1, 13, 23, 27, 36, 43, 75, 265

Coldstream Guards, 81, 156, 182
   see also British Army

Columbia/Columbian, 265

Comets (aircraft), 94

Committee for State Security (Komitet Gosudarstvennoy Bezopasnosti/Комитет государственной безопасности/ KGB) (Soviet), see KGB

Committee on the Judiciary (American), see United States Senate Committee on the Judiciary

Commons, House of, 89, 98, 161

Commonwealth, 3, 21, 27–8, 76, 82, 94, 96–7, 100, 134, 146, 151, 156–7, 180, 186, 192, 194–6, 218, 229, 246–7
   see also Foreign and Commonwealth Office

Commonwealth Crown Colony, 3

Communications Agency (American), see United States Communications Agency
   see also White House

Communist Party (Cypriot), 85

Congress (American), see United States Congress

Constantine I of Greece, King, 3

Constantine II of Greece, King, 44, 49–50, 141, 150, 165, 173, 252, 268

Constantine of Greece, Prince, see King Constantine II of Greece

Constantinople, 2, 32, 115, 277

Corfu, 127

Cox, Liz, 278

Crawford Jr, William Rex, 13–4, 20, 74, 217, 219, 221, 257–8, 264–5, 275, 277–8, 280, 292, 296

Crete, 4, 34, 105, 223

Crusaders, 4

Cuba/Cuban, 66, 140

Cuban Missile Crisis, 140
Cypriot Cabinet, *see* Cabinet
Cypriot Church, 80
Cypriot government, 18, 183
Cypriot High Commission, 96
Cypriot Ministry of Interior, 133
Cypriot National Guard, *see*
    National Guard
Cypriot navy, 133
Cypriot Orthodox Church, 1
    see also Church of Cyprus
Cypriot Parliament, 17, 99, 169
Cypriot police, *see* Police
Cypriot presidents, *see* President
    Archbisop Makarios III and
    President Nikos Sampson
    see also Acting President
        Glafcos Ioannou Clerides
Cyprus Broadcasting Corporation,
    80–1, 86
Cyprus Emergency, 5, 12, 273, 281–2
Cyprus Task Force, 93, 97, 103,
    116, 191
Cyprus, Archbishop of, 1
Cyprus, Church of, *see* Cypriot
    Church
    see also Cypriot Orthodox
        Church
Cyprus, Federated State of, 260
Cyprus, King of, *see* King James II of
    Cyprus
Cyprus, Republic of Northern, 269
Cyprus/Cypriot, *passim*
Czechoslovakia/Czech, 16, 52,
    116, 178

Dardanelles, 32
David, Wing Commander, 82, 85
Davies, (American) Ambassador
    Rodger Paul, 47, 66, 68–70, 72–4,
    97, 137–8, 163, 194–5, 216–8, 225–6,
    232–5, 258, 263–4, 268
Davies, Dana, 47, 137, 216, 233, 235
Davies, John, 47, 137, 216, 233, 235
Davies, Sally, 47, 233

Davos, Lieutenant General Ianos,
    159, 162, 164
Davy, Timothy, 32
Day, John, 46, 55, 63–5, 68, 70–1, 73,
    123, 212, 265, 294
Day, Sir Derek Malcolm, 13, 275, 278
de Lacy Le Cheminant, Air Chief
    Marshal Sir Peter, 92, 100, 168, 185
Dean, John, 39
Defence Committee (British), *see*
    British Defence Committee
    see also Cabinet
Defence Ministry (Turkish), *see*
    Turkish Defence Ministry
Defence, Ministry of (MOD) (British),
    see British Ministry of Defence
Defense (American), Department of,
    see United States Department of
    Defense
Defense Attaché Office (American),
    see American Embassy
Defense Intelligence Agency (DIA)
    (American), *see* DIA
Demirel, Major General Bedrettin,
    81, 157
Demirel, Süleyman, 240
Democratic Party (America), *see*
    United States Democratic Party
Denissis, Georgios, 76
Denktaş, Rauf Raif, 17–8, 30–1, 60, 66,
    81, 122, 177, 190, 195, 201, 203–204,
    209–11, 214, 219, 237, 242, 250, 252,
    254–7, 259–61, 269
Denmark/Danish, 32, 252
Devonshire, see HMS *Devonshire*
Dhekelia, Cyprus, 7, 22, 79, 126, 147,
    162, 180, 222, 226, 229
Dhekelia, RAF, *see* RAF Dhekelia
DIA (Defense Intelligence Agency)
    (American), 44–5, 67, 75, 117
Dillon, Robert 'Bob', 46, 55, 63–5, 68–
    9, 71–3, 93, 103–104, 114, 119, 121,
    125, 133, 265, 275, 280–1, 283–4
Dimitriou, (Cypriot) Ambassador
    Nikos, 73

Dimitriou, (Cypriot) Foreign
    Minister Dimis, 106, 260
Dimitriou, Panikos, 257
Dobbs, Mr, 287
Dobrynin, (Soviet) Ambassador
    Anatoly, 86–7, 281
Dodecanese, 64
Downing Street, England, 100,
    102–103, 125, 174, 282, 287
        see also British government,
        British Treasury, Cabinet
        and Whitehall
Dreamer's Bay, Cyprus, 77
Dring, Simon, 198
Dulles, Allen Welsh (CIA
    director), 44
Dunnigan, Thomas J., 279
Durham, England, 125
Dutch Embassy, 246

Eagleburger, Lawrence 'Larry', 111,
    175, 202
Eagleton, (American) Senator
    Thomas, 259
Ealing, England, 198
East Germany / East German, see
    Germany / German
East Wing, United States, 202
        see also Oval Office and White
        House
Eastern Mediterranean, see
    Mediterranean
EC (European Community), see
    European Community
Ecevit, (Turkish) Prime Minister
    Bülent, 30–4, 59–60, 80–1, 85–6, 89,
    93, 96–8, 101–103, 107–108, 110–1,
    113, 115, 118–21, 123–6, 133, 139,
    142–6, 148–54, 157–8, 161–2, 164,
    166–7, 170, 172, 176, 178–80, 182–3,
    185, 188–91, 193–7, 205–208, 210–3,
    215, 217, 219, 226, 228–9, 230–1,
    234–6, 239–40, 245, 247, 266, 282,
    287, 293
Ecevit, Mrs, 166

Economist (newspaper), The, 270, 273
EDEK (ΕΔΕΚ Σοσιαλιστικό Κόμμα /
    United Democratic Centre Union),
    12, 171
Eden, (British) Prime Minister
    Anthony, 24
Egypt, Sultan of, 2
Egypt / Egyptian, 2–3, 24, 27, 38, 50,
    75, 113, 137, 186, 210, 223, 242–3,
    245
Egyptian Embassy, 223
Egyptian presidents, see President
    Gamal Abdel Nasser and
    President Muhammad Anwar
    Sadat
Ehrlichman, John, 60
Eisenhower, (American) President
    Dwight D., 199
ELDYK (Ελληνική Δύναμη
    Κύπρου / Elliniki Dynami
    Kyprou), 78, 129
Eliot, T.S., 30
Elizabeth II of England, Queen, 32
Elliniki Dynami Kyprou (Ελληνική
    Δύναμη Κύπρου / ELDYK), see
    ELDYK
Empress Restaurant, United
    States, 154
England, Queen of, see Queen
    Elizabeth II of England
        see also British royal family
England / English, 2–3, 5–7, 17–8,
    21–2, 27, 30, 49–50, 58–9, 62,
    64–5, 73, 75–6, 79–80, 82–3, 86,
    88–90, 92–7, 99–103, 106–107,
    109, 111, 115, 117, 121, 123, 125–6,
    128, 130, 132–6, 139–41, 144, 146,
    157, 164–70, 174–5, 177, 179–80,
    182–3, 185, 187, 190–4, 196, 198,
    201, 211, 218, 221–2, 224–5, 227,
    229, 234, 236–9, 242, 246–7, 249,
    267–8, 270, 272–3, 275, 282, 287,
    290, 296
Ennals, (British) Foreign Minister
    David Hedley, 95–6, 237

Enosis, 4–7, 9–10, 12, 15–8, 20, 31,
    51–2, 56, 62, 81, 86, 91–2, 101, 115,
    125, 130, 132, 141, 160, 250
EOKA, 5–6, 12, 15, 17–20, 27, 47, 52,
    55–7, 59, 61–3, 66, 70, 73, 79, 81, 88,
    250–1, 268
EOKA-B, 15, 19–20, 47, 52, 55–7, 59,
    61–3, 66, 70, 73, 79, 81, 88, 250–1, 268
Epirus, Greece, 53
Erdoğan, Recep Tayyip, 266
Erim, (Turkish) Prime Minister
    İsmail Nihat, 51
Ersin, Lieutenant General Nurettin,
    113, 127
ESA (Ελληνική Στρατιωτική
    Αστυνομία), 19, 53
Esenbel, (Turkish) Ambassador /
    Foreign Minister Melih, 133,
    253–4, 256, 295
Estes, Luba, 262
Estes, Ron, 46, 63–4, 67, 71, 73, 256,
    262–3
Ethniki Organosis Kyprion
    Agoniston, *see* EOKA
Eton College, England, 30
EU (European Union), *see* European
    Union
EUR (Bureau of European Affairs),
    39, 42, 55, 57, 62, 84, 116, 133
Europe / European, 2, 12, 23–5, 28, 32,
    34, 38–40, 42, 55, 57, 62, 82, 84, 89,
    97–8, 101–102, 111, 116, 133, 139,
    150, 153, 180, 194, 214, 218–9, 231,
    249, 264, 266, 268, 273, 275, 288
European Affairs, Bureau of (EUR),
    see EUR
European Community (EC), 24, 98,
    101, 111, 150, 153, 214
European Union (EU), 266, 268
Evans, David M., 202, 290
Evren, Brigadier General Sabri, 127

ΕΔΕΚ Σοσιαλιστικό Κόμμα (EDEK /
    United Democratic Centre Union),
    see EDEK

Ελληνική Δύναμη Κύπρου (Elliniki
    Dynami Kyprou / ELDYK), *see*
    ELDYK
Ελληνική Στρατιωτική Αστυνομία
    (ESA), *see* ESA

F-14 (aircraft), 138
F104 fighter jets (aircraft), 149
Fahmi, Foreign Minister Ismail, 223
Falklands, 127, 267
Famagusta, Cyprus, 2, 14–5, 17, 26,
    56, 95, 113, 116–7, 122, 126, 128–9,
    134, 137, 147, 156, 161, 201, 204,
    211, 213, 222, 225–6, 230, 242, 251,
    257, 259
Far East / Far Eastern, 23, 247
Fatima plantation, Cyprus, 148
Fessus, Vera, *see* Vera Sampson
Finland / Finnish, 8, 182
Finnish prime minister, *see* Prime
    Minister Sakari Severi Tuomioja
First World War, 3–4, 29
Five Mile Beach, Cyprus, *see*
    Pentemille (Five Mile) Beach
Fleet Street, England, 222
Foot, Sir Hugh (Lord Caradon), 100
Ford Jr, (American) President Gerald
    R., 202–203, 205, 212, 215–6, 220,
    223–4, 227, 231, 235, 241, 243–4,
    249, 254–6, 259, 264–5, 271, 275,
    291, 294–6
Ford, Betty, 203
Foreign Broadcast Information
    Service, 162
    Foreign and Commonwealth
    Office, 21, 27–8, 76, 82, 94, 96–7,
    100, 134, 146, 151, 156–7, 180, 186,
    192, 194–6, 218, 229, 246–7
    see also Commonwealth
Forrestal, USS *Forrestal*
France / French, 24, 32, 38, 81–2, 113,
    117–8, 124, 141, 147, 150, 153,
    171–3, 177, 186, 190, 214, 218,
    228–9, 242, 245, 255, 264, 267–8,
    274, 284, 287

Franco, General Francisco, 75, 174
Frederica, Queen, 44
French Connection (film), *The*, 32, 274
French Resistance, 267
Fulbright, (American) Senator William, 241
Fyjis-Walker, Richard, 101

Gaddafi (Qaddafi), Colonel Muammar, 40, 102, 212
Geneva Declaration, 191–2, 198–9, 235
Geneva peace conferences, 183
Geneva, Switzerland, 156, 160–2, 174–5, 183–6, 188–92, 198–201, 203–204, 206, 209–12, 215, 217–8, 227–9, 235, 237, 246, 289–91
Georgia, United States, 83, 264
Georgitsis, Brigadier General Michalis, 69, 76, 128
Germanic tribes, 2
Germany/German, 5, 17, 24, 32, 36, 44, 75, 134, 147, 172, 210, 218, 247, 267
    East, 75
    West, 32, 44, 218, 247
Gibraltar, 3
Giorkatzis, (Cypriot) Interior Minister Polykarpos, 15, 18, 51
Gizikis, (Greek) President General Phaedon, 19, 58, 70, 72–4, 76, 83, 129, 144, 159–60, 165, 170–1, 173, 177
GOG (government of Greece), *see* Greek government
Goksan, Rear Admiral Emin, 116, 131
Gold, *see* RFA *Gold*
Golden Marina, Cyprus, 156
Good Friday Agreement, 267
Goodison, Sir Alan, 28, 97, 186, 211, 229, 237, 246, 267, 278–9, 283, 289, 293–4
Goodpaster, General Andrew, 180
Goodpath, General, 140

Goulden GCMG, Sir Peter John, 208–209, 224, 275, 291–2
Graham, Jay, 233
Grand National Assembly (Turkish), *see* Turkish Grand National Assembly
Grant, Lindsey, 33, 60, 66, 68–70, 72, 216, 235, 275, 278, 280, 292
Greco-Turkish War, 5
Greece, Government of (GOG), *see* Greek government
Greece/Greek, *passim*
Greek air force, 14, 156, 159
Greek Cabinet, *see* Cabinet
Greek Civil War, 12, 44, 49, 53
Greek Cypriot police, *see* Police
Greek Cypriots, 1, 4–8, 11–20, 22, 33, 51–2, 60, 65–6, 80, 82, 86, 91–2, 95–6, 106, 122, 124, 127, 134, 142, 152, 156, 158, 160–1, 170, 177, 184, 191–3, 207–209, 213, 217, 221, 226–7, 232–3, 236–9, 243, 246, 250–2, 255, 257–61, 269
Greek Embassy, 236
Greek Foreign Ministry, 66
Greek government, 10, 43, 52, 57, 69, 71, 76, 89, 106, 118–9, 145–6, 148, 150, 152, 154, 184, 192, 200, 235, 249
Greek Intelligence Service (KYP), *see* KYP
Greek islands, 35
Greek Mafia, 48
Greek military academy, 53
Greek military police, *see* ESA *see also* Police
Greek Ministry of Press, 235
Greek National Guard, *see* National Guard
Greek Naval Academy, 83
Greek Orthodox Church, 1, 17, 43, 66, 71
Greek Pentagon, 63, 129, 184, 223
Greek police, *see* Police
Greek Pools Football Agency, 56

Greek president, *see* President
   Phaedon Gizikis and President
   İsmet İnönü
Greek prime ministers, *see*
   Prime Minister Adamantios
   Androutsopoulos, Prime Minister
   Panayotis
Kanellopoulos, Prime Minister
   Georgios Papandreou and Prime
   Minister Eleftherios Venizelos
Greek royal family, 44, 50
      see also British royal family,
      King Constantine I of
      Greece, King Constantine
      II of Greece, King Paul I of
      Greece and Prince Philip of
      England
Grey Wolves, 29
Grimland, David, 233
Grivas, General Georgios 'George',
   5–6, 9–12, 15–6, 19–20, 46, 52–3,
   55–7, 129, 278
Gromyko, Andrei Andreyevich, 62
Grove, Brandon, 277, 279
Guarantee, Treaty of, 125, 128, 185,
   204, 206, 223
Guns, *see* Weapons
Gursel, Burak, 271
Guyer, Dr Roberto, 184
Güneş, (Turkish) Foreign Minister
   Turan, 80, 119–20, 125, 133, 136,
   143–4, 156, 172, 179–80, 183, 185–
   91, 197, 199, 201, 203–204, 206–14,
   225, 241, 290–1, 294
Gwertzman, Bernard, 229

Haig, General Alexander, 151, 202
Haldeman, Harry Robbins 'Bob', 60
Halton, RAF, *see* RAF Halton
Hamburg, Germany, 17
Hamilton Air Force Base, United
   States, 216
Hammarskjöld, Dag Hjalmar Agne
   Carl, 186
Hampstead, England, 267

Hampstead Heath, England, 268
Happy Valley (camp), Cyprus, 236
Hare, Paul Julian, 119–20
Hare, Raymond, 120
Harington, General Charles, 32
Hartley, Douglas G., 51, 275
Hartman, Arthur 'Art' Adair, 39, 57,
   61–2, 64–5, 93, 133, 139–40, 154,
   194–6, 200–206, 208, 219, 224–6,
   235, 240, 243, 264, 275, 278, 288,
   290–3
Harvard University, United States,
   30, 36, 45, 49, 119, 144, 263
Hattersley, (British) Foreign Minister
   Roy, 58, 62, 80, 227, 237
Hawaii, United States, 44
Healey, Chancellor of the Exchequer
   Denis Winston, 199
Heath, Edward, 23–4, 273
Heathrow Airport, England, 107, 266
Hellenic Army, 78
Hellenic Force in Cyprus, *see* ELDYK
Hellenistic nationalistic agenda, 54
Hellenistic region, 4
Henn, Brigadier Francis 'Frank', 80,
   90, 117, 162, 178–9, 273
Hermes, *see* HMS *Hermes*
Hermes, *see* Operation Hermes
High Bright Sun (film), *The*, 6, 274
High Commission, *see* British High
   Commission and Cypriot High
   Commission
Highland Light Infantry, 27
Hilton (hotel), Belgium, 253
Hilton (hotel), Cyprus, 198, 222, 252
Hitler, Adolf, 224, 231
   see also Nazis
HMS *Andromeda*, 136, 157–8, 168, 178
HMS *Brighton*, 136
HMS *Charybdis*, 22
HMS *Devonshire*, 99, 105, 136, 164,
   167–9, 198
HMS *Hermes*, 92, 99, 105, 136, 164,
   167–9
HMS *Onslaught*, 136

HMS *Rhyl*, 99, 105, 136, 157, 168–9, 198
HMS *Tiger*, 22
Hofburg Palace, Austria, 146
Hollywood, United States, 14, 39, 262
Holy Land, 2
Hong Kong, 23
Hood, Robin, 30
Hooper, Ambassador Sir Robin William John, 59, 83, 89, 106–107, 109, 131, 134, 146, 152–3, 171, 173, 218, 223, 237, 267, 280–1, 285, 287, 292
Hotel Excelsior, Italy, 246
Hotel La Reserve, Switzerland, 198
How the West Was Won (film), 42, 274
Howe, Michael, 61
Howe, Mrs, 61
Hulse Jr, Stacy Beakes, 45–6, 74, 114, 256, 262–3
Humphrey, (American) Vice President Hubert, 241
Humphrey, Andrew, 189
Hunt, Sir John, 247
Hunter, Colonel J.J.G., 192
Hyland, William G., 238, 256, 294
Hyperides, 17

Iberia/Iberian, 2
Idris of Libya, King, 40
India/Indian, 5, 17, 24, 28, 32, 40, 128, 219
Indian Army, 5
Indian police, *see* Police
Indiana, United States, 47, 231
Indonesia/Indonesian, 206
Ingersoll, (American) Deputy Secretary of State Robert 'Bob', 116, 118, 123–4, 138–40, 286
Inhan, Asaf, 128, 178–9
Inland Revenue Union, 21
Intelligence and Research Bureau (American), *see* United States Intelligence and Research Bureau

see also United States Department of State
Interior, Ministry of (Cyprus), *see* Cypriot Ministry of Interior
International Affairs Division (American), *see* United States International Affairs Division
Ioannidis, Brigadier General/General Dimitrios, 19, 22, 32, 35, 43–7, 52–64, 66–72, 74–7, 81, 84, 90–4, 98–100, 108–11, 114–5, 120–1, 129–30, 133, 144–5, 150–4, 159–60, 165, 170–1, 173–4, 184, 197, 223, 238, 256, 267–8, 279, 281
Ionian Islands, 4
Iran/Iranian, 23, 262, 266
Iran-Contra affair, 262
Iraq/Iraqi, 23, 206
Ireland, Republic of/Irish, 267, 273
see also Northern Ireland/Northern Irish
Irmak, Professor Sadi, 248, 250
Islam, 2, 29, 31, 183
see also Muslim
Israeli-Syrian war, 245
Israel/Israeli, 13, 24–5, 27, 38, 62–3, 75, 158, 181, 243, 245, 255, 265
Istanbul, Turkey, 30, 34–5, 80, 115
Işik, (Turkish) Acting Foreign Minister/Defence Minister Hasan Esat, 97, 108, 282
Italy/Italian, 2, 4, 24, 39, 41, 47, 50–1, 82, 107, 111, 120, 138, 140, 198, 222, 246, 262, 265, 295

İnönü, Battle of, 32
İnönü, (Greek) President İsmet, 32
İskenderun, Turkey, 96
İzmir, Turkey, 34, 131, 156

Jackson, Robert L., 43, 275, 279
James II of Cyprus, King, 2
Japan/Japanese, 85
Javits, (American) Senator Jacob, 219
Jeger MP (British), Lena, 22

Jessup, Colonel, 235
Jewish, 36, 47, 219, 226, 231
Johnson, (American) President
    Lyndon B. Johnson, 9–11, 24, 33,
    40, 104, 113, 151, 270
Johnstone, Colonel H.A., 227
Joint Intelligence Committee
    (British), see British Joint
    Intelligence Committee
Jordan, General Amos, 138
Jordan/Jordanian, 235
Judiciary Committee (American),
    see United States Judiciary
    Committee
        see also United States House of
        Representatives
Justice and Development Party
    (Turkish), 266
Justice Party (Turkish), 240

Kanellopoulos, (Greek) Prime
    Minister Panayotis, 171–2
Karamanlis, (Greek) Prime Minister
    Konstantinos G., 6, 49, 141, 145,
    150, 171, 173–4, 177, 182–6, 191,
    195, 197, 203, 209, 213, 215, 217–8,
    220, 223, 226–31, 238, 240–1, 243,
    246, 248–50, 252–4, 267–8, 289, 293
Karaoğlanoğlu, Colonel İbrahim,
    131, 142
Karpas Peninsula, 9
Keeley, Ambassador Robert V.,
    11, 277
Kennedy airport, United States, 108
Kennedy, (American) President John
    F., 37
Kennedy, (American) Senator
    Edward, 244
Kennedy, Charles Stuart, 45, 275,
    277–80, 283, 285–6, 288, 290, 295
Keo Brewery, Cyprus, 158
KGB (Комитет государственной
    безопасности/Komitet
    Gosudarstvennoy Bezopasnosti/
    Committee for State Security),
    262

Killick, Sir John Edward, 96, 146, 151,
    218–20, 237, 275, 283, 292
King Charles Street, England, 128
King, (American) Ambassador
    Barrington, 8, 41, 275, 277, 279
King's College London, 17
Kingsfield, Cyprus, 147
Kirby, Harmon Elwood, 42, 46, 55, 60,
    265, 275, 279
Kirca, Coşkun, 189–90
Kissinger, (American) Secretary
    of State Dr Henry, 24–5, 30,
    36–40, 42, 50, 55, 58, 61–5, 68, 72,
    75–6, 82, 84–7, 89–93, 96, 98–9,
    101–104, 107–108, 110–3, 115–9,
    121–6, 128–34, 138–40, 142–6,
    148, 150–4, 159–65, 170–5, 179–81,
    184, 187–91, 193–6, 200, 202–208,
    210–2, 215–20, 223–32, 234–8,
    240–9, 253–61, 264–5, 269–70,
    273, 279, 281–2, 284–8, 291–6
Kissinger, Nancy, 143, 153
Kition, Bishop of, 1
Klirou, Cyprus, 79
Knights Templar, 2
Kocatepe, see TCG Kocatepe
Kojak (television programme), 14, 274
Kokkina, Cyprus, 161, 211
Kombokis, Colonel
    Constantinos, 69
Komitet Gosudarstvennoy
    Bezopasnosti (Комитет
    государственной безопасности/
    KGB/Committee for State
Security), see KGB
Korea/Korean, 46, 114
Korean War, 46, 114
Koromilas, Peter, 74
Korutürk, (Turkish) President Fahri,
    86, 139, 203
Korydallos Prison, Greece, 268
Kos, 184
Kreisky, (Austrian) Chancellor Bruno,
    146
Krini air strip, Corfu, 127

Kubisch, Jack B., 203, 239–40, 263–4, 290, 294
Küçük, Dr Fazil, 6–7
Kurdish, 31
Kux, Denis, 290
Kykkos Monastery, Cyprus, 4, 16, 79, 86
KYP (Greek Intelligence Service), 44, 129
Kypraios, (Greek) Foreign Minister Konstantinos, 83, 89, 134
Kyrenia, Cyprus, 14, 26, 106, 113, 116, 122, 124, 128–9, 142–3, 152, 157, 159, 162, 166–9, 177, 193–4, 198, 251, 253
Kyros, Congressman Peter, 231

Комитет государственной безопасности (Komitet Gosudarstvennoy Bezopasnosti/ KGB), see KGB

La Bastille, 5
Labour Party (British), 21–2, 30, 174, 185, 196, 199
Lagakos, Efstathios, 72–3
Laird, (American) Secretary of Defense Melvin, 40, 273
Lake Geneva, Europe, 198–9
Lancaster House, England, 6
Lancing, (American) Secretary of State Robert, 63
Langley, United States, 64, 262
Larnaca, Cyprus, 16, 88, 95, 134, 137, 147, 236
Latin, 2
Le Monde (newspaper), 242, 273
Lebanon/Lebanese, 15, 137, 162–3, 235, 262, 265
Ledra Palace Hotel, Cyprus, 124, 147, 236
Lee, Flight Sergeant John 'Taff', 147, 157–8, 271
Leeland, Mr J.R., 279
Lefka, Cyprus, 204

Libya, King of, see King Idris of Libya
Libya/Libyan, 40, 102, 267
Lightnings (aircraft), 135–6, 167
Limassol, Cyprus, 19, 26, 61, 79–80, 82, 85–6, 88–9, 95, 127, 133–6, 158, 169, 257
Limassol Bay, Cyprus, 26
Lincoln, (American) President Abraham, 146
Lincoln's Inn, England, 17
Lincolnshire, England, 267
Lisbon, Portugal, 51
London Peace Conference, 3
London School of Economics (LSE), England, 22
London, England, 3, 6–7, 17–8, 21–2, 27, 30, 58–9, 62, 64–5, 73, 75, 79–80, 82–3, 88–90, 92–4, 96–7, 99–103, 106–107, 109, 111, 115, 117, 121, 123, 125–6, 128, 130, 132–6, 139–41, 144, 146, 157, 164–70, 174–5, 177, 179–80, 182–3, 185, 187, 191–4, 196, 201, 211, 218, 221, 224–5, 227, 229, 236–9, 242, 246–7, 249, 268, 270, 272–3, 275, 282, 290, 296
Lord, Bette, 154
Lord, Winston, 154
Lowenstein, Ambassador James G., 154, 200, 290
LSE (London School of Economics), see London School of Economics
Lunkov, (Soviet) Ambassador Nikolai, 151
Luns, Secretary General Dr Joseph, 61, 82, 223
Luqa airport, Malta, 94
Lusignan, House of, 2
Luton Airport, England, 76
Lyneham, RAF, see RAF Lyneham
Lysander (aircraft), 267
Lyssarides, Dr Vassos, 12, 81

Macedonia/Macedonian, 141
Macmillan, Harold, 22

Macomber Jr., William 'Bill' Butts,
  33–4, 67, 97–8, 119–21, 126, 133,
  142–4, 148, 170, 180, 202, 205,
  211,226, 231, 245, 264, 275, 284
Machine guns, see Weapons
Mafia, see Greek Mafia
Mahi (newspaper), 20, 273
Makarezos, Nikolaos, 49, 268
Makarios House, 5
Makarios III, (Cypriot) President
  Archbishop, *passim*
Malaysia/Malaysian, 265
Malta/Maltese, 3, 92–4, 116, 193, 247
Maltese prime minister, see Prime
  Minister Dom Mintoff
Mansfield, (American) Senator
  Mike, 241
Maresal Fevzi Çakmak, see TCG
  Maresal Fevzi Çakmak
Maria (maid), 234
Mariani, Ralph, 271
Marine Corps, see United States
  Marine Corps
    see also United States Marines
Marseille, France, 32
Marston, Brigadier H.H., 230
Martinique, 255
Maryland, United States, 47
Mason, (British) Secretary of Defence
  Roy, 92, 224, 282
Massachusetts, United States, 1, 244
Massachusetts, University of, 1
Maury Jr, John M., 44
Mavros, (Greek) Foreign Minister
  George, 171–2, 184–8, 190–1, 195,
  197, 199, 201, 204, 207, 209, 211,
  213–4, 223, 236, 241–2, 294
Mayfair, England, 96
McBain, Malcolm, 278
McCloskey, Ambassador/
  Ambassador at Large Robert 'Bob',
  15, 99, 111, 116, 121, 123–4, 126,
  155, 174, 275, 278, 285
McFarlane, Major Richard, 81, 86
McKenzie, Lieutenant Ian, 178

Mediterranean, 3, 7, 12, 23, 25,
  34–5, 39–41, 58, 65–6, 74–6, 80,
  93, 104–105, 111, 158, 174, 187,
  189–90, 194–5, 244–5, 260, 265, 267,
  273, 275
    Eastern, 3, 25, 39–40, 58, 65, 74,
      76, 104–105, 111, 194, 244–5,
      260, 275
Southeastern, 158
Mehmed II (Mehmed the
  Conqueror), Sultan, 2
Mehmed the Conqueror, see
  Mehmed II
Mekong Delta, Vietnam, 41
Menderes, (Turkish) Prime Minister
  Ali Adnan Ertekin, 6, 29
Mersin, Turkey, 96, 116, 149
Messalina cruise liner, 143
Methodism, 28
Metropolitan Museum of Art,
  The, 264
Middle East/Middle Eastern, 23, 25,
  27, 34, 38, 40, 44, 47, 55, 61–3, 75,
  98, 104, 114, 116–7, 162, 187, 200,
  217, 226, 247, 267, 272
Miles, (British) First Secretary
  Richard Oliver, 14, 22, 97, 278
Miles, Mrs, 14
Military police, see Secret military
  police
    see also Greek military police,
      Police and Royal Military
      Police
Mintoff, (Maltese) Prime Minister
  Dom, 94, 96
Missouri, United States, 203, 259
Mitchell, Clive, 135
Mitchell, John H., 60
MOD (British), see British Ministry of
  Defence
Monaco, 82
Monde (newspaper), *Le, see Le Monde*
Mons, Belgium, 136
Monte Carlo, Monaco, 82
Montreux Convention, 34

Morocco/Moroccan, 41
Morphou, Cyprus, 201
Moscow, Russia, 6, 12, 33, 37, 59, 75, 274, 287
    see also Radio Moscow
Mount Olympus, Greece, 135
Mount Troodos, Cyprus, 78, 257
Mouskos, Michael Christodoulou, see Archbishop Markarios III
Muslim, 2–3, 185, 206
    see also Islam
Mussolini, Benito, 41

NAAFI (Navy, Army and Air Force Institutes), 105, 148, 156, 226
Nasser, (Egyptian) President Gamal Abdel, 12, 24
National Defense University, United States, 264
National Front, 12, 15
National Guard, 8–12, 15, 19, 52, 56–7, 61–3, 66–70, 72–4, 76, 78–82, 85–6, 88–91, 93, 95–7, 100, 102, 105–106, 109, 111, 119, 126–9, 134, 136, 142–3, 146, 153, 156–7, 159–60, 163, 166, 168–9, 172, 176, 180, 199, 213, 222, 226, 230, 232, 250
Cypriot, 8–9, 12, 15, 19, 52, 56, 61–3, 66, 73, 78, 109, 111, 153, 166, 230
Greek, 57, 100, 102, 129, 199, 213
Greek-Cypriot, 19, 159–60
Greek-led, 10
National Organisation of Cypriot Fighters, see Ethniki Organosis Kyprion Agoniston
National Salvation Party (NSP), see NSP
National Security Council (American), see United States National Security Council
    see also Security Council
NATO (North Atlantic Treaty Organization), 8–10, 23–5, 31, 33–4, 38–40, 50–1, 59, 61, 64, 67–8, 82–3, 93, 111, 118, 130, 135–6, 141,

144, 150–1, 153, 160–1, 164, 168, 172, 174, 179–80, 189, 196, 199, 207, 210, 220–1, 223, 231, 240, 243, 249, 251, 253–4, 261, 267
Naval War College, 53
Navy, Army and Air Force Institutes (NAAFI), see NAAFI
Nazis, 36, 66
    see also Adolf Hitler
Near East Joint Intelligence (British), see British Near East Joint Intelligence (British)
Near Eastern Affairs, Bureau of, 39, 47, 64
Neff, Eric, 56–7
New Democracy Party (Greek), 248
New England, United States, 172
New York Times, The, 98–9, 110, 173, 229, 231, 276, 278, 280, 282–4, 287–8, 291–4
New York, United States, 14, 94, 96, 98–100, 108, 110, 118, 173, 184, 188–9, 206, 219, 229, 231, 241, 259, 264, 272–4, 276–8, 280, 282–4, 287–8, 291–4
Newport Beach, United States, 132
Nice, France, 82
Nicholson, Michael, 127, 285
Nicosia airport, Cyprus, see Nicosia International Airport
Nicosia General Hospital, Cyprus, 235
Nicosia International Airport, Cyprus, 26, 160, 175–6, 259
Nicosia, Cyprus, 1, 4, 7–8, 10, 13–5, 19–20, 22, 25–6, 28, 33, 46–7, 56–7, 60, 68–70, 72, 74, 77, 79, 88, 90, 105, 115, 117, 123–4, 127–8, 137, 142, 147, 153, 156–7, 160, 166, 175–8, 182, 185, 201, 208–209, 211, 213, 216, 221–3, 230–1, 235–6, 240, 251–2, 256–7, 259, 263, 279–80, 282–3, 289–90, 294
Nicosia, RAF, see RAF Nicosia
Nimrods, 116, 122

Nissi, Cyprus, 26
Nixon, (American) President Richard M., 24, 36–7, 39–42, 60, 65, 69, 72, 75–6, 99, 102, 108, 123–4, 128, 139–40, 144, 173, 181, 187, 191, 193, 199, 202–203, 212, 273, 282, 285–6
Nixon, Pat, 203
Nobel Peace Prize, 38
Noratlas fleet, 153
Nord Noratlas (aircraft), 153
Normandy, France, 235
North Atlantic Treaty Organization (NATO), see NATO
North Carolina, United States, 30
Northern Ireland/Northern Irish, 21, 62, 79, 204, 270
    see also Republic of Ireland/ Irish
Norway/Norwegian, 217
Norwegian Fjords, 217
NSP (National Salvation Party), 31
Nuclear weapons, see Weapons
Nuremburg, Germany, 267

Oakley, Robert 'Bob' Bigger, 103, 114, 119, 144, 154, 158–9, 194–5, 202–203, 224, 275, 283–4, 287, 289–90
Observer (newspaper), The, 62, 273
Ohio, United States, 55
Olcay, Osman, 118
Olna, see RFA Olna
Olver, Stephen, 28, 59, 66, 73, 79, 88, 95, 97, 99, 105–106, 119, 126, 147, 156–7, 168, 176, 178–9, 182, 193, 195, 237, 267, 279, 282–3, 289–90
Olwen, see RFA Olwen
Olympic Airways, 239
Onassis, Aristotle, 53
Onslaught, see HMS Onslaught
Operation Ablaut, 97
Operation Drop Star 4, 201, 203, 206, 214, 222, 228
Operation Hermes, 14
Operation Homestead, 191
Operation Niki, 153

Operation Skylark, 90
Oriental Studies, School of, 30
Ormsby-Gore, David, 23
Osmanli Turks, 115
Othello (book), 2, 274, 277
Ottoman Empire, 3, 29
Oval Office, United States, 61, 69, 199
    see also East Wing and White House

Pakistan/Pakistani, 23, 40
Palainis, Charalambos, 129
Palais de Nations, Switzerland, 185
Palestine/Palestinian, 55
Panayotacos, Constantine, 94, 118
Panhellic Socialist Movement (PASOK), see PASOK
Pantazis, Major Andreas, 79
Papadakis, Pavlos, 69
Papandreou, (Greek) Prime Minister Georgios, 9–10
Papandreou, Andreas, 41, 48–9, 172, 243, 248, 267
Papanikolaou, Lieutenant General Alexandros, 145, 159, 268
Paphos Free Radio, 81, 86, 88, 274
Paphos, Bishop of, 81, 86
Paphos, Cyprus, 1, 18, 26, 65, 81, 86–8, 90, 102, 142, 161, 274
Pappas, Thomas 'Tom', 42, 44
Paramali Forest (camp), Cyprus, 236
Paris Peace Accords, 38
Paris, France, 38, 113, 117, 141, 150, 153, 171, 173, 284, 287
Parliament, see Cypriot Parliament and Turkish Parliament
PASOK (Panhellic Socialist Movement), 248
Pattakos, Stylianos, 49–50, 268
Paul I of Greece, King, 44, 49
Pennsylvania, United States, 46
Pentadáktylos Mountains, Cyprus, 127
Pentagon Papers, The, 37
Pentemille (Five Mile) Beach, Cyprus, 124, 129

Persian Gulf, 23
Phantoms (aircraft), 106, 135, 179–80, 183, 185, 202, 206
Philip of England, Prince, 32
    see also British royal family and Greek royal family
Philip of Greece and Denmark, Prince, *see* Prince Philip of England
Phillips, Sir Horace Hyman, 82, 89, 92, 106, 117–9, 125, 133, 136, 157–8, 166–7, 169, 194, 196, 217, 237, 267, 273, 275, 285, 288
Piraeus, Greece, 41, 83, 151
Platoni Beach, Cyprus, 157
Platres, Cyprus, 134
Playboy (magazine), 20, 273
Police, 5, 8, 10, 12, 14–6, 19, 28, 43, 47, 52–3, 56, 61–2, 79, 81–2, 85, 137, 163, 173, 217, 221, 226, 232–4, 240, 250, 257, 263, 268
    Cypriot, 8, 10, 12, 15–6, 62, 81, 221, 233, 250
    Greek, 8, 19, 53, 233
    Greek Cypriot, 8, 233
    Indian, 28
    Turkish, 5
    see also Greek military police, Royal Military Police and Secret military police
Portsmouth, England, 21
Portugal/Portuguese, 51, 174
Potts, James M., 45
Pound, Ezra, 30
Pravda (newspaper), 59, 141, 151, 273
Presidential Palace, Cyprus, 74, 77–80, 86
Press (Greek), Ministry of, *see* Greek Ministry of Press
Princess Mary (hospital), 158
Princeton University, United States, 55
Progressive Party of Working People (Ανορθωτικό Κόμμα Εργαζόμενου Λαού/AKEL) (Cypriot), *see* AKEL

Pumas (aircraft), 136, 192

Qaddafi, (Gaddafi), Colonel Muammar, *see* Colonel Muammar Gaddafi
Queens, United States, 259

Radio Moscow, 59, 274
    see also Moscow
RAF (Royal Air Force), 7, 13, 17, 22–3, 25–6, 79, 82, 85, 88–90, 92–5, 105–106, 116, 122, 127, 134–5, 137, 147, 156–8, 162–3, 170, 178, 180, 183, 189, 193, 195, 202, 217, 222, 226–7, 229, 236, 246–7, 249, 251, 257, 267, 272, 275, 278
RAF Akrotiri, 13, 23, 25–6, 82, 85, 88–90, 122, 135, 147, 156, 158, 202, 222, 227, 249, 251, 257, 275
    see also Security Committee
RAF Dhekelia, 22, 79, 147, 162, 180, 222, 226, 229
RAF Halton, 135
RAF Lyneham, 95, 158
RAF Nicosia, 7, 79
RAF Scampton, 267
Rallis, (Greek) Minister Konstantinos, 129
Ramsbottom, (British) Ambassador/ High Commissioner The Honourable Sir Peter, 13–4, 65, 102–103, 108, 110, 117–9, 163–4, 174, 208, 210, 229, 237, 248, 278, 282, 284, 291, 294–5
Reagan, (American) President Ronald W., 265
Regent, see RFA *Regent*
Representatives (American), House of, *see* United States House of Representatives
    see also United States Judiciary Committee
Republican Party (American), *see* United States Republican Party
Republican People's Party (Turkish), 30

RFA (Royal Fleet Auxiliary), 136, 158, 168, 178
Rhode Island, United States, 53
Rhodes, Greece, 142–3
Rhyl, see HMS *Rhyl*
Richard I of England (Richard the Lionheart), King, 2
Richard the Lionheart, *see* King Richard I
Richards, Ivor, 118, 184, 295
Riddleburger, Toni, *see* Toni Stearns
Rifles, *see* Weapons
RN (Royal Navy) (British), *see* Royal Navy
Robert College, Turkey, 30
Rodman, Peter W., 37, 278
Rogers, (American) Secretary of State William, 40, 58
Roman Catholic, *see* Catholic
Roman Catholic Church, 3
    see also Roman Latin Church
Roman Empire, 2
Roman Latin Church, 2
    see also Roman Catholic Church
Romans, 2–4
    Rome, Italy, 4, 24, 41, 50, 198, 222, 246, 262, 295
Rosenthal, Benjamin, 259
Rossides, (Cypriot) Ambassador Zenon, 94, 108
Rota, Spain, 84, 138
Rouleau, Eric, 242
Round the Horne (radio programme), 125, 274
Rover, see RFA *Rover*
Royal Air Force (RAF) (British), *see* RAF
Royal Armoured Corps (British), 97
Royal Corps of Transport (British), 126, 136
Royal family, *see* British royal family and Greek royal family
    see also King Richard I of England (Richard the Lionheart), Prine Philip of England and Queen

Elizabeth II of England
Royal Fleet Auxiliary (RFA) (British), *see* RFA
Royal Fusiliers (British), 227
Royal Marines (British), 97, 105, 193
Royal Marines commandoes (British), 97, 193
Royal Military Police, 137
    see also Police
Royal Navy (RN) (British), 21, 149, 157, 166–7
Royal Pioneer Corps (British), 136
Royal Scots (British), 90, 137
Russia/Russian, 3, 6, 12, 33, 37–8, 59, 75, 91, 101, 164, 169, 231, 245, 262, 274, 287
    see also USSR (Soviet Union)/ Soviets

Sabre (aircraft), 124
Sadat of Egypt, (Egyptian) President Muhammad Anwar, 50, 243
Safronchuk, Vasily Stepanovich, 140
Salmina Towers (hotel), Cyprus, 156
Salonika, Greece, 83
Sampson (née Fessus), Vera, 20
Sampson, (Cypriot) President Nikos, 19–20, 56, 77, 81, 84, 86, 89, 91–3, 97–103, 108–109, 112, 117, 119, 125–6, 128, 130, 139, 151, 160, 162, 164, 169–70, 246, 268, 283
San Clemente, United States, 102, 113, 116, 123, 132, 138–40, 150, 203, 285–6
Sancar, General Semih, 80, 86, 113, 133, 168
Sarbanes, Paul Spyros, 47, 226, 255, 259
Savalas, Telly, 14
Scali, (American) Ambassador John, 118, 140
Scampton, RAF, *see* RAF Scampton
Scandinavia/Scandinavian, 50, 147
Schlesinger, (American) Secretary of Defense Dr James 'Jim', 125, 139, 150, 247, 284

Scorpions (tanks), 136
  see also Tanks
Scotland/Scottish, 90, 137, 235
Sea Kings (helicopters), 158
Second World War, 1, 4–5, 17, 21,
  23–4, 36, 38, 42, 79, 85, 101
Secret military police, 268
see also Greek military police, Police
  and Royal Military Police
Security Committee, 82
  see also RAF Akrotiri
Security Council, 40, 82, 84, 86, 88,
  94, 100, 108, 118, 120, 130, 140, 145,
  150, 154–5, 179, 184–6, 189–92, 204,
  206, 208, 228, 255, 276, 284
  see also National Security
    Council and United Nations
Senate (American), *see* United States
  Senate
Senate Committee on the Judiciary
  (American), *see* United States
  Senate Committee on the
  Judiciary
Seraphim, Archbishop, 66–7, 71,
  73–4, 177
Serbia/Serbian, 3
Severis, (Cypriot) Health Minister
  Zenon, 81
Seychelles, 5
Shakespeare, William, 2, 274, 277
Shuster, Alvin, 231
Sicily/Sicilian, 2
Silva, Walter J., 42, 275, 279
Sirmopolous, Colonel, 89, 136
Sisco, Joseph 'Joe' John ('Jumping Joe'),
  39–40, 42, 61, 68–9, 71, 73, 84, 98–9,
  102–104, 107–11, 113–21, 123–6,
  128–34, 136, 138–40, 144–6, 148–55,
  158–60, 162, 164, 174–5, 190, 194,
  207, 210, 212, 225, 265, 283–4, 291
Six-Day War, 25, 27
Sixth Fleet, *see* United States
  Sixth Fleet
SOE (Special Operations
  Executive), 267

South America/South American, 38,
  40, 75, 263
South European Department, 28
Southeastern Mediterranean, *see*
  Mediterranean
Southern Flank, 25, 40, 42, 272, 275
Soviet Embassy, 80
Soviet Union (USSR)/Soviets, *see*
  USSR (Soviet Union)/Soviets
    see also Russia/Russian
Spain, James W.S., 33, 275, 278, 286
Spain/Spanish, 44, 84, 125, 138, 174,
  262, 264
Spain, King of, *see* King Carlos of
  Spain
Special Operations Executive (SOE),
  see SOE
Spink, Air Marshal/Flying Officer
  Clifford 'Cliff', 135–6, 271
Spink, Catherine, 135
Spitfires (aircraft), 79
St James's, England, 96
St Patrick's (camp), Cyprus, 86
Stabler, Wells, 39, 57, 61, 73, 103, 111,
  116, 123, 228, 237, 240, 264
State (American), Department of,
  see United States Department of
  State
    see also United States
      Intelligence and Research
      Bureau
Stavrou, Georgios, 129
Stern, Laurence M., 272, 278, 287
Stern, Thomas, 277, 283
Stearns, (American) Ambassador
  Monteagle 'Monty', 172–3, 187,
  193, 238, 263, 273, 288–9, 296
Stearns, Toni (*née* Riddleburger),
  172–3
Stoddart, Ted, 198
Strasbourg, France, 81
Suez Canal, Egypt, 3, 24
Suez Crisis, 24, 113, 137, 186, 210, 245
Suffolk, England, 135
Sun (newspaper), *The*, 266, 273

Supreme Court (American), *see*
   United States Supreme Court
Surrey, England, 90
Sweden/Swedish, 14, 116
Swedish government, 116
Switzerland/Swiss, 6–7, 132, 141,
   156, 160–2, 170, 174–5, 183–6,
   188–92, 198–201, 203–204, 206,
   209–12, 215, 217–8, 227–9, 235, 237,
   246, 289–91
Syria/Syrian, 38, 62–3, 75, 81,
   243, 245
Syrian Embassy, 81
Syrian president, *see* President Hafez
   al-Assad

Tactical Reserve Unit, 16, 61, 79, 85
Taksim, 4
Talbot, (American) Ambassador
   Walter Phillips, 45
Tanks, 78–9, 129, 136, 182, 226–7
   see also Scorpions
Tasca, (American) Ambassador
   Henry Joseph, 41–3, 45–6, 52, 54,
   57–8, 63–71, 73, 84–5, 90, 92, 103,
   109, 111, 114–6, 126, 129–32, 134,
   138, 143, 146, 148, 153, 158–9,
   164–5, 171–3, 187, 193, 203, 238–9,
   256, 262–3
Tasca, Natalina, 41
Taylor Woodrow (company), 267
Taylor, Elizabeth, 14
TCG *Adatepe*, 149
TCG *Kocatepe*, 149, 178
TCG *Maresal Fevzi Çakmak*, 149
Tel Aviv, Israel, 158
Tetenes, Spyridon, 62–3, 71, 83
Texas, United States, 262
Thames Television, 226
Thasos, 54
Thatcher, (British) Prime Minister
   Margaret 'Maggie', 266
Thessaloniki, Greece, 42–3, 122, 223
Thọ, Lê Đức, 38
Thomas, Dylan, 30

Thrace, 33, 35, 54, 117, 145, 151,
   159, 223
Tiger, see HMS *Tiger*
TMT (Türk Mukavemet Teşkilatı/
   Turkish Resistance Organisation),
   5, 18, 116, 122
Togo/Togolese, 265
Tomkys, Roger, 97
Tomkins, Sir Edward Emile, 284, 287
Treasury (British), *see* British
   Treasury
Triantafyllides, (Cypriot) Chief
   Justice Michael, 81
Troodos Mountains, Cyprus, 4,
   79, 137
Truman, (American) President Harry
   S., 33, 43
Tuomioja, (Finnish) Prime Minister
   Sakari Severi, 8
Türk Mukavemet Teşkilatı (TMT/
   Turkish Resistance Organisation),
   see TMT
Turkey/Turkish, *passim*
Turkish air force, 149
Turkish Airlines, 257
Turkish army, 187, 217
Turkish Cabinet, *see* Cabinet
Turkish Cypriots, 1, 3–11, 13, 17–9, 23,
   26, 31, 53, 56, 60–1, 65–6, 80–1, 84,
   86, 92, 95, 102, 105–108, 110, 113,
   117, 122, 127, 129, 133, 135, 142,
   163, 170, 177, 179, 184, 195, 197–8,
   200–201, 203, 205, 207, 213, 218–9,
   231, 234, 236, 239, 249, 250–1, 257,
   261, 264, 269
Turkish Defence Ministry, 200
Turkish Embassy, 30, 110
Turkish Foreign Ministry, 149
Turkish government, 31, 108, 195,
   205, 267
Turkish Grand National Assembly,
   103, 117
Turkish High Command, 149,
   167, 180
Turkish navy, 131, 178

Turkish Parliament, 89, 247, 250
Turkish police, see Police
Turkish president, see President Fahri
    Korutürk
Turkish prime ministers, see Prime
    Minister Bülent Ecevit, Prime
    Minister İsmail Nihat Erim and
    Prime
Minister Ali Adnan Ertekin
    Menderes
Turkish Resistance Organisation
    (Türk Mukavemet Teşkilatı / TMT),
    see TMT
Turkish War of Independence, 32
Tyler, (American) Ambassador
    William, 237–8, 294

U2 stealth bomber (aircraft), 13, 25
UK (United Kingdom), see United
    Kingdom
Ukraine / Ukrainian, 169
Ulman, Haluk, 213
Umayyad Caliphate, 2
UN (United Nations), 5, 8, 14, 16, 18,
    26, 40, 51, 65, 67–8, 80–2, 86, 88,
    90, 94, 96–7, 100–101, 103, 105–10,
    115–7, 119, 128, 130, 136–7, 140,
    144–7, 152, 161–4, 167–8, 170, 172,
    175–6, 178–80, 182–6, 188, 191–3,
    199–201, 204–206, 208, 210, 212,
    216, 218, 224–5, 227, 229, 233–4,
    236, 239, 241–2, 245–6, 251, 255,
    257–8, 260, 269, 284, 292, 294
    see also Security Council
UNFICYP (United Nations
    Peacekeeping Force in Cyprus),
    8, 14, 26, 80, 90, 105, 115–7, 128,
    136, 140, 146–7, 161–2, 172, 175–6,
    178–9, 184–6, 191–3, 204, 206, 216,
    225, 229, 233–4, 258
Union of Soviet Socialist Republics,
    see USSR (Soviet Union) / Soviets
United Democratic Centre Union
    (ΕΔΕΚ Σοσιαλιστικό Κόμμα /
    EDEK), see EDEK

United Front, 15, 18
United Kingdom (UK), passim
    see also Britain / British
United Nations (UN), see UN
    see also Security Council
United Nations Peacekeeping
    Force in Cyprus (UNFICYP), see
    UNFICYP
United States (US) / American, passim
United States Air Force (USAF), 55,
    140, 167, 216
United States Central Intelligence
    Agency (CIA), see CIA
United States Communications
    Agency, 132
United States Congress, 41–3, 47–8,
    58, 116, 123, 159, 187, 191, 215, 220,
    226, 231, 236, 240–1, 243–7, 253–6,
    260, 266, 275–6, 286
United States Defense Intelligence
    Agency (DIA), see DIA
United States Democratic Party, 24,
    38, 60, 193, 231
United States Department of Defense,
    69, 138–9, 150, 159
United States Department of State,
    14, 30, 34, 36–7, 39–42, 46, 54–5,
    58, 60, 62–7, 70–2, 74–7, 84, 93,
    98, 103, 110, 115–7, 119, 122, 141,
    150, 154, 162–3, 172–3, 189, 200,
    207, 212, 217, 226, 229, 238, 247,
    256–7, 264–5, 271, 279–84, 287,
    290, 292–4
        see also United States
        Intelligence and Research
        Bureau
United States Embassy, see American
    Embassy
United States government, 57, 69, 72,
    91, 150, 181, 254, 259
United States House of
    Representatives, 39, 61–2, 65, 181,
    187, 191, 199, 241–2, 253
        see also United States Judiciary
        Committee

United States Intelligence and
   Research Bureau, 70, 72, 76, 238
   see also United States
      Department of State
United States International Affairs
   Division, 116
United States Judiciary Committee,
   39, 61, 65, 181, 187, 191
   see also United States House of
      Representatives
United States Marine Corps, 34, 272
United States Marines, 34, 272
   see also United States Marine
      Corps
United States National Defense
   University, 264
United States National Security
   Council, 84, 120, 145, 150
United States Navy (USN), 25, 41
United States of America (USA)/
   American, *see* United States/
   American
United States presidents, *see* Dwight
   D. Eisenhower, President Gerald
   R. Ford Jr, President, Lyndon B.
Johnson, President John F. Kennedy,
   President Abraham Lincoln,
   Richard M. Nixon, President
   Ronald
W. Reagan and Harry S. Truman
   see also Vice President Spiro
      Agnew and Vice President
      Hubert Humphrey
United States Republican Party, 24,
   181, 187, 199, 265
United States Senate, 39, 191, 219,
   242, 253, 276, 286
United States Senate Committee on
   the Judiciary, 276, 286
United States Sixth Fleet, 25, 34, 41,
   105, 114, 172, 200
United States Supreme Court, 65, 72,
   79, 123, 140, 181
Upper Volta, 265
Urquhart, Brian, 205

US (United States)/American, *see*
   United States/American
US government, *see* United States
   government
USA (United States of America), *see*
   United States/American
USAF (United States Air Force), *see*
   United States Air Force
USN (United States Navy), *see*
   United States Navy
USS *America*, 84, 138
USS *Forrestal*, 92, 105, 138
USSR (Union of Soviet Social
   Republics) (Soviet Union)/Soviets,
   9, 12, 19, 25, 31, 33–4, 36–40, 43, 51,
   59, 62, 64, 67, 71, 75, 80, 84, 86–7, 89,
   92, 94, 99, 105, 107, 110–1, 117–8, 132,
   140–1, 143, 145–7, 151–2, 161, 163–4,
   169, 188–9, 192–3, 205, 216, 218, 230,
   256, 262, 264–6, 281, 293, 299

Vakis, (Cypriot) Justice Minister
   Christos, 79
Vance, Cyrus, 11, 120, 270
Varnava, Antoinette, 233
VC10 (aircraft), 198
Veniamin, Chris, 70
Venice, Italy, 2, 82
Venice, Republic of, 2
Venizelos, (Greek) Prime Minister
   Eleftherios, 4
Vienna, Austria, 146, 151–2, 156,
   158–9
Vietnam War, 24
Vietnam/Vietnamese, 24, 37–8, 41, 61,
   172–3, 239, 242, 265
Virginia Tech college, United States,
   46
Virginia, United States, 46, 51, 258,
   272
Vlachos, Angelos, 211
Vulcans (aircraft), *see* Avro Vulcans

Waldheim, Secretary General Dr
   Kurt, 18, 82, 94, 108, 175, 179–80,

185–6, 193, 200–201, 204–206, 225, 292
Waldorf Towers, 243
Waller, John A., 64
Warburton, Miss A.M., 290–1
Warsaw Pact, 25
Washington College, United States, 265
Washington DC (Washington), United States, 6, 13, 24–5, 36, 38, 42–3, 45–6, 48, 50, 52, 57–62, 64–5, 67–75, 83–4, 86, 92, 94, 97–9, 102–103, 107–108, 110–1, 114–5, 117, 120–1, 123, 128, 132–3, 138–41, 143, 150, 154–5, 159, 161–4, 169, 171, 173–5, 177, 181, 184, 186–7, 191–4, 200, 202–203, 205, 207–208, 210–2, 216–8, 223, 228, 231, 234–5, 238–40, 242, 247, 249, 253–6, 260, 263, 265, 270, 273, 275–6, 279–84, 286–9, 291–6
Washington Post (United States), *The*, 69, 273, 276
Washington Summit, 38
Wasps (helicopters), 167
Watergate, 36, 38, 42, 61, 65, 69, 72, 75, 102, 104, 116, 124–5, 181, 188, 198, 200, 210, 220, 270
Watson, Helen, 137, 147–8, 271
Watson, Wing Commander Ken, 82, 137, 267, 271
Waynes Keep, Cyprus, 78
Weapons, 7–9, 11, 15–6, 23, 25, 27, 29, 34, 37–8, 51–2, 56–7, 65, 85, 95–6, 114–6, 124, 127, 129, 135, 149–52, 159, 162, 168, 178–9, 182, 188, 199, 204, 232, 234, 244
    American, 34, 244
    anti-tank, 204
    automatic, 8, 11
    bombs, 9, 15, 27, 29, 51, 124, 129, 135, 149, 152, 162, 179, 188
        atomic, 9
        car, 15, 51

Czech, 116, 178
guns, 85, 114, 124, 127, 182, 232, 234
    machine, 127
    rifles, 85, 234
    historic, 85
    Japanese, 85
    nuclear, 9, 23, 25, 34, 37–8, 150–1
    Turkish, 199, 124, 129, 135, 152
Weckmann-Muñoz, Dr Luis Jesús, 86, 88, 178
Welch, Kika, 262–3
Welch, Richard 'Dick', 262–3
Wessex (helicopters), 167
West Berlin, *see* Berlin
West Germany/West German, *see* Germany/German
Weston, Sir John, 22, 278
Whirlwinds (aircraft), 26, 90, 158, 162
White House, United States, 24, 36–40, 61, 113, 132, 151, 199, 202–203, 241
    see also East Wing and Oval Office
Whitehall, England, 6, 23, 90, 100, 110, 125, 185, 187, 215
    see also British government and Downing Street
Wilhelm I, (German) Kaiser, 3, 252
Will, John, 231
Williams, Ann, 123, 163, 233–5, 258
Williams, Ben, 163, 233–5
Williams, James Alan, 20, 47, 72, 123, 138, 163, 225, 230–5, 258, 275, 278–80, 284, 286, 293, 295
Williams, Laura, 258
Williams, Ray, 278
Wilson, (British) Prime Minister Harold, 21–4, 27, 58, 64, 89, 98, 100–102, 106, 113, 125, 174, 180, 184, 196, 199, 201, 218, 224–5, 228, 240, 243, 248–9, 265–6, 273
Wilson, Charlie, 262, 274
Wilson, John, 275

Wiltshire, England, 95
Wolf, John, 115, 132, 275, 284–5
Woodward, Richard 'Bob', 69, 274
Wright Abbey, 291
Wright, Mrs G.S., 279

Yale University, United States, 119
Yemen/Yemeni, 217
Yennadios, Bishop, 170

Yom Kippur War, 38, 55
Young, Major General Peter, 8
Yugoslavia/Yugoslavian, 124, 239, 287

Zachary, Dan, 275
Zumwalt, Admiral Elmo, 41
Zürich, Switzerland, 6–7, 132, 141, 170